Political Ethnography

4. März 2014

Political Ethnography

What Immersion Contributes
to the Study of Power

Edited by
EDWARD SCHATZ

Foreword by Myron J. Aronoff

The University of Chicago Press
Chicago and London

Edward Schatz is associate professor of political science at the University of Toronto. He is the author of *Modern Clan Politics: The Power of "Blood" in Kazakhstan and Beyond.*

The University of Chicago Press, Chicago 60637
The University of Chicago Press, Ltd., London
© 2009 by The University of Chicago
All rights reserved. Published 2009
Printed in the United States of America
18 17 16 15 14 13 12 11 10 09   1 2 3 4 5

ISBN-13: 978-0-226-73676-1 (cloth)
ISBN-10: 0-226-73676-8 (cloth)
ISBN-13: 978-0-226-73677-8 (paper)
ISBN-10: 0-226-73677-6 (paper)

Chapter 5 originally appeared in *Insurgent Collective Action and Civil War in El Salvador*, © 2003 Cambridge University Press. Reprinted with the permission of Cambridge University Press.

Library of Congress Cataloging-in-Publication Data
Political ethnography: what immersion contributes to the study of power / edited by Edward Schatz; foreword by Myron J. Aronoff.
    p. cm.
  Includes bibliographical references and index.
  ISBN-13: 978-0-226-73676-1 (cloth: alk. paper)
  ISBN-10: 0-226-73676-8 (cloth: alk. paper)
  ISBN-13: 978-0-226-73677-8 (pbk.: alk. paper)
  ISBN-10: 0-226-73677-6 (pbk.: alk. paper) 1. Political anthropology.
2. Political science. I. Schatz, Edward.
GN492.P655   2009
306.2—dc22   2009008192

CONTENTS

The workshop that gave rise to this exciting volume was one of the most intellectually stimulating symposia in which I have been privileged to participate during four decades as an academic. "Political Ethnography" was organized by Edward Schatz and took place in 2006 at the University of Toronto. I learned much from this cohort of gifted young scholars who represent the future of the profession and the promise that political ethnography will continue to gain recognition as a valuable approach in political science. Unusually for all too many academic conferences (and the edited volumes resulting from them), the participants in "Political Ethnography" shared a common approach despite their internal differences and were able to create what Dvora Yanow refers to in her chapter as an "epistemic community," which this book reflects and to which it contributes. Consequently, the volume reflects an intellectual exchange that, as a whole, is more valuable than the sum of its individual chapters.

The project of building conceptual and methodological bridges between anthropology and political science has been a major goal during my professional career. Various obstacles have hampered this project. For example, as I noted in my keynote address to the "Political Ethnography" workshop, paradoxically, as political scientists have become more interested in ethnography and in the concept of political culture, anthropologists have undergone agonizing soul-searching and in some cases scathing critiques of the value of both participant observation and the conceptualization of culture.[1] Also, unfortunately, many scholars do not read in subfields within their discipline other than their own specialty, much less across disciplinary boundaries. Another challenge is that multidiscipline identities and/or interdisciplinary approaches can be professionally marginalizing.

My own professional career is illustrative of the difficulties of bridging disciplines. I earned a Ph.D. in both anthropology and political science. Subsequently, as a Fellow of the Netherlands Institute for Advanced Studies in the Humanities and Social Sciences, I was introduced by one prominent Dutch political scientist to his colleague as "half a political scientist." By the same token, I have also been introduced as "half an anthropologist" by one prominent anthropologist to another. Apparently, if you are qualified in two disciplines you can attain a modicum of recognition in both fields, but are reduced to a half of each by some of your learned colleagues.

During my term as president of the Association of Political and Legal Anthropology (APLA), I succeeded in affiliating the organization with the American Anthropological Association. I also edited the journal *Political Anthropology*, which was for a period the official publication of the APLA. The first five volumes that I personally edited contained almost equal numbers of contributions by anthropologists and political scientists (as well as a couple of sociologists). The subsequent volumes, edited by anthropologists, were predominantly written by anthropologists. The journal that eventually became the official publication of the APLA (*PoLAR: Political and Legal Anthropology Review*) is now heavily dominated by anthropologists. The multidisciplinary fields that have established major centers in universities—such as gender studies, gay and lesbian studies, cultural studies, and subaltern studies—have tended to create their own jargon, journals, and self-referential discourse, making them no less (and in some cases more) insular than the traditional disciplines. The concerted effort it takes to successfully bridge and maintain communication across disciplinary boundaries without producing a new insular field is a daunting challenge reminiscent of the myth of Sisyphus.

Yet there are grounds for optimism. Hopeful signs of the opening up of American political science to the approach represented in this book include the proliferation of panels, roundtables, and papers on qualitative methods (most organized by the recently renamed section on Qualitative and Multi-Method Research), ethnography, and interpretation at the annual meetings of the American Political Science Association (APSA) and regional political science associations. My colleague Jan Kubik (a contributor to this volume) and I were asked by the program chairs of the 2007 annual meeting of the Midwest Political Science Association (MPSA) to organize a Political Anthropology section and were especially gratified by the number of bright graduate students and young scholars who expressed interest in it. The MPSA, which tends to be dominated by the American politics field, is sometimes considered to be the most professionally conservative of the regional political science associations. That its representatives took the initiative by inviting a new section dealing with political ethnography is particularly gratifying and promising.

Edward Schatz's excellent introduction to this volume outlines the parameters of agreement and disagreement among the contributors. The two "core principles" are that "ethnography requires participant observation" (immersion in the field of research); and that it requires "sensibility" to the meanings attributed by those observed to their political reality. There is a consensus that ethnography expands the boundaries of the "political" and provides a normative grounding for understanding politics (shared with the philosophical approach of political theorists). Ontological and epistemological differences between interpretive and positivist approaches characterized discussions in the workshop and are reflected in the contributions in this book. I consider this "conversation" to be among the great strengths of the book. Unlike most edited volumes, the chapters here reflect the give-and-take of discussions in which the participants actually *listened* to one another. For example, Schatz calls the reader's attention to the debate between "monism" and "dualism" over the role played by the researcher in the construction of knowledge.

Despite the gains made in recent years, this book argues that ethnography is generally underappreciated in academic political science. While some argue for useful synergies between approaches, others assume incommensurability between research traditions and caution against mixing them. Some fear, with justification, that mixed methods may relegate ethnography to an inferior, supplementary status. Clearly, much depends on the nature of the problem and the field under examination. While I strongly agree with Schatz in the conclusion of this book that one need not utilize multiple methods in all research, there are contexts and problems of investigation where they are not only useful, but perhaps essential. For example, in my graduate research, I felt the need to conduct a survey after extensive ethnographic fieldwork and to analyze the survey data using the most up-to-date statistical methodology at the time, partly in order to prove to the members of my Ph.D. committee that I had mastered the methods. My ethnographic fieldwork was an invaluable asset in designing the questionnaire and in interpreting the data. The quantitative analysis contributed important "hard" evidence in support of hypotheses derived from the interpretation of the qualitative data.

The kinds of problems politicians and political scientists confront throughout the world today, such as the challenges of democratization in deeply divided societies or the increasing salience of identity politics leading to a clash of cultures in an increasingly transnational world, require the kinds of understanding that can only be gained through ethnographic methods and more nuanced cultural understanding. There are encouraging signs at present that more graduate students and scholars in political science recognize this need. It is critically important that more courses be offered in political ethnography in political science departments. This book impressively helps fill a conspicuous void in persuasively making the case for the important contribution of political ethnography to our understanding of politics. I recommend it with enthusiasm and without reservation.

Note

1. A slightly revised version of my keynote address was published as Aronoff (2006). For a discussion of the various approaches to political culture, see Aronoff (2002).

ACKNOWLEDGMENTS

This book is the product of a collaborative effort that became institutionally visible with a workshop held in October 2006 at the University of Toronto. I am grateful to the Social Sciences and Humanities Research Council of Canada, the Connaught Fund, the Office of the Dean (University of Toronto at Mississauga), the Department of Political Science (University of Toronto at Mississauga), the Asian Institute, and the Centre for European, Russian, and Eurasian Studies (CERES) for their generous financial support. Cheryl Misak and Graham White deserve special mention for their enthusiasm about the project. In addition to the presentations of participants, the involvement of David Cameron, Sohini Guha, Elisabeth King, Jeffrey Kopstein, Michael Lambek, Tania Li, Vincent Pouliot, Susan Solomon, and Marie-Joelle Zahar greatly enriched our discussion. Janet Hyer, Larysa Iarovenko, Olga Kesarchuk, and Jana Oldfield of CERES ensured that the workshop ran without a hitch.

I personally owe a debt of gratitude to all the chapter authors, who worked with great dispatch and eagerness to produce the final product. John Tryneski of University of Chicago Press was enthusiastic about the project's merits and honest about avenues for improvement. Conversations with him were a delight. Additional conversations with James Scott, Lee Ann Fujii, and Patrick Thaddeus Jackson helped to sharpen the presentation of arguments. Anonymous reviewers for the University of Chicago Press offered insightful critiques and sensible advice that helped to make this a better book. Olga Kesarchuk, who came to be known among chapter authors as "eagle-eyed Olga," read each chapter carefully and provided excellent editorial and bibliographic assistance. As always, Lara Dominguez traveled with me through this project's many stages; I would long ago have gone astray without her.

This book is dedicated to our innumerable interlocutors in the "field" without whose involvement such an endeavor would be unthinkable.

Edward Schatz
Toronto, Canada
October 2008

Ethnographic Immersion
and the Study of Politics

EDWARD SCHATZ

As long as political scientists continue to study politicians, some of us certainly will want to collect data through repeated interaction with these politicians in their natural habitats.

—Richard F. Fenno Jr. (1990, 56)

When Richard Fenno studied U.S. politicians in their "natural habitats," he was exploring uncharted professional terrain. For decades, very few students of American political life had embraced approaches that encouraged close, face-to-face contact with the people being studied. The dominant perspective among Americanists that a political *science* should aspire to the research methods and designs prominent in the natural sciences meant little professional and institutional space for ethnography.

If political science had been a methodologically plural discipline, it would have embraced the value of ethnographic approaches. The study of politics in the 1990s and 2000s, however, suffered from a narrow view of what constitutes legitimate research methodology. Ignoring Feyerabend's warning that "the best protective device against being taken in by one particular language is to be brought up bilingually or trilingually" (Feyerabend 1979, 91, as quoted in Deising 1991, 50), many scholars were seduced by the "language" of the technological cutting edge. Made possible by unprecedented and widely available computing power, statistical techniques and the logic associated with them became hegemonic among students of politics.[1]

Whether or not this research produced substantive research findings that justified such an enthusiastic embrace,[2] the study of politics risked not capitalizing on its historic strengths—its eclecticism (Sil and Katzenstein

2005) and its ecumenicalism (Kasza 2001). It risked marginalizing long-productive, nonstatistical approaches as somehow "prescientific" or inherently "inferior." Prominent scholars who proclaimed the value of nonquantitative approaches in fact advocated their use only insofar as they served the purposes of a "quantitative worldview"—that is, as raw data that might eventually be reduced to quantities and subjected to statistical tests.[3]

Scholars who did not share the assumptions or predilections of dominant approaches pushed back, often under the mantle of "qualitative methods." Some argued that many important political phenomena lend themselves poorly to quantification (Kasza 2001). Others contended that widely used quantitative approaches can easily mislead—either because they underemphasize the path-dependency that characterizes the development of human communities (Pierson 2004) or because they make problematic assumptions about the homogeneity of variables (Ragin 2000; Schram 2004).

This push-back produced a variety of changes to professional political science and a series of fruitful and interesting, though ultimately unresolved, discussions about what the study of politics ought to look like (Monroe 2005). With the possible exception of the American politics subfield (where intellectual ferment about methodology and method remained less pronounced), scholars became increasingly interested in the "how" of political research to ensure a self-aware, and therefore more insightful, discipline.

Beyond "Qualitative" Methods

These were welcome changes, and the category "qualitative" proved useful in implementing them, but this book argues that it is time to get more specific. The word *qualitative* obscures much variety in approaches to inquiry. Beyond a basic family resemblance, interviews, historical process-tracing, archival work, discourse analysis, and ethnography (to name a few) are methods that are useful in different ways. In this volume, we take stock of one kind of "qualitative" work—ethnography—and ask what it has contributed to the study of politics and how it can become more useful in the future.

This endeavor began, as many do, informally.[4] Hallway discussions, chats at conferences, listserv threads, side conversations, and the like—many of them facilitated by the so-called Perestroika movement (Monroe 2005)—helped to crystallize what we might call, to take liberties with Benedict Anderson's (1983) phrase, an "imagined community." A web of common approaches to the study of politics linked many of us, although few had thought consciously about giving this group a name. Indeed, it would be an exaggeration to call it a community-in-waiting; if this community was constituted by a web, it was a web that strained to keep its integrity. In some cases, professional, generational, or geographic distances made it difficult to recognize the strands that existed. In other cases, philosophical commitments and prior training highlighted what individuals linked by the web had to *disagree about*, rather than what they had in common.

Frequent, public invocations of the category "qualitative" nonetheless spurred our sense of commonality. We knew from our readings, research, and training that ethnography has made and continues to make important contributions to the study of politics, even if mainstream social science sometimes leaves these contributions in shadow.[5] We also knew that ethnography and "qualitative" methods were not one and the same. In a series of conference panels, roundtable discussions, and a workshop, we sought to put our collective finger on the nature of these contributions.[6]

Ethnographic approaches have long informed political science—albeit from the margins—and especially so among those comparativists who conduct field research abroad. (Given the discipline's development, this has typically meant outside the United States). An early proponent of ground-level, field-based techniques, David Apter reflected on his suspicion of the grand theories that were popular early in his career, cautioning that "a global approach, whether dressed up in the language of structural-functional analysis or some other, would remain useful only superficially. One needed to know more—that is, to understand more deeply the specific context of events—a pull toward what is called 'area studies'" (Apter 1973, 5).

Although sensitive to context, Apter's ontology was a realist one; he took as relatively unproblematic the existence of a reality external to the observer that could, in its essential if complex features, be discovered. Capturing the thrill of discovery, he commented:

> Field work is exciting. It is like working with the pieces of a jigsaw puzzle. One gradually discerns a pattern. The rules for finding the pieces and interpreting the pattern—these are much more complex. For one thing, broad themes and large units are hard to fit into a narrow quantitative mode as such and need to be translated into indicator variables. These, while they may be capable of being programmed and manipulated, are rarely generalizable for the macro unit. Thus the search for ultimately quantitative, indicator variables capable of standing as surrogates for analytical ones became a long-time concern [of mine]. (Apter 1973, 5)

Most of today's political ethnographers would share Apter's attention to empirical complexity, even if they abjured his search for "ultimately quantitative . . . variables." Like Apter, James C. Scott, the comparativist scholar most associated with political ethnography, would call for greater nuance in our theoretical accounts, questioning the received wisdom about peasant rebellions (Scott 1985) and emphasizing the role that "hidden transcripts" (that is, conversations and interactions among members of subordinate groups) play in generating possibilities for resistance (Scott 1990). More than Apter, however, Scott engaged in participant observation as a technique; also, unlike Apter, Scott was uninterested in constructing crisply bounded quantitative data as a route to generalization or predictive theory. His substantive insights ultimately call into question the very possibility of predictive theorizing. Riding the tide of interpretivist ethnography in anthropology, Scott anticipated by at least two decades the emergence of a robust interpretivism in political science.

Comparativists have not had a monopoly on the political ethnographic tradition. Among the widely recognized contributors to the American politics subfield, for example, was Richard Fenno, whose willingness to follow politicians to their "natural habitats" has already been noted in the epigraph. While Fenno's substantive insights about Congress have been absorbed and considered by others, the subfield's mainstream has nonetheless been uninterested in engaging the challenges implied by Fenno's epistemology.

This book builds on the tradition of political ethnography, asking what role ethnography plays and what value it potentially brings to the study of power. Put most directly, we argue that close, person-to-person contact that is attuned to the worldviews of the people we study is invaluable for a science of politics. Taken as a whole, the volume suggests that ethnography helps ensure an empirically sound, theoretically vibrant, epistemologically innovative, and normatively grounded study of politics. This empirical, theoretical, epistemological, and normative added value exists for those working from a variety of ontological starting-points and using a range of epistemologies. The chapters that follow will flesh out these claims.

Beyond this core agreement, however, we disagree about much. Like any vibrant community, ours is rife with internal debates, discussions, and tensions. The intellectual common ground we discovered quickly gave way to the constructive airing of differences. In this volume, then, we seek *both* to represent the utility of ethnography for the study of politics *and* to highlight key axes for debate and discussion. We agree that any attempt to grapple with the value of ethnography must be true to the internal diversity that constitutes a web of political ethnographers.

What Is Political Ethnography?

How do we define the contours of political ethnography? In cultural anthropology, where ethnographic approaches are *de rigueur*, dissensus reigns about what constitutes, and ought to constitute, the approach. Its character is similarly contested in this volume. Nonetheless, we might discern two core principles undergirding our understanding of political ethnography. The authors of the following chapters embrace these two principles in varying proportions and with varying degrees of enthusiasm. Some scholarship is ethnographic in *both* ways, but only one of these two principles needs to be present for a work to qualify, by this volume's definition, as ethnographic.

First, most scholars equate ethnography with participant observation. That is, immersion in a community, a cohort, a locale, or a cluster of related subject positions is taken to be the *sine qua non* of the approach. The volume's subtitle highlights the centrality of such immersion.[7] The premise is that one must be "neck-deep" in a research context to generate knowledge based on that context. This characterization, of course, is merely a starting-point. It conveniently brackets important questions: does valid observation always require participation? Of what duration and intensity should participant observation be? How much immersion is necessary, appropriate, ethical, and fruitful? What kinds of knowledge can be generated through the use of such methods? These are natural questions to ask, and anthropologists for decades have addressed them in serious and sustained ways.[8] It says much about the sociology of academic political science that we feel a need to advance such a fundamental claim about ethnography's value. We hope that, once the discipline no longer views participant observation as a marginal research method, it will confront these bracketed issues.

A second and less common understanding of ethnography also emerges in this volume. In this understanding, ethnography is a *sensibility* that goes beyond face-to-face contact.[9] It is an approach that cares—with the possible emotional engagement that implies—to glean the meanings that the people under study attribute to their social and political reality.[10] Thus, while some scholars equate ethnography with participant observation, one may nonetheless abstract *from* participant-observation qualities that inform a more general ethnographic sensibility.

If ethnography is a sensibility, participant observation is only one among the methods that might be used. Close familiarity with and analysis of any collection of human artifacts (texts, cultural products, and so on) can generate an ethnographic study by revealing the meanings people attribute to the world they inhabit. It is in this sense that James Scott's (1998) *Seeing Like a State*, although itself not the direct product of participant observation "in the field," is infused with a profound ethnographic sensibility, detailing the inner logic that guides modern states in their efforts to remake physical and social space. It seems unlikely that a scholar could operate with an ethnographic sensibility without having at some point conducted participant observation; indeed, Scott's ethnographic sensibility emerged from previous work (Scott 1985, 1990) that relied centrally on immersion.[11] Nonetheless, the two understandings of ethnography—one as ground-level method, the other as sensibility—are conceptually distinct.

If an understanding of ethnography as participant observation is more traditional, an understanding of ethnography as a broad sensibility emerges from the challenges of studying the contemporary social world. As global links become more vibrant and complex though technological, cultural, and ideational change, traditional forms of participant observation must be modified. As Comaroff and Comaroff (2003, 151) ask, "How—given that the objects of our gaze commonly elude, embrace, attenuate, transcend, transform, consume, and construct the local—do we arrive at a praxis for an age that seems . . . post-anthropological?" In chapter 1, Kubik details how once-strong standards among anthropologists for the duration of field research and for the type of immersion conducted have given way to more flexible and more diffuse norms implied by the term *sensibility*.[12] Moreover, the term *sensibility* goes at least partway to transcending artificial distinctions between fieldwork and deskwork, between research site and site of analysis, between researcher and researched, and so on—distinctions that are hard to sustain in a world that defies these binary distinctions. It also avoids reducing ethnography to the *process* of on-site data collection. *Sensibility* implies epistemological commitments that are about more than particular methods; in this sense, an ethnographic study usually employs multiple tools of inquiry.[13]

The notion of an ethnographic sensibility that pays attention to the perspectives of the people being studied nonetheless generates several conundrums. First, it implies a dichotomy between an insider and an outsider, a dichotomy that may mislead. After all, people are "insiders" or "outsiders" by degree in any named group or community; to study them requires varying mixtures of what Geertz (1973) called "experience-near" and "experience-distant" approaches. Membership in any community or category comes in shades of gray.[14] One is a feminist, a capitalist, a casino waitress, a "kill-line worker" or in the president's "inner circle" by degree and only at particular times in particular places. The invocation of such categories must not imply an unchanging essence or permanent membership; those who invoke them must do so for representational convenience. The same is true for the ethnographer herself, as Lorraine Bayard de Volo demonstrates in chapter 10 based on contrasting immersive studies—one on Nicaraguan mothers and another on cocktail waitresses in Nevada casinos.

Moreover, analytic categories that imply that a community contains an inner essence often overestimate the stability of meaning and identity, and underestimate internal variety and contradictions, as Lisa Wedeen details in chapter 3. When so-called insiders inhabit such a changeable, internally variegated, and layered reality, a different analytic vocabulary is required.

Nonetheless, the category of "insider" may have heuristic value. In any given time and place, there are those who could be provisionally called "insiders" if their status is stable enough to generate durable meanings. The scholar with an ethnographic sensibility tends to rely on these individuals to construct her descriptive account and explanatory framework. This does not mean that she rushes to accept at face value the testimony of her interlocutors. (She might proceed using Ricoeur's [1970, 32–35] "hermeneutic of suspicion.") Rather, it means that she begins with a basic assumption— that immersion generates information. Whatever motivates her interlocutors—a generosity with time, a personal or professional interest in the scholar's activities, pure curiosity, the thrill of contact with an outsider, an intention to deceive, an attempt to insert the outsider into micro-level political dynamics, or something else entirely—the interlocutor presents self and fact to the scholar, and the scholar's task is to make sense of the information contained in this presentation.[15]

But, while one can and should be skeptical about aspects of individual testimony, and while one can and should dismiss what some interlocutors offer as simply wrong-headed, ill-conceived, or otherwise a "dead end" from the perspective of a given research project's central objectives, a general sympathy for interlocutors is nonetheless the hallmark of ethnographic research. An ethnographic study—all else being equal—is likely to grant descriptive and/or explanatory priority to the ways in which "insiders" on the whole understand their existence. Imagine a hypothetical researcher who, though intending to conduct an ethnographic study, genuinely does not enjoy spending time with particular individuals (local strongmen, perpetrators of violence, corrupt police officers, and extremist ideologues come to my mind, though this is at root a normative question). Since an ability to sympathize lies at the core of ethnography, conducting a study that relied on ethnographic contact with such individuals would be practically and sometimes ethically difficult.

A second conundrum regarding this sensibility is its diffuse nature. If identifying a threshold past which a researcher becomes a "participant observer" is difficult, this is even more the case for an ethnographic sensibility. Especially in this second sense, there is in practice no "pure" ethnography. There is only a sliding scale of commitments that necessarily fall short of the ideal type.[16] Indeed, what constitutes an "insider" perspective (or an "outsider," for that matter) depends on the blind spots in a particular research agenda; varying degrees of immersion can generate crucial insights whose importance depends upon the state of existing knowledge on particular topics, as Cédric Jourde demonstrates in chapter 9 with regard to knowledge of "Islamism" and "authoritarianism." Whether a given piece of research is ethnographic in this sense implies a claim about what a given epistemic community does and does not know.

The contributions to this volume are as diverse as are our understandings of political ethnography. First, we span the subfields of political science. Some projects emerge from subfields like comparative politics, where ethnographers for decades remained productive, if underappreciated, contributors to a variety of topics. Others represent subfields such as American politics and public administration, where scholars working in the ethnographic tradition continue to swim against the professional tide.[17] Second, some—though not all—contributors use the term *ethnographic* to describe their own work. Elisabeth Wood (chapter 5), Timothy Pachirat (chapter 6), and Katherine Cramer Walsh (chapter 7) fall into this category. Others, such as Jourde, characterize their own work as "ethnographic" in some qualified sense. Still others avoid invoking the term or otherwise distance their work from the tradition. In chapter 4, Cyrus Ernesto Zirakzadeh, although emphasizing a micro-level perspective, space for human agency, and multiple contingencies, does not use the term *ethnography*. (Nonetheless, his field research was, by most understandings, clearly ethnographic. As if to underscore the point, Zirakzadeh flees a hail of police rubber bullets and, in doing so, forges common cause with the Basque nationalists he sought to study—in ways that recall how Geertz and his wife found themselves fleeing a police raid on a village cockfight [Geertz 1973].) At the Toronto workshop, Michael Schatzberg expressed tongue-in-cheek discomfort about being strongly identified with a particular epistemic community, introducing himself with a mock confession: "My name is Michael, and I am not a political ethnographer." Corey Shdaimah, Roland Stahl, and Sanford Schram in chapter 12 offer the strongest departure from the ethnographic tradition. Arguing that interpretivist commitments (including an essentially top-down mode of theorizing and conducting research) characterize political ethnography, they prefer to identify with the tradition of "participatory action research," which—they argue—gives greater opportunity for "bottom-up" research than does political ethnography.

While some use the term *ethnography* and its cognates, others modify the term, and still others do not use it, diverse ways of imagining one's research do not negate a core similarity of approach that animates the contributions. Rather, they underscore that political ethnography is practiced in shades of gray.

Given such shades of gray, it is crucial to ponder what ethnographic immersion is *not*. As Dvora Yanow notes in chapter 13, when scholars conduct interviews, they may or may not be proceeding ethnographically. Similarly, although a survey researcher may engage people face to face, their relationship remains razor-thin. Much more revealing information often emerges when, as Walsh puts it, the survey "interview is over and the laptop cover is down." Nor is fieldwork synonymous with immersion. Fieldwork that is ethnographic must occur in the nearest possible locale. Living in a five-star hotel disembedded from the social life of ordinary people is unlikely to produce ethnographic insights (unless, perhaps, if one studies the life-world of the wealthy or those hotel workers who serve them).[18] Long duration in the field is likewise insufficient; if the researcher is not equipped with ethnographic skills and tools of inquiry, he may build knowledge, but not of an ethnographic sort. Finally, in-depth interviews, when conducted as a part of a multiple-method research design that seeks to mine these interviews for particular information rather than insider meanings and perspectives, are unlikely—in and of themselves—to produce ethnographic research. Indeed, whenever ethnographic techniques are subsumed by different, nonethnographic sensibilities or techniques (for example, Laitin 1998; Varshney 2002; Collins 2006), their character changes fundamentally (Schatz 2007). Thus, being "neck-deep" in insider worldviews is an ideal type, and some work simply falls on the nonethnographic side of a broad spectrum of political research.

This book does not pretend to cover "best practices" of ethnographic immersion. In a discipline that is increasingly self-conscious about methods and methodologies, many students and scholars seek to go beyond widely available "how-to" manuals.[19] Nor can they learn to do research from the "just so" stories that often accompany scholars' descriptions of their research.[20] Rather, they want in-depth examination of the philosophical underpinnings, epistemological realities, and practical challenges that particular approaches pose. Thus, the chapters that follow are not idealized versions of political ethnography. They embrace (some of) the messiness that is ethnographic practice and consider ways to harness this messiness to improve leverage on political questions. To reveal ethnography as it is genuinely practiced in the study of politics is this volume's goal.

What Immersion Contributes

With their overlapping (though not coinciding) understandings of political ethnography, the volume's contributors agree that a study of politics with insufficient space for ethnographic approaches is an impoverished, academic affair. So, what does immersion contribute? Part 3 showcases some contributions; other chapters provide additional examples. For present purposes, we might group ethnography's value for political science into four clusters.

First, ethnography produces detailed evidence of the sort that can flesh out, or call into question, generalizations produced or meanings assigned by other research traditions.[21] To take some of the central concerns of political science, if the study of justice, freedom, democracy, or order is to mean anything, it must take into account individuals' lived experiences and how they perceive these abstractions. Do property rights produce empowerment, as a broad literature claims? Shdaimah, Stahl, and Schram usefully scrutinize this causal story in part using ethnographic data. Do people support social movements because of prior ideological commitments, as is often assumed? Bayard de Volo critically assesses this assumption. If popular understandings of "democracy" vary from society to society, what are the implications for democratic theory (Schaffer 1998)? These and other questions can be productively engaged with micro-level evidence of the sort that ethnography provides.

Empirical soundness contributes to theoretical vibrancy. A theoretically vibrant social inquiry does not rest content with asking the same questions in the same ways. Although one need not abandon a baseline expectation that knowledge can cumulate, a research program that grinds along in the same paradigm risks becoming trivial. Ethnography often expands—indeed, it often explodes—how we understand the boundaries of the "political." Thus, in chapter 8 Schatzberg considers soccer and sorcery to be eminently political topics; Enrique Desmond Arias in chapter 11 describes how everyday violence that occurs outside the analytic vision of those focused on formal democratic institutions nonetheless lies at the heart of Latin American politics; Pachirat in chapter 6 suggests that keeping uncomfortable political matters from public scrutiny is itself an act of power; and Walsh in chapter 7 calls into question the common notion that public opinion is "that which surveys measure," showing the dynamic and textured process by which opinions are formed and re-formed.

Third, ethnography holds out the promise of epistemological innovation.[22] Research conducted at close range invites the researcher to "see" differently; heterogeneity, causal complexity, dynamism, contingency, and informality come to the fore. Presented with these different social facts, the ethnographer may re-envision her path to knowledge construction. Instead of resting content with broad categories, she searches for subtypes and sub-subtypes, and generates "problematizing redescriptions" (Shapiro 2004). Instead of testing elegant causal chains, she views complex configurations of factors that combine and recombine in a striking variety of ways. Rather than seeking covering laws, she prefers concatenated theories. Rather than viewing a context as containing static content, she trains her lens for constitutive processes that capture dynamism. And rather than concentrating on macro-structural factors, she seeks to carve out a space for human agency.

Fieldwork is often humbling, and humility can spur different ways of thinking about knowledge production. Jessica Allina-Pisano, for example, in chapter 2 describes the kaleidoscope of interests, perceptions, actors, and discourses that define most research sites and make descriptive accuracy challenging to achieve.[23] Indeed, most ethnographers could probably recall, presumably with some horror at their own naïveté, having learned that an interlocutor had deliberately misrepresented the truth. This realization is both liberating and troubling. It is liberating, since the scholar feels suddenly free from the clutches of a "lie." It is troubling because it raises fundamental questions about the veracity of other testimony. Other aspects of field research—the timing of one's presence at the research site, one's personal characteristics that facilitate access to certain kinds of information and foreclose access to other kinds, and any number of other contingencies—produce an awareness of "researcher effects" and the impossibility of complete knowledge. If knowledge is viewed as fragmentary and partial, one might redraw the line between expert and nonexpert. How best to redraw this line is a matter of some debate, but ethnographic inquiry recommends attention to this sort of epistemologically fresh thinking.

Finally, ethnography provides normative grounding to the study of politics. Scholars interested in abstract thinking (as we are prone to be) run the risk of losing sight of the normative concerns that originally motivated them; they can get lost in conceptual disputes and methodological technicalities. By contrast, ethnographic study contains the potential to *care* for people on a continual basis, as is evident in Pachirat's and Bayard de Volo's chapters.[24] While not a substitute for training in moral or political philosophy, ethnography has the central virtue of keeping the researcher in touch with the people affected by power relations.

Axes of Contention

Yanow suggests that ethnographers use a "yes, and" approach to their work: that is, they build on what people, texts, or the field site bring up (often unexpectedly), rather than negate or refuse these offers. A similar, additive approach is on display here, but this does not mean that this volume's ethnographers agree on everything. In fact, while we have much in common, at least three axes of disagreement run through this volume.[25]

Interpretivist vs. Neopositivist Epistemology

Introduced in Part 1 of this volume, the first axis of debate mirrors larger meta-theoretical concerns in the discipline. To what kind of science does ethnography contribute? Is ethnography best understood as part of an interpretivist or a neopositivist research program?[26] Kubik details how in cultural and social anthropology, ethnography's "mother" discipline, the approach has made major and admirable intellectual contributions on both sides of this ontological and epistemological divide.[27] But, as contrasting chapters by Allina-Pisano and Wedeen show, important philosophical and practical differences characterize the two uses of ethnography.

Both Allina-Pisano and Wedeen imply the existence of a social reality that is complex, multivocal, and multilayered, but their uses of ethnography diverge. Using the language of Günter Grass, Allina-Pisano suggests that ethnography's core added value lies in its ability to "peel the onion skin" of reality—to get closer to its essence with every swipe of the paring knife. Her vivid examples from fieldwork show that facts are often elusive, and her search for small-t truths (rather than Truth) is one that revels in complexity and nuance. She remains committed, however, to a "correspondence" understanding of truth, in which a claim is true based on its correspondence to an objective reality.

Wedeen, by contrast, invokes the language of "performances," suggesting that there is no pristine reality separate from the researcher that is essentially discoverable; what is discoverable is the type of performance that the researched choose to offer the researcher. These performances constitute the quotidian practices that are "intrinsic to, not separate from, daily life." In short, while Allina-Pisano argues for a context-specific, micro-level, nuanced search for truth that looks for causality behind performances, Wedeen cautions that any search for truth must take care not to run aground on problematic ontologies and power-laden epistemologies.

Ethnography, then, is used differently in each case; each scholar answers differently the question, "What value do insider voices offer?" For Allina-Pisano, these voices are useful to the extent that they help bring the scholar into closer proximity to (some reasonable estimate of) a correct answer to whatever question is being asked. From this perspective, testimony is to be mined for its truth-value. For Wedeen, by contrast, voices are less usefully understood as insider or outsider, as accurate or inaccurate; rather, each voice can be interpreted for what perspectives, practices, and assumptions it reveals. Wedeen's interpretivism hesitates to pass judgment on the truth-value of testimony, but rather seeks to link these testimonies to prevailing social discourses.[28] Allina-Pisano's ethnography is likewise predicated on sensitivity to the perspectives, practices, and assumptions of her interlocutors, but she is explicit about a preference to use this sensitivity as leverage for adjudicating among truth-claims.

The volume's other chapters also face this core debate. Most contributors prefer an interpretivist epistemology, though a long history of realist ethnography within anthropology reminds us of a need to historicize this preference. Using viscerally effective examples from an "industrialized slaughterhouse," Pachirat underscores a key insight of interpretivist ethnography: one's truth-claims are fundamentally affected by the relationship between researcher and researched. If the former's position changes, so does his understanding of the social world. Likewise, Schatzberg displays a fundamental interpretivism. Showing that sorcery has long been, and remains, a central feature of the political landscape in Congo, he does not pass judgment on those who believe in sorcery any more than upon those who believe in rational-choice theory.

Being an interpretivist does not preclude the possibility of advancing truth-claims. Indeed, for the interpretivist, we can only discern what is "real" by taking people's worldviews seriously; after all, such worldviews lie at the core of the social construction of reality (Berger and Luckmann 1967). Thus, for Schatzberg, sorcery is real if it has discernible effects on politics and society—effects that his chapter documents. For Yanow, echoing a "consensus" understanding of truth, truth-claims are intersubjectively produced within epistemic communities that offer their own standards and evaluative criteria. In this understanding, judgments about research quality are both possible and necessary. An "anything goes" relativism does not rule the roost.

Some chapters are consistent with, and engage crucial aspects of, what might be considered a qualified neopositivist research agenda. This is not the dogmatic, narrow-minded neopositivism depicted in some polemics.[29] Rather, it is a qualified version that uses attention to detail to generate middle-range theories, that considers cumulative knowledge a possibility worth pursuing, and that is optimistic about the scholar's potential to offer contributions. For example, Wood explicitly seeks to use her ethnographic material about El Salvador to produce general knowledge about the "micro-foundations of collective action." She feels motivated to address and capable of speaking to broader debates in comparative politics. Jourde's use of the term *unidentified political objects* reflects an ontological position that lends itself to such a qualified neopositivist approach. Arias, in his forward-looking "research agenda" for the study of Latin America, emphasizes middle-range theorizing and recommends unleashing the activities of ethnographers in a coordinated, multiple-site effort to produce empirically grounded, but general knowledge.[30]

Like many debates, this one is often argued at the margins. Those ethnographers who assume a qualified neopositivist position produce research that is ultimately much closer to that of interpretivist ethnographers than to that of most rational-choice theorists or advocates of a "quantitative worldview." Likewise, the interpretivist ethnographers here have at least as much in common with their qualified neopositivist ethnographer counterparts as with many postmodernists. Both sides admit that untold complexity inhabits the social world; they agree that ethnography helps make sense of it.

The Role of the Researcher

A related debate concerns the role the researcher plays in the construction of knowledge. Most ethnographers are sensitive to how their presence in the research site alters their appreciation of a research topic; indeed, ethnography is premised on the notion that direct engagement with people being studied produces knowledge. But can knowledge be meaningfully abstracted from the encounters between researcher and researched that produced it? All agree that when the ethnographer immerses himself in a research context and insider viewpoints, the *possibility exists* that he will produce more grounded truth-claims than the scholar who does not engage in immersion. What they disagree about is how to maximize the analytic leverage of ethnographic immersion.

Some contributors take philosophical inspiration from Nietzsche's sardonic commentary on the impossibility of "immaculate perception." In this view, no spectator-like, neutral gaze is possible in a quest for knowledge. Knowledge is coproduced in unique, often fleeting, power-laden, and deeply context-dependent relationships. It is more than subjective; it is intersubjective, coconstituted by a variety of subjects engaged in a thicket of multiple, overlapping forms of communication. Patrick Thaddeus Jackson (2008) calls this position "monism," since an essential separation of the "seer" and the "seen" is impossible.

From this monist perspective, ethnography's role is not so much to produce abstract knowledge as to provide new ways of seeing and thereby challenge existing, often hegemonic, categories of practice and analysis. The ethnographer is necessarily embedded in a variety of relationships (with colleagues, with the people being studied, with a broader society) that exert a profound impact on any claim to truth. To wish that it were otherwise is to cling to a naïve and outdated notion of science. For the monist, any truth-claim is necessarily "partial"; one cannot metaphorically check one's partiality at the door. Recognizing this partiality is the route to powerful insights about social and political life. Among the contributors to this volume, Pachirat, Walsh, and Wedeen most clearly espouse this position.

Jackson's (2008) opposite perspective is "dualism." Dualists argue that knowledge can potentially be separated from the world that produced it; in its neopositivist variant, general, decontextualized knowledge can be created through a careful and incremental search for small-t truths.[31] Dualist ethnographers remain sensitive to "researcher effects," but such effects may be identified and isolated, and their effect on knowledge production minimized. The job of the ethnographer is to become aware of what these researcher effects are and to estimate their impact. This, in turn, is a signal to the epistemic community that the knowledge generated might need to be corrected by shifting it in one analytic direction or another—the equivalent of a statistician shifting a curve by a standard deviation. Allina-Pisano most directly articulates a dualist position, rejecting epistemologies that rely on faith commitments more than on standards of evidence.

In-depth discussion of the philosophical positions associated with these arguments would take us far afield. For present purposes, these perspectives imply different types of commitment to "first-person research," the title of Part 2 of the volume. In a pure sense, all research is first-person to the extent that it is conducted by individuals (or, more rarely, individuals collaborating in teams). Some scholars, however, foreground their own personal characteristics, predilections, aspirations, and experiences that infuse the knowledge-generation process.[32] Others, operating either from a philosophical dualism or from an awkwardness about revealing personal information, prefer to put the first-person "I" into the background. Arias and Wood, in their respective chapters, take this approach. It is hard to imagine research projects more physically demanding and emotionally trying than ethnographic work on violence and civil war, and yet the first-person voice appears relatively more muted in their respective accounts. By contrast, Pachirat emphasizes that his varied personal experiences in the industrialized slaughterhouse informed the knowledge he produced on the topic.

These considerations about the first-person "I" are not limited to the research design phase, the fieldwork phase, or the writing-up phase; rather, they shape scholars' entire career paths. As Zirakzadeh shows in his chapter, what kind of knowledge is produced on any substantive topic (in his case, about the Basque region of Spain) is crucially linked to a broader array of background factors and choices made in the course of personal and professional development. While Pachirat covers micro-level contingencies that affect what knowledge is produced, Zirakzadeh puts into the foreground an array of key meso- and macro-level contingencies.

Those monist researchers who emphasize that their research is conducted in the first person face an additional set of questions. This type of first-person research is likely to treat "objectivity" as, at best, an elusive goal; to many monists, research can serve political goals as much as scientific ones. The impossibility of "[separating] power and surveillance from the gathering of ethnographic information" (Rosaldo 1986, 92) gives new meaning to the word *political* in "political ethnography." While *political* usually refers to the object of study—politics—for many monists, this adjective modifies the effect that *any kind of research* has on the world of which it is an essential part. Pachirat demonstrates this centrally. Shdaimah, Stahl, and Schram take the point a step further by engaging in advocacy with the people they study.

Ways Forward

Those who conduct ethnographic work about politics do not exist in a professional or intellectual vacuum. While one could always find examples of those who put on intellectual blinders to pursue, single-mindedly, their own vision, as a rule ethnographers are an open-minded lot. Being open-minded means being exposed to, and in some cases conducting on one's own, research that derives from quite varied epistemologies and/or uses equally varied methods.[33]

But what place should ethnography have in the study of politics? To argue, as this volume does, that ethnography has been generally under-appreciated in academic political science is to make a claim about the sociology of a discipline. The chapters herein offer some of many possible pre-scriptions to treat what ails political science.

Some contributors suggest that the attention to the micro-level that ethnography brings is compatible with standards of research used across social-scientific inquiry. Arias, for example, emphasizes a need for ethnographers to produce cross-site comparisons and begin to generalize from their data—an argument that King, Keohane, and Verba (1994) would support. Similarly, Wood implies that ethnographic work that attends to a research design emphasizing variation can generate better causal theories. Some authors imply that ethnography's attention to meaning-making can be taken too far and therefore prove self-defeating. Without a way to discern fact from fiction, knowledge claims may drift with the political tides, argues Allina-Pisano. Similarly, Shdaimah, Stahl, and Schram contend that without a way to speak in the language of hard "facts," scholarship cannot call upon those with the power to solve the concrete problems of specific communities. For these scholars, ethnography brings different sensibilities and an atypical level of analysis, but it is essentially conducive to a Popperian attempt at incremental theory building.

If standards are shared, the possibility exists for useful synergies between ethnographic and nonethnographic work. In other work that addresses a largely neopositivist audience, Bayard de Volo and Schatz (2004) suggest that ethnography can assist scholars who seek to trace causal chains, check analytic reasoning, and pinpoint behavioral outcomes. Indeed, many have incorporated elements of ethnographic inquiry into multiple-methods research projects (for example, Stokes 1995; Laitin 1998; Varshney 2002; Shdaimah, Stahl, and Schram, this volume), seeking to combine the epistemological advantages of each. The implication is that if a scholarly approach is akin to a "language" (Feyerabend 1979), every scholar should be multilingual, as each aspect of political life requires a different language to decode it.

Others provide a different way forward. Here, Yanow is most explicit. Addressing those ethnographers who are interpretivists,[34] she contends that they constitute a distinct epistemic community with distinctive, shared standards. Speaking to the ethnographer who is writing a research report, she asks, "What do readers need to find in a manuscript to convince them that it meets the criteria of this epistemic community for doing and being good scientific work?" To meet the criteria that a reader accepts as valid is to persuade.

Yanow's perspective implies a degree of incommensurability between various research traditions and counsels caution against the mixing of approaches, a point I consider in the concluding chapter. For me, ethnography should be part of a methodologically plural body of research about politics, but this pluralism should principally reside at the discipline-wide level. Mixing methods derived from different epistemological traditions within single research projects may relegate ethnography to the status of "summer intern" (Hopf 2006, cited in Pachirat, this volume).[35] Put differently, such mixing runs the risk of misaligning ontology and epistemology (Hall 2003). In this sense, a metaphorical "multilingualism" should occur across the discipline.

Finally, while most contributors see a need to devote energy toward the professional development of ethnographers and the promotion of ethnography in the discipline, some demur. Rooted in a pragmatist, problem-solving tradition, Shdaimah, Stahl, and Schram are more interested in addressing the particular, concrete problems of the people they study.[36] Indeed, they are skeptical of ethnography's ability to avoid being "top down" in its treatment of the people being studied and suggest that promoting problem-driven research would obviate the need for any explicit support of nonmainstream epistemologies and ontologies.

Role of the Editor

While I will not dwell on it, a few words are warranted about the choices I have made as editor of this volume. Of the background conditions, environmental factors, and specific choices that affect the final product, two in particular deserve mention.

First, whom does the volume exclude or include? Beyond the usual constraints dictated by colleagues' workloads and travel schedules, I wanted to speak to political scientists by detailing the contributions that *political scientists* have made via ethnography.[37] I also wanted a volume that would represent the major subfields of the discipline. The lack of a contribution from an international relations specialist had much to do with how unfortunately rare ethnography is in that subfield, a crucial fact that I take up in the volume's conclusion.[38]

But who is a political ethnographer? I have suggested that "pure" ethnographic work is hard to come by, especially in political science departments. Thus, selection included people who might describe themselves, as has Lee Ann Fujii (personal communication), as conducting "ethnography lite." But, as Rasing (1994, 2) reminds us, "It is not necessary to be an ethnographer to make valid ethnographical observations. A keen interest in people, an inquisitive mind and a sensitivity to the truth are of relevance."

Rather than seeing those who deviate from "pure" ethnography as conducting a watered-down version of the real thing, I seek to mine their work to see what they contribute to particular research programs.

Second, am I a political ethnographer? To an extent I am, but my empirical work (for example, Schatz 2004) has incorporated ethnographic methods and sensibilities only partially. Like Zirakzadeh, my hesitancy to embrace a "purer" version of ethnographic inquiry stemmed from my training. While I was schooled in an eclectic study of politics, I calculated that I ought not to go "too far" away from what I perceived to be mainstream political science. I now realize that this choice stemmed from an incomplete understanding of the discipline and its possibilities. Thus, one of the central motivations for this volume is purely selfish—to learn from my colleagues what ethnography can contribute to political research and to imagine different possibilities for my own work.

Organization of the Volume

Part 1 introduces the central ontological and epistemological issues associated with conducting ethnographic work. In chapter 1, Kubik provides a background philosophical discussion that sets the stage for appreciating ethnography's contribution to both neopositivist and interpretivist research programs. In chapter 2, Allina-Pisano, through a series of vignettes, illustrates the virtues of ethnography for improving the quality of data and gaining better traction on mainstream social science research problems. In chapter 3, Wedeen elegantly and powerfully argues that ethnography's central virtue lies in its value as an interpretive tool—to enhance our understanding of "performative practices."

The chapters in Part 2 demonstrate that all research is conducted from the first-person perspective and highlight questions of background predisposition, positionality, and research design. Zirakzadeh in chapter 4 provides an honest accounting (beyond what most scholars ever produce) of how he, in essence, stumbled upon the value of ethnographically informed research techniques. In chapter 5, Wood details the value of ethnographic material in discovering the logic by which people mobilize in advance of, and during, civil war. She shows that to discover this logic requires an ability to listen assiduously and interpret thoughtfully, based on a grounded sense of how memory is constructed during and after wartime. In chapter 6, Pachirat offers a detailed description of his research in an industrialized slaughterhouse in the U.S. Midwest and, in the course of it, makes a powerful argument for the value of a researcher's partiality.

Part 3 offers a sampling of the many contributions of ethnographic research to our understanding of power. In chapter 7, Walsh shows how a field like public opinion research—long dominated by survey research methods—overlooks the insights from ethnographic research to its own detriment. In chapter 8, Schatzberg challenges readers to broaden their understanding of politics by considering how the supernatural might have an impact on political and social life. In chapter 9, Jourde demonstrates how rudimentary blind spots in the literature on authoritarianism and Islamism can be remedied through an ethnographic sensibility. In chapter 10, Bayard de Volo details how two very different research projects began to remedy fundamental shortcomings in social movement literature and feminist theory, respectively.

Part 4 asks what place ethnography has and should have in the discipline. In chapter 11, Arias proposes a research agenda that would fundamentally transform, and ground, the study of Latin American politics. In chapter 12, Shdaimah, Stahl, and Schram, based on multiple-method research conducted on homeownership in Philadelphia, emphasize the limits of an ethnography that would be content to reveal insider perspectives. In the problem-driven tradition of the pragmatists, they not only advocate the *perspectives* of the people they study; they directly seek to help solve everyday problems. In chapter 13, Yanow provides an insightful and engaging set of instructions to would-be writers, readers, and reviewers about key elements of an ethnographically conducted interpretive study. She emphasizes that research involves not just a "double hermeneutic," in which researchers interpret the interpretations produced by the researched (Giddens 1984), but a triple one: the writer and reader also create a relationship based on interpretation. Her chapter, in the tradition of Feyerabend, emphasizes how communication between epistemic communities is required for ethnographic studies to enjoy the legitimacy they deserve. Recognizing the various strains of political ethnography, the conclusion asks what kind(s) of ethnography would best suit the study of politics.

Notes

For their insightful comments on a draft of this introduction, thanks to Jessica Allina-Pisano, Lorraine Bayard de Volo, Lee Ann Fujii, Patrick Thaddeus Jackson, Cédric Jourde, Timothy Pachirat, Vincent Pouliot, and Dvora Yanow.

1. This was especially true in the United States, whose political scientists have disproportionately driven trends in the discipline. Rational-choice scholarship also offered a type of mathematically driven reasoning, but since it was relatively unconcerned

with producing empirical research, I leave it to the side in this discussion. See Green and Shapiro (1996).

2. This embrace of statistical approaches was highly selective and typically based on a large-n, variable-oriented, linear, and probabilistic orientation that precluded other statistical approaches. On a more recent revival and development of Boolean techniques and their potential for studying the social world, see Brady and Collier (2004).

3. I have in mind King, Keohane, and Verba (1994). George Thomas (2005, 855) raises the opposite possibility—that "if social science has a unified logic, it is found in approaches traditionally associated with qualitative methods rather than statistical inference." See also Brady and Collier (2004). The phrase "quantitative worldview" comes from McKeown (2004).

4. For a similar, recent consideration of political ethnography, largely by sociologists, see Qualitative Sociology (2006). Auyero (2006a, 257) begins the special issue of that journal with the sentence: "The revival of ethnographic research within sociology is undisputed." Political science, by contrast, has not yet experienced such a revival to the same extent, although a variety of intellectual and professional initiatives suggest that such a revival might be expected.

5. Some of us received training in ethnographic methods via neighboring disciplines, especially anthropology and sociology. Others, such as Zirakzadeh (chapter 4) are essentially autodidacts.

6. The workshop was held at the University of Toronto in October 2006.

7. Thanks to Lisa Wedeen for suggesting that *immersion* replace *insider perspectives*, which was used in the Toronto workshop.

8. Kubik in chapter 1 offers a *tour d'horizon* of the anthropological literature on ethnography that considers these debates.

9. I borrow *sensibility* from Pader (2006), although her use of the term is different from that offered here.

10. As Lorraine Bayard de Volo highlights in chapter 10, emotional engagement with the people being studied can be as useful as it is inevitable.

11. The ethnographic work of political scientists Lloyd and Susanne Rudolph (e.g., 2003) and Myron Aronoff (1974, 1989, 1993) could be characterized similarly.

12. See also Burawoy et al. (2000).

13. Participant observation is itself a cluster of closely related techniques. See, for example, Jorgensen (1989).

14. I have in mind not formal membership, such as when one pays dues to an organization, but rather "belonging" to a group or category. For valuable methodological implications built upon this core insight about shades of gray, see Ragin (2000).

15. Lee Ann Fujii (2007) calls the information gathered from such presentations "metadata," since they are often contained at a level of abstraction higher than that of the factual information informants impart. In a related vein, Pouliot (2008, 5), argues (after Bourdieu) for approaches that help to discern "what agents think *from* (the background of know-how that informs practice in an inarticulate fashion)," rather than simply "what agents think *about* (reflexive and conscious knowledge)."

16. Garfinkel's (1984 [1967]) "ethnomethodology" might approach such an ideal type, but few political scientists—indeed, few cultural or social anthropologists—are committed to the deeply inductive enterprise that he offers.

17. Americanists who use participant observation include Fenno (1990), Glaser (1996), Soss (2000), Walsh (2004, 2007), and Warren (2005).

18. On "wealthology" (the study of the rich), see, for example, http://www.cultureplan ning.com/html/wealth.html (accessed 1 August 2007).

19. For "how-to" books, see Fetterman (1989) on ethnography and Spradley (1980) on participant observation.

20. In my own "methodological appendix," I did not resist the temptation to neaten up—for the purposes of presentation—what was a very messy research process. See Schatz (2004, appendix).

21. I suggest in this volume's conclusion that ethnographic inquiry is more likely to call into question broad generalizations from other research traditions than to confirm their validity. Thus, ethnography is well positioned to generate what Ian Shapiro (2004) calls "problematizing redescriptions."

22. Thanks to Patrick Thaddeus Jackson for stimulating this line of thinking.

23. That achieving descriptive accuracy is no mean feat calls into question the common-place among political scientists that description is somehow a lower order endeavor than explanation. For one version of this commonplace notion, see King, Keohane, and Verba (1994).

24. For a cautionary tale that speaks to the potential for ethnographic approaches to serve the interests of the powerful, see Asad (1973). Ironically, Shdaimah, Stahl, and Schram's chapter argues that ethnography's ability to champion the people being studied is laudable but does not go far enough.

25. Thanks to Jessica Allina-Pisano for stressing the need to cover these disagreements as a way to move discussion forward.

26. Thanks to Patrick Thaddeus Jackson for suggesting that *neo-* precede *positivism*, since the philosophical differences from the earlier positivism are notable.

27. Kubik, in fact, adds a third and more recent tradition: postmodern ethnography.

28. For a fuller explication of interpretivist research, see Yanow and Schwartz-Shea (2006).

29. For well-balanced and nonpolemical discussions of the merits and demerits of the neopositivism in King, Keohane, and Verba's *Designing Social Inquiry*, see Johnson (2006) and the contributions to Brady and Collier (2004).

30. For a similar argument concerning the study of "intense, multifocal events," such as protest demonstrations, see Mazie and Woods (2003).

31. Jackson also discusses critical realist and Habermasian "dualism," which generate a research dynamic different from the one I identify here with neopositivist dualism.

32. For this reason, many of the chapter contributors reference themselves. Citing one-self is, of course, a time-honored practice among scholars, but it is particularly ap-propriate for many ethnographers who believe that the first-person singular should not be excised from the text.

33. Mixing methods that share a family resemblance is not the same as mixing episte-mological positions, a point I detail in the book's conclusion.

34. Kubik in chapter 1 reminds us that ethnography may be interpretivist, realist, or postmodernist.

35. This issue is covered by the contributions to Qualitative Methods (2006).

36. For a fuller explication of this position, see Flyvbjerg (2001).

37. Much border-crossing blurs the category "political scientist," but all of the contrib-utors except Shdaimah and Stahl either work in political science departments, were trained as political scientists, or both.

38. Prominent exceptions include Barnett (2003), Hopf (2002), and Autesserre (2006).

PART ONE

Two Traditions of Political Ethnography

The chapters in Part 1 trace two broad traditions of political ethnography—a realist and an interpretivist one. Jan Kubik in chapter 1 details some of the principal contributions of each of these two traditions, emphasizing that while political scientists tend to imagine ethnography as necessarily interpretivist, ethnography has been used in a striking variety of ways, even in its "mother discipline" of anthropology. Indeed, Kubik adds a third and more recent tradition—postmodern ethnography—which presents new challenges and opportunities for students of politics.

In chapter 2 Jessica Allina-Pisano provides a series of fieldwork-based vignettes that highlight the value of realist ethnography. Arguing that realist ethnography can provide one way of adjudicating truth-claims and negotiating power-laden situations, she suggests that political ethnographers should not abandon their claims to "small-t" truth; their methods and approaches—among them, their attention to many layers of interpretation that characterize human communities—are in fact uniquely suited to discovering these truths.

In chapter 3 Lisa Wedeen offers an interpretivist understanding of what political ethnography can do, arguing that the ethnographer is well positioned to shed light on "performative practices." She distances the ethnographic project from the language and conceits of behavioralism, emphasizing that individuals do not simply "behave"; rather, they "practice" in ways that are unique to human beings. Moreover, people "perform"—that is, their perspectives are not pristinely isolated and waiting to be discovered by the researcher; rather, they are in motion and emerge in the process of human expression.

ONE

Ethnography of Politics: Foundations, Applications, Prospects

JAN KUBIK

Today's political science is a massive, multistranded research enterprise whose complexity defies succinct characterization. It is therefore difficult if not impossible to provide a simple and concise answer to the question, "What is the use of ethnography for political scientists?" It depends on the aim of the research project, the specific ontological assumptions about social/political reality, and the particular conception of ethnography. Since it is impossible to consider all possibilities in a single chapter, I delimit the scope of my remarks to two *problématiques* that are central to the comparativist enterprise: the significance of the cultural aspect of social reality and the consequences of the recent turn from macro- to micro-levels of analysis (Elster 1985; Geddes 2003). I focus discussion on the subfield of comparative politics, since it has been the site of most ethnographic work conducted within political science. It is also the subfield I know best.[1]

The relative utility of ethnography is closely related to our understanding of politics. March and Olsen (1989, 47–48) typify a commonplace, *materialist-institutional* understanding by suggesting, "The organizing principle of a political system is the allocation of scarce resources in the face of conflict of interests." This is a time-honored way of thinking about politics, for, as March and Olsen observe, "a conception of politics as decision making and resource allocation is at least as old as Plato and Aristotle."

Yet March and Olsen are keenly aware of a significant shortcoming of this conception: "Although there are exceptions, the modern perspective in political science has generally given primacy to substantive outcomes and either ignored symbolic actions or seen symbols as part of manipulative efforts to control outcomes" (1989, 47). Not all politics can be reduced to competition over material resources; indeed, much of it concerns the struggle over collective identity, including often deadly contests over the meaning of symbols signifying this identity. Dirks, Eley, and Ortner (1994, 32) develop this thought further:

> Politics is usually conducted as if identity were fixed. The question then becomes, on what basis, at different times in different places, does the nonfixity become temporarily fixed in such a way that individuals and groups can behave as a particular kind of agency, political or otherwise? How do people become shaped into acting subjects, understanding themselves in particular ways? In effect, politics consists of the effort to domesticate the infinitude of identity. It is the attempt to hegemonize identity, to order it into a strong programmatic statement. If identity is decentered, politics is about the attempt to create a center.

Such centers emerge and disintegrate as a result of specific actions by concrete actors who propose, disseminate, and interpret cultural meanings encoded in a variety of symbolic ways. To study such processes, political scientists—at least those who recognize that any attempt to propose and propagate a vision of collective identity, and thus any "cultural" effort whose aim is endowing human (particularly collective) action with meaning, is *par excellence* political—must move beyond the *materialist-institutional* perspective and employ a *symbolic-cultural* approach.[2] And within such an approach "the researcher should ask whether the theory is consistent with evidence about the meanings the historical actors themselves attributed to their actions" (Hall 2003, 394). For researchers who embrace ontologies that include the "meaningful" layer of reality, ethnographic approaches emerge as promising tools for studying politics.

If we understand politics as, in some important measure, *locally* produced, we again might turn to ethnography. Indeed, attention to the microlevel of analysis constitutes an important trend in today's study of politics (Geddes 2003). Game-theoretic ambition to develop a concise theory of politics (Bates et al. 1998) and a more sociological quest to identify micro- or meso-level mechanisms governing social and political life (Tilly 2001) share an assumption that progress in the social sciences is more likely when our analytic gaze is focused on the details of concrete interactions rather than the workings of "large" structures. Thomas P. O'Neill Jr.'s memorable quip that "all politics is local" captures this idea.

This turn to the local coincides with renewed interest in observing "actual" human behavior: students are increasingly admonished to focus on the "real life" interactions of people in "real time," rather than on interactions of variables in abstract theoretical spaces.[3] Hall captures this perspective:

> The systematic process analyst then draws observation from the empirical cases, not only about the value of the principal causal variables, but about the processes linking these variables to the outcomes. . . . This is not simply a search for "intervening" variables. The point is to see if the multiple actions and statements of the actors at each stage of the causal process are consistent with the image of the world historical process implied by each theory. (2003, 394)

This attention to the *symbolic-cultural* and to the *local*, micro-scale, and "actual" should make political scientists hungry for more ethnography, a research tool well suited for addressing these emergent concerns.

But we need to pause to consider the intellectual, philosophical, and epistemological origins of the long and tangled traditions of ethnographic inquiry before we can appreciate ethnography's potential value for the study of politics.

The Promise of Ethnography

Most writers posit participant observation as the defining method (or technique) of ethnography (Bayard de Volo and Schatz 2004, 267; Tilly 2006, 410). Below I investigate the usefulness, if not indispensability, of ethnography for studying a reality that is construed as meaningful ("ideal"), processual ("diachronic"), and interactive. Suffice it to note here that ethnography's usefulness for studying "constructed" realities has been demonstrated in sociology (where it serves as an auxiliary tool) and anthropology (where it is the principal tool), and should thus be examined by political scientists, particularly comparativists, who are often admonished to take culture seriously (Norton 2004; Chabal and Daloz 2006; Harrison and Huntington 2000; Rao and Walton 2004).[4] In sociology, it supplements various interpretive techniques (for example, content or textual analysis) in studies that treat cultures as assemblages of (broadly understood) texts; in anthropology, it is indispensable for studying culture in action.

But ethnography obviously can be and has been employed by more positivistically oriented researchers. It is thus imperative to outline the differential uses of ethnography in positivistic and interpretivist research programs. Let us begin in ethnography's "maternal" discipline, cultural/social anthropology. To be sure, culture is not the only object of this discipline, which is composed of several, partially separate intellectual traditions, to some extent overlapping with "national" schools.[5] An exhaustive discussion is beyond my scope, but it is worthwhile to highlight one distinction: while the "British" have developed *social* anthropology, the "Americans" tend to practice *cultural* anthropology. Beyond semantics lie fundamental ontological, epistemological, and methodological issues. In a nutshell, while the "British" generally tend to focus their efforts on studying *social structures* and their "political" dimension (initially in non-Western societies), the "Americans" tend to construe the object of their studies as *culture(s)* and the multiple ways in which culture interacts with power. These different definitions have consequences for the nature of specific projects, their conceptualizations, and methodologies. But at the same time these two traditions have something in common: they both approach politics as an aspect of social relations that needs to be studied in practice, *in statu nascendi*, through extensive fieldwork centered on (preferably long-term) participant observation.

What ethnographers observe (via participation) depends on the particular school or research tradition. By and large, while "British" lenses "detect" structure, "American" ones are fitted for studying culture. Significantly, both "structure" and "culture" can be and often are these days defined in a constructivist manner. It is enough to consider Giddens's theory of *structuration* or Bourdieu's theory of *practice*—both *par excellence* constructivist conceptions of social structure. Moreover, at least since the wave of postmodern critiques, we know that "objects" of study do not exist out there, in an "objective reality," ready to be "discovered"; rather, they are coconstituted by the two (or more) participants in a *research interaction*.

Ethnography as a method (participant observation), therefore, is not limited to the study of culture. Just as many interpretive studies of politics rely on participant-observation, noninterpretive studies use the same method (for example, studies of organizational structures, informal networks, or economic exchanges). At the same time, not all interpretive studies of power and politics are ethnographic (Bayard de Volo and Schatz 2004, 267). In fact, most are not. Table 1 illustrates these distinctions, based on examples drawn mostly from comparative studies of politics.

Most research in political science is based on a naturalist ontology of the social and does not rely on participant observation; the work of Przeworski and his collaborators (2000) on the relationship between economic development and the survival of political regimes is exemplary. Such work is also practiced to great effect in the broadly defined area of "political culture"; consider the large-n studies of Inglehart and his collaborators who

Table 1

		Preferred Ontology of the Social and the Attendant Epistemology/Methodology	
		Meaningful/ Interpretivist	Natural/Positive/ Noninterpretivist
Research Technique	Participant Observation	Aronoff (1989); Kertzer (1996); Wedeen (1999)	Malinowski (1922); Laitin (1998); Fortes and Evans-Pritchard (1940)
	Nonparticipant Observation	Kubik (1994); Edles (1998); Bonnell (1997); Chabal and Daloz (2006); O'Neill (1999)	Most political science; Przeworski et al. (2000); Petersen (2001)

survey "values" of the world's population. Also, most work in game theory is noninterpretive, as it is built on deductively derived models of purportedly universal motivation mechanisms. Some game-theoretic work is sensitive to local contexts and is "ethnographic" in its tenor, although it does not typically use participant observation. (Petersen's work, for example, deals with past events, as I discuss below). The second category features naturalist/positivistic works that rely on participant observation but do not provide interpretive accounts of the social worlds actors live in. Much of classical British social anthropology belongs to this category. Most influential works in comparative politics that rely at least partially on participant observation belong to the naturalistic, noninterpretive genre, though some—such as Laitin's influential 1998 study—are close to the boundary between interpretive and noninterpretive types of work.

The third type includes works that are interpretive but do not use participant observation. Bonnell's (1997) analysis of Soviet posters as tools of power, Edles's (1998) work on the symbolic dimension of Spanish democratization, or my own study (Kubik 1994) of Polish Solidarity's symbolic challenge to the hegemonic power of the Communist Party belong to this type. Finally, works belonging to the fourth type combine interpretive epistemology with participant observation as the main method. Consider Aronoff's (1989) study of the inner workings of the Israeli Labor Party, Kertzer's (1996) detailed reconstruction of the Italian Communist Party cell's operation in a local setting, or Wedeen's (1999) analysis of everyday, counter-hegemonic challenges to Hāfiz al-Asad's power in Syria.

To summarize: as a method,[6] ethnography is used to study culture (meaning systems) or other aspects of the broadly conceived social, such as economy, power (politics), or social structure. Its essence is participant observation, a disciplined immersion in the social life of a given group of people. Ethnography is sometimes erroneously equated with (1) in-depth interviewing (as opposed to administering surveys); (2) case studies (as opposed to large-n statistical studies); (3) process tracing (as opposed to finding correlations); and (4) interpretation of meaning (as opposed to the "naturalistic" study of "objective" social facts). Studies based on these four methods are not necessarily ethnographic; they become so when they rely on participant observation of considerable length.[7]

An answer to the question "What is ethnography good for (in the study of power and politics)?" depends not only on the definition of ethnography, but also on the conception of a discipline (its ontological and epistemological assumptions) within which it is defined and practiced. Because the track record of ethnographic work is more robust in anthropology than in political science, let me examine what it has contributed to each of three broad traditions of political anthropology: positivistic, interpretive, and postmodern.[8]

Ethnography in Positivistic (Political) Anthropology

In this section I take stock of the contributions that traditional, positivistic ethnography has made to the study of power. I do so to emphasize a central point: ethnography can benefit positivistic research agendas at least as well as it can contribute to interpretive ones. Thus, as Allina-Pisano shows in chapter 3, ethnography has a long tradition of working in a "realist" vein.

Political anthropology is a subdiscipline with a distinguished tradition of realist inquiry. Many illustrious nineteenth-century scholars (most prominently Maine, Spencer, Marx, Morgan, and Tylor) studied non-Western political systems and, particularly, their evolution.[9] They can be seen, therefore, as precursors or early practitioners of the discipline. But the modern field of political anthropology is often said to have emerged with the publication in 1940 of *African Political Systems,* edited by M. Fortes and E. E. Evans-Pritchard. All studies reported in that volume were based on extensive ethnographic fieldwork, but, by contrast to today's anthropologists—who would emphasize the cultural specificity of each case—the editors made an explicit effort to strip all social processes of "their cultural idiom" and reduce them "to functional terms" to generate comparisons and arrive at generalizations (quoted in Vincent 1990, 258). At the time of the volume's publication, anthropology (including political anthropology) was still predominantly characterized by its focus on non-Western, "exotic," or at least "marginal" societies. As Vincent (1990, 24) notes, "Not until the 1950s, in the face of challenges from other disciplines on the eve of their massive intervention in the anthropological domain, did anthropologists make manifest that 'anthropology is characterized by a set of methods rather than bound by a subject matter' (Bohannan 1967, xiv)."

Ethnography and the Study of Power

Long before Foucault made it fashionable, ethnographers were tracking down the exercise of power within the interstices of official structures, behind the veil of various officialdoms, and in ostensibly apolitical spaces and domains. But, perhaps more important, there is no other method that can allow researchers to study power *in statu nascendi* in all settings, formal and informal, and—particularly—to reconstruct the *informal workings of formal power structures*.

Ethnography is thus used to map out the multiple layers of power within complex bureaucratic structures and to complement if not supersede reconstructions of "modern" power generated by other methods. For example, Wedel et al. (2005) detail the anthropology of policy making in complex, modern organizations; Abeles considers the workings of the European Parliament (1992) and the European Commission (2004); Aronoff (1989) explores the Israeli Labor Party; Bailey (1983) unravels the politics of various committees (at parliaments, governments, universities, and so on); Wedeen (1999) focuses on the intricate mechanisms of resistance in authoritarian Syria; and Gaventa (1980) highlights the politics of inequality in an Appalachian valley.

Likewise, ethnography seems indispensable to the study of collective action; no other method can better expose mechanisms of the important, early stages of mobilization (Blee and Currier 2006). Petersen (2001) uses an "ethnohistorical" approach to reconstruct the mechanisms of anti-Nazi mobilization in Lithuania in the 1940s. He begins by modeling the sociological mechanisms and group features that help explain why individuals in certain communities (at certain times) rebel against oppressors, while others remain passive or collaborate. His model specifies such attributes of the community as (1) the initial distribution preferences and constraints concerning the risk of rebellion; (2) the types of norms (of honor or family obligation, for example) that define the types of subgroups; and (3) the distribution of those subgroups within the larger community. Petersen divides mobilization into two stages: from passivity to resistance, and from resistance to rebellion. Then, he considers separately the problem of rebellion's sustainability. For each stage or problem he identifies a different set of mechanisms and shows how they reinforce each other, propelling the process forward (to rebellion) or backward (to collaboration).

Since Petersen studies past events, he cannot employ participant observation, but he collects and interrogates his data *as if* they were generated by such a method. The ethnographic tenor of his study does not come, therefore, from participant observation, but rather from an *ethnographic problematization and framing* of the work.[10] He sets out to study the details of community organization and uses all available information not only to reconstruct actors' views and preferences, but also to map out their actions within the local structures that both empowered and constrained them, and to identify the mechanisms that make mobilization possible. His is a quintessentially ethnohistorical, indeed ethnographic, project.

Ethnography and Game Theory

Ethnography is particularly well suited to test the limits of rationality in game-theoretic models, which otherwise run the risk of circular reasoning. As Morrow proposes: "Rational behavior means choosing the best means to gain a predetermined set of ends. It is an evaluation of the consistency of choices and not the thought process, of implementation of fixed goals and of the morality of those goals" (1994, 17). But to determine whether such consistency exists, researchers often infer both the *intention* to employ certain means and their *actual employment* from observing *ex post facto* the very same action. To determine an actor's rationality, one would have to first infer that an actor *intended* to employ certain means to achieve a given goal; then observe the *actual* means employed; and finally *compare* the two. Such tests of rationality are rare, perhaps because the ethnographic method is seldom used in studies relying on game-theoretic models.

Ethnography and the Study of Social Structure

Any full understanding of power requires an understanding of social structure, which is both a product of and a constraint on individual and collective action. Traditional ethnography makes at least three contributions in this area. First, while focusing on small-scale phenomena, ethnography allows the researcher to see the way social structure actually works in people's daily lives (say, how a position in class structure influences one's life choices; see Willis 1981 or Sider 1986). Second, it contributes empirical material to the study of one of the thorniest problems of social theory: the relationship between structure and agency. By observing people up close, ethnographers can gauge the "structural" limitations actors face, reconstruct the range of strategic choices they have, observe their actual action, and assess its possibly transformative impact on structure. Third, ethnography is the best method of studying the complex interplay between (formal) social structure and (informal) social organization.[11]

Ethnography's contribution to the study of the relationship between formal and informal institutions should be carefully appraised by political scientists, as this relationship has been one of the hallmarks of new institutionalism. In a path-breaking and influential study, the economist Douglass North shows that economic behavior is shaped by both formal and informal institutions (1990, 4).[12] Positing that economic performance is determined by a complex interplay of three factors—demography (human capital), the stock of knowledge (including everyday beliefs), and the formal institutional framework—North (1997, 14) warns that "we know very little about this interaction." Participant observation is well suited to studying the complex interplay of such factors.

Ethnography and the Study of Social Process

Research methods typical of political science, such as opinion surveys, periodic collection of economic statistics (usually aggregated on a yearly basis), or pooled expert opinions on institutional changes (also routinely aggregated and reported yearly; see the World Bank or Freedom House) *register the occurrence of change*; they do not *specify the mechanisms of change*. As political science faces increasing calls to turn from macro- to micro-levels and to study actual mechanisms, the value of ethnography should become apparent. As Trickett and Oliveri (1997, 149) argue, "ethnography can capture the dynamic of change in ways that snapshot surveys using pre-established dimensions and response categories cannot." Ethnography allows researchers to reconstruct the manner in which large-scale social processes (say, postcommunist transformations) actually occur and how they constrain or empower people in their daily lives. It is, after all, the reproduction and transformation of daily lives that are observable, not "structural change."

Ethnography can also detect how the macro- and micro-dynamics of change may be out of step. Introducing a collection of ethnographies about postcommunist transformations, Burawoy and Verdery opine:

Our view of the relation between macro structures and everyday practices is that the collapse of party states and administered economies broke down macro structures, thereby creating space for micro worlds to produce autonomous effects that may have unexpected influence over the structures that have been emerging. . . . It is precisely the sudden importance of micro processes lodged in moments of transformation that privileges an ethnographic approach. (1999, 3)

Significantly, they do not merely signal the differential rhythms of macro- and micro-changes; they claim that the often overlooked and/or unintended micro-processes may influence, derail, or even halt macro-changes. Such observations dovetail with recent writing on the mechanisms of social change in historical sociology and historically oriented comparative politics.[13]

Finally, ethnography is critical for identifying the sources of impending change. Norton (2004, 41) observes that since change often comes from the periphery, it is important to "recognize the power of liminal, or marginal, groups. . . . Because they stand on the boundaries of identity, they are often central to debates over those boundaries."

Ethnography and the Study of Political Economy

Bird-David observes, "A diversity of exchange forms had been reified by anthropologists into either 'gift' or 'commodity,' while in the concreteness of social life—among indigenous people as among Westerners—there are multiple kinds. These have to be studied, too" (quoted in Herzfeld 2001, 111). To study economic transactions in isolation from their cultural and social contexts entails a risk of serious distortion. Aware of this, most anthropologists rely on ethnography to advance what has come to be known as the "substantivist" conception of economy (as distinct from the "formalist" view derived from neoclassical economic theory).

The distinction between substantivist and formalist definitions of economic activity was first introduced by Karl Polanyi (1957):

The two root meanings of "economic," the substantive and the formal, have nothing in common. The latter derives from logic, the former from fact. The formal meaning implies a set of rules referring to choice between alternative uses of insufficient means. The substantive meaning implies neither choice nor insufficiency of means; man's livelihood may or may not involve the necessity of choice and, if choice there be, it need not be induced by the limiting effect of "scarcity" of the means. (1957, 243)

In the same essay he observed:

> The human economy, then, is embedded and enmeshed in institutions, economic and noneconomic. The inclusion of the noneconomic is vital. For religion or government may be as important for the structure and functioning of the economy as monetary institutions or the availability of tools and machines themselves that lighten the toil of labor. (1957, 250)

This distinction can be understood ontologically, methodologically, and historically. In ontological terms, the substantivist (holistic) approach treats economic activity as an "aspect of social life rather than a segment of society" (Plattner 1989, 14). Accordingly, the economic domain is construed as inseparably embedded within other domains; it cannot be fruitfully analyzed in isolation. Formalists, by contrast, conceptualize economic activity as a separate domain (segment of society) with its own, specific mechanisms, best specified by neoclassical microeconomics.

Substantivists claim that since economic activity is usually (or always)—even in the capitalist system (see Narotzky 1997; Gudeman 2001)—embedded in social, cultural, and political contexts, it has to be studied sociologically/anthropologically/ethnographically (in its full social context).[14] For their part, methodological formalists attempt to apply the methods of modern microeconomic analysis to non-Western societies. They assume that "individuals in every culture exercise rational choice in a means-ends, constraints, and opportunities framework" (Plattner 1989, 13). They propose that the economic domain can be usefully isolated from other domains of social life (religious, familial, and so on) in every society and people can be always studied as "utility maximizers."

Historically, the distinction is sometimes said to separate modern societies that operate on the market principle from other societies where the market principle either is absent or is inseparably intertwined with other principles (moral, familial, or statist). While many people subscribe to some version of an evolutionary paradigm, believing that societies move from a substantivist to a formalist phase, ethnographers have problematized this claim. For example, anthropologists who study postcommunist transformations have shown that the "progress" from ex-communist substantivism to neocapitalist formalism at best is uneven, slow, and full of reversals. Moreover, to survive under adverse conditions, people create and maintain complex networks that can be conceptualized as "economic" only at a risk of serious conceptual stretching. The extensive and empirically convincing literature on this phenomenon is found mostly in anthropology

(Humphrey 2002; Burawoy and Verdery 1999; Buchowski 1997), but also sociology (Stark and Bruszt 1998) and political economy (Woodruff 1999; Blyth 2002).

These insights about postcommunist transformations follow on the heels of a long anthropological tradition of recognizing complex relationships between economy and culture. Beginning in the 1960s, anthropologists using ethnographic evidence wrote books with titles like *Political Economy and Culture of . . .* showing, for example, that while in practice economic relations tend to be complex and multistranded, in ideology (of capitalism or communism) they appear as separate and single-stranded. In a recent, sophisticated ethnography of family firms in Italy, Yanagisako (2002, 13) performs a similar service, showing that even today, "family and kinship processes, relations, and sentiments are crucial for the production and reproduction of all forms of capitalism, whether family capitalism or nonfamily capitalism"—in spite of a prevailing discourse that normatively separates "family" from "business" relations. It is hard to imagine how such a demystification of the dominant view of economic activity could have been accomplished without ethnography. Significantly, this realization has already filtered to the World Bank, as a path-breaking volume indicates (Rao and Walton 2004).

From the onset of anthropology (political anthropology in particular), ethnography has been successfully employed to locate power in hardly accessible or atypical places, beyond the world of formal institutions. And as cultural/social anthropology has come to be defined by its method rather than its object, its preoccupation with marginal or peripheral phenomena has continued. Thus, the major contribution of traditional positivistic anthropology—via ethnography—is to the study of power and politics *outside* of centers and mainstreams, within a complex *interplay* with economic and cultural processes, and in locations and crevices where the exercise of power or authority is often *invisible* to other disciplines.

Interpretive Ethnography: The Study of Meaning (Culture) in Action

Wittgenstein should perhaps be declared a patron saint of the ethnographic study of meaning, as he emphasized that the meaning(s) of a sign (word, picture, and sound) is best determined through studying its use, its employment in social practice. As I demonstrated earlier, ethnography and interpretation are not necessarily paired; quite often they are not. But their combination allows for the reconstruction of how culture (the meaning-creating machine) operates in practice, and how the actual production and interpretation of meaning are practical activities, often central to both power struggles and economic maneuvers, and shot through with emotions.

There are many definitions of culture; ethnographers need one that goes beyond treating it merely as a symbolic structure. The Comaroffs (1992), for example, speak about meaningful (37) or symbolic practices (35) that constitute culture construed as a "semantic space, the field of signs and practices, in which human beings construct and represent themselves and others, and hence their societies and histories. It is not merely an abstract order of signs, or relations among signs. Nor is it just the sum of habitual practices. Neither pure langue nor pure parole, it never constitutes a closed, entirely coherent system. Quite the contrary: Culture always contains within it polyvalent contestable messages, images, and actions" (1992, 27).

Contests within this semantic space are by their nature political, as they often constitute attempts to achieve legitimacy or to establish collective identities (nation, class, gender, race) and endow them with an aura of naturalness. Can societies and their politics, permeated by such symbolic struggles, be studied in the same manner as "natural systems" examined by the "hard" sciences? Sahlins (2004) argues that Thucydides in *The Peloponnesian War* provided a positive answer to this question, thus setting Western social science on a naturalist course. Since Thucydides, the debate between naturalists and antinaturalists has run through almost the entire course of Western social reflection. In the second half of the nineteenth century naturalism and antinaturalism in the social sciences were defined and deliberated with great clarity by such German scholars as Heinrich Rickert, Wilhelm Windelband, and Max Weber (for overviews see Palmer 1969; Bleicher 1980; Bambach 1995).

Perhaps the most influential among them, Wilhelm Dilthey (see, for example, Dilthey 1976), proposed a sharp distinction between the "positivistic" (*Naturwissenschaften*)[15] and the "humanistic" (*Geisteswissenschaften*) disciplines, defined the "proper" method of the latter as interpretation (*Verstehen*), and sharply differentiated it from explanation, the proper procedure of the former. Clifford Geertz revived this distinction in his trendsetting 1973 volume, as he famously declared: "Believing, with Max Weber, that man is an animal suspended in webs of significance he himself has spun, I take culture to be those webs, and the analysis of it to be therefore not an experimental science in search of law but an interpretative one in search of meaning. It is explication I am after, construing social expressions on their surface enigmatical" (1973, 5).

Today, while some argue for a basic unity of the "scientific" method (King, Keohane, and Verba 1994; Miller 1987), the question remains: given that social activity entails human agents producing, receiving, and interpreting meaning systems, does social research require specifically tailored techniques? It is a complex debate that has been recently reviewed (Taylor 1971; Yanow and Schwartz-Shea 2006; Gerring 2001; Henderson 1993; Fay 1996; Little 1991, 1998). Nor is it merely a methodological (how to study something) debate; it is also—if not primarily—epistemological (what are the conditions of knowability of certain types of objects?) and ontological (how are the objects of knowledge "actually" constituted?) (Hall 2003).

Many thinkers have articulated unequivocal ontological-epistemological antinaturalist answers to these questions, the clearest of which may be that offered by Thomas and Znaniecki (1918–20). What has come to be known as the "Thomas theorem" is usually formulated as: "If men define situations as real, they are real in their consequences." Already in the early 1920s both Thomas and Znaniecki offered an extensive set of comments on this proposition, emphasizing that social reality is constructed by humans (in their case, ethnic Poles in Poland and in the diaspora). This essentially phenomenological position was later developed by Berger and Luckman (1967) and eventually spilled over to other disciplines in various forms of constructivism. In this way, a strong philosophical position emerged that combines *constructivism* as an ontological stance with *interpretivism* as an epistemological-methodological position.

Political scientists hotly debate whether "subject-dependent realities" (as opposed to "objective realities") are the proper subject matter and thus what tools of inquiry are appropriate.[16] Meanwhile, much of sociology and almost all of cultural/social anthropology are *de rigueur* constructivist, as are, basically by definition, cultural studies, much of feminist work, and art history.[17] Significantly, this embrace of constructivism often leads to ethnographically inflected inquiry in these fields. Anthropologist Richard Shweder (1997), for example, defines ethnography as a "species of qualitative research" that, by definition, deals with "qualia" whose ontological status often remains undertheorized as researchers focus on narrow methodological rather than ontological/epistemological issues:

> I propose that the tension between quantitative and qualitative turns less on methodological issues than it does on one's answers to questions about how to best study subjectivity and how to best study realities that are perspective and context dependent. Basically it is the difference between studying something that exists regardless of your's [sic] or anyone's reactions to it, and

studying things that come into real existence by virtue of their meaning and the perspective that is taken on them. (1997, 160)

Sociologist Andrew Abbott (2001a, 61) argues that constructivism (or "constructionism," as he calls it) is characterized by idealism (attention to how reality is mediated by interpretation), diachronism (attention to process), and interactionism (attention to social interaction as constitutive). It seems that any investigation guided by Abbott's idealism, diachronism, and interactionism is more likely to succeed when the researcher privileges a micro-level (over macro-level) approach, as actual people need to be observed in real-life situations.

Interpretivism in cultural anthropology had its heyday in the 1970s and the early 1980s. The masters of interpretive or symbolic anthropology— Clifford Geertz, Victor Turner, Marshall Sahlins, Edmund Leach, David Schneider, and Mary Douglass—proposed rich and multifaceted theoretical frameworks for studying the complex relationship between the political and the symbolic; the essence of this relationship was captured by the title of Abner Cohen's seminal *Two-Dimensional Man: An Essay on the Anthropology of Power and Symbolism in Complex Society* (1974). Through careful conceptualization and detailed ethnographic fieldwork, these (and many other) scholars showed that culture is not an immutable, monolithic terrain composed of structured configurations of symbols and signs, available for (contemplative) interpretation; it is rather a complex set of signifying practices through which humans collectively create the worlds they inhabit and within which they compete for power and material advantages.

Since the 1980s interpretivism has changed, mostly under the impact of the postmodern challenge, but it has retained its viability as a research program not only in cultural or political anthropology (for example, Kwon 2006), but also in other disciplines, including political sociology (Ashforth 2005) and comparative politics (Wagner-Pacifici 1986; Fernandes 1997; Edles 1998; Chabal and Daloz 2006).

Ethnography of Nation-Building

Much of the competition for symbolic power and cultural hegemony remains inscrutable for such standard methods of political science as surveys or institutional analysis. Interpretive ethnography offers a solution. Take, for example, the study of nation-building, one of the central preoccupations of today's comparative politics (Smith 2004). It is hard to imagine a method other than ethnography that would highlight and clearly demonstrate that national-level meaning-formation and similar local-level processes are often incongruous and, if related, their relations are complex.[18] Herzfeld (1997) investigates the relationships between national and local levels of identity formation and shows that there is no single logic that would apply to the formation of "national identity" in all locations where this process takes place. Gagnon (2004) shows how ethnic identities of "Serbs" and "Croats" are formed, re-formed, and deformed through a series of mobilizations and demobilizations whose local and national rhythms vary considerably. Interpretive ethnography can capture this variation.

Interpretive Ethnography and Democratization

Interpretive ethnography has also made critical contributions to the study of democratization. For example, by showing that "democracy" is interpreted and thus practiced in many different ways that depend on local cultural contexts (Wedeen 2004; Paley 2002), ethnographically inclined researchers help us understand why democracy-promotion projects built on decontextualized, universalistic assumptions are beleaguered by often insoluble problems.

Ashforth's (2005) nuanced and multilayered ethnography shows that the fragile legitimacy of South African democracy is seriously threatened by the persistence of witchcraft.[19] As the country undergoes rapid political and economic change, many people, particularly in poorer areas such as Soweto, feel increasingly insecure and unsure why the benefits of post-Apartheid development are sparse and slow in coming. They also feel jealous of those whose life fortunes have improved. To deal with insecurity and a growing sense of injustice, they look for explanations offered by their own culture, in which personal misfortunes are attributed to evil acts of witches. This culture also suggests a remedy: affected individuals or communities need to enlist the help of traditional healers. But the healers' authority challenges the efforts of the new, democratically elected, and "modern" government to achieve legitimacy. As Ashforth puts it:

> Belief in witchcraft presents severe challenges for the project of democratic government within a modern state. A democratic regime cannot acknowledge the legitimacy of "informal" efforts to seek justice in the face of witchcraft, but if authorities prevent communities from securing their own forms of justice while refusing to address the underlying problem of occult violence, they open themselves to the charge that they are either ignoring the dangers facing the community or in league with evil forces themselves. (2005, 314)

Ashforth's study demonstrates that the "top down" *political* logic of democratizing projects often clashes with the "bottom up," usually local, *cultural* mechanisms that dictate the meaning of democratization for the "target" populations. Insensitivity to such localized cultural understandings often derails or deforms even the most promising democratization projects.

Interpretive Ethnography and the Politics of Collective Memory

Kwon (2006) provides another example of the clash of between national- and local-level logics in a study examining collective memory and its impact on regime consolidation in Vietnam. Again, ethnography proves indispensable. The Vietnamese, whose society had been ripped apart by devastating wars, have recently engaged in the rebuilding of their country's social and cultural fabric. In a society whose edifice rests on a base of multigenerational kinship regulated by elaborate rituals, this is a particularly demanding task. The ritual reconstruction of lineages that were destroyed by "bad deaths" that occurred "in the streets" (while the proper location for dying is "at home") is fraught with difficulties. Death outside of the culturally legitimated locations disrupts the viability of family units grounded in the cult of ancestors. Given that family units are the building blocks of social order, a society that lost hundreds of thousands of its members in ritually uncontrolled conditions, either as soldiers on battlefields or as victims of killing fields, is unbalanced. Reburying under the "proper" conditions can "re-fit" ancestors into their "rightful" ritual locations and thus restore social order.

This is exactly where the state's politics and the culture of lineage and community clash. The communist authorities of Vietnam, although reluctantly supportive of society's self-healing efforts, are also interested in the victims of the foreign invasions. Reburying can become a political ritual that promotes the regime's interests; the dead are splendid candidates for hero worship. But the cultural logics of hero worship, championed by the regime, and cults of the ancestors, needed by the families, are at odds. Engaging in the latter can undermine the regime's claims to legitimacy and weaken the nation-building potential of official heroism.

Kwon contributes to the literature on the relationship between the politics of memory formation and the struggle for political legitimacy (see, for example, Davis 2005) and confirms that the study of this relationship is seriously flawed when cultural mechanisms involved in this process are abstracted away. But he insists that collective memory is always formulated according to specific cultural rules in concrete social locations and constructed on several levels, at different scales, often simultaneously. The political and cultural logic that governs this construction at the national level, where it contributes to the regime's self-legitimizing efforts, can be undermined or annulled by the local, regional, or familial processes of collective memory formation.

Interpretive Ethnography and Comparisons

What about the relationship between (ethnographic) interpretation and comparison, a chief task of comparative politics? Within traditional positivistic anthropology, participant observation was seen as a reliable and unproblematic tool for collecting data that were directly fit for comparisons and generalizations, but the interpretive turn undercut this methodological optimism. As Holy aptly puts it, while in positivistic anthropology "generalization was seen as problematic, description was not" (1987, 4), "subjective" or "interpretative" anthropology problematized description as it moved from "the theory of social facts as things to a theory of them as constructions" (5). Constructivism made comparisons dubious, and the word "comparison has completely disappeared from the vocabulary of methodological discourse" (6–7).

Such a conclusion may sound ominous to the practitioners of comparative politics, but in all fairness many of them have arrived at a similar position (Bowen and Petersen 1999; Smith 2004; Wedeen 2004; Chabal and Daloz 2006), prefigured in the work of a philosopher who once took a good critical look at their practices (MacIntyre 1978). Comparativists, whose field has been stretched—in Collier's seminal formulation (1993)—between case studies and large-n studies, used to search for a "scientific" salvation in the direction of an "ever larger n." These days, however, many of them opt for a method of "small scale controlled comparison," which promises that "through a focus on process and mechanism within the detailed study of the cases, much of the complexity of political life can be addressed while maintaining an ability to generalize" (Bowen and Petersen 1999, 11).

To summarize: interpretive ethnography based on participant observation of semiotic practices delivers important and original bodies of knowledge for research programs founded on three commitments: (1) *constructivism/ interpretivism* (interpret—not just explain—actions that are "meaningful" to actors), (2) *ontological realism* and an attendant epistemology (focus on actual actions of real people, rather than variables),[20] and (3) *micro-scale* (observe actual, "small-scale" settings and reconstruct relevant mechanisms).[21] These three commitments undergird a research agenda that is indispensable in a world that stubbornly refuses to be rationalized and homogenized and in which the politics of identity is pervasive.

Postmodern/Multi-Sited/Global Ethnography

It is paradoxical that when some political scientists have begun turning toward ethnography, anthropologists have thoroughly reevaluated, and often scathingly critiqued, the method that traditionally is the *raison d'être* of their discipline.[22] With the postmodern turn, ethnography has been faced with new tasks; its role in the study of power therefore needs to be examined afresh. As I will suggest, a "reformed" ethnography remains just as relevant to the study of power as ever.

The reexamination of ethnography's value has been propelled by a double engine of *postmodernism* and *globalization*. The former cast doubts on the epistemological adequacy of social-scientific methods, particularly their claims to "objectivity," "detachment," and the possibility of "accurate" representations of reality; the last of these accelerated a reconceptualization of the object of study by discarding earlier conceptions of "ethnographic" realities as isolated and self-enclosed systems.

Debate about the relative (de)merits of "ethnographic" representations of reality has been particularly heated since the publication of *Writing Culture: The Poetics and Politics of Ethnography* (1986), whose authors examine ethnography as a literary genre belonging to a broader category of "scientific" writing. Crapanzano, for example, criticized Geertz for being too domineering and not allowing enough space in his narrative for the natives' unfiltered voices: "Despite his phenomenological-hermeneutical pretensions, there is in fact in 'Deep Play' no understanding of the native from the native's point of view. There is only the constructed understanding of the constructed native's constructed point of view. Geertz offers no specifiable evidence for his attributions of intention, his assertions of subjectivity, his declaration of experience" (1986, 74). Postmodernists challenge the authorial authority of the interpreter, the hero of the interpretive turn. They posit that ethnographic texts should be polyvocal, allowing the "natives" to speak in their own voices and to represent (textually, narratively) themselves.[23] While very few scholars would relinquish control over their texts, the idea that the work should allow the reader to "hear" the natives' own conceptualizations of reality is not alien to many practitioners of today's comparative politics (Laitin 1998; Wedeen 1999; Ashforth 2005). It is, however, clear that the postmodern critiques of ethnography as a genre of writing have not fundamentally changed the way most social science narratives are composed. Nor have they diminished interest in ethnography as a research method, although globalization has called for its overhaul.

Globalized World: From Structures to Flows and Networks

The image of structure in today's social science has lost its once formidable luster as it has been challenged by the images of networks (Castells 1996), assemblages (Sassen 2006), flows, and scapes (Appadurai 1990). This has put a new set of demands on the methodology of empirical investigation. What should we do, for example, with a time-honored, grand binary opposition: system versus life-world (Habermas), which echoes Marx's own distinction between base and superstructure? Marcus astutely observes that "the distinction between lifeworlds of subjects and the system does not hold, and the point of ethnography within the purview of its always local, close-up perspective is to discover new paths of connection and association by which traditional ethnographic concerns with agency, symbols, and everyday practices can continue to be expressed on a differently configured spatial canvas" (1998, 82). Such a perspective produces an image of social reality as a flat plane, composed as a mosaic of pieces of various sizes, complexly interconnected, and subjected to increasingly rapid recombinations; the older, Marx-inspired vision of a hierarchically ordered reality (a "causally" weighty base at the bottom and a somewhat less consequential superstructure at the top) is passé. One consequence of this remapping is a call for ethnography to focus on complex interactions of economic, social, political, and cultural processes, without *a priori* privileging causally any of them.

Power in the Globalized World

In a path-breaking formulation, Foucault proposed that the study of power needs to focus on its exercise or actualization(s) "in the complexities of everyday practice" (Herzfeld 2001, 122). This premise has long guided ethnographers and has produced eye-opening results; the postmodern situation has added a layer of complexity. Having been asked to look for power literally everywhere, ethnographers now face the task of tracking it down inside extensive, often hidden networks that connect actors through increasingly *globalized webs* of influence, dependence, and assistance. As localities have become increasingly discourse-based and "virtual," actors can escape (at least partially) the exercise of power by their direct "local" superiors by engaging in Internet-empowered, transnational networks (see Tarrow 2005 for an overview). Ethnographic studies of such networks are not easy, but they are much needed.

Identity and Globalization

We learned some time ago that the stability/permanence of identity must not be *a priori* assumed, but empirically determined. It is therefore helpful to conceptualize politics in such a manner that the struggle for identity becomes as central to it as the struggle for scarce resources.[24] This new concept is most powerfully articulated by Dirks, Eley, and Ortner, who construe politics as a struggle to stabilize collective identity around a symbolically established center (1994, 32). Sometimes such a center is formed; sometimes it is not. It has also become clear that "resistance in the struggle to establish identity does not rest on some nostalgic bedrock of tradition or community, but arises inventively out of the same deconstructive conditions that threaten to pull it apart or destabilize what has been achieved" (Marcus 1998, 74). The postmodern turn makes the task of studying such *processes of invention and stabilization* even more demanding: the formation of identity needs to be caught *in statu nascendi*, as various flows intersect in a single locale and/or are traced down through several locations/locales. Again, it is hard to imagine a method better suited for such a task than ethnography, perhaps pursued at multiple sites, as I discuss below.

Ethnography and the Global-Local Dynamic

In this increasingly globalized world, researchers face a methodological challenge: ethnography, designed to study the structuring of social life, power, and the formation of identity in "small" locations, has proved inadequate for studying the world of (fast) global flows of goods, services, and information; migrating populations; and shifting meanings. As the Comaroffs observe:

> The economies of signs and practices have to be situated in the intimacy of the local contexts that gave them life. At the same time, they require to be inserted into the translocal processes of which they were part *ab initio*: processes—commodification, colonization, proletarianization, and the like— composed of a plethora of acts, facts and utterances whose very description demands that we frame them in terms of one or another Theory of History. (2003, 161)

The "terrain" ethnographers are supposed to investigate needs to be reconceptualized so they can situate the object of their study (a small community) within a translocal field of political, economic, and cultural forces. The work to address this need began in the 1970s. Paradoxically, as some political scientists began moving their discipline from *macro* (structural historical studies) to *micro* (game-theoretic work on the individual calculation and the growing interest in the small-scale mechanisms of politics),[25] anthropology in the hands of many of its leading practitioners was already traveling in the opposite direction.

By and large, this movement from micro- to macro-level in anthropology has had two major phases:[26] (1) the *world-system phase*, inspired mostly by Wallerstein (1974) and Frank (1969), and arguably culminating with Wolf (1982); and (2) the *globalization/postmodern phase*, epitomized most distinctly by the critical works of Clifford and Marcus (1986) and Marcus (1998). The theoretical tenor of the first phase was decisively materialist, (neo-)Marxist, while the second wave was primarily culturalist, as its practitioners pushed the interpretive turn in the social sciences to its limits (and perhaps beyond). During this phase, anthropologists set out to demonstrate how local structures and cultures are influenced and shaped by larger structures, such as states, class structures, and the world system of (mostly economic) interdependencies.

The second phase was marked by the theoretical implosion of the whole repertoire of such "traditional" concepts as the binaries of micro/macro, system/worldview, or center/periphery, and the concept of a clearly bound cultural whole. Accordingly, ethnography and fieldwork had to be reinvented again. In Trouillot's words: "The problem is not fieldwork per se, but the taking for granted of localities upon which the fetishization of a certain kind of fieldwork was built and the relationship between . . . supposedly isolated localities and supposedly distinct cultures" (2003, 125). To answer this challenge, methodologists and practitioners propose ethnography that is *postmodern, multi-sited,* and *global.*

Postmodern Ethnography

Trouillot argues that the conceptualization of ethnography as a method focused on the study of small, relatively homogeneous communities has prevented anthropologists from achieving the proper understanding of the relationship(s) between the broader *world* (however it is conceptualized) and specific *location*. This blinded them to the phenomena that constitute the bread and butter of today's social science: the expansion of capitalism and its "local" consequences, colonialism and postcolonialism, migrations, and globalization(s). Postmodern sensitivity demands that location be construed not as a relatively bounded and separate whole, but as a place where various flows intersect.

According to Marcus, postmodern ethnography needs to be sharply distinguished from what he calls positivistic or "realist" ethnography. Specifically, three dimensions of ethnographic inquiry need to be reconceptualized: the spatial, the temporal, and perspective or voice (1998, 62).

First, the concept of community "in the classic sense of shared values, shared identity, and thus shared culture" (Marcus 1998, 62) needs to be replaced with the concept of "multi-locale, dispersed identity" (1998, 63), constructed, often simultaneously, by often mutually independent flows of cultural material, complex political configurations, and economic relations. Marcus argues, "It is the burden of the modernist ethnography to capture distinctive identity formations in all their migrations and dispersions" (1998, 63).

Second, to "(post)modernize" the temporal dimension of ethnography, Marcus asks that we replace dominant "Western historical metanarratives" that have routinely served as a historical background for many scholars with local histories and carefully reconstructed local collective memories. He contends, "The past that is present in any site is built up from memory, the fundamental medium of ethnohistory" (64).[27]

Finally, the traditional ethnographic perspective, heavily indebted to the concept of structure (social or semiotic), needs to be replaced with the concept of "voice." For Marcus: "Voices are not seen as products of local structures, based on community and tradition, alone, or as privileged sources of perspective, but rather as products of the complex sets of associations and experiences which compose them" (66). As I understand this postulate, today's increasingly mobile people need to be studied as members of (several) networks and participants in (several) flows, rather than as products and producers of clearly identifiable structures. Table 2 summarizes Marcus's distinctions.

Most political scientists and anthropologists who accept at least some postmodern insights about the constructed and increasingly fluid makeup of identity are aware that from time to time ethnographic studies reveal the emergence of rather "solid" entities: dispersed and incongruous identities become communities, localized collective memories captivate us as metanarratives, and voice freezes into structure. They warn, however, that this needs to be empirically demonstrated rather than a priori theorized.

Table 2

Three Dimensions of the Ethnographic Subject	Realist Ethnography	Modernist Ethnography
Space	(Relatively closed) community of shared values (culture)	Multi-locale, dispersed identity
Temporal	"Western" metanarrative as a background story	Localized collective memory
Perspective	Structure (social or semiotic)	Voice

Multi-Sited Ethnography

For Trouillot, multi-sited ethnography is an improvement, since it is "a partial answer to the ethnographic trilogy (one observer, one time, one place)" (2003, 125). But, how would one conduct a multi-sited ethnography? Marcus proposes seven strategies: (1) follow the people; (2) follow the thing; (3) follow the metaphor; (4) follow the plot, story, or allegory; (5) follow the life or biography; (6) follow the conflict; and (7) conduct a strategically situated (single-site) ethnography (1998, 89–99). There is no room here to characterize them all. Instead I briefly illustrate their usefulness by reconsidering one of the key tasks of ethnography: tracking down power in unusual and marginal places (for example, among the subaltern).

Marcus suggests that the primary task of cultural/political anthropology is the reconstruction of a complex dialectic of *resistance and accommodation* as marginal or subaltern people try to come to terms with the pressures of political and/or economic globalization. This framework, in his mind, has served realist ethnography well, at least since the first "wave" of globalization of anthropology in the mid-1970s. The postmodern world, however, calls for its retooling. Most important, the multi-sited ethnography that traces multiple loci of action undermines the binary conceptualization of the dominant versus the marginal (subaltern). It not only calls for a more systematic focus on the powerful (and on ethnographic studies of what they actually do and think), but, more important, it prods the researcher to look for as many sites of power and counter-power exercise as possible (see also Gledhill 2000). As a result, "questions of resistance, although not forgotten, are often subordinated to different sorts of questions about the shape of systemic processes themselves and complicities with these processes among variously positioned subjects" (Marcus 1998, 85).

Global Ethnography

"New" ethnography, in addition to being postmodern (in Marcus's sense) and multi-sited, is also supposed to be global. Building on his earlier work on the extended case study method (1998), Burawoy (2000, 26–28) articulates four methodological guidelines: (1) "the extension of the observer to the world of the participant" (the essence of participant observation); (2) "extension of the observations over time and space" (following subjects through complex and increasingly global networks); (3) "extending from micro processes to macro forces" (relying on a theoretically informed model of the external forces whose contingent character needs to be grasped); and (4) "extension of theory" (avoiding the "straitjacketing" power of theory by the incessant, mutually correcting dialogue of theory and data).

Studying politics in the world inhabited by increasingly mobile and globalized populations calls for new concepts and methods. Ethnography that is multi-sited, global, and sensitive to postmodern concerns is an intriguing new tool. But it seems that it is particularly effective when it combines new research concerns with the tested techniques of traditional positivistic and interpretive ethnographies.

Conclusion

The usefulness of ethnography for comparative politics and political science in general cannot be assessed without realizing that there is no single ethnography, but several different types of ethnography. In this chapter I outlined three types: positivistic, interpretive, and postmodern (including multi-sited). Each is associated with a different ontology of the social, and each can help political scientists in different tasks.

Positivistic ethnography is indispensable for studying *overlooked* (informal dimensions of) power (Abeles 2004); *hidden* (faces of) power (Lukes 1974; Gaventa 1980); *inaccessible* (mechanisms of) power, for example in early stages of protest mobilization (Bayard de Volo and Schatz 2004, 269); ostensibly *inconspicuous resistance* to power (Scott 1990); *ambiguous* (effects of) power exercise (Wedeen 1999); and *cultural construction* of agents and subjects of power (Mahmood 2005).

Interpretive ethnography is crucial for exposing the relations between power and meaning in concrete situations. Its significance for political analysis has become clearer as a growing number of political scientists—particularly in comparative politics—work within a constructivist paradigm and design their research programs around such principles as *ontological realism, constructivism/interpretivism,* and *micro-focus* on "small scale" mechanisms.

Postmodern ethnography is central for capturing the dynamics of power and identity in an increasingly interconnected and globalized world. Multi-sited ethnography, attentive to the novel (gradually more virtual) ways of constructing collective identities and focused, *inter alia,* on the increasingly transnational and translocal nature of political and economic transactions, is a promising addition to the methodological armamentarium of today's social science.

Notes

I would like to thank Mike Aronoff for comradeship, inspiration, and patience. This piece owes a lot to him. Many thanks to Michal Buchowski, Amy Linch, Lisa Wedeen, Dvora Yanow, and my students for extremely useful comments on earlier drafts of this text. Edward Schatz's guidance and inspired editing were indispensable.

1. For examples of ethnographic work from other subfields, see the chapters in this volume by Pachirat, Walsh, and Yanow, as well as Shdaimah, Stahl, and Schram.
2. Aronoff (1991); Chabal and Daloz (2006); Edles (1998); Wedeen (1999, 2002); Johnson (2003). For an innovative marriage of formal modeling and interpretive/symbolic analysis in the field of international relations, see O'Neill (1999).
3. Geddes (2003, 23) puts it well: "Although multiple regression is an excellent tool for testing hypotheses, it is not always a good image to have in mind when trying to explain something complicated, because it focuses attention on the identification of causal factors rather than on how the causal factors work."
4. For excellent overviews of up-to-date conceptualizations of culture, see Swidler (1986); Sewell (1999); Wedeen (2002).
5. One might identify specific characteristics of at least four schools: German, French, British, and American (Barth et al. 2005). But even if such a nation-based typology is rejected as simplistic, three distinct trajectories can be distinguished (Barnard 2000; Vincent 1990). Barnard proposes to isolate: (1) the "French" sociological tradition running from Montesquieu via Saint-Simon, Comte, and Spencer to Durkheim and Mauss; (2) the "British" tradition, founded by Ferguson and Smith and running, *inter alia,* via Maine, Morgan, Tylor, and Frazer to Malinowski and Radcliffe-Brown and their students; and (3) the "American" tradition, also having Montesquieu as its founder, but running through Humboldt, Grimm, and Bastian to Boas (the most influential thinker here), Kroeber, and Lowie (Barnard 2000).
6. Ethnography is also a genre of writing, as I discuss in the section on postmodern ethnography.
7. In his introduction, Schatz argues that some work that uses nonparticipant observation may nonetheless have an ethnographic *sensibility,* insofar as it focuses on "insider" perspectives. Given my equation of ethnography with participant observation, I leave this possibility to the side.
8. These three traditions emerged in the indicated order, but currently all of them are practiced.
9. See Vincent (1990, 33–77).

10. This is akin to what Schatz in this volume's introduction calls an "ethnographic sensibility."

11. The distinction between social structure and social organization has been most famously introduced and analyzed by Raymond Firth (1951). On Firth see Vincent (1990, 331) and Barnard (2000, 125).

12. A similar idea is formulated in the work of historical institutionalists (Thelen and Steinmo 1992, 2–3) and in some game-theoretic analyses (Fearon and Laitin 1996).

13. See Pierson (2004); Mahoney and Rueschemeyer (2003); Ekiert and Hanson (2003); Abbott (2001b).

14. In more general terms, substantivist approaches tend to conceptualize human relations as multistranded and complex, while the formalist approaches emphasize single-stranded relations, depending on the issues that are studied.

15. Anthony Giddens succinctly characterizes positivism: "In nineteenth-century social philosophy and social theory positivism was in the ascendant, if positivism is taken to mean two things. First, a conviction that all 'knowledge,' or all that is to count as 'knowledge,' is capable of being expressed in terms which refer in an immediate way to some reality, or aspects of reality that can be apprehended through the senses. Second, a faith that the methods and logical structure of science, as epitomized by classical physics, can be applied to the study of social phenomena" (1976, 130).

16. Constructivism has become an accepted and vibrant option in many branches of political science. See, for example, Blyth (2002) in political economy or Adler (2002) and Klotz and Lynch (2007) in international relations.

17. As Tobin (1999, 1) writes, "Paintings, as is the case with all cultural production, are not merely reflections of larger social and economic forces; they participate in the production of meaning, in the dynamic construction of identities, and in the structuring within discursive fields of particular positionalities."

18. Yet not long ago Wilson observed that "the dialogical relationships between the creation and re-creation of national and cultural identities and the same processes at local levels have too long escaped critical ethnographic investigation" (1990, 160).

19. For a discussion of the political impact of witchcraft elsewhere in Africa, see Michael Schatzberg's contribution to this volume.

20. Following Hall (2003), I understand realism as an ontological stance, assuming that social reality is constructed out of actions of real people, not operations of variables. The attendant methodology requires that, as a minimum, values of variables are "translated" into actions of actual people in "real" contexts.

21. Moreover, ethnography is the best method to observe meaning-production and meaning-decoding via nonverbal mechanisms that are often employed to communicate and exercise power but also to challenge it through counter-hegemonic displays and performances. As Trickett and Oliveri demonstrate, an "ethnographic approach can help discern the meaning of practices that people do not or cannot fully describe through verbal means" (1997, 149).

22. Consult, in particular, Clifford and Marcus (1986) and Marcus and Fischer (1999).

23. As Tyler explains, postmodern ethnography privileges "discourse" over "text," it foregrounds dialogue as opposed to monologue, and emphasizes the cooperative and collaborative nature of the ethnographic situation in contrast to the ideology of the transcendental observer (1986, 126). While the questions of textual representation of social reality have been seriously debated in history (White 1978), sociology, and anthropology (Clifford and Marcus 1986), political scientists seem far less preoccu-

pied with studying the impact of the manner in which this reality is represented in their texts on their knowledge (though see Patterson and Monroe 1998).

24. For an enlightening discussion, see Brubaker and Cooper (2000) and the Harvard Project on "Identity as a Variable": http://www.wcfia.harvard.edu/misc/initiative/identity/.
25. See, for example, Geddes (2003); Laitin (2004); Little (1998).
26. Vincent (1990, 388–402); Marcus (1998, 79–80); Trouillot (2003, 120–21).
27. This call to rethink the relationship between history and memory has been recently heeded by sociology, history, and cultural studies; there has been a renaissance of writing on historical memory.

TWO

How to Tell an Axe Murderer: An Essay on Ethnography, Truth, and Lies

JESSICA ALLINA-PISANO

In August 2000 and again in 2005, the scientific journal of record *Nature* ran articles about "political scientists." The scientists in question were evolutionary biologists who had stepped outside their role as researchers to speak out against efforts by proponents of the intelligent design movement, who wanted their theory of creation taught in public schools alongside Darwinism (Gewin 2005). Around the same time, while teaching a seminar on nationalism at a liberal arts college in the northeastern United States, I encountered a dean who urged me to "allow the debate" as my undergraduate students contested not how or why, but whether the Third Reich had killed millions of Jews.[1] The intelligent design movement's attempt to cast its claims, based in biblical revelation, as a competing theory to be considered in science classes alongside research-based consensus,[2] together with the putative "debate" posited in the Holocaust denial literature, highlights a more general problem in the production and transmission of knowledge: amid a societal commitment to epistemological pluralism, how ought we to adjudicate truth claims about the world?[3]

In a world of epistemological pluralism, truth claims may have no ontological status: all claims and perspectives can be treated as *ipso facto* equally valid. As a result, they may be adjudicated in the political arena, subject to bald contests of power rather than analytical acumen or specialized knowledge evaluated within a common framework of accepted standards of research. There is arguably a danger in such instances that populism of the moment, or of a specific segment of society, may overcome knowledge that has been accrued, tested, and improved by communities of scholars over decades or generations.

The political context of these conflicts between particular truth claims, while anchored in a specific historical moment, points to a more general epistemological challenge for ethnographers working within interpretivist traditions of social inquiry. Interpretive approaches narrate alternative epistemologies, telling us a great deal about how human beings understand and constitute the world. However, for problem-driven research (Shapiro 2005), there is also a need for approaches that can help social scientists reliably adjudicate truth claims about the world. If social research is to speak to real-world questions, it must include tools that allow its practitioners not only to make observations about how people think about and constitute their world, but also of the material conditions and social structures within which they make their choices.

Interrogation of the subject-object relationship is a central preoccupation for any researcher interested in careful and rigorous research. However, researchers focusing on certain types of questions may wish to place principal emphasis not on analysis of the subject-object relationship, but on making observations that are as "theory neutral" as possible (Wendt and Shapiro 1992) and from there, establishing causality. To put it a different way, social science in general and the study of politics in particular may sometimes require a commitment to uncovering truth—truth in the sense of *Beim Haüten der Zweibel* (Peeling the Onion), rather than sacred revelation—in addition to elucidating social meaning.[4]

Toward a Realist Ethnography

Ethnography is better positioned than other qualitative social science methods to do precisely this—to peel the onion. All modes of knowledge production are in some way subjective, but the ethnographer is equipped to contextualize and interpret her subjectivity: to be conscious of the ways that her position conditions the observations she makes.

As Kubik notes in chapter 1, ethnography is especially good for examining politics in the margins and interstices of political life, including that broad swathe of politics that occurs outside of, parallel to, or unseen within formal institutions. In contexts where informal practices drive formal politics (Ledeneva 2006), where political actors deliberately hide their activity (Allina-Pisano 2004), or where the politics of less powerful people are the object of study (Scott 1990), ethnography may be the best or even the only viable approach. Where partially hidden, power-laden processes drive economic distribution, as under customary law, informal patron-client relations, "corruption," and other regimes of reciprocity, ethnography may likewise be of particular help in uncovering causal mechanisms.[5]

The essential problem associated with truth claims made through ethnographic study is endemic throughout the study of politics: if the act of observation shapes the object of observation, then there is no "neutral" evidence. And if neutrality is deemed necessary for advancing causal claims, then no avenue of inquiry remains open to the scholar except deductive thought—and then only once its necessarily subjective first principles have been adopted. The notion that truth claims must, by definition, be founded upon "theory neutral" observation cedes nearly all ground in the production of knowledge to formal modelers and rational-choice theorists.

If, however, as most philosophers of science since Kuhn (1962) would hold, observation is necessarily mediated by the act of observing, the study of problems in the world is possible primarily through an interpretive lens. In most formulations, an interpretive lens offers alternative epistemologies but no ontological claim to truth or objective description as such. For many social scientists, this is problematic for a number of reasons, not the least of which is that rational-choice theorists have themselves returned, of necessity, to the empirical world in order to narrow the domain of their claims: as others have argued, rational-choice approaches without reference to context produce not meaningful theory, but a single explanation for everything, everywhere (Green and Shapiro 1996).

This chapter makes a case for ethnography with a realist sensibility. It does not deny the value of interpretation in ethnographic approaches to social research. On the contrary, it suggests that an understanding of the ways in which people think about their world can be a necessary condition for the collection and use of reliable empirical data about them. In other words, it suggests not only that ethnography is capable of making meaningful contributions to social research, but also that it offers advantages for adjudicating truth claims and establishing causality that other approaches do not. Further, this approach builds upon longstanding traditions in social research: fieldwork-based research exploring local political and moral economies long has been a staple of political science as well as social anthropology.[6]

Following Shapiro's understanding of scientific realism in general, realist ethnography proceeds from two assumptions: that "the world consists of causal mechanisms that exist independently of our study—or even awareness—of them," and that ethnographic techniques "hold out the best possibility of our grasping their true character" (Shapiro 2005, 8–9). A realist ethnographer draws inferences not only about what political actors say they do, but also what she observes them doing.[7] That observation, however, is necessarily conditioned by familiarity with the context that shapes the social meaning of action. In the language of many of my Russian-speaking interlocutors in research, the ethnographer can offer a *vzgliad so storony*, an informed outside view. Such an approach allows the scholar to attend to the role of language in constituting social reality, but it does not require that she bracket material or structural factors.

Demands for theory-neutral observation, common in the field of political science in North America, have resulted not only in a practical problem for knowledge generation, but also in a bifurcation of social inquiry: with some exceptions, formal theorists and empiricists of various persuasions study formal institutions and the people that populate them. To the extent that those institutions tend to be loci of social, political, and economic power, the study of formal politics is the study of the powerful. And because those who study political elites often cleave to epistemologies that admit to ontological truth, their research findings are articulated as truth claims about the world.

In contrast, the ethnographic tradition of studying people at societies' margins, of examining the politics of the subaltern, most comfortably embraces interpretive approaches to knowledge. This approach recognizes self-understanding and social construction as the primary domain of social inquiry. The claims of this research thus center on the production of social meaning—how people see the world, and how those self-understandings constitute reality. The result is that while social research about the powerful claims a monopoly on the production of facts and causal inferences, research about the relatively powerless offers alternative epistemologies but not competing, or corrective, facts.

However, the study of the margins is important not only for communicating and interpreting the voices of less powerful people, but also because the knowledge produced in the margins may sometimes be, in the world of truth claims, more accurate than that generated in the center. People in the margins may have more than "another perspective" to contribute; as actors close to local processes of political change, they sometimes have more detailed information about certain types of phenomena than do political and social elites. Similarly, where key political processes unfold in the interstices of formal institutions (Ledeneva 2008)—in the hallway, on the telephone, over a drink—ethnography offers an opportunity not only for enriching our understanding of perspectives on politics, but also for identifying otherwise elusive causal mechanisms, for more firmly establishing what happened and why.

Realist ethnography charts a middle course between ostensibly "theory neutral" and "theory laden" observation.[8] A realist approach acknowledges the role of the ethnographer in coconstituting the reality he studies.

It does not, however, presume that the ethnographer's presence will always meaningfully alter the causal mechanisms being observed; the ethnographer must use her knowledge of context to reflect upon the specific ways in which her presence is likely to have shaped the evidence.[9] Thus, realist ethnography refers to the process that guides research and writing, not to the product itself.[10] The extent to which the ethnographer's presence influences others' behavior and elicits performances for the ethnographer may vary depending on the chosen field sites, as well as on the ethnographer's position in local and global hierarchies of social, economic, and political power. In the ethnographic tradition that takes a single, small village as its object of study, the researcher's presence may be likely to influence the reality being observed to a greater extent than would be the case in a field site defined by mass demonstrations.[11]

Ethnographers cannot control for the effects of their presence on their interlocutors, but ethnography is better suited than other varieties of social science to identify the specific ways in which the researcher's presence shapes evidence. In other words, unlike many of their counterparts engaged in other types of social research, ethnographers are, with their contextual knowledge, in a position to know which types of biases their presence is likely to introduce. In most cases, research based upon statistical analysis cannot account for such effects, as users and compilers of databases are usually different individuals, and even collectors of statistics may not be sufficiently embedded in local realities to discern the ways in which numbers might be intentionally or unintentionally altered in the process of transmission. For example, it is well known in postsocialist contexts that businesses or government offices often keep more than one set of (different) books, but this does not necessarily change how users of databases treat aggregate commercial or government statistics. Likewise, in countries where communications infrastructure is radically uneven, there are likely to be substantial differences in regional figures that may have little to do with anything beyond an electricity outage, the absence of a copy machine, or some other obstacle that affects the collection and transmission of data but leaves no trace of the nature, magnitude, or direction of the bias introduced.

Ethnography is most often associated with participant-observation research, but participation in fieldwork settings need not implicate the researcher in the cocreation of social reality any more than an unobtrusive "neutral" presence would. Indeed, sometimes evidence-gathering without active participation can be more disruptive than silence. This may be particularly the case in postauthoritarian contexts. For example, once, at the end of a long day of meetings and conversations in post-Soviet eastern Ukraine, one of my interlocutors reprimanded me for my lack of engagement at that moment: "You're like a ghost. And we don't like ghosts." Here, people interpreted my silence not as serious scholarly attention or fatigue, but as public comportment reminiscent of a member of the secret police engaging in surveillance.

Through a series of fieldwork-based vignettes, this chapter examines the kinds of claims realist political ethnography can make. These vignettes are drawn from research on land privatization in rural communities in the former Soviet Union between 1997 and 2006. During that period I conducted participant-observation, interview, and documentary research in an effort to uncover the incentives and causal mechanisms that, at the local level, drove shifts in postsocialist property regimes. This research was multi-sited, providing a view onto the beliefs and actions of different actors involved in the privatization process. I lived on a former collective farm to observe the process of farm reorganization at close range; I attended the meetings of farmers' organizations to try to understand the challenges faced by people who were trying to obtain and use land; and I spent time in county and regional offices, where I watched and listened to those charged with distributing land.

The chapter aims to show through narrative what sorts of things ethnography can tell us that other qualitative methods cannot.[12] The ideas presented here cohere around the problem of using "face value" statements in research. In particular, how do we interpret evidence produced by our interlocutors if our intent is not only to uncover the self-understandings of our subjects, but also to adjudicate and make truth claims about political and social phenomena? While the following discussion concerns truth claims, I do not propose here a paradigm for translating ethnographic work into generalizable theory: all theory based on ethnography is synecdoche—but so, on the other hand, is all theory based on random quantitative sampling.

If, in Robert Darnton's (1984) terms, minor episodes can illuminate the ways historical actors viewed their world, I suggest that such episodes can offer windows onto political realities that, in the absence of ethnographic knowledge, otherwise would remain hidden from view. The following vignettes engage the relationship between power and evidence. The first reflects upon the process of research, rather than presenting research findings. It highlights the epistemological challenges of doing fieldwork, illustrating how interpretation without adequate ethnographic knowledge can contribute to the reproduction of status quo power relations. The second vignette provides an example of how reading interview texts divorced from ethnographic context can lead to wrongheaded conclusions. The third shows how participant-observation research illuminates the power relations that underlie competing truth claims. The fourth vignette suggests ways in which ethnography can help us identify ritual speech and read between the lines to uncover both social meanings and aspects of institutional change.

Vlad the Researcher

Toward the end of a period of research in a country of the former Soviet Union, I requested that a colleague at a local institute help me identify a student research assistant to copy newspaper articles on land reform. I had begun this job myself some time before, but field interviews increasingly occupied my time, and I had a limited number of months to complete that stage of my research. At that time, in this particular country, female university students faced a highly restrictive labor market in which employment often required extreme compromises of individual dignity. Job advertisements for foreign as well as domestic companies were explicitly directed toward young men, while the few ads for young women enumerated precise body measurements and required that applicants have "no hang-ups." Knowing this, I specified that I would prefer to hire a young woman. Instead, my colleague presented me with a male undergraduate—a student she knew and wished to help—for the job. He was qualified for it, and I hired him.

Vlad was a second-year student with an odd demeanor. Despite manifold obstacles to obtaining newspaper articles, including far-flung libraries, incomplete holdings of periodicals, and the ever-present problem of copying articles in libraries where reproduction services were understaffed or nonexistent, Vlad executed the task well. We met every week or two at the institute, where he presented me with a stack of articles that I would read and file with my other research materials.

Some time into his work with me, Vlad announced that he would be away for a week or two. He needed, he said, to "visit his grandmother" in another region. His grandmother was ill, and no other family members were available to care for her. We made arrangements to meet again when he returned.

That week, the local television news covered a real-life horror story. The body of a murder victim had been discovered at a market on the city outskirts, where it was being sold by the kilogram. Initial reports suggested that the murderer knew the victim, and that the murder had occurred following a personal dispute over money—in this case, three hundred dollars.

Not long after the television broadcast, I received a call from my colleague at the institute, who requested that we meet immediately. An hour later, as we strolled through a park, my colleague told me that Vlad had been named the main suspect in the market murder. He was being held and questioned by the police. My colleague added that I was no longer welcome to meet with Vlad at the institute, and that I should find a different meeting place. In particular, my colleague emphasized that because Vlad had my business card with my local phone number written on it, I should not be surprised to receive a call from the detective in charge of the investigation.

A week later, Vlad called to arrange a meeting. I was unwilling, under the circumstances, to identify a private meeting spot. However, in a context in which some categories of people targeted by the authorities routinely fell through the cracks of the court system, and where more informal mechanisms of seeking justice and retribution were not unheard of, I was equally unsure about a public meeting. I chose a nearby café, where I settled up with and said good-bye to Vlad, who expressed interest in staying in touch with me. I did not hear from the authorities before I left the country a week later, and I have not spoken with Vlad or my colleague since that day.

This episode raised a number of questions that required immediate answers. Most crucially at the time, from the standpoint of the researcher, where does the truth lie, and if Vlad were the murderer, did he still need money? Here were two competing, incommensurable narratives: short of stretching the ironic trope to its conceptual limits, I saw no way to frame both Vlad's narrative (I am going to visit my grandmother) and my colleague's (Vlad is being held by the police on suspicion of being an axe murderer) as different understandings of the same core event. The existence of alternative epistemologies was both logically impossible and morally unacceptable. Furthermore, for practical reasons I could not remain agnostic on the question of what had happened.

In a modern perversion of Pascal's wager—it is safer for me to commit myself to the belief that Vlad is an axe murderer and live my life accordingly than it is to harbor doubt—I chose to act in response to my colleague's version of events, rather than Vlad's. This represented a compromise on my part. I lacked sufficient knowledge to make an informed judgment: I made my decision about likely truth on the basis of my colleague's authority, not firsthand knowledge. This decision was driven by practical, not intellectual concerns, but it was nonetheless an attempt to establish causality and adjudicate a truth claim on the basis of incomplete knowledge. Turning the analytical lens on myself, I surmise that I chose to accept my colleague's version of events not only for, in the American satirist Stephen Colbert's formulation, its "truthiness,"[13] but also because there was no obvious danger to my-self in doing so (whereas the risks of association with Vlad were unknown but potentially serious). Furthermore, I shared multiple social ties with my colleague, and this likely influenced my response. I knew both my col-league and Vlad individually, but my colleague and I had a dozen other ac-quaintances in common. I was friendly with one member of my colleague's family and had worked with one of my colleague's coworkers. I had no in-formation about the nature of Vlad's relationship with my colleague, or why my colleague had insisted I hire Vlad and not someone else.

Although I was embedded in some of the social relations that consti-tuted my colleague's and Vlad's world, I was not embedded deeply enough. I knew no one in Vlad's circle other than my colleague. To my knowledge, I had not met the person who had been killed. Had I been more famil-iar with Vlad's circle of friends, I might have noticed if one had gone miss-ing. In this situation, I faced a practical need to adjudicate truth claims, but I lacked deep ethnographic knowledge of the relationships that could have cast light on the question at hand. With better contextual knowledge, I would have had a stronger empirical basis for my conclusion: either one of Vlad's friends was missing, or none was. Lacking that information, I made a choice that seemed safer: to accept the story as told from above.

Most positive social science positions the researcher as a mid-twentieth-century Switzerland. While embeddedness in any community creates biases in the researcher, the absence of ethnographic knowledge creates its own bias. Without such knowledge, we are likely to make judgments based on whatever evidence is most easily accessible. In the case of Vlad, the author-ities had a ready-made—and, to my mind, plausible—narrative available for consumption. Vlad, in contrast, had provided only a thin story that held up weakly—both in aesthetic terms and analytically, in view of the claims made by my colleague and, putatively, by the state. This is in some ways no surprise: it may be the case that the production of narratives to explain and excuse itself is the ordinary condition of power. If this is so, social science research without ethnography risks reproducing the status quo power rela-tions that feed it.

DT

At end of the 1990s homemade signs could be seen all along the Ukrai-nian stretch of international highway E40. The highway enters Ukraine at the Polish border near the city of L'viv and winds through western Ukraine

to the capital, Kyiv. From Kyiv, the road continues across the eastern territory of Left Bank Ukraine to Kharkiv before it turns southeast through the
Donbas to the Russian city of Rostov. In the east, the signs, small squares of
cardboard propped on chairs in front of houses that closely line the road,
read *"Kupliu DT"* ("I'll buy diesel fuel"). The acronym *DT* stands for diesel,
or *dizel'noe toplivo*. The Russian verb and abbreviation were intelligible to
nearly all who used this portion of the road.

Such signs could be found both along major highways and along some
back roads in Ukraine: they signified difficult times and a fortuitous location on a road along which fuel trucks traveled. The informal diesel trade
went unrecorded by any legally registered enterprise or government organization. Nonetheless, its survival depended on the roads, trucks, and fuel of
the formal economy: people living along such roads purchased diesel from
supply trucks passing through and resold it locally at a slightly higher price.
On the reverse side the handwritten cardboard signs nearly always read:
"I'll sell diesel fuel."

In early spring of 2000 I passed several such signs during a visit to a remote district of eastern Ukraine. A Russian-speaking passenger in my vehicle—a professor of philosophy at an agricultural institute and officer
of an organization that assisted local farmers—wondered aloud what the
signs meant. He added that he thought *DT* might mean *dorozhnyi transport*,
or automotive transportation. In his mind, the cardboard signs read: "I'll
buy your car."

A similar reference appeared in popular culture just a few days later. This
reference, aired on national television, likewise suggested a certain distance
from rural concerns on the part of the urban intelligentsia. The broadcast
was a contest of a popular Russian-language genre of improvised comedy
skits. It included a reference to the same confusion expressed by the professor of philosophy: "I put diesel [*soliarku*] in the car instead of gas [*toplivo*]. I
thought *DT* meant *devianosto tretii* [93 octane]."[14]

Neither my passenger nor the comedic butt of his own joke possessed
knowledge necessary to interpret the abbreviation correctly—the way its
user intended it to be read.[15] The comedy skit, which was a riff on Soviet
versus post-Soviet driving cultures as well as urban-rural cleavages, suggested that such ignorance was presumed to be widespread enough among
a particular portion of society to amuse a television audience. But most
Russians and Ukrainians familiar with rural life or with automobiles would
have recognized the acronym *DT*. Even someone unfamiliar with the meaning of the acronym but knowledgeable about rural economic conditions
would have guessed at least one truth: that the vast majority of village resi-

dents, including those engaged in the informal diesel trade, would not have so much free capital as to purchase a vehicle from a passerby.

By many measures, the professor of philosophy would seem to have been an expert on rural affairs. He was, after all, a founding member of a rural nongovernmental organization and the type of professional to whom Western scholars and lending institutions routinely turn for local information. I happened to recognize his mistake because I conducted research on farms and frequently discussed diesel prices with tractor operators and farm chairmen, and also because I drove a Russian vehicle and regularly used gas pumps in the area. In the absence of contextual knowledge gained through participant-observation research, however, I might have accepted the philosophy professor's statement at face value, as an accurate interpretation of textual meaning for the signs' intended audience.

For a social scientist, the analytical consequences of such a judgment could be potentially serious. If one takes *Kupliu DT* to mean "I'll buy your car," and if one sees such signs at regular intervals along a highway, two logical inferences likely result: first, that there is a large informal market in automobiles; and second, that people living along the E40 live fairly wealthy lives in which cash is widely available and the risk of spending money on a car with an unknown mechanical history is not a grave concern.

Further, if a social scientist conducting qualitative research solely in the form of interviews had spoken with the philosophy professor and accepted his interpretation of *DT*, these inferences might shape her interpretation of subsequent interview texts. In the light of the philosophy professor's interpretation, would the former mechanic who lives in a house where a *DT* sign has been posted be presumed to be lying when he describes the enormous expense and difficulty involved in commuting to his job in a nearby town? What about the pensioner next door who cares for her granddaughter after the deaths of her daughter and son-in-law and who laments her complete isolation and difficulty making ends meet? Is she merely "putting on the poor mouth"—performing poverty for the benefit of the researcher? How would the researcher decide?[16] Ethnography has a role to play in interpreting such a lamentation if social inquiry is to be concerned not only with how the pensioner sees or presents herself, but also with the economic consequences for her village and the world if she—as one of hundreds of thousands, if not millions like her—is unable to provide an education for her granddaughter. Here, the type of knowledge acquired through ethnography allows the researcher to discern more intelligently the material condition of such a village street, and to avoid a misinterpretation that might so easily be produced through the use of other qualitative methods.

Plov

Near the end of the 1990s I lived for a time on the territory of a Russian collective farm undergoing privatization. I was there to study the process of land distribution at close range. The village attached to the farm sat in a wooded area dotted with lakes, a showpiece of natural beauty and a popular local destination for hunting, trapping, and fishing. However, the peace of the landscape for people, if not for animals, seemed at odds with social life in the village, in which some people seemed to lie to one another about everything.

Like life in other small places with scarce resources, village society meant a kaleidoscope of fabulae—a positivist's nightmare. The benches lining picket fences where old women shelled peas were carnivals in the Bakhtinian sense, as tales of the director's investments, the neighbor's cow, and the "American" villager's lottery-won green card were spun into gossip that challenged village hierarchies. In such an environment, where village-level great power politics seemed to govern every public utterance, it was difficult to know which statements might have been tactical maneuvers directed toward neighbors, and which were performances with my presence as a researcher in mind.[17] In that village, the benches outside each fence together constituted the space that Scott identifies as the site of reproduction for private subordinate speech—the hidden transcripts of the dominated (Scott 1990, 70–107). However, even among relative equals—subordinates who lived autonomous lives in one sense but whose ability to heat their homes or travel to the hospital depended to a large extent on the farm director's goodwill—performances were often contradictory.[18]

As I interviewed or spoke with dozens of people on the farm; attended early morning meetings of farm specialists, at which the farm director set out the problems and tasks for the day; chatted for hours with the director's secretary; went swimming with the older women's singing and drinking group; hitched rides with people my own age when, after a day in town, I could avoid the 7-kilometer walk to the village from the bus turnoff on the highway; and on weekends went to the farm disco where "old maid" eighteen-year-olds hoped for love or at least marriage, I wondered how I would begin to understand how privatization was changing life in the village.

Part of my answer came after an ill-fated picnic by the river one afternoon. A relative of my host had, in the summer heat, killed a duck the day before and hung it in her yard. That afternoon, she built a small fire and briefly cooked the fowl. Duck fat was mixed with rice to make *plov*, and every member of the party washed it down with copious amounts of moonshine made from sugar beet. Only I abstained from drinking, as I had scheduled a meeting with the farm director for the end of the day. When I returned from the meeting with the farm director, my host asked me if I had told him where I had been that afternoon. I said I had not, and she replied, "Correct."

Clarity about political economy in the village arrived in the following days, as I fell seriously ill. In the first days I passed through the usual stages of acute food poisoning, made worse, among other things, by the absence of access to a stove where I could boil (and thus render potable) water from the shallow village wells. A hard knock to the head as I stumbled into the latrine at an incorrect angle and made contact with a length of metal supporting the roof added a concussion to the mix, and it was time to travel to a city hospital.

Upon my return, an entire landscape of power in the village unfolded before my eyes. In my absence, a set of stories had emerged about what had happened to me: what I had eaten, where I had eaten it, who had prepared it, whether I was really sick, where I was being treated, whether I had gone to the city hospital, which of the folk medicine practitioners had visited me and what they had prescribed, and whether I was ever coming back. I heard some of these narratives directly, as people described what they had heard and asked me about it. I heard others indirectly, through gossip networks in the village. For the first time since I had arrived in the village, I alone knew what had occurred, if not all of the social implications of the event. This allowed me to map out who had told what to whom and to identify some of the loci of discursive and material power in the village.

The woman who prepared meals in the small kindergarten kitchen where I ate had been placed in the most awkward position. The kindergarten was believed to possess the cleanest kitchen in the village, and all guests of the farm were required to eat there. In the neighbors' view, it was she who had "shamed" me (*pozorili Dzhesiku*), so she instructed me with a counter-lie, "Don't tell them you ate in the kindergarten." Otherwise, she warned, the place would be closed down for days as a sanitary crew worked, and she would lose her job. The person who had served the guilty portion, meanwhile, denied ever having fed me when she spoke with a neighbor who was close to the farm chairman. In this case, my temporary vulnerability laid bare not only the ways people in the village understood their own vulnerability, but also how others responded to it.

Without this genre of knowledge, it would have been difficult fully to understand key components of village social relations that shaped the privatization process at the local level. The nature of the farm director's power over certain members of the community, as well as the complex webs of reciprocity that tempered that power, became clear only after this episode. Here, a new social position not only revealed a different type of information, but also brought to my analysis of property relations a more sensitive instrument for measuring power and negotiation in the village.[19]

In other words, participant observation research made possible analysis that could not have been achieved in any other way. While this research revealed a shifting terrain of power relationships, it did more than show me how people understood their social positions. It also showed how specific power relationships structured performance, illuminating villagers' precise points of strength and vulnerability: the pensioner who had to remain in the chairman's good graces in order to have coal for the winter; the schoolteacher who could afford to give me a 5-liter jar of milk for making *prostokvasha*, a sour milk product useful for recovering from food poisoning; and the drinking, singing *babushki* who after long, hard lives formed a tight, mutually supportive social network that allowed them the freedom to worry about pleasing no one but each other.

Yevhen

A realist approach to ethnography, even as it may be principally concerned with causal mechanisms and truth claims, nonetheless requires that the ethnographer be equipped with the type of knowledge that characterizes interpretivist approaches. In particular, in order to make reliable observations, the ethnographer must be able to distinguish ritual speech from original narrative, as well as to interpret the social meaning of texts.

In July 2006 I interviewed Yevhen, a sixty-year-old man selling a pile of what looked to be the previous year's root vegetable harvest. Yevhen had a vegetable stand—two wooden boxes covered by a dishtowel—alongside a road that runs through his village in eastern Ukraine. Yevhen had come to eastern Ukraine from the Crimean peninsula on the Black Sea. He worked in the village for years, and then commuted to a nearby city to work in a bicycle factory. After the Soviet collapse, in his words, "the state seized" his savings. His wife had worked in the local collective farm kindergarten after suffering an injury to her leg, but many kindergartens were closed during *perestroika* and she lost her job: "She was let go [*sokratili ee*] and that was it." During the ensuing period, land shares were distributed, but there was no information available to her about it at the time, so she did not receive land.

In 2006 there was no collective agricultural enterprise in the village, but there was a farm with "one boss" (*odin khoziain*), who was "some kind of deputy" head of state administration in the provincial capital. Somehow, after some manipulation of farm finances, the boss had managed to pay off farm debts. Yevhen had a land share: at first, he had 8 hectares of land, but later he lost 2 hectares. He received 700 to 800 *hriven'* (about 150 dollars) in land rents for his 6 hectares, "not in cash but in food [*produktami*]." At home, his wife's "tears fall because there's no [land] share." It cost him 700 to 800 *hriven'* each year to have his household garden plowed.

As Yevhen described it, people had "already thoroughly robbed [*perevorovali*] the collective farm," and "there are none of our people there. They are people who were brought in [*oni privoznye liudi*]." Even though "we built the *kolkhoz*," Yevhen and his coworkers received nothing from it. When asked what prevented him from starting his own farm, he replied, "Fuel prevents me. Machinery prevents me. Before, there was interest" in private farming, but now "we're not building but destroying. Everything is destroyed like after the war." In 2006 there were no lights on the roads and "there's no gas." There was, however, a "good school" in the village through eleventh grade, the last year of secondary school in Ukraine.

As Yevhen spoke, a couple in their early twenties drove up to the small store behind his stand. Observing their Cabriolet convertible, Yevhen compared their situation to that of the men down the road who work twelve hours a day and are paid 260 *hriven'*, or about fifty dollars, each month. Yevhen remarked that the heads of people like him are filled with concerns about money: "you sit at home and think about how to get money to buy pants for your grandchildren so they can go to school." As I departed, Yevhen presented me with two apples from his stand and instructed, "Tell them there's nothing good here, nothing good."

I reconstructed the previous narrative from my notes, after I had asked Yevhen to tell me about his experience of village life and land reform in Ukraine. I have reported the elements of Yevhen's story in the order in which he gave them. This interview was unusually short, lasting only about twenty minutes, and I have not spoken with Yevhen before or since then. Yevhen declined to be recorded as we spoke, a preference that did not distinguish him from hundreds of others whom I have interviewed in this region of rural Ukraine and in other postsocialist societies. I have thus included only those fragments that I was able to transcribe verbatim, and so I have reported his speech in the third person. I do not know Yevhen's real name. Most people in low-status positions in post-Soviet Ukraine are reluctant to identify themselves, even with the assurance that their statements would be reported anonymously. For them, danger resides not so much in the publication of their statements abroad as in their local circulation: Yevhen's wife might not like to be seen as weepy, his grandchildren as poor, his neighbors as thieving, or his local boss as shady or stingy.

Several other people were present as Yevhen spoke. It was easy to remove these individuals from my report of Yevhen's narrative, erasing them like Soviet leaders photographed on Lenin's tomb or, in Kundera's formulation, Clementis on the balcony of the Prague palace (Kundera 1979, 9).[20] The person who drove me out to the village was the regional head of a national voters' rights organization. In recent years, he had spent time on the road "giving lectures" to rural people about land reform. At several junctures, he interrupted Yevhen to challenge him on his interpretation of one point or another—usually just when I wanted to ask Yevhen what I saw as an important question of clarification. Other people, primarily urbanites who had stopped to inspect Yevhen's onions, carrots, and apples on their way to collect water from a natural spring down the road, moved in and out of the conversation.

Yevhen's story appears to be a personal narrative, a radically abbreviated version of a life history filtered through the voice of a political ethnographer. However, certain elements of his story are not personal at all. Instead, they are part of both broader social narratives and a liturgy of lamentation that is shared, above all, with outsiders.[21] In Hayden White's terms, Yevhen's trope in this interview is tragedy (White 1978). Viewed through the lens of White's philosophy of history, and presuming a degree of conscious storytelling on Yevhen's part, Yevhen selected elements of his past to support this mode of narration. In other words, the sequence of detail is crafted for the purpose of singing a tale of woe in the face of economic liberalism.

I suggest this may be the case because every element of Yevhen's story saturates post-Soviet social space and is reproduced in conversation repeatedly, often using the very same words. Over a decade and more of studying rural politics in Russia and Ukraine, and over the seventeen-year period during which I have conducted research in post-Soviet countries, I have come across the statement, "everything is destroyed, like after the war" hundreds of times. It may very well be true that some individuals in rural eastern Ukraine look around them at wasted farmland, ruined buildings, and broken people, and conclude that their landscape indeed resembles a world of sixty years before, when Hitler's armies and Soviet forces had only recently vacated land where they had lingered in front-line battle and occupation for over a year. But it is also true that this trope has become part of the post-Soviet cultural landscape and can be repeated without thinking, substituting, in Arendt's (1994) formulation, cliché for thought. In Yevhen's case, he was an infant and a toddler in the years following what came to be known as the Great Patriotic War. It seems unlikely that his description proceeds directly from personal observation and experience: rather, he is drawing upon a shared social metaphor.

Conversely, Yevhen's description of his wife crying over her loss of land seemed, to my mind, implausible. It is, of course, possible that she did mourn the absence of a land share, and that the additional land rent income would have made all the difference for the couple. But in years of conversations with land shareholders in the region, I have never come across such open regret in the face of dispossession. It was the exceptional quality of this statement that raised my suspicions about the character of Yevhen's words as a performance for a foreigner. Against the background of other statements that are *too often* uttered, the question arises: how familiar or unfamiliar must an element of narrative be in order to have the ring of truth?

The thorny methodological and epistemological issues Yevhen's story raises are part of a broader problematic. If the purpose of political ethnography is not only to offer alternative epistemologies in the form of shared understandings, but also to gain an understanding of social reality (the ultimate goal, as I understand it, of realist social science) and some purchase on causality, what can this brief exchange with Yevhen reveal? Is there anything about his narrative that would show "what happened and why"? Can his individual account be aggregated in any meaningful way, if the story he tells about his life partakes in established social narratives? What can a practitioner of realist ethnography learn from this?

Some truth about power relationships can be read between the lines of his story.[22] For example, Yevhen seems to have reason to believe that he should not identify the characters in his drama. With the exception of one mention of "the state," Yevhen does not name the agents of change in his experience. Instead, he uses passive or impersonal constructions to describe action: "she was let go," "thoroughly robbed," "people were brought in." He notes that he lost land but does not specify how or why, or who now owns it. In one instance, the subjects of action are inanimate objects: "Fuel prevents me. Machinery prevents me." The practice of avoiding attribution of responsibility is a Soviet discursive tradition, but it is also characteristic of subordinate populations more generally.[23] That Yevhen speaks in this way strongly suggests a lack of social power—a hypothesis corroborated by the condition of his carrots.

Key parts of Yevhen's story not only echo conventional narratives of post-Soviet life, but also suggest individual variations of historical experience already established through the accumulation of ethnographic and documentary evidence.[24] Dispossession through exclusion from the community of beneficiaries of postsocialist distribution and privatization, consolidation of managerial power in the hands of outside figures, the reduction of land share holdings at the margins, cashlessness and labor migration, disintegration and dismantling of rural factor endowments, income inequality, and the destruction of socialist-era property are by now uncontested phenomena in postsocialist rural politics (Allina-Pisano 2008; Creed 1995; Humphrey 2001; Verdery 2003).

Clearly, the researcher must be aware of the existence of broad social narratives in order to interpret individual statements intelligently and situate them within a field of social-scientific knowledge. For this reason, it may not always be possible to interpret meaningfully the texts of open-ended interviews without the type of knowledge that ethnographic research can provide. Because of the existence of social narratives, the texts that result from open-ended interviews have a form that precedes their content (White 1987). A social scientist seeking to discern individual experience or counter-hegemonic discourse must know that form well enough to distinguish ritual speech that captures *Zeitgeist* from individual speech that means to convey information about specific experience.

To put it a different way, ritual speech tends to be marked by repetition across individual narratives. The *gute Mensch* Stasi agent character in Henckel von Donnersmarck's screenplay *Das Leben der Anderen* (The Lives of Others) provides a useful description of a related phenomenon when he observes that persons telling the truth under interrogation reformulate their story each time they tell it, producing slight variations in each repetition. In contrast, persons who are lying (for whatever reason) do not: they tell precisely the same story each time, often using the same words.[25] In the face of an ethnographer's request for information, repetition may mark the telling of a shared social narrative, while departures from such a script may signal an account intended to describe individual experience.[26]

Yevhen's narrative also points to the necessity for ethnographers to understand the world of politics and policy in the metropole in order to interpret their interlocutors' statements. Yevhen's words taken at face value, in isolation from knowledge of formal institutions, convey only partial knowledge. For example, the state did not, technically, "seize" his savings. Rather, amidst the hyperinflation and currency devaluation following the Soviet collapse and the implementation of structural adjustment policies, state banks temporarily froze assets as the currency plunged, leaving the population with savings that lost all value. Yevhen, like most others of his generation, experienced this policy as seizure—a characterization that is not only a representation of his worldview, but also an expression, couched in metaphor, of a reality shared by all, as seen from below.

Conclusion

This chapter has suggested that a realist approach to ethnography can illuminate truth claims and identify causality more reliably than some other types of qualitative social science inquiry—whether in the world of individual action (here, murder) or economy (informal petroleum trade). In addition to enriching social research with the elaboration of alternative epistemologies, ethnography can contribute in important ways to debates about causality within positivist social science traditions. Realist ethnography also can provide contextual detail to illuminate the informal power relationships that underlie formal politics, as in the village networks that shaped privatization. Finally, armed with knowledge of social narratives, the realist ethnographer can extract truth claims from field notes and interview texts in much the same way that practitioners of other approaches use documentary evidence to build and test arguments.[27]

Ethnography and ethnographically informed qualitative research provide windows onto hidden politics and an opportunity to recalibrate the vision of histories and explanations as told from above. Work that is close to the source, whether in villages or the halls of legislatures, can reveal incentive structures, causal mechanisms, and patterns of action that drive formal politics, telling us not only how their meaning is understood, but also how they work. In this sense, ethnography can provide not only a different view, but also a view that more fully and accurately expresses the content and meaning of politics.

Notes

I would like to thank the anonymous reviewers at University of Chicago Press, Edward Schatz, and the participants in the Workshop in Political Ethnography for helpful suggestions—in particular, Lisa Wedeen, Tim Pachirat, and Jan Kubik for challenging questions and criticism that contributed to and helped sharpen the argument. Conversations with James C. Scott, Tracy Mc-Donald, and Susan Solomon inspired the presentation of fieldwork vignettes in this chapter. This chapter is the product of a series of conversations about social science epistemology and fieldwork with Eric Allina-Pisano and André Simonyi, who contributed to the ideas presented here.

1. It should be noted that such a move is not solely the product of right-wing politics. Here, the "hermeneutics of suspicion" (Ricoeur 1970) accommodates the hermeneutics of belief.

2. When discussing the conflict between this particularistic interpretation of a biblical text and the field of evolutionary biology, one should bear in mind that neither of these worldviews addresses the question of the origin of life. Rather, they both make claims about change in the physical world over time.

3. I do not intend to suggest any affinity between Holocaust deniers and proponents of intelligent design. However, their epistemologies have two things in common: first, an approach to knowledge that privileges *a priori* belief over evidence; second, a rhetorical strategy of using pseudo-empirical methods to convince others to adopt their beliefs.

4. *Beim Haüten der Zweibel* (Peeling the Onion) is the title of Günter Grass's 2006 autobiography in which he reveals, among other things, his wartime participation in the Waffen SS.

5. This is the "substantivist" study of economy that Kubik contrasts with neoclassical theory in chapter 1.

6. A list of such research would be long. The work of James C. Scott provides but one example. In socialist and postsocialist societies, authors conducting ethnographic research (or research with what might be termed an ethnographic sensibility), such as Katherine Verdery, Michael Burawoy, Kate Brown, and Alena Ledeneva reveal causal mechanisms even as they examine layers of social meaning. In this volume, chapters by Elisabeth Wood and Katherine Cramer Walsh exemplify this approach.

7. However, realist ethnography need not fall into the trap of attributing false consciousness to political actors (see Scott 1990, 70–107).

8. See Wendt and Shapiro (1992) for a discussion of scientific realism in the context of political science.

9. For a discussion of this proposition in another field, see Brewer and Lambert's (2001) discussion of conditions that shape degrees of "theory ladenness" of observation in cognitive psychology.

10. On process versus product in scientific realism, see Shapiro (2005, 9).

11. It seems possible, in addition, that ethnographers may sometimes overestimate the extent to which our interlocutors care what we think.

12. For a brief explication of how ethnography differs from other tools of qualitative social science research, see Bayard de Volo and Schatz (2004).

13. "Truthiness," as used by Colbert, means the quality of being known from the gut, rather than the head (*The Colbert Report* 2005).

14. In North America, 89 octane; octane numbers are calculated differently in different countries.

15. The *DT* sign provides an illustration of the type of text that can be an appropriate object of realist analysis: it is an object "out there" that has a single, unambiguous meaning for the author and intended reader.

16. For a satirical exploration of this practice, see O'Brien (1996).

17. Here, I do not presume, though neither do I exclude, a binary consciousness that admits to a distinction between authentic or "true" thought or speech, and dissimulation. Works that suggest the existence of such a dichotomy include Scott (1990) and Wedeen (1998). Alexei Yurchak (2003) offers a critique of this approach.

18. On this point, see Ortner (1995).

19. Timothy Pachirat powerfully examines the effect of position on knowledge in his chapter in this volume.

20. The imagined scene on the Prague balcony may offer a more appropriate analogy

than Soviet-era photos, for the individuals erased from Yevhen's narrative nonetheless leave traces in it, like the hat of Clementis that remains on Gottwald's head.

21. On conversational rituals in a Soviet context, see Ries (1997).

22. See Timothy Pachirat's chapter for another example of how ethnography can allow the researcher to read power relationships between the lines.

23. For an exploration of this subject in the Ukrainian media, see Ryabinska (2006).

24. This instance could be interpreted as support for Schatz's contention that some ethnography serves only to correct perspectives already established by other methods. See Schatz (2007). However, the use of ethnography for this purpose in this instance does not render it useless for establishing truth claims and causality more generally, as in the following examples.

25. The implication here—that in post-totalitarian contexts, the ethnographer and the policeman have much in common—is hardly an original suggestion. While the product of ethnographic work differs in several important ways from state surveillance—ethnographers' interlocutors are not identified, and the results of research are not secret—the close formal resemblance, *as it may be experienced by those who interact with ethnographers,* should condition our reading of ethnographic texts. The farmers with whom I interact in postsocialist societies regularly draw this connection, and as one of my Moscow colleagues in the natural sciences recently commented in reference to my research, "well, you're almost a spy [*razvedchik*]."

26. This accounts for one of the problems encountered by ethnographers in places where ethnographic research has been done before: over time, people develop narratives that they then produce when prompted by the presence of a notebook and pen, or of a voice recorder. Elisabeth Wood further discusses issues of memory and testimony as evidence in chapter 5 of this volume.

27. The production of knowledge through ethnography is heir not only to the interpretive tradition of recent decades, but also to the more ancient practices of observation and recording executed by more conscious servants of power: the scribes, administrators, and officials who tracked, recorded, and filed their notes about the world around them.

THREE

Ethnography as Interpretive Enterprise

LISA WEDEEN

Fieldwork has a particular Victorian-era history, one characterized, according to Henrika Kuklick (1997, 48), by "expectations that personal growth (of an implicitly masculine sort) could be effected through pilgrimages to unfamiliar places, where the European traveler endured physical discomfort and (genuine or imagined) danger." Emerging out of developments among Victorian naturalists, fieldwork came to be a "defining property of membership" in various disciplinary communities. In geology, zoology, and biology, and eventually in anthropology, students of natural history who turned to the field in the nineteenth century established standards for what was regarded at the time as an explicitly scientific enterprise (48–49), one that required the presence of experts *in situ*.

Take the example of organized fieldwork in biology. Whereas naturalists had previously relied on theories put forth by armchair scholars who hired middle-class adventurers to collect data, by the late nineteenth century, scientists came to believe that persuasive analysis had to be done by the ones who had gathered the data on which generalizations were based (Kuklick 1997, 49). Thus beginning in the 1870s, field stations were established in Europe and the United States to serve a burgeoning international community of scientists, enabling them to examine "living creatures instead of preserved specimens" (49–50). Well-known anthropologists, such as A. C. Haddon and Franz Boas, came out of this tradition, beginning their careers as natural scientists whose work in the field facilitated their transformation into sociocultural anthropologists who could explain variations within the human species as adaptations to geographical conditions. (Haddon, a former zoologist studying coral reefs, actually introduced the term *fieldwork* into anthropology [50].) As anthropology developed a distinct identity among the fields of natural history, the naturalist ideal of studying "primitive humanity in its natural state" became the discipline's foundational methodological purpose: "fieldwork in anthropology came to share with fields such as primatology the requirement that its subjects be directly observed in their natural surroundings" (Gupta and Ferguson 1997, 6).

My point here is not to rehearse anthropology's intellectual genealogy—George Stocking (1968, 1983, 1992) has done a masterful job of that—but to show that ethnography, far from being pitted against prevailing understandings of science, was originally a product of scientific developments. In mainstream political science, the view of ethnography's possible contributions to knowledge has come to rest on this older version of fieldwork's compatibility with the natural sciences, an affinity that sociocultural anthropologists have challenged over time. Particularly in the 1960s, preeminent anthropologists started interrogating the history of their discipline, discussing its complicity in imperial projects and domestic social control, its tendencies toward exoticism and its assumptions about "otherness," its troublesome figurations of race, its vexed connections to positivism, and the problems its central term *culture* posed conceptually, methodologically, and politically.[1] By the late 1970s and early 1980s, these conversations produced a spate of literature on the difficulties of doing fieldwork at all, and they encouraged a reflexivity (a reflection directed back at the discipline and its practitioners) that inserted the anthropologist self-consciously into the ethnography itself.

Political scientists began abandoning anthropology at this time. Monographs practicing reflexivity often devolved into what has been disparagingly called by scholars and journalists "navel gazing," and political science's own commitments to the scientific enterprise did not fit well with this turn. By the late 1980s, however, anthropologists had largely overcome the ethnographic crisis generated by their radical interrogation of the discipline's foundations and premises. Today, anthropology in no way entertains the notion of an objective observer, central to the naturalism of old, nor does it betray the hyper-preoccupation with the individual anthropologist's own experience in the field, so characteristic of the 1970s and early 1980s.[2] Instead, and largely as a result of Foucault's influence, we find an abiding attention to *epistemological* reflexivity, to the ways in which concepts and styles of reasoning, as well as scholarly commitments, are historically situated and enmeshed in power relationships.[3] Unlike the testimonial writings that made the ethnographer *as person* a primary object of her own narrative, the Foucauldian turn allowed anthropologists (as well as historians and philosophers) to analyze the discursive and institutional dynamics of scholarly production. Instead of searching for truths, Foucauldian analysts examine how truth-claims work.

I want to suggest that political scientists deserted anthropology just when anthropologists were generating important epistemological lessons about reflexivity and power—the latter being a primary concern of politics. Those lessons invite asking important questions such as: What sorts of disciplinary practices give particular research questions and methods the imprimatur of excellence, while others are deemed unworthy? What are the practices that bound and normalize a discipline, enabling certain kinds of knowledge to thrive, while foreclosing or deauthorizing other ways of knowing? What are the institutional conditions of fieldwork's intellectual production, in particular? In the following sections I do not tackle these questions directly, but use them as an orienting device, as a way of considering political science's interests in science, the possible relationships to ethnography in light of these scientific convictions, and strategies for pursuing ethnographic work in the discipline. I then identify some problems with current conceptualizations of ethnography among political scientists and offer suggestions for addressing them.

In more schematic terms, this chapter is divided into two parts. Part one begins by focusing on Gary King, Robert Keohane, and Sidney Verba's *Designing Social Inquiry* (1994) in order to exemplify how political science operates as a discipline, reproducing the norms, prohibitions, conventions, and constraints that generate standards for identifying expertise. I then locate interpretive social science within political science, explaining what an interpretive enterprise means and entails. Part two turns to the specifics of interpretive ethnography, questioning some of the ways in which ethnography has been appropriated by political science and, in doing so, making a key distinction between performance as an event and the performative as a specific logic of social interaction. I conclude by suggesting the added value of ethnographic approaches.

The Discipline's Interests in Science and Interpretive Alternatives

From its inception in 1903 to the present, the American Political Science Association has been the site of repeated attempts to "transform the study of politics into an independent science" (Ross 1991, 288). Despite important variations among positivists and significant disagreements between positivists and nonpositivists (including disputes about what *positivism* means), the concept of science adopted in these efforts has generally entailed separating facts from values, identifying purportedly lawlike principles governing political action, formulating hypotheses and posing alternatives to them, and subjecting all propositions to empirical tests.

Although standards of rigor are in part a technical matter, subject to debate in any context (from poetry to physics), in political science, arguments about scholarly rigor have generally accompanied efforts to unify the discipline across subdisciplinary and methodologically diverse boundaries. A case in point is the exceptionally influential book by Gary King, Robert Keohane, and Sidney Verba, *Designing Social Inquiry* (1994).[4] I think it is fair to say that no book in recent years has been as powerful as this one in authorizing experts and disciplining the discipline. By 2001 more than 20,000 copies had been sold; the book had already been reprinted six times; and 518 libraries had purchased it.[5] Insisting that differences in traditions within the discipline were simply *stylistic*, the authors sought to produce a unified epistemological and methodological community, one in which the scientific methods familiar to quantitative researchers would also become the norm in qualitative studies. The unity sought by KKV was not, therefore, based on the idea that qualitative work could be both nonscientific and legitimate. The claim, rather, was that there is simply no political science worthy of the name that does not conform to the putatively generalizable scientific strictures they defined.

According to KKV, the "best qualitative research," like quantitative research, operates with "the same underlying logic of inference." This logic of inference, whether causal or "descriptive," can be made "systematic and scientific." Indeed, its value relies on its claims to the scientific method. Although the authors concede that not all questions of abiding concern for politics can be covered by learning the rules of inference, "the rules are relevant to all research where the goal is to learn facts about the real world." The "real world" remains underspecified in the authors' account, but by drawing a sharp distinction between "what is" and "what ought to be,"[6] and by insisting on a strict separation between the "philosophical" and the "empirical," they formulate the real world as that which is constituted by the "rules of inference." Questions about "agency, obligation, legitimacy, citizenship, sovereignty, and the proper relationship between national societies and international politics" are located outside the domain of proper scientific inquiry (all from KKV 1994, 6). The KKV approach thus reproduces a classic intradisciplinary divide between political science and political theory, reading the manifestly political concerns of theory out of the discipline of political science.

The belief that such an approach is ontologically adequate may signal the authors' unacknowledged metaphysical commitments. Certainly such a conviction seems to limit the range of possibilities open for rigorous work in political science. For KKV, "the distinctive characteristic that sets social science apart from casual observation is that social science seeks to arrive at valid inferences by the systematic use of well-established procedures of inquiry" (1994, 6). "Good research," for which the authors use "the word 'scientific'" as the "descriptor," is work that adheres to the dictates of explicitly scientific research (7). "Valid inferences" are those established by scientific work, which is the guarantor of objectivity.[7]

KKV's methodological treatise thereby rests on familiar understandings in the discipline: they not only assume the intrinsic worth of scientific studies, but also posit a specific and by no means self-evident understanding of science as a practice based on a clear divide between empirical facts and philosophical values. Science, in their view, requires testable, falsifiable hypotheses; an acknowledgment of the tentative nature of findings; and (therefore, arguably) an emphasis on methods over results. Worried that the absence of consensus about what social science *is* necessarily entails disagreement about what constitutes good work or shared standards, the authors ignore underlying philosophical problems raised by their position, attempting to impose a specific type of rigor on the discipline at the expense of other rigorous forms of engagement with politics. In this sense, the book fit well with a number of books in the 1980s and 1990s, many of which lamented the divisions within political science and insisted on the methodological assumptions of the natural sciences.[8] Although *Designing Social Inquiry* has yet to create the desired consensus, the book has arguably been more successful than any other in specifying the terms under which scholarly work would be taken seriously in the field. *Designing Social Inquiry* has produced guidelines for hiring and tenure decisions, as well as for what is sayable and practicable in the discipline.

Interpretive social science receives little recognition in *Designing Social Inquiry*, and its methods are rarely taught in political science qualitative methods seminars more generally.[9] This neglect may have to do with the divergent ways interpretive and scientifically minded political scientists view categories of fact, the nature of evidence, and possibilities for objectivity. Rather than claim that science moves us toward a fully adequate description of social life, interpretivists of various stripes are often more interested in understanding how it is that scholars in the discipline have increasingly believed this progress to be under way (see Poovey 1998, 7). To borrow from Foucault, interpretivists tend to question the "kind of power that is presumed to accompany . . . science" (Foucault 1980, 84). They are therefore committed to thinking through the assumptions undergirding the production of lawlike principles supposedly governing human behavior, which is to say, to dealing with the philosophical questions the scientific approach tends to dismiss from consideration.

As a rubric, the term *interpretive social science* can refer to a variety of epistemological, methodological, and political commitments—and, indeed, may be too elastic to be of great use. The "interpretive turn" is sometimes invoked as a synonym for the "culture turn" (Hunt and Bonnell 1999) and at other times as a synonym for "hermeneutics" (Rabinow and Sullivan 1987; Geertz 1973, 1980). It sometimes means a commitment among practitioners "to violate the positivist taboo against joining evaluative concerns with descriptions of fact" (Rabinow and Sullivan 1987), and it sometimes connotes a belief that such a divide is impossible to sustain in practice, so that normative claims and factual statements necessarily infuse one another.

Nevertheless, there are at least four characteristics uniting interpretivists across their differences. We have already dealt with one primary feature: *interpretivists view knowledge, including scientific knowledge, as historically situated and entangled in power relationships.* Power is generally not simply about leverage in such accounts, but also connotes intersubjective relationships that are diffuse, omnipresent, and often acephalous. Foucault, for example, traces how power works in excess of state institutions or particular elites, operating through discursive processes that suffuse all aspects of life. Power passes through institutional spaces as well as micro-spaces of health, education, science, theories of language, and ordinary communication. It is located in and generated through social-scientific categories and the assumptions underlying them; in legal definitions of personhood and their widespread dissemination; in the administrative routines of colonial bureaucrats; in psychological understandings of madness, sex, and family; in practices of worship; in activities of peer review; and so forth.[10] In this sense power is hard to measure, although it is observable. Moreover, observations are not objective or external to the conditions that produce scholars doing the observing.

Second, interpretivists are also constructivists in the sense that they see the world as socially made, so that the categories, presuppositions, and classifications referring to particular phenomena are understood as manufactured rather than natural. There is no such thing as ethnicity or race, for example, outside of the social conditions that make such classifications meaningful. What counts as a phenotypical distinction or a "cultural difference" is a product of the discursive and institutional environment within which such distinctions make sense. The title *How the Irish Became White* (1996) exemplifies this interpretivist sensibility. Although a number of social scientists avow constructivist commitments, the radical constructivism of many interpretivists entails privileging the history of categories over the fact of groups. This attention to classification invites interrogating how social scientists themselves stabilize or fix categories of group affiliation—how analysts help to produce groups as substantial entities through their scholarly practices. The task of an interpretivist is often to analyze the sort of work categories such as "black" and "white" or "Sunni" and "Shi'a" do, while accounting for how they come to seem natural and taken for granted, when they do. By engaging in this work, interpretivists do more than reveal how scholars reify categories, they also offer a rich, robust understanding of social and political life.

Third (and related), interpretivists tend to eschew the individualist assumptions that characterize much rational-choice and behaviorist literature. Although some interpretivists do stress the importance of agentive individuals (e.g., Bourdieu 1977), others question the very meaning of agency, or they compare divergent, historically contingent notions of what counts as agentive action (Butler 1997; Asad 2003; Mahmood 2005). Despite this range, no interpretive social scientist could assume, as many rational-choice and strategic-action theorists do, a maximizing, cost-benefit calculator who can be divorced, for the sake of general propositions, from actual historical processes. Ideas, beliefs, values, "preferences," and decisions are always embedded in a social world, which is constituted through humans' linguistic, institutional, and practical relations with others (Wedeen 2002).

Fourth, interpretivists are particularly interested in language and other symbolic systems, in what is sometimes termed "culture" in the literature.[11] Despite conceptual ambiguities inherent in the term, promising developments in practice-oriented anthropology have led *culture* to be understood and operationalized as "semiotic practices." Culture as semiotic practices can be thought of as an abstract theoretical category, a lens that focuses on meaning, rather than on, say, the fact of prices or the tallying of votes (Sewell 1999; Wedeen 2002). I am not arguing that votes and prices have no meaning, but that a semiotic practical approach would study these phenomena in terms of the distinct meanings they index and generate, while an economist might take prices, and a political scientist, votes, at face value. It is worth noting that the term "meaning" is at once entirely taken for granted in the social sciences and deeply contested across theoretical paradigms within interpretive social science. For the purposes of clarity here, I understand meaning to be "the economy of signs and symbols in terms of which humans construct, inhabit, and experience their social lives (and thus act in and upon the world)."[12] A formulation of culture as meaning-production also refers to the work symbols *do*—how symbols are inscribed in activities that operate to produce observable political effects (see Wedeen 2002). Here *work* might be most fruitfully understood, as it is in Foucauldian discourse analysis, as two-pronged. First, it may be seen as an examination of a text's or an ideology's logics—the assumptions the discourse implies, its context-dependent uses, and the possibilities it forecloses. Second, it might be seen as an investigation into the rhetoric's effects—the ways in which that discourse is mediated, reiterated, and transmitted; how it becomes subject to risks through repetition; and how it is assessed and resignified over time by and through elite-inspired organizations, extraordinary events, and everyday, embodied activities.[13] Discourse analysis, as opposed to a more natural scientific commitment to method, is scarcely conceivable independent of context; it relies ultimately on a sensitive, if not empathic, understanding of the conditions under which a discourse is produced, as well as of its effects in the world. Ethnography is one particularly good way of grasping a discourse's observable effects. A discourse analysis is an especially effective way of identifying the implications of ethnographic work. Perhaps for these reasons, scholars interested in "culture" as semiotic practices have often been drawn to ethnography.

Although interpretive methods of various sorts have typically been sidelined in the discipline, recent efforts to produce "valid social knowledge" (Laitin 2003, 170) have prompted appeals for the adoption of mixed methods, and this has included the incorporation of "narrative" methods, especially ethnographic ones. The Institute for Qualitative Research Methods—now the Institute for Qualitative and Multi-Method Research, based in Syracuse, New York—even changed its name and mission statement to capture this trend in the discipline. The Qualitative Methods section of the American Political Science Association has followed suit, appending "multi-method" to its title as well. For the former ethnographer David Laitin, narrative approaches are by themselves inadequate. When combined with large-n statistical work and formal models, however, they can help generate robust findings (discussed by Pachirat, this volume; Hopf 2006). Laitin (2003, 175) advocates for "productive complementarity" among these three different conceptual and methodological orientations, a call presuming that the facts gathered by fieldworkers can be isolated from their meaning in context; that words such as *theory* do not themselves contain important, historically changing assumptions about knowledge, stature, and modes of inquiry; and that systematic knowledge is the kind that counts (Poovey 1998, 1). My point is not that such assumptions are wrong. Rather,

I am suggesting that calls for "productive complementarity" tend to subordinate the epistemological concerns of "narrative approaches" to the aims of science. Ethnography is often deployed in the service of the very sorts of objectivist aims that current ethnographic approaches in anthropology undermine. And ethnography is seen as the least prestigious method, treated as the "summer intern" (Hopf 2006) to the "senior partner" of formal methods.

Claims that ethnography is not a coequal method in political science and the epistemological contradictions that emerge as a result of mixing methods suggest at least three strategies in response. First, one might embrace the "productive complementarity" Laitin champions, conceding that what ethnography does, given the objectives of science in the discipline, is to fulfill the roles Laitin and others outline for it. In other words, one can choose to bracket the epistemological tensions. Ethnography then becomes a "plausibility test" for the predictions put forward by formal models; it is a means of identifying possible causal mechanisms linking statistically significant independent and dependent variables; it is also a way of "fleshing out residuals which may have not been captured by statistical models or which may not (yet) be amenable to measurement and statistical analysis" (Laitin 2003, 179). One might acknowledge that this is precisely what ethnography can do for a subset of scientifically minded scholars, and that the problem is not with the roles designated, but with the value assigned to those roles. In other words, one could choose to identify with the purposes of ethnography (as stated by Laitin and others) but not with the value ethnographic work has in political science.

Second, one could ignore or selectively address methodological challenges, while pursuing the research problems that make one curious and happy. For a political ethnographer, that would undoubtedly require ethnographic work, with the worthiness of such work perhaps being demonstrated in the findings generated or by the questions raised. Pursuing substantive "puzzles" that are answered compellingly with ethnographic work is one way to advertise the strengths of ethnography, to clear space for ethnographic commitments and activities, without confronting all the academic debates about methodological virtue. Substantive problems particularly congenial to ethnographic study include questions of how political identifications are established; how rhetoric and symbols not only exemplify but can also produce political compliance; why some political ideologies, policies, and self-policing strategies work better than others; what terms like *democracy* and *religion* mean to political actors who invoke or consume them, and how these perceptions might affect political outcomes;

and why particular material and status interests are taken for granted, are viewed as valuable, or become available idioms for dissemination and collective action.[14]

Third, one might consider doing ethnographic work on the discipline—analyzing the ways in which particular terminology and communities of argument operate in political science. Such an ethnography might entail participant observation in faculty meetings, immersion in off-campus graduate student environments, or an analysis of the micro-dynamics and broader debates characteristic of conferences and lectures. This ethnography might be combined with an attention to the work particular categories or phrases such as "valid social knowledge" *do* in context, permitting us to ask questions such as these: What counts as valid and as knowledge? What even constitutes a problem requiring a solution? When and why do these problems come to the fore, and what sorts of implications do they have for our understandings of politics? What vocabularies authorize expertise, and why? These questions presume interrogating a natural sciences view of what social science is.

To be clear: I am not championing the pursuit of any one of these strategies over another. Nor are they necessarily mutually exclusive. An ethnographer might choose to translate her findings into the language Laitin suggests, highlighting, for example, her project as one that explicates causal mechanisms. This strategy will require neglecting certain epistemological concerns, but perhaps only temporarily. She might also embark on an analysis of the relationship between a given concept and the styles of social-scientific reasoning that stabilize it, for example. Each strategy can contribute insightfully, individually or in tandem, to debates in the discipline. Ethnographic work and interpretive studies more generally have a place—indeed, multiple places—in the study of politics. They can enrich ongoing debates in the discipline, while also raising questions about the underlying assumptions that structure those debates.

Ethnography as Sensibility and Activity

Within interpretive social science, ethnography has a particularly prominent place and a long scholarly provenance. There is, of course, ethnographic work that is not interpretive and interpretive work that is not ethnographic (Kubik, this volume).[15] We already saw how ethnography emerged out of field methods associated with the natural sciences, for example, and its place in the largely interpretivist discipline of anthropology remains both central and vexed.[16] Yet interpretivist ethnographies allow us to see how an often antipositivist episteme need not lead to the abandonment of empiricism (see Morris 2007, 38; Derrida 1976 [1967], 162). Ethnography is an especially good way to gain insight into actors' lived political experiences, to observe how people make sense of their worlds, to chart how they ground their ideas in everyday practices and administrative routines, and to analyze the gap between the idealized representation and actual apprehension of events, people, and political orders. It would even seem that an ethnographic approach is required to address the difficulties of what Timur Kuran (1995) calls "preference falsification," by offering a way to figure out what people are thinking when they falsify their preferences in public. Ethnography gives us insight into the underlying attitudes of citizens, into the shared (but not necessarily official) meanings they assign to phenomena. Ethnography also charts the forms of contestation and sources of unbelief that may be particularly difficult to discern in authoritarian regimes. Ethnography permits us to register competing histories "as they happen" (Caton 2007).

As scholars of ethnography in political science have noted, doing interpretivist ethnographic work requires a distinct "sensibility," what the oft-cited anthropologist Daniel Miller (1997, 16–17) identifies as a "particular perspective"[17] comprising the following "commitments":

1. "To be in the presence of the people one is studying, not just the texts or objects they produce"
2. "To evaluate people in terms of what they actually do, i.e. as material agents working with a material world, and not merely of what they say they do"
3. To have a "long term commitment to an investigation that allows people to return to a daily life that one hopes goes beyond what is performed for the ethnographer"
4. To engage in a "holistic analysis, which insists that . . . behaviors be considered within the larger framework of people's lives and cosmologies."[18]

Miller's is a helpful list, and most of the commitments do seem to be constitutive of the ethnographic enterprise. But ethnographers in political science tend to endorse this list too readily, and I want to discuss some of the problems it brings to the fore. On reflection, for example, the fourth commitment may not be valid without qualification: the object of study identified in some ethnographic works is more holistic than it is in others. Some ethnographers underscore the ruptures, the ambiguity, and the fragmentary character of social life rather than striving for semiotic coherence, if that's what Miller's holism implies.[19]

Here, however, I want to focus briefly on Miller's third commitment and the lines of inquiry it invites us to pursue. The third commitment implies that the ethnographer cannot know the whole story, which seems correct and salutary. It also helpfully registers a difference between ethnography and other kinds of fieldwork, for intrinsic to the former is a long-term commitment to people and place. Because people under study may alter their behavior when in the presence of researchers, Miller's third commitment suggests that one of the ethnographer's tasks is to be aware of possible discrepancies, making sure his fieldwork has enough depth to distinguish actions he observes from what might have occurred in his absence.[20] But commitment three also hints at a tension in Miller's formulation, one that speaks to the general limitations of viewing ethnography as spectatorship and "informants" as performers. On the one hand, Miller recognizes that aspects of an "informant's" interiority and of her experiences of daily life will not be available to an ethnographer—and I would add, arguably to anyone else. (Psychoanalysis teaches us that some emotions, thoughts, and motivations may not even be accessible to the "informant" herself.) On the other hand, one of the advantages of ethnography is that extended participant observation requires an enmeshment in the social, semiotic world under investigation. And this saturation entails, as Bayard de Volo and Schatz note (2004, 267), particular activities, such as "learning a local language or dialect; participating in the daily life of the community through ordinary conversations and interaction; observing events (meetings, ceremonies, rituals, elections, protests); examining gossip, jokes, and other informal speech acts for their underlying assumptions, recording data in field notes." Commitment three suggests that the ethnographer and the people he studies live in a necessarily bifurcated world: there is actual daily life and there is the world performed for the ethnographer, an implication that undermines the advantages of depth central to ethnographic work. Theatrical metaphors also reproduce a flawed understanding of power relationships, as if there were an on-stage and an off-stage, a fake or scripted actor and an authentic self, a strictly bounded public domain and a private one (for an extended criticism of theatrical metaphors, see Mitchell 1990; Abu-Lughod 1990).

This critique reminds us that the ethnographic activity of participating in the daily life of a community (however broadly or narrowly construed), including the sensibility that attends such engagement, generally takes place against the backdrop of a theory of interpretation—a particular understanding of what meaning is and how language operates. Different theories (structuralism, hermeneutics, poststructuralism, deconstruction) have divergent accounts of how and why discourses work, how they are received and evaluated, how they suffuse institutions, and how (or whether) they can themselves be generative. For example, some theoretical orientations help us analyze a discourse's causal effects, while others focus on felicitous conditions; some are geared toward responding to "why" questions, while others deal with "how" ones. A causal question was at the forefront of my first book, *Ambiguities of Domination* (1999), which examined the "cult of personality" around Syrian President Ḥāfiz al-Asad (in power 1970–2000)—all the rhetorical practices and imagery that substituted for discussion of substantive political issues in public. I argued that this official rhetoric worked to enforce obedience, induce complicity, and structure the terms within which transgressions could take place. The "cult" generated the guidelines for public speech and action while atomizing people from one another; it tired people out, taking language that could have once seemed politically inspiring and rendering it absurd. My new book *Peripheral Visions* (Wedeen 2008a) also registers the effects of discourse, but the emphasis here is on practices as performative, as capable of summoning selves (and groups) into existence. In contrast to theatrical metaphors of performance, the idea of performativity here is that the actions performed are intrinsic to, not separate from, daily life. Selves, on this account, do not exist, as if in some authentic mode, independently of the actions by which they are constituted.

An emphasis on "performative practices" requires the elaboration of both terms. First, *practices*: Practices are actions or deeds that are repeated over time. They are learned, reproduced, and subjected to risk through social interaction.[21] Practices, like actions (as opposed to "behaviors"), are also, in the sense I use the term, unique to human beings. Like actions, they involve "freedom, choice, and responsibility, meaning and sense, conventions, norms, and rules" (Pitkin 1993, 242). They may be self-consciously executed, but they need not be. They tend to be intelligible to others (including the ethnographer) in context-dependent ways. Practices, like human actions, are ultimately "dual," composed both of what "the outside observer can see and of the actors' understandings of what they are doing" (Pitkin 1993, 261; also discussed in Wedeen 2002). Ethnographic work is especially capable of working productively with this dualism and the tensions it evokes, because the ethnographer is positioned both to register the categories a community uses (its "categories of practice") and to enjoy the distance necessary to develop relevant analytical categories (Brubaker 2004). For example, *democracy* can connote what citizens of a polity say it means, such as contested elections, or radical redistribution, or anticommunism (or communism), or disorder. *Democracy* can also be an analytic category that indicates—given the grammar of the word and its scholarly uses over time—agonistic deliberation; equality of condition; rule by, of, and for the people; and/or accountability. Some of these notions of the term overlap with ordinary language uses, but not all. A project that pays attention to ordinary language use (for example, Schaffer 1998; Paley 2002) may or may not be compatible with an analysis that foregrounds the existence of democratic practices, where democracy is a category of analysis rather than the term "natives" use to describe what they are doing (Wedeen 2007, 2008a). A particularly robust category of analysis will attend to the etymology of the word, its conceptual grammar, and the puzzlements it has produced over time.

Second, *performative*: The word *performative* was initially invoked by J. L. Austin to describe particular kinds of speech acts in which the utterance is the act itself: "I promise" or "I protest" or "I bet" are examples of performatives.[22] Derrida's use of *performativity* to refer to an "iterable practice" (1988) has been adopted by subsequent theorists to articulate a theory of self formation in which the iterative character of speech and bodily practices constitute individuals as particular kinds of social beings or "subjects." Through the repeated performance of practices, in this view, the person's desires, understandings, and bodily comportment come to acquire a particular, recognizable form (Butler 1993, 1997; Mahmood 2005, 162–63; see also Bourdieu 1991).[23] This literature allows us to focus on the ways in which the category of the national citizen, for example, relies on performing norms and activities associated with nationalism, such that the category comes into being, at least in part, through these performances. Nationalist actions, in this light, may be understood as performatives because they enact that which they name, a national self or "subject."[24]

Emphasizing practices as "performative" speaks to substantive concerns that are relevant not only to interpretivists but also to social science more generally, such as how to study "identity" or how to think about "subjectivity." And here, too, the role of ethnography is important. Rather than think of identities as antecedent facts about people that help determine their actions, we might follow Hannah Arendt in her understanding of identities as what results from public speech and action; *through* public words and deeds, actors "make their appearance" in the world (Arendt 1958, 179). As Patchen Markell notes, "one important consequence of this is that identity, for Arendt, is not something over which agents themselves have control. Because we do not act in isolation but interact with others, who we become through action is not [simply] up to us; instead, it is the outcome of many intersecting and unpredictable sequences of action and response, such that 'nobody is the author or producer of his own life story'" (Markell 2003,

13).[25] By emphasizing the "performative" aspects of identity formation, one can show not only that nationalism is actualized in nationalist practices, for example, but also that national persons themselves are formed by the speech and embodied acts associated with nationalism (such as pledging allegiance to the flag, singing the national anthem, drawing a map, or using the word *we* to talk about a country's foreign policy). Similarly, it is not simply that the merits of democracy cause or are realized in particular kinds of democratic acts, but also that democratic persons are themselves constituted through the doing of democratic deeds.[26] These deeds are not embellishments of a democratic order independently existing, but rather are instances of democracy itself. Democratic practices can exist outside a democratic regime. And regimes coded as democratic may be missing crucial aspects of democratic life (understood in terms of the word's grammar and uses—aspects such as agonistic debate; continual accountability; ongoing, fulfilling participation in political affairs; and/or universal equality). The "observation" part of *participant observation* suggests that ethnographers can observe the ongoing work of nationalism and democracy, to name two examples, by watching how people get constituted through these activities.[27] The "participant" part of the term suggests that the ethnographer herself can be affected by—indeed, coformed anew through—these interactions. In this view, the ethnographer can produce rigorous knowledge in part *because* she participates.

This approach to discursive practices does not imply that nationalist persons believe in nationalism or that people acting democratically are necessarily emotionally committed to democracy. If, in interpreting actions in this way, I privilege intelligibility over deep-seated meanings, I do so for the reasons I think Miller attempts to express in specifying commitment number three: intelligibility does not presuppose grasping an inner essence or getting into the heads of informants, understood as captive minds of a system, but rather centers on the ways in which people attempt to make apparent, observable sense of their worlds—to themselves and to each other—in emotional and cognitive terms. In stark contrast to grasping an inner essence, such a conceptualization of meaning requires us to discover what in fact we know (that children are saluting a flag or ballots are being checked and counted, for example) and what we need to know (what work this flag salute or ballot tallying is doing in the context in which it is going on).[28] By analyzing the context-specific logics of these activities and their effects, we can avoid assuming that elections necessarily imply democracy or that they are even the best way to ensure the values of accountability and participation. Such an inquiry then prompts us to ask questions about the conditions under which specific material and semiotic activities emerge, the contexts within which they find public expression, the consequences they have in the world, and the irregularities they generate in the process of reproduction. Focusing on the logics of a discourse and its political effects might be compared to enhancing visual resolution in the natural sciences: it adds value to scholarship to the extent that it allows for more nuanced, valid understandings of politics that are capable of unsettling previous beliefs and affecting our prior assumptions about the world.

Conclusion

Ethnographic observations can generate counterintuitive findings or confirm previous research. They can raise questions about the concepts and paradigms currently informing social science projects and invite novel ways of imagining the political. They can negotiate the tensions between the particular lived experience of social actors and the analytic categories we use to generalize about them. Such work might be folded into agendas and utilize vocabularies typical of mainstream political science; it can also reach out beyond the boundaries of the discipline and strive for new forms of interdisciplinary conversation. Interpretive social science does not aspire to the objectivity of the field sciences of old; nor should its commitments to reflexivity necessarily entail inserting the "I" of the observer into the narrative about the field. One can assume the coformation of ethnographer and local actors without having to narrate that experience as therapy. Such a predilection had political scientists fleeing from anthropology after Geertz.[29] Weaving empirical evidence into theoretically motivated findings generally presupposes activities other than the interviews political scientists tend to designate as fieldwork, however. Political scientists would therefore be well served by familiarizing themselves with debates in the discipline of anthropology, as well as with ethnographic methods. For ethnography as sensibility and activity implies the possibilities and pleasure of serendipitous encounter, the commitments to long-term engagement with places and inhabitants, and an abiding attention to what people say and do—as well as an appreciation, crucial to politics, that what people say is a form of doing in its own right.

Notes

The author would like to thank the participants at the NSF workshop on Qualitative Methods (May 2005), colleagues who participated in a workshop held at the University of Toronto entitled

"Political Ethnography: What Insider Perspectives Contribute to the Study of Power" (October 2006), and panelists at the Midwest Political Science Association's annual conference (April 2007). I am also indebted to John Comaroff, Michael Dawson, Daragh Grant, Rohit Goel, Rosalind Morris, Don Reneau, and Edward Schatz for helpful suggestions.

1. See, for example, Dell Hymes's call to rethink anthropology's imperial roots (1972; see also Asad 1973; Gough 1968; Fabian 1983; Stocking 1992). All are cited in Morris (2007, 34).

2. This is my periodization, but it fits well with most accounts of the discipline.

3. Rosalind Morris (2007, 33) suggests that there may be an affinity between Foucault's concept of episteme and American anthropology's notion of culture, especially under the influence of structuralism, that explains anthropology's receptivity to Foucault's thought.

4. Hereafter referred to as KKV. This section is a slightly revised excerpt from Wedeen (2006); a more in-depth discussion of KKV can be found in Wedeen (2008b).

5. Keisha Lindsay supplied this information through a WorldCat search (June 2001) and through a telephone interview with Eric Rohmann, sales director, Princeton University Press, 11 June 2001. Although KKV claim that their "goal is practical: designing research that will produce valid inferences about social and political life" (3), several commentators, some of whom support the enterprise, have likened the project to a religious one: a "missionary effort" (Shively 1995); a book that has "the aim of evangelizing" (Rogowski 1995, 467); a "homily," one that "puts forth a simple straightforward faith" (Brady 1995, 12). These are all cited in James Johnson's excellent essay (2006). That essay differs markedly from my analysis of KKV here, in that the former argues directly with the text rather than analyzing how the book "works" in the Foucauldian sense. In other words, Johnson does not bracket whether the text is good or bad, but argues that the authors' theory of inquiry impedes our ability to make sense of successful quantitative analyses and of causal explanation. He also argues that it fails in its mission to "impart intellectual unity to the discipline of political science" (224). I am more interested in asking why and how that unity matters.

6. For a sophisticated discussion of the distinction between is and ought, see Pitkin (1993 [1972]).

7. For a fascinating study of the history of objectivity and its gradual identification with science *tout court*, see Daston and Galison (2007).

8. The most obvious text lamenting a "discipline divided" is Almond's (1990). One of the most oft-cited critiques of *Designing Social Inquiry* is Brady and Collier (2004). King's *Unifying Political Methodology* (1989) is an effort to unify statistical methods in political science. *Designing Social Inquiry* is more ambitious.

9. There are a few pages on interpretation beginning on page 38 of KKV. Clifford Geertz is discussed on pages 37, 38–40, 232, and 233.

10. The three sentences on Foucault are from Wedeen (2008a, chap. 4).

11. These four points are excerpted from and an elaboration of Wedeen (2006). See, too, Wedeen (2004). The last point has been dealt with at length in Wedeen (2002), so I am not going to rehearse those arguments here.

12. These are John Comaroff's words, email correspondence (25 January 2009).

13. These points are taken from Wedeen (2008a), especially the introduction and the conclusion.

14. This list is excerpted from Wedeen (2002).

15. There are obviously many interpretive works that are not ethnographic. By ethnographies that are not interpretive, I have in mind works (early structural-functionalist and Manchester school network analyses offer pointed examples) such as Fortes (1945, 1949), Kapferer (1972), and Krige and Krige (1943). Kapferer's network analysis of an African factory, for instance, reduces interactions, which are taken largely at face value, to abstract network morphologies that are then used to explain political outcomes such as strikes. As John Comaroff (personal communication) put it to me, "a quantum of transactions, unmediated by their meaning, congeals into patterns, which are the object of analysis." Similarly, structural functionalists (e.g., Krige, Radcliffe-Brown, Schapera et al.) asked questions to obtain "native" data on practices. Native responses were taken as indicative of the values they held. Nobody asked why, or what those statements meant, or what motivated them. The researcher then compared informants' answers to patterns of social practice in order to devise ethnographic generalizations that could then be narrated (by the researcher) as "systems" and "structures." For example, the ethnographer might ask informants what the rules governing devolution of rank were. If the natives said that male primogeniture was the pattern, then that was the ethnographic generalization. The researcher then counted cases in which it happened, and noted the deviation from the pattern, and how it was dealt with—and then wrote secondary rules. The result was ethnography. Again, there was no discussion of what those rules meant (in the case of rules involving devolution of status, an interpretive account might have included the rearrangement of power relations or a discussion of factional alignments). In these noninterpretive ethnographic accounts, the outcomes tended to be rationalized to fit the rules *ex post facto*. An interpretive ethnographer, by contrast, would look for the meaning of these rules in political communication, in the restructuring of power relations, in public discourses about staffing regimes, and so on. Despite variation among interpretivists, most contemporary ones would see these rules as variable, historically constituted, and subject to risk. To put it plainly: noninterpretive ethnography focuses on presumed values, and then looks for structure and system. An interpretive ethnography centers on meaning, and at least in many instances, on process and history. Special thanks are owed to John Comaroff here.

16. Sociocultural anthropology dominates the discipline these days. Many of the top departments no longer have physical anthropologists, in fact.

17. In political science, see Pader (2006); Yanow (2006a); Pachirat (this volume).

18. This list is cited in MacDonald (2001, 72) and in an earlier version of Pachirat's chapter for this volume, although Pachirat (rightly, in my view) omitted a cumbersome "of" from the second commitment.

19. There are a wide variety of works on resistance in anthropology, and I mention just a few here: Comaroff and Comaroff (1991, 1995); Comaroff (1985); Abu-Lughod (1986); and Abu-Lughod's essay criticizing anthropological preoccupations with resistance (1990). There are also scholars inspired by Foucault's writings on historical rupture (e.g., Messick 1993). Comaroff and Comaroff's "Ethnography on an Awkward Scale" (2003) deals with some of the issues brought to the fore by the effects of globalization, the recent historicization of the discipline, and the questioning of what counts as "the field." Key ethnographic texts that also raise these issues include Mazzarella (2003); West's recent book (2007); and West's monograph (2005). Of particular note, too, is the Derridean-inspired work of James Siegel (1998; 2000 [1969]; 2006).

20. Thanks are owed to an anonymous reviewer for this reading.

21. This section on "performative practices" is excerpted and modified from Wedeen (2008a). A variety of scholars have noted that practices are subjected to risk because their very iteration creates possibilities for intervention, action, innovation, and subversion. On subversion see, for example, Butler (1993, 1997); for an account emphasizing improvisation, see especially Bourdieu (1977, 1991). The anthropologist Marshall Sahlins also shows how the reproduction of rituals, customs, and cosmological narratives places them at risk (1981, 1987).

22. For a discussion of Austin's problems in distinguishing performatives from descriptive statements, see Pitkin (1993, 38). See also J. L. Austin (1961; 1965).

23. Significantly, there are also critical differences among these theorists. Butler remains close to Austin in *Bodies that Matter* (1993) and *Excitable Speech* (1997), but Derrida's deconstructionist argument is specifically targeted at Austin's failure to understand that "the boundary between text and context is not so easily drawn," as Rosalind C. Morris has pointed out to me (personal communication). Moreover, Derrida's notion of iterability, which Butler embraces, differs from Bourdieu's practice-oriented theory. The Derridean (and to some extent Austinian and Butlerian) notions get away from the simple logic of "reproductive enactment," to borrow Morris's (1995) term, and can thereby stress the creative gestures and multiple possibilities for innovation and subversion. This latter critique of Bourdieu may not be fair, given his attention to improvisation, but the general point holds: theories of performativity tend to emphasize reproduction or to see iteration as an opportunity for fresh political possibility.

24. See also Bourdieu's discussion of the performative (1991, especially 220–28) and Brubaker (2004).

25. The insertion of "simply" is mine, not Markell's. Arendt's words, cited in Markell's quotation, are from Arendt (1958, 184).

26. I am not presuming here that we have to share an understanding of what these democratic deeds are, or who controls the terms of their definition; Wedeen (2008a, chap. 3) deals with these latter issues explicitly.

27. See Wedeen (2008a) for a discussion of the ambiguity in the notion of constituting selves.

28. These are all examples from Wedeen (2002).

29. By "after Geertz" I mean that political scientists tended to ignore anthropologists other than Geertz by the late 1970s, after Geertz had published his influential *Interpretation of Cultures* (1973).

PART TWO

First-Person Research

All research is conducted by people, even if research reports in some traditions place this in the background. Political ethnographers, by virtue of their close interactions with ground-level processes and interlocutors, are frequently reminded of the role played by individual choices (by the researcher and by the researched), ground-level contingencies, and a variety of background factors. Their awareness brings sensibilities that are often absent in other traditions.

In chapter 4, Cyrus Ernesto Zirakzadeh reflects on his intellectual journey of a quarter-century, emphasizing the tensions produced when constellations of professional requirements misalign with a scholar's intellectual sensibilities. His is the kind of transparent, first-person journey to ethnography to which many other political ethnographers working in political science departments might relate.

While Zirakzadeh foregrounds his first-person experiences, Elisabeth Wood in chapter 5 alludes to her own experiences less frequently. Instead, she focuses on the firsthand experiences of her interlocutors—people who suffered through a brutal civil war in El Salvador. Although Wood could not be a participant observer in a conflict that had already ended, she conducted in-depth interviews, selected participant observation of community meetings, and participatory mapmaking workshops as a way to reconstruct insider perspectives on insurgent collective action. This work, while not produced by pure participant observation, reflects a desire to study people from the nearest possible vantage point. As a result, their testimony provides ample raw material for theorizing the role of ordinary people in insurgency.

In chapter 6 the nearest possible vantage point brings Timothy Pachirat to the "kill floor" of a slaughterhouse in the U.S. Midwest. In this setting, Pachirat demonstrates that the position of the researcher reveals a range of sedimented power relations and conceals others. Only by changing his position in relation to the researched can the scholar begin to unravel the multiple layers of power that are exercised in any given setting. This implies that simplistic notions of pure observation—

the *sine qua non* of the researcher-researched dichotomy and the heart of reigning versions of the social-scientific method—are deeply problematic. Pachirat's solution is to embrace, rather than reject, his partiality. Recognizing that partiality is the natural state of affairs for any observer, he demonstrates, is the first step toward an understanding of real-world truths.

FOUR

When Nationalists Are Not Separatists: Discarding and Recovering Academic Theories while Doing Fieldwork in the Basque Region of Spain

CYRUS ERNESTO ZIRAKZADEH

How should we integrate the insights of theories we learn in the classroom with the views of participants in politics? Can we simply discard and view reality cold, without the images, categories, and words that our professional vocabularies provide us? Or, if by chance we choose to take advantage of our scholarly traditions, which of our inherited concepts should we employ?

Rather than discuss the process of concept adoption (and adaptation) abstractly, I shall recall my first attempt to listen carefully to participants and to relate their knowledge to the concerns of established political scientists. From this case study, some practical trade-offs and dilemmas may come to light. These include the challenges of reconciling the long-term and large-scale concerns of many academics with the short-term intentions and local objectives of many political actors; balancing the deterministic tone of political sociology with the ubiquitous choices and contingency that actors perceive; and concisely portraying the shared political beliefs of opposition groups during times of intense internal debate and widespread ideological creativity.

Acquisition of a Theoretical Option

At the end of the 1970s, I was a doctoral student at the University of California at Berkeley, preparing for fieldwork in the Basque region of Spain—a territory that many nationalists call Euskadi Sur. My motivation was partly career driven. The job market for new Ph.D.s in political science was tight, and I needed an "angle" to survive as an academic. Comparatively little had been published about Iberian politics (although a handful of eminent scholars studying regimes either were describing Spain as a paradigmatic example of a breakdown of an authoritarian regime, or were analyzing Spain for lessons about the founding of a liberal democratic regime). For an ambitious young scholar, Spain appeared understudied, a place about which a green academic might quickly make a mark. The trick (the survivalist side of my mind whispered) was to think about Spain in a manner that would interest older, more established scholars. It was, after all, important to secure approval from the professionally influential.

Nondegree temptations to think differently abounded, however. Spain held a special place in my mind. It symbolized a land of New Left ideals, to which I—a former participant in a cooperative housing experiment in Ann Arbor, Michigan, and in antiwar and anti-Shah demonstrations at the University of Michigan and Stanford University—was personally wedded. During the 1930s, anarchist experiments in the countryside and in major cities, such as Barcelona, terrified both Western bankers and Soviet commissars (according to Bookchin 1977, Chomsky 1967, and other commentators sympathetic to experiments in participatory democracy). George Orwell (1952) learned about Trotskyism and anarchism while in Spain. Perhaps while conducting fieldwork, I could take a break now and then, and look at remnants of a revolutionary upheaval that I had long admired from afar.[1]

Then there were profoundly personal motivations fueling my desire for fieldwork in Euskadi Sur. Being a first-generation U.S. citizen, I repeatedly had noticed while growing up that U.S. citizens of European descent had not always welcomed my devoutly Catholic mother (from Guatemala) or my headstrong atheistic father (from Iran) with softly socialist sympathies. My parents, wishing me a happy life, had worked hard through my infancy and childhood to rid me of overt signs of difference, such as "funny accents" and stiff hair. Partly out of fear of being shunned and partly out of desire to take advantage of the open avenues available to a well-educated suburbanite, I had spent a quarter-century learning how to behave like a person of northern European descent. I was rewarded for my efforts to assimilate with steady academic and professional advancement. Going to Spain and observing the arguments and behavior of Basque nationalists seemed an emotionally safe method to wrestle with my nagging feelings of guilt about my abandonment of my parents' heritages.[2]

Facing pressures to complete the dissertation in a hurry (my wife and I were gamely raising a two-year-old in a partly converted fieldworkers' mess hall) and drawing on very limited financial resources, I decided to travel to Euskadi Sur for just one summer. My dream was to distribute a concise three-page research instrument among diverse political activists to test a set of sociological hypotheses about Basque politics that some well-known scholars in the United States had been developing. Having read the extant scholarly literature in English on Basque nationalism and on the sociological origins of nationalist movements, I felt sufficiently prepared to analyze distant events.

Novelist Margaret Shedd, who died the year my dissertation was approved, provided my entry point into the world of Basque politics. Shedd was a "Red" writer in northern California with a long history of involvement in socialist politics. She had acquired fame in the Basque region for her novel (in English) about the infamous "Burgos trial." The name refers to a series of events that began when security forces arrested and tortured several young Basque men and women affiliated with the nationalist organization ETA (Euskadi ta Askatasuna, or Basque Homeland and Freedom), and then subjected them to a military tribunal that imposed severe sentences, including capital punishment. Shedd's book, which openly sided with the ETA suspects, pulled no punches: it was an indictment of the Franco regime. In retrospect, I realize that the novel, and the letter the author penned on my behalf to her friends in the Basque region, contributed to my deviation from a fairly straightforward research agenda. Shedd facilitated my exposure to events and incidents that were important to local Basque activists but that were far from the political concerns of the U.S. academy.[3]

At the time, most English-language social scientists and political commentators were not particularly interested in the goals and perceptions of local Basque activists per se; more salient were the topics of regime stability and regime change. In addition, most students of Iberian politics desired a peaceful transition of the peninsular political order from its Francoist, authoritarian past to a European-like pluralist regime. Hence, they interpreted events in the Basque region within a broader story about democratization. The struggle for constitutional liberties and rule by an elected parliament gave local events in the Basque region their significance. Scholars wanted to know whether the activities of Basque nationalists advanced the realization of a liberal-democratic Spanish nation-state. The answer was almost universally no, leading to the use of derogatory terms, such as *extremists* and *millennial,* to label the Basque nationalists who either called for immediate political independence or refused to denounce particular acts of violence by their compatriots (Linz 1980, 20, 43–51; Medhurst 1982, 235–61; Payne 1976, 76–102; Payne 1979, 169–70).

Social scientists in the United States were never simply teleological thinkers, however. They also embraced a causal argument that made sense of extremist behavior in Euskadi Sur and rendered it less surprising and unexpected. Prominent Iberianists who often wrote in English, such as Juan Linz (1973, 78–83), Ken Medhurst (1982, 239–42, 248–9), and Stanley Payne (1976), interpreted Basque nationalism as a form of xenophobic and backward-looking politics fairly common in rapidly industrializing territories during the early and mid-twentieth century. Their argument paralleled a broad scholarly consensus about the dangers of rapid modernization: regardless of where on the globe, artisans and owners of small farms, small workshops, and small stores feel threatened by the sudden secularization of local spiritual thought and culture; by the establishment of large public and private bureaucracies (in lieu of small-scale, personal ties); by the rapid growth of cities; and by the rise of novel and gigantic economic forces (big businesses, global markets, and organized labor).[4] Dizzied, unanchored, and vulnerable, members of the traditional middle classes in the Basque region (like their counterparts elsewhere) sought emotional refuge in romanticized images of the past and joined political parties committed to purging recent social changes from their homeland. There is nothing particularly puzzling, then, about the "extremist" nationalist politics in Euskadi Sur. Basque nationalists (like the German Nazis, the Italian Fascists, and the supporters of Senator Joseph McCarthy in the United States) were disoriented burghers and small farmers bucking modern social trends.

This theory matched what I knew about Basque history. The city of Bilbao (the most populous urban center on Spain's northern coast) had industrialized rapidly during the late nineteenth and early twentieth centuries, and by mid-century was the steel, naval, and mining center of Spain. It was in Bilbao that Sabino de Arana, son of a socially downward-moving businessman, articulated the first version of Basque nationalist ideology. Furthermore, the two northernmost Basque provinces (Vizcaya and Guipúzcoa) were also the most industrialized and commercial provinces of Euskadi Sur and, coincidentally, where most acts of political violence by nationalist groups, such as ETA, occurred. The two southern provinces (Alava and Navarra), in contrast, remained overwhelmingly rural and fairly nonindustrialized, although the provincial capitals enjoyed influxes of foreign capital and a growth spurt between 1965 and 1975. Here, violence was less common, and support for nationalist organizations less widespread. Thus, the spatial distribution of economic development corresponded to the spatial distribution of extremist behavior, suggesting to me: "Voilà! The modernization thesis works!"

Given the scholarly consensus about how rapid modernization feeds extremist politics, and given my basic knowledge of Basque economic de-velopment, my plan was simple. I would talk to fifty to a hundred local political activists from different parts of Euskadi Sur. After I returned to Berkeley, I would look at the survey results and explore statistical rela-tionships between the respondents' stated political beliefs and their social backgrounds. I anticipated that my correlations would mostly match con-ventional wisdom. I also secretly hoped that there would be one or two un-expected anomalies that would allow me to draw on my knowledge of the history of Western political and social thought, and demonstrate my crea-tivity.

Learning to Discard Theories

My first few weeks in the Basque region were, frankly, frustrating because of difficulties in gaining access to a "representative sample" of Basque patriots. The political climate was not hospitable to survey research. Although the Spanish government had adopted a new northern European–like consti-tution, which contained promises of civil liberties and included an elected parliament, in the four provinces that constitute Euskadi Sur police officers continued to patrol city streets with their hands near the triggers of auto-matic weapons; miniature tanks continued to roam the streets; and states of exception and martial law were periodically declared. In this situation of ar-bitrary arrests and ubiquitous symbols of repression, local residents did not immediately trust strangers (who could be informers). When I discussed the idea of impartial social science and promised to protect the anonymity of all respondents, my professional courtesies met awkward silence.

My problems were compounded by my political naïveté. Thanks to my mother's friendship with a high-school teacher from the United States who routinely took his students to Spain for summer trips, I had secured a sec-ond letter of introduction that garnered me access to political conservative circles in the Basque region. I had been initially pleased with the letter be-cause it would (I thought) ensure a broad range of interviewees. I would have a "control sample" against which to assess the responses of the na-tionalists.

That second letter of introduction, in fact, enabled me to peek into the world of right-wing Basque politics. This in turn helped me realize that the region's political struggles involved clashes of feelings, interests, and goals that are absent in the modernization literature, and entailed policy controversies and social organizations that are overlooked in analyses of regime change. For instance, in Pamplona (the capital of Navarra), I attended a Sunday mass for Catholics sympathetic to the arch-conservative organization Opus Dei. After the service, a local Basque business executive offered to drive me around town. His car had a pistol in the glove compartment, in case (he told me) members of ETA jumped him. As we rode, he pointed to a group of people near a working-class housing complex who were enjoying an outdoor barbeque. My host commented that it was a typical neighborhood-association gathering, and then added, in effect, "That's the trouble with supporters of ETA. They complain that they are exploited and mistreated by the wealthy, but their large stomachs show that they are overfed."

The comment was revealing for many reasons (perhaps the least of which was my host's predictable failure to entertain another hypothesis: large bellies can be the result of high-starch diets, which nonwealthy people sometimes perforce adopt). More important for purposes of my intellectual growth was his observation that ETA might have organizational ties to local working-class culture. The social phenomenon he mentioned in passing—the *asociaciones de vecinos*, or neighbors' associations—was at that time almost never discussed in U.S. academic literature about Spanish politics. The day after our drive, I began to collect reports from local newspapers and newsmagazines on the *asociaciones de vecinos*. I learned that they had been legalized toward the end of the Franco regime and had flourished in Bilbao, Pamplona, and other Basque cities for about a decade. The *asociaciones de vecinos* were not only recreational groups. They also lobbied the regime for public services; provided myriad services (including education, sanitation, and medical care) to impoverished immigrant neighborhoods; and took to the streets when civil liberties were being blatantly violated. What, I began to wonder, could the *asociaciones de vecinos* have to do with the militant nationalist group ETA?

In addition, my host's repeated caricatures about the unreasonable expectations of poorer Pamplonians brought to the forefront of my thinking the conflicting images of economic justice within Euskadi Sur, where class awareness and consciousness seemed high, and interclass relations appeared strained. The theme of class conflict, however, was largely absent from mainstream U.S. academic literature about Basque nationalism, which to this day is much more about the speed of the region's economic development than about possible maldistribution of wealth and income. For most scholars, the only social class within the region worth analyzing was the traditional middle class.

During my two weeks in Pamplona, opportunities to meet with ETA sympathizers and former members were few and far between. My problems arose from many sources. First, I was physically darker and blockier than Basques who, for me, resembled northern Europeans in their light skin coloring, their nonbrown eyes, and their narrow and finely chiseled facial features. Second, I was linguistically an outsider, since I speak Spanish with a Central American accent. Finally, I had obvious connections to right-wing politicians in town. Consequently, whenever I tried to strike up a conversation about current events in a corner bookstore, my friendliness was unreciprocated. Most customers left the store and waited outside, while the owner and I arranged to have books mailed to the United States.

I did hold a forty-five-minute interview with one woman who, according to the conservative business owner who had befriended me, was said to be a former member of ETA. She told me much about politics within the *asociaciones de vecinos*, their complex relationship to ETA cells during the Franco regime, and their role in recent events, including what she viewed as the antecedents of a recent antigovernment and pro-ETA riot that had coincided with Pamplona's famous running of the bulls. A few days after the interview, she was arrested, and I never saw her again.

Perhaps my most extended conversation with local residents who condoned ETA took place at a dinner with the owner of a modest barbershop (a member of the region's traditional petite bourgeoisie?), who said that he once had sympathized with ETA. After dinner, he and his wife retired, and his younger brother and I talked for a while. The brother gave me a glossy dossier, which had been covertly published by and distributed among friendship circles and the *asociaciones de vecinos* in Pamplona. It discussed the origins of the recent riot where some citizens had shouted, "Long live ETA!" According to the news articles reprinted in the dossier, police misconduct—specifically, the firing of rubber bullets into an unarmed crowd within a bullring—had sparked the days of trashing and burning of cars and stores.

Near the end of my stay in the city, I visited the provincial headquarters of the Communist Party because I had read a detailed article about factions within Basque nationalist politics written by a CP member. The scene was briefly disorienting to me because of the heavy security outside the main door and the festive atmosphere within (including travel posters to attract members to vacation excursions). I chatted with a couple of organizers about the town's electoral politics, its recent economic growth (several international corporations had opened plants in the outskirts), its current labor turmoil (a one-day general strike took place during my visit), and about the appeal of ETA in the newly constructed working-class neighborhoods that encircled the city.

By the end of my stay in Pamplona, I realized that ETA was much more multidimensional and programmatically eclectic than U.S. academic literature had suggested. I also realized that "modernization" did not capture the economic issues that concerned local residents. The region's recent economic development was not simply fast paced; practical problems were being generated, as well as issues of distributive justice. A plethora of parties, unions, and associations had formed in every major Basque city to respond to the housing shortages, unsafe work conditions, boom-and-bust cycles, rising unemployment, and heavy pollution. The voices and views of Basque politics were more numerous and diverse than I had expected.

Building Bridges to ETA Sympathizers

By the time I reached the Bilbao metropolitan area, which would become my home base for almost six weeks, I had decided to jettison my survey. I had discovered that whenever I used it—for example, with the chief pollster for the Basque Nationalist Party—my battery of questions (for example: How intensely do you feel about independence? How would you classify yourself in terms of class status?) bored the respondents. The survey had little to do with how nationalists (and local residents in general) saw themselves, understood their political disagreements, and defined their political options. I concluded that if I were to write a dissertation that would be meaningful for everyday people (a legacy of my New Left background that I could not shake), I had to find a way to represent the world that captured participants' understandings, feelings, and choices.

After I arrived, I severed all ties with right-wing parties and rented a room in a nationalist hotel in the city's Casco Viejo (or old downtown). Most of the major antigovernment political bars (Trotskyist bars, anarchist bars, Herri Batasuna bars) were located nearby, as was a park where nationalist periodicals were readily available, where political rallies were held, and where posters announcing political meetings could be easily viewed.

Despite the half-dozen acquaintances I had made, courtesy of Shedd, my evenings were lonely, and I experienced little success in meeting activists at local political taverns.[5] After two weeks, my isolation abruptly ended. By accident, as I was returning from watching a nationalist demonstration in the newer downtown (where banks and department stores are located), I found myself on the wrong side of a line of police officers, who were firing rubber bullets to disperse a crowd. My survival instinct led me to join some young people who were crouching in doorways and seemed to know what they were doing. We scampered from building to building. They mistook my act of sheer desperation as a sign of solidarity. As I entered a bar that evening for my nightly try at conversation—a project that I fully expected to end in futility once again—a dozen or so people approached me and started to talk. The next morning my hotel mailbox was packed with pamphlets, alternative newspapers, and invitations to public events. My survey had died, but I was collecting unexpected information.

I suddenly was invited to several local party headquarters. My favorite probably was the Trotskyist hovel, largely because of its archives with many years of newspaper clippings carefully arranged in cardboard boxes, and partly because Trotskyists' curiosity about U.S. politics led to a friendly, relaxed exchange of opinions. I also developed a rapport with the Trotskyists when seemingly minor coincidences led to laughter. For example, they liked my brightly colored shirt and asked where I had bought it so they could get some for an upcoming street event (unfortunately for them, I had bought it a few months earlier in the United States).

During my visits with Trotskyists at their headquarters and homes, I came to appreciate the breadth of ETA activists because the Trotskyists were one of the splinter groups within ETA (they constituted the so-called ETA VI) and their political goals and tactics included neither total separation of Euskadi Sur from Spain nor armed struggle. They favored, instead, the creation of a social-democratic enclave within Iberia in which neighborhood marches for municipal services, wildcat strikes, boycotts, and other disruptive but nonlethal forms of street agitation would flourish. The Spanish state, from their perspective, was inevitably and incurably oriented to capitalist development and regimentation of the workforce. Better to turn one's back on the state and cultivate more local and informal political gardens.

The flip side of access to the Basque Left was that centrist parties, including the electorally powerful Basque Nationalist Party (PNV), suddenly refused to allow me access to their second-tier officials, including their pollsters and electoral strategists. In the United States, most scholars and journalists label the PNV as politically moderate in tactics (because it avoids gunplay) but as sometimes extremist in its goals (because some PNV factions desire complete secession from Spain and unification with Basque provinces on the other side of the French border). Few U.S. writers doubt that the party deserves attention because it is the longest lasting of the numerous nationalist parties in Euskadi Sur, the most popular party among voters in the region, and the most visible and active party within formal government institutions. Consequently, I had spent weeks cultivating rela-

tions with PNV activists at all levels and from diverse factions. While previously social scientists within the PNV had generously given me access
to their exit-poll results and their neighborhood-by-neighborhood tabula-
tions of votes for successive elections, now I could not enter their offices.

So my collection of material remained one-sided. Now I was receiving
documents from the so-called Abertzale Izquierda (or "Basque Patriotic
Left," a vernacular term for the loose coalition of participants, followers,
and sympathizers of different wings of ETA), rather than from either the
ideologically bourgeois and sociologically middle-class PNV or the conservative managers of big businesses in Pamplona. Through the reams of
material that I was slowly gathering, I began to see Basque nationalist politics in a very different light. The politics no longer appeared to take place
amid a large-scale, regionwide transformation of a premodern society into
a commercial, bureaucratic, industrial, urban, and secular one. Ideas, institutions, and organizations seemed ephemeral. Parties, unions, newsmagazines, neighborhood associations, and other political organizations often
appeared and disappeared in the course of a few years.

My perceptions of salience, scale, and time were dramatically changing.
Basque politics now seemed primarily to involve a new set of street-level
episodes and small, local organizations. When talking about politics, residents were mainly concerned about problems coming to their attention
within the past weeks and months: the impending completion of a nuclear-
energy plant on the outskirts of Bilbao, the release of workers from a Bilbao
steel mill, the shortage of medical services and schools in the working-class
shantytowns on the Left Bank of the Nervion River (a major waterway that
snaked through the metropolis), and the periodic meanderings of Gypsy
families through working-class neighborhoods, where they were harassed
by nonaffluent but homeowning families.

Further, as I explored bookstores and kiosks, I realized that local writers (whose publications were either overlooked or neglected within the U.S.
academy) were discussing Basque nationalist politics as open-ended and
unpredictable.[6] While U.S. scholars saw violent actions, such as bombings
and kidnappings, as sociologically predetermined, local writers saw a much
more contingent world. While U.S. scholars saw continuity over time in
terms of nationalist violence—with killings, bombings, and kidnappings
forming a lethal social and cultural pattern that would persist and perhaps
intensify—local observers were prone to see a series of discrete events, each
partly reversing and contradicting what had occurred before. To give a taste
of what I was uncovering, I shall briefly describe the *asambleas* of ETA, a
topic marginalized if not ignored in most English-language scholarship.

ETA *Asambleas,* or Local History Uncovered

According to writers in Euskadi Sur, between 1959 and 1980 ETA held more than a half-dozen official leadership meetings (*asambleas*) of ten to twenty persons to determine the group goals, strategy, and tactics.[7] At each gathering, the assembled discussed what ETA's several hundreds of members, who were spread across the region and organized in cells of three to six members, were to do. Consensus was usually elusive. Moreover, officially adopted positions changed dramatically from one *asamblea* to the next. Typically, an alliance of leaders mustered enough votes to nominally pass its agenda at a meeting. Then, a subset of the defeated factions would form a cabal, monopolize the next *asamblea*, and pass policies that supported its vision. A few years later, a counter-coup would jettison many previous ideas and adopt a few strikingly novel proposals and concepts. Through this process of initiatives, reversals, setbacks, and accretions, the thinking of the "ETArras" (as they were called and called themselves) not so much "evolved" as shifted.[8]

Attendance did not falter, despite the absence of consensus. Murmurings and reversals were acceptable to participants because revolutionary hopes were high. Between 1960 and 1980, it seemed as if the Franco dictatorship was finally in its last throes and a new political order would soon be crafted. Almost every leader of ETA, regardless of his or her distinctive political aspirations, believed that to affect the course of history, one needed to collaborate with other militants, regardless of their convictions.

Why could the ETArras not agree on a program? One might view the disharmony as evidence of stubborn contrariness, possibly suggesting emotional instability and personal insecurity (images compatible with the modernization thesis). Yet on further reflection, the pandemonium within and among the *asambleas* has another explanation. Coming from different towns and hiding from the police, many members of ETA were strangers to one another. Moreover, coming from different occupations (including farming, industry, education, and religion), levels of intellectual training, and political experience, the activists held opinions, values, and expectations that often diverged and sometimes clashed. As well, the organization's office personnel underwent rapid turnover. The Spanish police hounded the ETA leaders who led the movement's various "fronts." Security forces arrested and incarcerated not only ETA combatants carrying sidearms, but also writers who composed the movement's outlawed publications, covert labor organizers who planned demonstrations, and recruiters of new members. Many leaders sooner or later were either killed, thrown in jail and tortured, or forced to flee the Peninsula. Then a younger generation of activists would take office and would act in accordance with their own experiences, values, and political calculations.

As they met and listened to one another, activists sometimes discovered that they truly disliked the programs and aims of their comrades. Before the Fifth *Asamblea*, for example, many older ETA members openly expressed frustration with younger authors and editors whose handling of movement publicity was colored by a European New Left perspective. The movement's broadsheets and pamphlets said that the region was already a place of heavy industry and extensive commerce and there was no turning back; that Basque workers and residents in general desired greater expressive rights in daily life and opportunities for workplace comanagement; and that radical nationalists should seek not political and cultural separation from Spain but a modicum of constitutional autonomy within the Spanish state and then work with progressive groups in other parts of Spain and Europe for a creative and unregulated society. Opponents of the New Leftists arrived at the Fifth Assembly armed with dossiers with which to expel leaders of the publicity front before they had an opportunity to defend their actions. When sympathizers of the New Left writers protested such conniving and attempted to walk out, they were placed under house arrest, and the meeting proceeded under the orchestration of the conspirators (Unzueta 1980).

By the mid-1970s, at least three major ideological currents competed for influence within the movement.[9] One stressed the need to work with clandestine communist, Trotskyist, Maoist, socialist, and anarchist parties within Spain and to organize the region's sizeable industrial working class and the growing number of college-educated white-collar employees. The goal of these ETArras was gradually to create a democratic and socialist state for the region that, ideally, would become the vanguard of progressive politics and economics throughout Europe.

Another ETA current looked with trepidation upon the industrial workers (many of whom arrived from non-Basque-speaking parts of Spain) and called for the resuscitation of the region's native language and culture. While the proletariat wing of ETA was generally amenable to Basque regional autonomy within a federated Spain, the culturally sensitive ETArras desired total independence, as well as the purging of non-Basque habits from the territory.

Last but not least, there were the so-called Third Worldist activists who were inspired by national liberation movements around the globe, from Cuba to Algeria to Vietnam. These ETArras argued that the organization should facilitate the formation of a populist alliance of Basque-speaking small producers and exploited industrial workers, and should provoke a mass uprising by means of armed attacks on government figures. In theory, the attacks would prompt a violent backlash by the Franco dictatorship. Indiscriminate state repression, in turn, would motivate the normally cautious to rebel. According to a theory of escalating violence (popularly known as the action-repression-reaction cycle), sooner or later the Spanish state would find military occupation of the Basque region too costly and would withdraw, leaving the Basque people free to determine their own postcolonial political and economic order.

Each ideological current contained mini-factions that disagreed on how to respond to fast-moving changes in Spanish politics that immediately preceded and followed Franco's death in 1975. They also disagreed on how best to respond to the global economic recession of the 1970s, to surges in unemployment and bankruptcies, and to other hardships in the economically diverse Basque region, which included isolated farmsteads, small-scale manufacturing towns, and enormous centers of heavy industry with shipyards and steel mills. Then, there were disputes within each faction about which street-level activities were de facto permissible and would become legal in the near future (a succession of state officials varied in their enthusiasm for enforcing laws about censorship, public assembly, and the use of police torture).

During the 1970s leaders of the Spanish government wavered between liberalization and crackdown. Scores of ETA cells meanwhile continued to act autonomously to evade police infiltration and arrest. Cells experimented with different methods of mobilization and, occasionally, armed action. The result was a mishmash of peaceful and quasi-legal labor organizing, defiant promotion of non-Castilian culture, and gunplay (Amigo 1978).

The radical nationalist coalition, in the end, could not endure as a loose federation of local, autonomous cells. A few small teams of ETA activists, acting independently of the organization's purported leadership, carried out audacious murders, such as the bombing of the car carrying Franco's handpicked successor, Carrero Blanco. By the close of the 1970s, more than sixty people were dying each year due to actions by ETA armed cells. The government responded by arresting suspected ETA activists and sympathizers, and suspending the already flimsy civil liberties that had been granted to labor and neighborhood organizers. The increased repression further fragmented the organization. Some cells (especially those engaged in labor organizing) called for an end to armed action. Others called for an escalation in the scale and scope of violence. Still others took complicated (and perhaps confused) positions between pacifism and militarism.

After more than a decade of uneasily living together, members of ETA permanently divided themselves into separate organizations engaged primarily in electoral and legislative politics, labor organizing, the rejuvenation of regional culture, or guerrilla warfare.[10]

Finding a Scholarly Audience, Sort Of

The information that I was collecting on the ideological debates within ETA and on the role of local social institutions and policy issues in ETA's heated disagreements over armed action was not what I originally had been seeking. Moreover, it was not what interested scholars in the United States. They wanted first and foremost to talk about regime change and, second, to portray violence by members of ETA as a regrettable but explicable phenomenon. The pressing practical question for democratically oriented scholars was how best to contain extremist behavior, which was, sociologically speaking, only to be expected. What should government officials do? To borrow Howard Zinn's (2006, 105) phrase, English-speaking scholars wanted to "airbrush" Basque political history, making it less puzzling, contingent, and unpredictable, and therefore within the control of state officials.

Contrariwise, inside the Basque region, historians and journalists (many of whom were former ETA activists) published interpretations in which the *asambleas* appear as major determinants of ETA's long-term evolution. These writers viewed participants in ETA as capable of choosing and reassessing goals, aims, and strategies, and as chief determiners of the organization's fate. If activists who attended the *asambleas* had chosen to act differently, the history of ETA (including its use of violence) would have changed markedly. Large-scale cultural and economic trends did not cause members of ETA to embark on a journey of violence. There was no material determinism.

When I returned to the United States, I brought with me boxes of newspaper clippings, local periodicals, and books by regional authors. The next few years proved exasperating for me and my faculty advisers as I tried to piece together a story about a multitude of parties, factions, labor organizations, and protest campaigns that did not fit neatly into a tale about modernization. Having learned to see the world from the vantage points of some of the actors, I believed that the social changes in the region were too complex to fit into the unidimensional modernization model; that the range of political options people were choosing was shaped by more than rage against modernity; and that the nationalists' agendas involved much more than degrees of separation from the Spanish state. Questions about nuclear power, women's rights, economic recovery, and labor organization were at least as salient in the nationalists' propaganda and in their supporters' minds. My advisers feared that I was producing unstructured reportage. Without a parsimonious model to inform my findings, my dissertation would resemble (in the unforgettable words of one adviser) "scrambled eggs."

Grasping for any theoretical framework, I called on my undergraduate training in Marxist economic and political thought at the University of Michigan and began to organize my findings in terms of responses to distinct modes of production. The notion of uneven capitalist development provided a set of contextual categories to describe the unions, general strikes, *asociaciones de vecinos*, right-wing town parties, producer cooperatives, and other actors and events that I had uncovered. Compared to the parsimonious and linear logic of modernization theory, the categories of core, periphery, and semi-periphery, of precommercial and commercial agriculture, and of monopoly capitalism provided more ways to classify social issues and describe local problems.

Moreover, I chose not to advance a socially deterministic argument. I did not say that the peculiar economic conditions in Euskadi Sur fixed the nature of political programs and organizations in the region. Rather, I argued that economic conditions provided experiences (both problems and opportunities) against which people invented and revised political programs and organizations. Despite the Marxist scaffolding, the spirit of my interpretation was highly voluntaristic and democratic, as I insisted that people freely and endlessly create and jettison political projects, notions, and beliefs.

Employing Marxist and neo-Marxist world-system classifications of types of capitalist economy, I was able to publish some of my earliest findings in interdisciplinary journals and anthologies (Zirakzadeh 1985, 1989). My relatively conventional Marxist language perhaps helped my readers relate my discoveries to their own substantive interests involving other times and places.

Still, my tale lacked overall coherence. Anyone who read my work closely could tell that under the familiar language about classes and economic structure, I was conveying an image of nearly orderless conflict among ephemeral groups and nearly anarchistic politics. It was an image of local-level politics in industrializing societies that, I later discovered, was being advanced at roughly the same time by some notable Leftist scholars opposed to structural Marxism, including political scientist James Scott (1985) and historian E. P. Thompson (1978), who insisted (correctly, I was coming to believe) that everyday people make their own political visions independently of the wishes and efforts of elites and nation-states.

A few years after my dissertation was approved, I attended a conference about "the frontiers of social-movement theory" in Ann Arbor. There, U.S. sociologists who had secured tenure and who were slightly older than I was—for instance, Doug McAdam, Sidney Tarrow, Myra Ferree, and Aldon Morris—publicly declared that modernization theory was passé and that theories of middle-class angst and "extremism" misrepresented the goals, motivations, and pragmatic decision-making processes within twentieth-century social movements.[11] I found the conference liberating because at long last, I had met a group of respected and established scholars who treated modernization theory with the same disdain that I did and who were for the most part committed to New Left ideals and concerns.[12] After the conference, I began to incorporate the ideas and logic of McAdam, Tarrow, Ferree, Morris, and others into presentations of my fieldwork. The result was my first book (Zirakzadeh 1991), which explains, through detailed descriptions of traditions of protest in the Basque region, why modernization theory is not useful for understanding contemporary Basque politics.

Even so, I remained uneasy. Part of me knew that I cleaved to the newly formed academic group out of unhealthy resentment. I praised the Ann Arbor writers because their enemy—modernization explanations for "extremism"—was mine. This, I secretly knew, was not a good reason to embrace an entire theoretical orientation, which had a specialized jargon, unexamined philosophic assumptions about the stability of group identity and solidarity, and a fascination with the role of leaders, called movement entrepreneurs, who intellectually guided and amassed resources for social movements.

In particular, the literature on social-movement theory for me posed a new conceptual problem involving the nature of culture. According to the Ann Arbor generation of social-movement theorists, ideas about justice and strategy sometimes can "put fire in the belly" and prompt action. Ideas are, psychologically speaking, among the preconditions for collective action. I certainly found this hypothesis plausible. The Ann Arbor group also argued that a subset of incendiary notions can be found in the widely accepted store of ideas of every society, and that movements often attract followers by employing ideas that already are widely believed. This argument also made sense to me.

I balked, however, at two additional hypotheses: (1) that a self-conscious subset within a movement (sometimes called "movement entrepreneurs") develops ideas for the entire movement; and (2) that for a movement to exist and expand, there needs to be agreement within it on images of justice and strategy. According to the Ann Arbor tradition of analysis, movements are internally homogeneous in terms of predominant beliefs, as a leadership cadre self-consciously combines beliefs into a single package (or "master frame") that other activists and major factions in the group accept with minimal opposition. These additional hypotheses jibed neither with what I had observed in Euskadi Sur, nor with my own experiences with New Left organizations. ETA was, culturally speaking, not unitary, ideologically cohesive, or top-down in terms of the dissemination of ideas. Nor did I find these features within Ann Arbor's Students for a Democratic Society, Berkeley's Caucus for a New Political Science, or the University of California's Association of Graduate Student Employees.[13]

As I began to study social movements around the globe, I reached the conclusion that in terms of movement culture, many (if not most) modern social movements have family resemblances to ETA. In its ideological heterogeneity, organizational decentralization, and intra-organizational pluralism, ETA shares much with the Greens in Germany (Markovits and Gorski 1993), Solidarity in Poland (Garton Ash 1991), and the Students for a Democratic Society in the United States (Gitlin 1980). In the language of social-movement scholarship that existed prior to the Ann Arbor meeting, the Basque liberation movement was a "segmented," "polycentric," and "reticulated" organization composed of diverse groups with complex ties to other political organizations, and with multiple, diverse, and often competing local leaders and centers of influence (Gerlach 1971).

To rethink my own view on social-movement culture, I began to explore research by political and cultural historians that the Ann Arbor social-movement writers were not discussing seriously or at length. Essays on movement culture as "free spaces" (where local followers second-guess and resist the ideas of nominal leaders and submit their own innovative notions) by Alan Brinkley (1981), Sara Evans (1978), Lawrence Goodwyn (1978), and Robin Kelley (1990) pointed to a more polymorphous and dynamic image of culture, in which subgroups within society are constantly employing and subverting inherited ideas. The British cultural-studies tradition (Chambers 1986; Hebdige 1979; Turner 1996) likewise viewed culture as malleable by all persons. A country's "national culture" should not be viewed as fixed and logically coherent, the cultural-studies folk insist; instead, culture is best understood as a logically pell-mell mix of stories, images, and terms. From the

British popular-culture analysts and the U.S. historians of popular culture, I was learning to see culture as a loose terrain of words, images, and symbols susceptible to rearrangement and redefinition by innumerable and (from an outsider's perspective) often anonymous people.

Again, I was finding myself in an intellectual maelstrom. If I were correct in interpreting culture as a set of constantly questioned and rearranged sensibilities and points of view (and not as a set of slowly changing and largely unquestioned customs, habits, and traditions), could I say anything about culture besides ephemeral and locally diverse truths? And if culture is constantly constructed not only by government elites and movement entrepreneurs but also by anonymous people who hold neither offices nor titles in political organizations, can there be more than disorder in political history? Can we say much more than that political projects throughout society are in constant flux and that in all organizations—even protest movements—there is an element of Babel?

Conclusion

My quarter-century journey to and from Euskadi Sur has led me to appreciate the contingent and pluralistic aspects of contemporary politics. I have lost faith in parsimonious causal theories—whether the modernization thesis of older social scientists, the social determinism of more mechanistic versions of Marxism, or the master-frame theories of the Ann Arbor generation of social-movement theorists. None, in my opinion, accounts for the complexity, decentralization, dynamism, and multivocality of local politics in the Basque region (or elsewhere).

As a result, I have gradually abandoned the hunt for widely applicable generalizations. After all, if it is difficult to make predictive statements about a single historical and regional case because a multiplicity of actors appear (each with a distinct and constantly evolving agenda, interacting and individually contributing to but never determining historical outcomes), why should we believe that we can easily find parsimonious causal hypotheses that fit *multiple* cases? Stated differently, why should we expect less complexity and indeterminacy when we look at a large collection of events instead of one? Peter Hall's (2003) suggestion about interpreting political conflict as long, complex, nonrepetitive sequences of choices and events makes more sense to me than do efforts by some scholars to discover enough parallels between political conflicts in different times and places to construct a large set of analogous cases and then explore the set for probabilistic hypotheses via regression techniques.[14]

Although I have lost faith in parsimonious causal theory, I find the notion of complete randomness, which Nietzsche and some Romantic poets periodically advanced, equally unappealing. Human initiatives have consequences, after all. Occasionally, an initiative secures the actor's goals as planned. Sometimes, however, an initiative ironically begins a series of events that subvert the actor's goals; and sometimes, an initiative brings about a condition that no one had anticipated. Outcomes result in part from the complex developments that predate and exist alongside the choice being made, and in part from other people's actions in response to the choice. Noting how every action is embedded in layers of social relations and then tracing the sequence of events, actions, counteractions, reversals, and (finally) long-term consequences can teach us simultaneously about the centrality of choice in human affairs and about our limited control over the future.[15]

My current methodological preference is to look at political events closely, identifying persons who are acting, moments of choice, and the contingent nature of every event with regard to antecedent events and subsequent ones. I increasingly believe that useful political analysis requires attention to the manipulation of cultural artifacts, which sometimes proves successful and sometimes does not. Culture must be understood anthropologically and democratically, as the result of the capacity in *all* humans to adjust their beliefs, construct words, and coin images. This highly fluid, nonstructural understanding of culture obviously complicates the study of political history because it requires an acceptance of the openness and unpredictability of life: in principle, nothing—goals, tactics, and decision-making processes—is immune from change because humans, unlike rocks, can assess their current condition and attempt to change it.[16]

The establishment and promotion of a political anthropology that looks closely at choice and at linguistic and artistic[17] innovations seems invaluable for political science today, when scholars tend to be overly sympathetic to assumptions of ideological conformity within parties, movements, and other forms of popular politics. But there are costs to viewing political history as radically contingent. Businesses and states offer professional opportunities and monetary enticements to scholars who can represent humans as pliable and uncreative subjects, akin to blank pages upon which a government can write orders without fear of resistance.[18]

Moreover, it is easier to assert that one is being sensitive to contingency and complexity than to be so in practice.[19] Whenever a researcher is writing an account, it is impractical and perhaps impossible to be sensitive to all voices. To compose a story, one must choose whose tale to tell. Some voice or viewpoint must set the parameters of the study. By what criteria will the choice be made? Whose perspective will provide the framework for understanding events? Whose understanding of reality will be privileged?

Finally, there is the challenge of training one's cultural ear to listen to different sides in politics. The range of disagreements, aspirations, and interests that we can discern will depend in part on our exposure to academic theory. But even more important is our personal history—especially the issues that over the years we've come to take seriously. My history in New Left politics, my experience with embracing and rejecting alternative national traditions, and my exposure to theories of Marxism all played a role in what I saw, understood, and could describe. If I had been a woman, had formal training in folk culture, and had more personal acquaintance with the world of high finance, I would have seen and noticed different events. We can expand our range of understandings before we enter the world of others, yet we will always suffer from some shortsightedness and points of blindness.

To report the diverse political positions that people develop, debate, and adopt is no easy task. Challenges and disincentives abound. A choice, nonetheless, remains. Whether we follow those often well-paid and eminent scholars who view humans as objects of external forces—or follow less mainstream and less widely read scholars who highlight human inventiveness—is ultimately up to us.

Notes

1. I was not the only graduate student in the 1970s with New Left sympathies who saw the 1930s Spanish Revolution as worth celebrating and pondering. Contemporaries whose doctoral research was spurred in part by affinity for the Spanish anarchists include political scientist Martha Ackelsberg (1991) and historian Temma Kaplan (1977).
2. Further complicating my feelings were my parents' own examples and choices. To cite but one illustration, my Guatemalan mother exhibited distrust of Mexicans and Chicanos. Her Guatemalan pride had a decidedly non-Latino component, which only further confused my efforts to answer "who am I?" and "who are my people?" Adding in the inevitable challenges of being raised a devout Catholic yet having an Islamic father who loved Sufi music and poetry, I was (and remain) a bubbling cultural stew lacking a clear-cut sense of ethnic identity.
3. As a result of serendipitous misunderstandings, Shedd's friends in the Basque country incorrectly introduced me by telephone and through street gossip as the *son* of Margaret Shedd. Fortunately, this led to considerable access for me because her romantic rendering of the ETA nationalists had generated a good many fans in the region. These sorts of unpredictable yet crucial developments that occur in the field are seldom examined in graduate courses on methodology.

4. For elaborations and criticisms of such logic, see Halebsky (1976); Kimmel (1990, 53–82); and Rogin (1967).

5. It did not help that I was a teetotaler and ignorant of bar decorum and the differences among various alcoholic drinks. By the time I returned to the United States, I was accomplished in ordering gin-and-tonics and striking up conversations with bartenders. The art of making friends in unfamiliar settings should be covered in methods courses, at least for those planning to conduct interviews and to engage in field observation.

6. While I was conducting fieldwork, Robert Clark (1984) at George Mason University was completing a manuscript on ETA that would prove groundbreaking in Basque studies partly because of his sensitivity to local political dynamics.

7. For overviews of the diverse decisions made at the *asambleas*, see Garmendia (1980); Bereciartu (1981); and Letamendia (1977).

8. For detailed descriptions, see Amigo (1978); Iriarte (1980); Iturrioz (1980); and Unzueta (1980).

9. Since the mid-1980s this threefold classification of the major ideological currents within ETA has become standard in English-language studies (Clark 1984; Zirakzadeh 1991).

10. For memoirs that illuminate the disillusionment among former ETArras, see Amigo (1978); Emparanza (1980); and Garailde (1980).

11. For a sample of the conference's papers, see Morris and Mueller (1992). For a later debate over the value of the Ann Arbor tradition of social-movement theorizing, see Goodwin and Jasper (2004).

12. Of course, my classmates and I in graduate school at Stanford and Berkeley often criticized modernization theory. But there was a whiff of parricide in our attacks. In retrospect, I am not sure that we were fully convinced by our arguments. Were we just enjoying the opportunity to say that our intellectually imposing teachers were "obviously" wrong?

13. For a fuller discussion of my unease with framing analysis and my efforts to find an alternative, see Zirakzadeh (2000); Payerhin and Zirakzadeh (2006). For other early critiques of master frames and framing analysis, see Benford (1997); Steinberg (1998).

14. It is not possible within the limits of this essay to expatiate on the implications of Hall's vision. Curious readers should visit his piece as well as other proposals from the "historical sociology" tradition (Mahoney and Rueschemeyer 2003).

15. William Sewell's (1996) event analysis, which combines "radical contingency" with a sense of multiple actors and historical sequence, resembles what I have in mind. Sewell and I differ, however. I see less continuity in history than he does and many more "sudden breaks" (his expression; I prefer the phrase "moments of cultural innovation").

16. For illustrations of how I incorporate culture, contingency, and choice into my work on social movements, see Zirakzadeh (2004, 2006).

17. Say, visual and musical expression.

18. For more on the politics of studying behavior rather than action, see Scott (1998, 309–57) and Amadae (2003).

19. See Schatz's concluding chapter in this volume, on some of the trade-offs involved in conducting research.

FIVE

Ethnographic Research in the Shadow of Civil War

ELISABETH JEAN WOOD

We feel a great patience. If we forget what we have suffered, it will come again. We want to press for change, we can't forget all we've suffered.

—*Campesina*, Tenancingo, 1987

We have lived the deepest truth of the war.

—Cooperativist, Los Horcones, 1992

What accounts for the emergence of a powerful insurgent movement in a country where quiescence had long been the response of the rural poor to social injustice? Why would many poor people run extraordinarily high risks to support the rebels despite the circumstances of civil war and state violence? Why would others decline to do so? I sought an answer to this puzzle through ethnographic research in militarily contested areas of El Salvador between 1987 and 1996. The body of this chapter first appeared in my *Insurgent Collective Action and Civil War in El Salvador* (Wood 2003), a work that explores the micro-foundations of collective action during civil war.

The material I gathered through interviews with approximately two hundred residents of *campesinos* (both participants and nonparticipants in the insurgency), participant observation of meetings and social gatherings, and participatory mapmaking workshops furnished the core evidence for the argument I made in the book.[1] My insurgent informants made it clear to me that moral commitments and emotional engagements were principal reasons for their insurgent collective action during the civil war.[2] Before the war, many participated in a social movement calling for economic reform and political inclusion because they had become convinced that social justice was God's will. As government violence deepened, some rural residents supported the armed insurgency as an act of defiance of long-resented authorities and a repudiation of perceived injustices (particularly brutal and arbitrary state violence). Participation per se expressed outrage and defiance; its force was not negated by the unlikeliness of victory and in any case was not contingent on one's participation. Through rebellion, insurgent residents asserted their dignity in the face of condescension, repression, and indifference. As state terror decreased, insurgent collective action spread across most of the case-study areas once more as residents occupied properties and claimed land for insurgent cooperatives. They did so despite their already having access to abandoned land because they took pride, indeed pleasure, in the successful assertion of their interests and identity, what I term the *pleasure of agency*. To occupy properties was to assert a new identity of social equality, to claim rights to land and self-determination, and to refute condescending elite perceptions of one's incapacities. In short, insurgent supporters were motivated in part by the value they put on being part of the making of history.

Thus, ethnographic data were essential to my documentation of patterns of civilian support for the insurgents, the emergence of a new political culture among supporters that reinforced insurgent collective action, and the causal role of state violence in both. The persuasiveness of my book's argument also rested on the inadequacy of alternative explanations, which I assessed by analyzing the variation across my five case-study areas in both patterns of participation and political economic conditions, using political economic as well as ethnographic data.

The case-study areas jointly met the following research criteria. Because the central issue was that of support for an insurgency, the case-study areas had to be *contested* regions where both participants and nonparticipants were present. Areas where one side or the other generally maintained control would not serve, as that meant, in the Salvadoran context, that only supporters of the controlling party would be visible to the researcher (whatever their private preferences). Each area had to be reasonably accessible to me in my small truck and should be politically manageable (that is, only one or two of the five insurgent factions should be active there). Across the case-study areas, I also sought variation in the social relations that prevailed before the war so that I could assess the relevance of classic theories of peasant rebellion.[3]

In terms of ethnographic method, my book drew more on formal interviews than many ethnographic works, for several reasons. Comparison across the case-study areas was essential to the research design, and relevant events such as land occupations took place simultaneously in all areas, so prolonged, sequential participant observation in a single area or a few areas was not an option. Moreover, access to the case-study areas was often difficult—indeed, at times impossible due to combat operations. My understanding of the history of local communities, residents' perceptions of that history, and the evolution of local political culture drew necessarily on group interviews and extended oral histories, as well as on participant observation, particularly of the relations between members of the guerrilla forces and local residents. Thus, the mix of ethnographic methods and the types of data gathered represented a compromise between the needs for multi-sited and for in-depth local research with an ethnographic sensibility, despite less sustained participant observation than a single site would have allowed.

In the chapter reprinted here (with only minor modifications), I analyze the difficulties in gathering and interpreting ethnographic material in the challenging circumstances of political violence and polarization (see also Wood 2006 and Wood 2007). In particular, I discuss how the new, insurgent political culture enabled my research: rural supporters of the insurgency were eager to tell their story, to have the history of the war in their communities written down.

To explore why some *campesinos* rebelled in contested areas of El Salvador before and during the civil war, my principal research strategy was to ask participants in the insurgency why they supported it, and to ask others why they did not. For revolutionary social movements, this is not usually done; the scholarly analysis of peasant rebellions, revolutions, civil wars, and even some social movements often relies on official or elite sources. In particular, as Nancy Bermeo (1986) and Nora Kriger (1992) argue, the study of peasant insurgency often relies not on the accounts of peasants themselves but on the memoirs of elite revolutionary leaders, who are usually from a different class, or on macro-level data.[4] One reason, of course, is that peasant actors are often illiterate or semi-literate and leave few written accounts of their actions, although oral sources in the form of stories and songs may be very rich. Participant accounts, be they elite memoirs, the few biographies of peasant participants available (which were often dictated to journalists or other literate interlocutors), or other accounts based on oral histories, rarely address social science concerns of how representative the narrator is or whether alternative accounts better explain available evidence.

In the absence of participant accounts, one alternative in studying historical instances is to infer the logic of insurgency from the "prose of counterinsurgency" (Guha 1983): the records of judicial, colonial, and other governmental authorities are read for insight into subaltern motives and beliefs. Not all states engaged in counterinsurgency produce the kind of records that facilitate such a rereading of official sources, however. Before and during El Salvador's civil war, those suspected of subversion by government agents were only in extraordinary circumstances processed by courts or other judicial bodies. Police and other security forces left few records of detentions, torture, or disappearances. (Nor were records of the Salvadoran military detailing particular operations available at the time of the writing of *Insurgent Collective Action*.) Of the few such records that existed, many were destroyed in order to render postwar investigation of human rights violations and other abuses of power more difficult. While human rights organizations kept records of violations as best they could, their records of rural events are very incomplete. Given conditions in the countryside, records exist only for those events that occurred where witnesses willing to report abuses resided. Such witnesses (often local priests or nuns) would have to run the risk of reporting an abuse by telephone and then meeting a human rights investigator locally, or of traveling to human rights offices in San Salvador. As a result, most violent events in the case-study areas went unrecorded.[5]

Nor do survey data provide much help in analyzing the course of the civil war. While a few surveys of households in contested areas were done by government agencies or other researchers for various reasons toward the end of the war, they usually gathered data on the composition of households, whether homes had access to potable water and schools, and the sources of income. In any case, residents' willingness to respond to questions concerning the history of the war in their own community and their own participation or not in political violence depends on a relationship with the researcher that is more personal than is possible in survey research.

The civil war in El Salvador offers the opportunity to analyze grassroots accounts of revolutionary participation using methods similar to those frequently used in the study of ordinary social movements. *Insurgent Collective Action* draws principally on open-ended interviews with rural residents, both participants and nonparticipants in the insurgency, in the Tenancingo and Usulután case-study areas. (I offer detailed discussion of the criteria for their selection in Wood [2003, chap. 3]). In this chapter I discuss the challenges of ethnographic research in areas of political violence and the strategies I pursued to meet them as well as possible.

Social Processes of Memory Formation

Non tutto quello che si racconta in questo libra è vero; ma tutto è stato veramente rac-contato. [Not all that is recounted in this book is true, but everything truly was so recounted.]

—Alessandro Portelli, *Biografia di una Città* (1985, 18)

For *Insurgent Collective Action*, I asked *campesinos*, participants and non-participants alike, landlords, and military officers questions concerning local conditions before the war; the local history of the war, including violence by both sides; and the emergence of new local organizations. That this analysis relies principally on open-ended interviews of course raises difficult issues of interpretation. The responses to my questions were shaped by three factors: the accuracy and intensity of the respondent's initial memories, the subsequent shaping of those memories through social and cultural processes, and the respondents' objectives in the ethnographic setting of the interview itself. I discuss each in turn.

First, recent laboratory studies that test for accuracy of recall of images and events that vary in intensity ("arousal" in the language of this literature) and pleasantness or unpleasantness ("valence") have found that images and events that rank as highly intense (in a variety of cognitive and biological measures) tend to be better remembered in both the short and long term than less intense images and events.[6] This appears to be true whether the stimuli are pleasant or unpleasant; there is some additional but debated evidence that unpleasant stimuli are better remembered than pleasant stimuli of the same intensity. What these laboratory studies suggest (but do not show, given the many differences between the laboratory and actual settings) is that the violent events frequently witnessed or participated in during civil war are the type—highly intense and most often very unpleasant—that are most likely to be well remembered.[7] For example, in one experiment, two groups of subjects were shown films that were identical except that one version contained a violent event midway through, while the other contained a parallel but nonviolent event (Bornstein, Liebel and Scarberry 1998). The subjects shown the violent version had better recall of the middle scene than subjects shown the nonviolent version, but they had less recall of what came before and after. This is not surprising: those who suffer from posttraumatic stress disorder are haunted by intrusive memories and nightmares—they often remember too much of their past experience, not too little.

Second, memories of political events, however well the events are initially remembered, may be later reshaped by social and cultural processes that affect which memories are retained, which emphasized, and which forgotten.[8] An example of the shaping of memory by subsequent experience is Leigh Binford's finding that witnesses in northern Morazán a decade later blamed the government's Atlacatl Battalion—notorious in the area for having killed more than a thousand people in 1981 at El Mozote—for several killings of *campesinos* that occurred *before* the battalion was even founded (1996, 105). Another example comes from Italy. Alessandro Portelli (1991) compared oral history accounts of the death of the worker Luigi Trastulli at the hands of a special police force in Terni, an industrial town in central Italy, with other sources. Workers he interviewed decades later remembered that during a protest against layoffs in 1953, Trastulli had been shot high against a stone wall with arms outstretched in a Christ-like position. The militant labor movement, they recalled, had fought all the harder after his death. According to contemporary judicial and journalistic accounts, however, Trastulli was shot in 1949 at street level with no memorable pose and there was little labor mobilization in response. Portelli argues that the labor movement's quiescent response to Trastulli's death was not consonant with the movement's culture, requiring the translation of the event in memory to circumstances in which the movement was more militant. Cultural norms may thus result in the suppression of some memories or expressions as unacceptable. In Sultanpuri, a neighborhood of Delhi, Veena Das (1990, 390) found distinct patterns of mourning by surviving relatives of communal violence: for example, younger widows were not allowed to mourn at all. She suggests that social structures intervene in the way that emotions such as guilt and sorrow are formed, "the way in which the world can be reformulated," and therefore how narratives can be told. In particular, memories of wartime events may be shaped by postwar outcomes, for example, by disappointment in the failure of a postwar government to deliver on redistributive goals promised in negotiated peace settlements.[9]

Third, the telling of personal and community histories in an ethnographic setting is also shaped by the respondent's personal and family trajectories through the war, by his or her present political loyalties, beliefs concerning the likely consequences of participating in the interview and of expressing particular views, and present personal objectives—all as informed by his or her understanding of the purpose of the interview. Political opinions may be systematically misrepresented out of security considerations, particularly in the context of civil war. Narratives may reflect self-aggrandizing motives, as respondents tell stories in which their roles are exaggerated or indeed entirely recast. Claimed motivations may be reconstructions that attribute a post hoc coherence to events by placing them in relation to a presumed goal (Markoff 1996, 603). Portelli (1997) points out that while oral history interviews are a personal exchange between the interviewer and interviewee, they are also testimonies intended as public statements and thus involve interpreting and legitimizing past actions and perceptions.

Moreover, because the telling of stories of past injustice and resistance shapes *present* propensities for mobilization and political identities, they may be told for precisely that purpose, rather than to convey accurate accounts of events as remembered. One result may be erroneous stories of origin, as in the case of Rigoberta Menchú, whose life history recounted in her *I, Rigoberta Menchú* to a Venezuelan anthropologist was not literally true although certainly representative of the violence during that period in the Guatemalan highlands (Stoll 1999). Another example comes from the U.S. civil rights movement, whose stories of origin (Polletta 1998a, 1998b) often overlooked the previous activism and training in civil disobedience of Rosa Parks before she initiated the Montgomery, Alabama, bus boycott of 1955 by refusing to move to the back of the bus. Those stories also frequently and erroneously claimed that the occupation of luncheon counters to protest segregation were spontaneous rather than organized activities.

Divergent memories of events of the Salvadoran civil war, I found, sometimes reflected these processes of memory formation. The bombing of Tenancingo in September 1983 provides a dramatic example. The FMLN attacked the municipal center despite the presence there of the well-trained and heavily armed Jaguar Battalion, commanded by a Captain Calvo. After his troops were trapped in the town, the town was bombed for several hours by government aircraft, an action that Americas Watch (1986, 157) at the time described as the "war's single most devastating attack," which left at least seventy-five civilians dead.[10] In interviews four years later, all respondents recalled the event with horror—and profound fear that the same thing might happen again—but the particular tale told appeared to reflect the political loyalties of the teller.

Survivors supportive of the FMLN reported that, when faced with imminent defeat, Calvo

locked himself and approximately forty soldiers into the Church. He called in the Air Force, saying that he was lost and that all those moving around the church were guerrillas. But they weren't just guerrillas, but civilians running crazy through the streets. The Green Cross [the domestic equivalent of the Red Cross] wanted to take the civilian population from the town, but a guerrilla stopped them, warning them that they would be bombed. They didn't try it, but another group of civilians did, fleeing down the road. A plane bombed them—children, women, and men. They bombed houses, streets, everything. All this didn't stop the FMLN—they captured Calvo and the forty soldiers from the church and spent the night in the town. . . . We later learned that the soldiers were freed some months later. (Interview with resident, Tenancingo, 1987)

Several Tenancingo residents told similar versions with varying degrees of apparent trauma.

One person, whom I came to consider one of my most informed and reliable respondents in Tenancingo, told me that he had later heard over the radio an audiotape of a pilot circling over Tenancingo calling his base for instructions, stating that those he saw on the streets looked like civilians. The response of his commander was to order him to bomb whomever he saw moving. As the likely source for the airing of the tape was one of the FMLN radio stations, I was skeptical. (I did not ask whether that was in fact the case, as it would implicate him politically in a way inappropriate at that time. I later came to believe that was indeed the source.) However, Jesuit scholar Ignacio Martín-Baró reported much the same thing:

I remember hearing a recording of a conversation between the pilot of a Salvadoran bomber and his commanding officer at the base. The pilot, who was flying over the town of Tenancingo, saw a group of people in a state of panic seeking cover in the local church and transmitted to the officer that they were civilians so he could not bomb them. But, from the command post, the officer insisted that "anything that moves is the enemy," that they were nothing but "subversives" and, therefore, that the pilot must bomb. (Martín-Baró 1988, 338)

A Belgian journalist who worked with the ERP for three years in Usulután states explicitly that she heard the tape on Radio Venceremos (Lievens 1988, 87–88). Whether the tape was in fact a recording of radio transmissions between the pilot and the base (which I judge likely, as Martín-Baró would have been skeptical), the conversation is etched in the memory of some Salvadorans, among them some Tenancingo residents.

Some interpretations emphasized the heroism of guerrilla forces in Tenancingo; one bordered on the mythical. According to a written, apparently eyewitness, account that circulated soon after the bombing and that was shown to me in 1987, the members of the Green Cross did retreat with the group and

> with megaphones called to the pilot to stop the bombing, but he didn't and dropped a bomb on them, killing eighteen persons there alone. My aunt, my cousin, and their sons died there; another cousin [would have died] inside [her pregnant mother], who fell dead from the shrapnel. But a passing female guerrilla that might have been a nurse said she had to save the life of the baby. She took out a knife and opened my cousin's side and took out the daughter. She cut the umbilical cord and gave her to another aunt to take to Cojutepeque where she was cared for. And by a miracle of God she is safe and well.[11]

In this account, not only did the Air Force overlook the presence of civilians in the town, but a guerrilla fighter literally produced life out of the suffering endured. Another Tenancingo resident reported in a 1989 interview that an entire family was killed except for a fetus who was saved. His repeating this story was particularly interesting, as he was not an insurgent supporter. Perhaps he had read this account and believed it; in any case he reported it as something he knew to be true. Still another resident stated in a 1989 interview that an entire family, including a pregnant woman, had been killed, but did not mention the saving of a fetus.

"Memories" held by members of the Tenancingo elite—none was present at the time of the bombing—tended to be very different. For example, one wealthier resident claimed—and seemed to sincerely believe—that guerrilla combatants captured Calvo and forced him to call in the Air Force to bomb the town, thus attributing moral responsibility to the FMLN while admitting the Air Force had bombed the town (the FMLN did not have planes or helicopters). Such beliefs persisted despite the long-standing acceptance of responsibility for the bombing on the part of the military itself. Colonel Domingo Monterrosa, the commander of the Atlacatl Battalion that moved into the area soon after the attack, was reported to have said to the surviving residents of Tenancingo, "Here we all lost, we lost and you lost, but you must understand that it was an exception and that the bombing occurred because the lives of the soldiers were in danger."[12] General Adolfo Blandón, Armed Forces Chief of Staff at the time, reiterated to me the military's responsibility in a 1987 interview:

It was my fate to be commander of the army when the worst that could happen to a town happened. . . . [After the first attack] we were able to arrange things a bit . . . and things were going forward when there was another confrontation. There was also an aerial action. It was an error.

Thus both government and insurgent supporters told narratives consonant with their political beliefs and loyalties.

As evident in these varied memories of the bombing of Tenancingo, processes of the social construction of memory are very salient in war narratives, particularly when storytellers participated in or supported political violence. Statements of past motivation may reflect present ambivalence concerning the justification of violence (Portelli 1997, 138). Statements in interviews with supporters of the insurgency concerning motivation for actions carried out some years earlier may be particularly subject to interim processes of both individual and social selection as ongoing dialogue within families, organizations, and communities reshapes initial impressions into social memories. Motivations claimed in interviews may be ex-post rationales for participation, whose real reasons lie elsewhere.

Moreover, silences in interviews may be as significant as the events related. When Kay Warren returned to the village in highland Guatemala where she had done ethnographic research before the civil war, she was struck by the "strategic ambiguities" in narratives concerning the local history of violence (for example, "they burned, they killed . . ." with the identity of "they" left unrevealed [1998, 110]). Those who could not understand the implication of such ambiguities were "by definition strangers with whom it was not wise to share information" (1998, 94). Villagers were reluctant to discuss the violence in any detail, offering generalizations in response to questions. The violence of the civil war had split families and communities, with the result that her respondents lived in a world of betrayal and existential dilemmas captured in phrases such as "we don't know who is listening" and "one did not know who was who" (1998, 107–8). Such silences may be particularly important for the ethnographer, as when villagers in the northern highlands of Peru proudly told how a group of purported thieves had been beaten and stabbed to death but neglected to say that one had been a young teenager (Starn 1999, 82–85), or when Chinese villagers who were displaced by a hydroelectric dam in central China were silent about traumatic village events during the Cultural Revolution (Jing 1996, 56). Moreover, silences in narratives may evoke corresponding silences by ethnographers. Linda Green did not feel free to pursue certain topics with the Maya war widows she interviewed; in particular, she could not ask widows whose husbands had been killed by the army about the photograph on the wall of a son in an army uniform: "I would give them the opportunity to say something, but I felt morally unable to pursue the topic" (Green 1995, 112–13). Thus the usual tension in the interpretation of oral history interviews—between the need to reconstruct events and the need to understand respondents' representations of those events—is sharpened in the aftermath of conflict and violence (Portelli 1997, 146).

There is an additional danger in relying on what Charles Tilly calls "standard stories," those frequently told by participants in a social movement (Tilly 1999). Such reliance may result in the analyst's neglect of causal mechanisms such as structural and demographic factors that may not be well captured in the personal narratives of histories of individuals and communities. Nonetheless, the choice to participate in a movement or not to do so rests on the perceptions and interpretations of structures and processes by individuals (shaped, to be sure, by their participation in organizations). Scholarly analysis of such perceptions and interpretations necessarily relies in part on the reports of potential participants in interviews, memoirs, and similar sources.

Research Method

My interviews took place during the Salvadoran civil war and the subsequent, initially precarious, cease-fire in politically polarized areas that suffered severe political violence. The interviews addressed the very issues of political opinion and participation that generated and reinforced that violence. The interviews and associated fieldwork thus required "certain precautions and incredible delicacy" (Adler 1992, 229). Among other things, such fieldwork raises challenging issues of personal security (for those interviewed, but also for the researcher) and the confidentiality of interview records. As Linda Green (1995, 1999) explores in her work on war-torn areas of Guatemala, violence and terror often leave behind a legacy of silence, fear, and uncertainty that can be deeply corrosive of self-confidence, trust, and hope. These field conditions made necessary research procedures—in particular, for informed consent to participation in the research—that emphasized the voluntary nature of participation in interviews and the confidentiality of informant identities.[13] These concerns are not unusual in ethnographic research, of course, but their importance is much deepened in the context of research on civil war and political violence. For example, I informed all respondents that I was interviewing people across the political spectrum. I did so because I judged that knowledge important for their informed consent as well as their decisions about what to say and what not to say. Moreover, respondents' understanding that I was doing so would protect me from misunderstanding should participants of one side see me interviewing adherents of the other. Of course, my interviews with both sides were undoubtedly shaped by this knowledge.

Despite these difficulties, over 200 *campesinos* were interviewed at length, many repeatedly over a period of four or five years in a variety of settings, both individual and collective. Initial interviews with insurgent supporters in a particular area usually occurred with a small group of leaders of the principal local organization (a federation of cooperatives or a land defense committee). They usually started with an introduction by a person known to them (typically a representative of a nongovernmental organization with long-standing contacts in the area).[14] This initial interview, usually a long discussion of the purpose of the project and of issues of security and confidentiality, was essentially a vetting of my research project by these local leaders.[15] In all cases, these local representatives agreed that their organizations would participate in the research project, and arrangements for interviews with members were made.

Subsequent interviews were usually extended conversations with small groups of activists concerning the history of their community during the civil war, the founding of local organizations, and their perceptions of contemporary political issues. Local leaders preferred that initial encounters be group rather than individual interviews, a process I understood as a further vetting of me and the project, a further assessment of its likely consequences, and an assertion of their control over the process. I later interviewed many members individually (and some repeatedly) in private settings; no obstacles or conditions were imposed on these interviews by anyone to my knowledge. Given the substantial degree of violence, political tension, and uncertainty around the themes of this study in the recent past, I promised I would not reveal the identity of those with whom I spoke (except in the case of a few political elites). While from the present vantage point this may seem an unnecessary precaution, it is a pledge which I have honored. For this reason, I characterize interviews only by the role of the interviewee (*campesino*, landlord, ERP commander, and so on) and the year and location in which the interview occurred.

However, one disadvantage of my reliance on local opposition organizations for initial contacts with insurgent *campesinos* was that I interviewed fewer women than men: while many women participated in the organizations, they tended to be less active than their male counterparts, and few were leaders. In group interviews I did my best to ensure their speaking, but they were often interrupted repeatedly. I also interviewed at length a dozen women in private settings about their experiences during the war, but because I particularly sought to know the history of the emergence of insurgent organizations, I inevitably relied more on men.

In these circumstances of recent political violence and enduring political polarization, I did not attempt to construct representative samples of local respondents. I did, however, interview the members of a wide range of organizations. Of the ten cooperatives established by the government as part of the 1980 counterinsurgency agrarian reform in the Usulután case-study areas, members of six were interviewed. Of more than forty insurgent (as opposed to agrarian reform) cooperatives in those areas, members of thirty-two were interviewed. Representatives of nearly all other *campesino* political organizations active in the Usulután case-study areas, including those founded by the government in the aftermath of the agrarian reform, were interviewed. In Tenancingo, leaders and members of a variety of organizations were interviewed, in both group and individual settings. Dozens of meetings of organizations in both Usulután and Tenancingo were also observed.[16]

Nor did I attempt to conduct field research in an area where insurgent activities were entirely absent (which would have been the ideal research design, as it would have added a clearly contrasting case). Ethnographic research on such politically sensitive questions during the civil war in areas of uncontested government and landlord control would have been dangerous for those interviewed. That I could carry out such research in contested areas was an achievement of the insurgency: rebellion had carved out a political "space" of relative autonomy (Adler 1992).

In the case-study areas, I interviewed *campesinos* who did not participate in the insurgency where and when I could. As nonparticipants generally did not belong to organizations (except small evangelical sects in some cases), it was more difficult to obtain introductions that they would trust. As a result, most of my interviews with twenty-four nonparticipants took place in small towns such as Tierra Blanca, Tenancingo, and Santiago de María, where I stayed with individuals trusted by many nonparticipants (in two cases local Catholic nuns, in one case a European development expert). These interviews usually took place in private, one-on-one settings in the case of *campesinos*; in official, sometimes group, settings in the case of mayors and other officials; and in private homes and offices in San

Salvador and other cities in the case of landlords. I also interviewed residents of two types of sites of likely nonparticipation: government-sponsored repopulated towns in Suchitoto and agrarian reform cooperatives in western El Salvador.

Interviews across this range of political allegiances during a bitter civil war proved possible for various reasons. International attention on the reconstruction of Tenancingo, which included significant European funding and press coverage, may have raised the costs to both the FMLN and the government of hostility to an academic researcher. That the researcher conducting the interviews was not from El Salvador but from the United States may also have contributed to the project's feasibility, particularly given the importance of U.S. funding to the government and the attention given to harassment (by either side) of U.S. and European citizens. That the ceasefire was in place during much of the Usulután research made travel to those areas less precarious than it would have been earlier. Finally, with a few minor exceptions, I had excellent luck: I was never caught in the wrong place at the wrong time. Such luck is a not-to-be-underappreciated aspect of fieldwork in settings of political violence (Sluka 1995).

I believe my research in contested areas was possible for a more profound reason. My inquiries met with the enthusiastic collaboration of many residents of contested zones (and of nearly all those approached in San Salvador as well), irrespective of class, occupation, or political affiliation. Residents acted on a willingness (perhaps even a need in some sense) to discuss with an outside researcher their own history and that of their families and communities.[17] Perhaps this willingness is a measure of the trauma and change brought by the war. Those interviewed frequently expressed a desire for their story to be told, that some account (or accounting) be made of the local history of the civil war. For example, one Tenancingo resident not allied with any political faction told me in 1987, "The people here are suffocating from the cries and shouts that we cannot speak. It suffocates. It does me good to talk to someone—I can't speak to people here about these things." One leader of the Land Defense Committee of Las Marías, a longtime insurgent activist whose involvement began with his training as a catechist in the mid-1970s, remarked:

> Just a comment on your project: I understand that you are asking us to consider participating in the construction of what we might call a history of the war in the conflicted zones. [pause] There are no more hidden things. We have suffered so; it would be right that there be such a history. What a period

we have lived through! The *campesino* does not have the capacity to do it; you engage with such things more there [in the U.S., in U.S. universities]. But it is something we have lived and we are still living. I don't know where to start.

This willingness of many residents of contested areas to talk about their personal and community histories at length with a researcher is common to many other ethnographies of civil wars. Green found that many of the Maya war widows she interviewed, including some she came to know very well, would tell her their stories over and over (1995, 115). In her analysis of the civil war in Mozambique after independence, Carolyn Nordstrom suggests that because the experience of violence is profoundly personal and linked to processes of self-identity and personhood, narratives of political violence are also attempts to find a meaningful way to deal with experience and to organize experience after the fact, and thus respondents exhibit what appears to be a "need to talk and talk" (1997, 3-4, 21-22, 79). Das suggests that survivors of communal violence in Sultanpuri agreed to interviews because "all this signified the fact that their lives held a meaning, and that their suffering would not go untold" (1990, 395). Marcelo Suárez-Orozco argues that narratives of political violence, known in Latin American literature as *testimonios* (testimonies), are rituals "of both healing and a condemnation of injustice—the concept of testimony contains both connotations of something subjective and private and something objective, judicial, and political" (1992, 367).

Yet the statements that Salvadoran insurgent *campesinos* made in interviews were concerned not only with violence. While most stories they told began as histories of injustice, violence, suffering, and loss, many continued as proudly told stories of the achievements of opposition organizations during the conflict—of land occupied and defended, of new organizations founded, and of new identities asserted. The *campesinos* recounted these achievements with enthusiasm, interrupting each other to cap the last story with the next. With groups I interviewed repeatedly over months and sometimes years, support for this project was particularly evident on my return after an absence. I would often be met with shouted greetings such as "Well, Elisabeth, do we have something to tell you!" or (to each other) "What did we say we should remember to tell Elisabeth?" These assertions of pride contrast sharply with those gathered in many ethnographies of civil war and political violence.

Redrawing Boundaries: The Mapmaking Workshops

A place on the map is also a place in history.

—Adrienne Rich (1986, 212)

At the level of open defiance, the mapping of revolution and riot is a reminder of the contingent nature of sovereign authority and the controverted character of sovereign power. By directing attention to issues of social distribution, mapping can also open the politically charged question of social justice.

—Jeremy Black (1997, 77)

In analyzing the course of the civil war in the case-study areas, I rely in part on the maps drawn for my book in 1992 by a dozen teams of *campesinos* from across Usulután in three workshops I convened in that year. I asked representatives of a dozen cooperatives to draw with marker pens on large sheets of butcher paper maps of their localities showing property boundaries and land use before and after the civil war. Drawn collaboratively by at least two and usually several members, in a process interspersed with much discussion of the history of the area as well as gossip, jokes, and teasing of one another (and of me), the resulting maps document how *campesino* collective action literally redrew the boundaries of class relationships through their depiction of changes in de facto property rights and patterns of land use in the case-study areas during the war. The accuracy of the claims by these cooperative leaders to occupy extensive areas of land in 1992 was confirmed by my own travel and observation in the case-study areas and by examination of the archives of landholding and land claims data maintained by the FMLN, the government, and the United Nations during the postwar process of adjusting property titles.[18]

These maps are therefore quite different in origin and purpose from most maps, which are usually the product of efforts on the part of expanding empires or consolidating states to centralize power, define frontiers, and regulate property rights (Harley 1988; Black 1997). The security interests of the U.S. Department of Defense in El Salvador, for example, led to the production of a number of maps of El Salvador, including one map of Usulután on which the many hacienda airstrips were carefully marked. To take another example, cadastral maps (maps of properties, often linked to a property register for tax purposes) reemerged in Renaissance Europe, as maps of private estates proved useful to asserting land claims or settling property disputes. They were later deployed by states to plan land reclamation (as in the Netherlands), collect taxes, manage state resources such as royal forests, and distribute land to settlers in colonies (Kain and Baigent 1992). Such maps were, of course, used to the advantage of some against the interests of others and in "portraying one reality, as in the settlement of the New World or in India," helped obliterate the old (Kain and Baigent 1992, 344). Indeed, Michael Biggs argues that the development of modern cartography contributed to the concept of the modern state as a *territory* over which the state held a monopoly of violence: the development of maps reshaped state lands into territory, a homogeneous and uniform space with boundaries (1999, 385). In short, maps are not just strategic but also cultural constructions. Maps not only reflect cultural practices of their producers, revealed by analyzing what is included and excluded (for example, whether or not places important to subordinate but not dominant social groups are named, how images are presented in relation to one another, and so forth); they may also have enduring cultural consequences.

Maps are not always produced in the service of the powerful. Sometimes (as here) they are produced by subordinate social actors or by civil society organizations contesting dominant values (as in many environmental maps [Black 1997]). Among the Beaver tribe of northeastern British Columbia, for example, some elders draw "dream maps" that indicate not only hunting trails and territories but also routes to heaven (Brody 1982). When mapping is a consistent cultural practice, anthropologists sometimes try to account for that fact. Robert Rundstrom (1990) argued that the Inuit of northwestern Canada and Alaska produce accurate and detailed maps, not because they need them for hunting more than other societies that do not produce them, but because mimicry is a prime cultural value that runs throughout their culture. Mapmaking by indigenous or peasant actors often occurs in the course of conflict with state authorities over land or other resources, as in the case of conflict over reed beds in Lake Titicaca (Orlove 1991, 1993) or over the consequences of the Alaska Highway natural gas pipeline for the traditional hunting territories of the Beaver (Brody 1982).

In this case, the willingness of insurgent *campesinos* to draw the maps reflected their assertion of contested property rights at the end of the civil war. Drawing such maps involved considerable sacrifice of work time on the part of individuals (with no recompense except, in some cases, a meal of beans and tortillas) and forgone opportunities on the part of the *campesino* organizations: each pair of maps took two full days to draw, given the unfamiliarity of the task. Despite this time commitment, cooperative members participated with remarkable enthusiasm; only one of twelve pairs of maps was not completed. Perhaps the process evoked what Dolores Hayden (1995,

9) calls "the power of place," the power of ordinary landscapes to "nurture citizens' public memory." Moreover, for all participants the process required a willingness to engage in the challenging task of conceptualizing familiar terrain in entirely new terms. For the many semi-literate and illiterate participants, the mapmaking workshops were the scene of difficult—and public—struggles with unfamiliar tools. One elderly mapmaker, the president of a cooperative in northeastern Usulután, unaccustomed to holding a pencil, traced an elaborate tapestry of small and medium holdings with his forefinger; his grandson carefully drew a line in its wake. While I promised that the maps would be returned to the communities, which may have provided some incentive, my impression was that the mapmakers were motivated primarily by their commitment to recounting their history.

Mapmaking was thus not an existing cultural practice but an artifact of my research.[19] A few of the mapmakers were familiar with maps, particularly those who worked closely with local FMLN commanders whom I observed to use fine-scale topographic maps (usually much creased and held together by layers of tape). Most certainly appeared to be natural cartographers; indeed, one developed an innovative projection in his maps (detailed in *Insurgent Collective Action* [Wood 2003, chap. 7]). But mapmaking was not something any of them had previously attempted.

Nonetheless, the maps reveal much about the history of the case-study areas, particularly the patterns of land occupation and use (Wood 2003, chap. 3), and also the perceptions and values of their makers (Wood 2003, chap. 7). Honoring an often-regretted but ethnographically correct pledge, I returned the maps to the mapmakers out of respect for their insight, gratitude for their taking the time, and hope that the maps might prove useful. Reproduced in *Insurgent Collective Action* are photographs of the original maps (tacks pinning the maps to the wall are visible on some maps) that were then digitally restored to a quality close to the original maps. (Color versions may be seen online at the website http:www.cambridge.org/us/features/wood.)

This willingness to collaborate in interviews and workshops reflected in part the isolation of many of these communities during the war. In interviews with members of organizations in San Salvador that frequently hosted international visitors, there was often a distinctly professional tenor to testimonials offered, as if a script were being played once again. In contrast, Usulután had been little visited by journalists, and to my knowledge, sustained research concerning the history of the war had not been carried out there. Few of the landlords interviewed had ever been approached for their opinions. Tenancingo, the site of a unique reconstruction project supported by European donors, had been visited by journalists, development specialists, and diplomats in the first few years of the project, but few lingered long enough to interview residents other than a few members of the community council. While my initial interviews with community leaders had the feel of an oft-told story, in subsequent interviews this initial script was abandoned and more complicated stories were told (for example, patterns of violence were more convoluted in later narratives).

Conclusion

Clearly, the interviews and maps that *Insurgent Collective Action* was based on must be interpreted carefully. This is particularly true for interviews concerning the history of the contested areas of Usulután, which is largely constructed from interviews carried out just before the end of the war. While some of the salient events had occurred quite recently, others dated back to before the war or to its early years. That the intervening years and experiences reshaped perceptions of earlier events is true of Tenancingo as well. Although interviews began there in 1987, the history of the early years of the war relied on the memory of interviewees (but to a significantly lesser extent, given the greater availability of human rights records for events there). And interviews were inevitably affected by the political context in which the interview occurred. Some interviews that I conducted with insurgent *campesinos* in the first few months of 1992, for example, clearly reflected the spirit of euphoria and victory prevalent throughout the case-study areas in the first weeks of the cease-fire. Later interviews with the same informants reflected a more sober and considered assessment of the achievements of the insurgency.

A possibly mitigating factor is that many interviewees claimed never to have told the story of their community before, which would suggest that explicitly social processes of memory formation had not been particularly strong in the case-study areas. On the other hand, because some interviews were with groups of *campesinos*, the interview itself was an instance of the process of the social construction of memory and political identity. The mapmaking workshops were explicit exercises in social memory, as participants recalled events of the civil war and discussed and celebrated its legacy as they drew. The maps, like all maps, "act as a form of memory" (Black 1997, 93).

To the extent possible, the oral testimonies gathered were compared with one another and discrepancies were explored in subsequent interviews. Because interviews with key respondents in both Tenancingo and

Usulután were repeated over several years, it was possible to construct histories of both areas that were less shaped by immediate political processes than histories relying on interviews gathered during a single period would have been, and to later fill in some of what had initially been silences.

I also drew on other sources, including interviews with landlords of properties in the contested areas (eleven of them, of whom seven were landlords of large properties in the case-study areas), pastoral agents of local parishes, FMLN commanders (sixteen of them, including twelve mid-level ERP commanders in Usulután, five of whom I interviewed on several occasions), Salvadoran military officers (three colonels responsible for government forces in the case-study areas and two generals), staff of several nongovernmental organizations, officials of the Salvadoran government and of the U.S. Agency for International Development, and staff of the U.N. Observer Mission in El Salvador. Corroboration was also sought in documents produced by human rights organizations (principally, Americas Watch and El Rescate, a U.S. solidarity and human rights organization that compiled data gathered by Salvadoran human rights organizations, particularly the human rights office of the Archdiocese of San Salvador, and reports appearing in the press), and by Salvadoran and foreign nongovernmental organizations, including the publications of the Universidad Centroamericána José Simeón Cañas, the national press, the United Nations, the Salvadoran government, and the U.S. Agency for International Development.[20] I also analyzed a rural household survey carried out at the end of war, the results of postwar elections, and databases documenting evolving agrarian property rights during and after the war. Finally, I illustrated the book's central argument with a formal model (Wood 2003, appendix).

So whether the reasons for participating in collective action expressed by many insurgent *campesinos* in interviews (and inferred from interviews by me) constituted an essential part of their reasons for participation at the time of the actions cannot be directly inferred, given the intervening processes of social construction of memory. Yet memories do not evolve randomly; the deviation of memory from fact illuminates values and beliefs. The retrospective nature of some interviews and the coloring of accounts of the past by the perceptions of the present are not just inevitable complications of my reliance on interviews, but also provide direct evidence of one legacy of the civil war, the reshaping of political culture in the contested areas of El Salvador. According to Luisa Passerini (1980, 10), "oral sources are to be considered, not as factual narratives, but as forms of culture and testimonies of the changes of these forms over time." I return in the final chapter of *Insurgent Collective Action* to these issues of interpretation and show that the reasons for insurgent collective action evident in retrospective interviews reflected emotional and moral reasons for rebellion earlier in the war.

The political and logistical conditions for field research vary significantly across civil wars (and across regions within each war). The dominant pattern of limited and selective violence during the latter half of the Salvadoran conflict—with the significant exception of the response by the state to the FMLN's 1989 offensive—contrasts sharply with the patterns of violence in many other civil wars (and with the violence early in the Salvadoran war). In many wars, leaders exercise little control over armed followers; armed factions perceive few constraints, either ideological or practical, on their use of violence; armed groups rely on the use of indiscriminate terror (particularly if their goal is to control resources or to carry out a campaign of ethnic or political cleansing) or on the kidnapping of foreigners to finance their activities. In some wars, the multiplicity of factions makes difficult any sustained presence of researchers in relevant areas of the country. Thus for logistical, security, or ethical reasons, field research of the kind described here may not be possible in many civil wars.

In retrospect, I am aware of many mistakes I made during my field research, of which two deserve mention. I wish I had better recorded the comments, jokes, and discussions that occurred during the map-drawing sessions. I was slow to understand their value, as I saw the maps as mere representations of land claims rather than as documents demonstrating the emergence of a new political culture. I also came to wish that I had interviewed more *campesinos* who did not support the insurgency, as the material I gathered from this group was generally less rich than what I collected from supporters. I also wish I had reflected more explicitly on the many ways in which participant observation informed my interpretation of all ethnographic data gathered. Despite these limitations, I believe that my informants, both supporters of the insurgency and nonsupporters, have much to teach us about collective action before and during civil war.

Notes

1.   In referring to poor rural residents as *campesinos* (literally, "of the countryside"), I follow their own usage. The word is not well translated by "peasants" as most of those who refer to themselves as *campesinos* are not owners of smallholdings but aspire to be. *Campesino* refers to a person who engages in agricultural activities, who

may be a landless day-laborer, a permanent wage employee, or a farmer working a smallholding, but not an owner who hires significant numbers of wage laborers.

2. For a parallel discussion of what sustained mobilization in support of the Sandinistas in Nicaragua, see Bayard de Volo, this volume.

3. However, this research design emerged through a more convoluted process than this indicates, as explained in chapter 3 of *Insurgent Collective Action* (Wood 2003).

4. This characterization of the literature on peasant rebellion as relying on elite sources loses much of its force if such rebellions are seen as the outgrowth of social movements, many of which have been extensively studied using participant accounts.

5. While the report of the Truth Commission contains much information on certain high-profile human rights cases and lists thousands more in the annexes to the report, the coverage of Usulután is strikingly poor, apparently because the dominant faction there, the Ejército Revolucionario del Pueblo (Revolutionary Army of the People, ERP) did little to encourage residents to report violations to the commission.

6. See the reviews by Margaret M. Bradley (1994) and Charlotte van Oyen Witvliet (1997). My attention was first brought to this literature by an analysis of narratives told by Lithuanians of the violence there during and after World War II by Roger Petersen (n.d.).

7. A distinction should be made between memories of past political *attitudes* and of intense political *events*. While memories of political attitudes appear to be particularly malleable, those of former political protests are more reliable (Markus 1986, 40–41).

8. The literature on social memory and narrative is vast. I have found the following particularly helpful: Portelli (1991, 1997); Halbwachs (1992); Passerini (1992); Jelin (1996); Polletta (1998a, 1998b, 1999); and Auyero (1999). See Olick and Robbins (1998) for a recent review of the literature.

9. Leigh Binford (2002) argues, for example, that some of the disillusionment expressed by some former members of the Frente Farabundo Martí para la Liberación Nacional (Farabundo Martí Front for National Liberation, FMLN) may reflect such disappointment. Nora Kriger's finding (1992) that Zimbabwean peasants were coerced into supporting the liberation forces may reflect such disillusionment (her interviews were conducted several years after the end of the war).

10. Reputable human rights sources disagree about the number killed during the attack and response. Americas Watch (1986, 79) claimed in 1986 that approximately 100 had been killed but later revised that number to 75 (1991, 53). In both documents, Americas Watch states that 35 civilians were killed when a plane dropped a bomb on the group retreating with the Green Cross. Tutela Legal, the human rights organization of the Archdiocese of San Salvador, estimated the number of dead at 175 (cited in Pearce 1986, 201).

11. *"Narración sobre los sucesos que pasaron en Tenancingo"* (Narration of events that occurred in Tenancingo), an eyewitness testimony signed *"un hijo de Tenancingo,"* undated but apparently written soon after the bombing, which was given to me in 1987 by a Tenancingo resident.

12. According to a newspaper report published in the Nicaraguan newspaper *Barricada*, 30 September 1983.

13. Research was carried out under protocols approved by the human subjects research review committees of the University of California at Berkeley, Stanford University, and New York University.

14. I usually succeeded in persuading the person who introduced me to leave after doing so. I was the only outsider present at all subsequent interviews. While this entailed my traveling alone through the case-study areas, that was preferable to the uncertainty that the presence of another outsider would introduce into the interview setting.

15. See Adler (1992) and Sluka (1995) for discussion of vetting processes in the contexts of ethnographic research with trade unionists in South Africa and nationalists in Northern Ireland, respectively.

16. Observing meetings of insurgent organizations took up much more of my time in the case-study areas than the reader would infer from their relative absence from the pages of my book. They were, however, very important for my credibility with insurgent interviewees and for my sense of relations between leaders and members.

17. Some of those interviewed might have been initially motivated by some hope that collaboration with the research might bring some material benefit. I did my best to discount such hopes in the informed-consent procedure that I went through, though of course I cannot know that I succeeded. In any case, no such benefits materialized; those I approached for a subsequent interview nonetheless appeared ready to participate again.

18. I also attempted to compare the maps to aerial photographs taken before the war by the Ministry of Agriculture. Approximately two dozen of the properties photographed fall in the Usulután case-study areas, of which eight were claimed by cooperatives at the end of the war. Of these eight, two were drawn for me by cooperative members. Unfortunately, due to the poor resolution of the original ministry photographs (or perhaps the quality of copying of those photographs since), only the general shapes of properties were more or less recognizable, and detailed comparisons with the mapmakers' maps were not possible. The *campesino*-drawn maps were roughly similar to the aerial photographs of these two properties.

19. While a form of mapmaking appears to have been practiced in pre-Columbian times in Mesoamerica (Harley 1992, 524–26), I am unaware of any evidence that rural communities retained the practice in the late twentieth century in what is now El Salvador.

20. For example, the history of Tenancingo after 1986 is documented by a wider range of sources thanks to the resettlement project and the resulting attention of nongovernmental and international agencies to the district.

SIX

The Political in Political Ethnography: Dispatches from the Kill Floor

TIMOTHY PACHIRAT

I would like to insist on the embodied nature of all vision.

—Donna Haraway (1991, 188)

Neutrality in fieldwork is an illusion.

—John Van Maanen (1991, 40)

Immediately in front of me, a painted plywood sign reads, "Great Plains Packing Company." Beneath the big block letters are two thick, black arrows pointing in opposite directions. Beside the first arrow, pointing to the right, are the words, "Front Office; Sales; Visitors." The second, pointing to the left, reads, "Employment; Shipping." Unlike the curving driveway and manicured lawn to the right, a small rectangular trailer on raised cinderblocks confronts anyone turning left. Behind it stands a chain link fence topped with three strands of barbed wire. My feet follow the left arrow. I am here to participate, not visit.

—Author's fieldnotes, June 2004

What is the meaning of the "political" in political ethnography? One answer is that it signifies the unique contributions that ethnographic research can make to our knowledge about politics. In contrast to a model of political inquiry (Laitin 2003) that subordinates ethnography as "summer intern" to the "senior partners" of formal and statistical analysis, proponents of political ethnography often argue for its intrinsic, stand-alone potential to generate knowledge about politics and power (Hopf 2006, 18). The extended participant observation and sustained immersion of political ethnography encourages an emic perspective that reemphasizes human agency and lived experiences, captures insider perspectives and meanings, and privileges rather than suppresses conflicting interpretations and descriptions (Shehata 2006; Bayard de Volo and Schatz 2004; Kubik, this volume; Wedeen, this volume). It also carries with it the capacity to challenge the very boundaries of the political (Scott 1985; Jourde, this volume). Political ethnography is *political* precisely because of its unique potential to both illuminate politics and challenge established conceptions of its boundaries.

While necessary and important, this meaning of the political in political ethnography is, in and of itself, incomplete. In this essay, I advance a second meaning that recognizes the embodied nature of ethnographic research and the relationships among perspective, power, and the ethnographic voice that this entails.[1] In addition to extending our knowledge about politics and power, the ethnographic process *itself* is political insofar as fieldwork inevitably locates the ethnographer within networks of power. Because "in ethnography, the ethnographer's self becomes a conduit of research and a primary vehicle of knowledge production" (Shehata 2006, 246), this second meaning of the political in political ethnography invites—even requires—the ethnographer to account for the partiality of perspective that shapes her voice. Rather than "claim[ing] the power to see and not be seen, to represent while escaping representation" (Haraway 1991, 188), it encourages a commitment to theorize the role of the ethnographer in the ethnography, something often referred to as reflexivity (Alvesson and Sköldberg 2000).

Although the importance of reflexivity has long been central to discussions of both the practice and the writing of ethnography in anthropology (Clifford and Marcus 1986; Geertz 1988; Tsing 1993) and sociology (Burawoy 1998), political science's attention to reflexivity in ethnographic research has been, with one important exception (Shehata 2006), largely scant and negative.[2] The discipline as a whole is still skirmishing over the legitimacy of the *first* meaning of the political in political ethnography—that is, whether or not stand-alone ethnography indeed has something valuable to contribute to our knowledge about politics[3]—and the *second* meaning of the political, with its focus on theorizing the role of the ethnographer in the ethnography, is either ignored entirely or explicitly cited as an obstacle to legitimizing ethnography in political science.[4]

In what follows, I speak to this deficit by drawing on my recent fieldwork in an industrialized slaughterhouse located in the Great Plains of the United States to underscore the importance of foregrounding relationships among perspective, power, and sight. My fieldwork demonstrates that reflexivity—defined as explicit attention to the role of the ethnographer in the ethnography—is not merely incidental to ethnographic research, an unavoidable and unfortunate byproduct of the fact that in ethnography the ethnographer is the primary instrument of research. To the contrary, it shows that the role of the ethnographer in the ethnography can be a *productive and necessary* source of reflection and analysis, rather than a shortcoming to be silenced or downplayed.

Given this aim, the remainder of the chapter proceeds as follows. I begin by contextualizing my fieldwork, briefly sketching its aims of contributing to our knowledge about politics and expanding the boundaries of the political. Next, I show how these aims were furthered because of explicit, reflexive attention to my role in generating ethnographic knowledge. Finally, I conclude by suggesting that the second meaning of the political in political ethnography is integral to its first meaning, underscoring the potential contributions reflexive political ethnography might make to our understandings of politics and power.

Context and Aims: The First Meaning of the Political

From June 2004 to May 2006, I conducted field research on industrialized slaughterhouse work in the Great Plains of the United States. For the first five and a half months of this period, I worked full-time on a slaughterhouse kill floor for nine to twelve hours each day (starting between 5:00 and 7:00 a.m. and finishing anywhere between 4:00 and 6:30 p.m.), Mondays through Fridays, with the possibility of mandatory overtime on Saturdays. The slaughterhouse employed over eight hundred workers, the large majority of whom were immigrants from Central and South America, Southeast Asia, and Africa. Approximately twenty-five hundred cattle per day were killed and processed at the slaughterhouse, which shipped meat to various distributors within the United States and internationally. I spent the last eighteen months of my time in the field conducting, on a much less grueling schedule, participant-observation research and interviews with community and union organizers, slaughterhouse workers, U.S. Department of Agriculture (USDA) federal meat inspectors, cattle ranchers, and small (custom) slaughterhouse operators.

Titled *Killing Work: Industrialized Slaughter and the Politics of Sight* (forthcoming, Yale University Press), this project takes the industrialized slaughterhouse as an exemplary case (Flyvbjerg 2001) of everyday, hidden, and *violent* labor, and explores the empirical and normative implications of a vast majority of people relying on a politically and economically disenfranchised minority to carry out a repetitive labor of violence on their behalf. At its core, the project is animated by an interest in understanding the delegation and execution of violent labor in modern society through the perspective of lived experience, both my own and those of fellow slaughter-house workers.

Drawing on my fieldwork, the project makes two broad claims reflecting the first definition of the political in political ethnography. The first is that the study of the division of labor through the lens of efficiency misses its centrality as a mechanism of power in society. Taking the industrialized slaughterhouse as a key example of, and exemplary metaphor for, the ways in which power is articulated through the division of labor and space in modern society, my work replaces the lens of efficiency with the lens of power and, as a result, encourages us to think differently about both the division of labor and our conceptualizations of power. While prior literature has made arguments about the relationships between power and the division of labor on a normative and theoretical plane (e.g., Walzer 1983; Rueschemeyer 1986; Young 1990; Berliner 1999), my project explores this relationship through the ethnographic perspective of lived experience and does so specifically as it relates to the relationships between repugnance, confinement, and the normalization and routinization of violence.

Specifically, I draw on my ethnographic fieldwork to posit a twofold geography of sight. The first operates between the slaughterhouse and society at large, serving to segregate and neutralize the violence inflicted on humans and other animals behind the physically and socially opaque walls of the slaughterhouse. The second operates within the industrialized slaughterhouse itself. Even within a zone of confinement largely opaque to the outside world, there exists a minute partitioning of labor and space that allows for different degrees of physical and moral distancing from repetitive acts of violence. Finally, by turning to the attempts of broad-based community organizing groups to draw attention to industrialized slaughterhouses, the project sketches and problematizes what I call a "politics of sight," or concerted, organized attempts to create ruptures in zones of confinement, to render the hiddenness of the repugnant visible in an attempt to produce political and social change.

Each of these three components—the geography of sight mediating society's relationship to the work of industrialized killing as a whole, the geography of sight at work within the slaughterhouse itself, and the politics of sight that seeks to render the repugnant visible—relies centrally on extended immersion and intensive participant observation as a way of contributing to our knowledge of how violence that is seen as both essential and repugnant to modern society is organized, disciplined, and regulated.

Further, by using political ethnography to critically redescribe a common and everyday phenomenon—the industrialized production of meat redescribed as the delegation and confinement of state-sanctioned violent labor in civilized society—my work implicitly argues for the importance of problematizing everyday, and therefore more normalized and naturalized, instances of power relations. At first glance, there is nothing obviously political about the industrialized slaughterhouse. Unlike war, executions, torture, imprisonment, and other acts of violence that are self-evidently political, the industrialized slaughterhouse remains firmly rooted in the terrain of the everyday, an element of the taken-for-granted world not especially worthy of attention from students of the political. By demonstrating how the industrialized slaughterhouse illuminates the division of labor and space as mechanisms of power, however, my political ethnography implicitly seeks to expand the boundaries of what is typically understood as "political."

Perspective, Power, and the Ethnographic Voice: The Second Meaning of the Political

The insights gained from my fieldwork resulted directly from my role as an active participant embodied in particular locations. To illustrate the importance of the second meaning of the political in political ethnography, I now offer a reflexive account of the five and a half months I spent working on the kill floor. This account underscores the importance of explicit attention to relationships among perspective, power, and the ethnographic voice, and the way these relationships shape not only *what* is seen (a question of access), but also *how* it is seen (a question of the production of ethnographic knowledge itself).

My ethnographic encounter with the industrialized slaughterhouse was from the very start fraught with questions of location. Contemporary industrialized slaughterhouses in the United States are extremely fragmented, both horizontally, through the minute division of labor and the accompanying partition of physical space within the slaughterhouse, and vertically, through a strict power hierarchy codified most visibly in hard-hat colors but also present in other, less immediately legible ways. This fragmentation forced me to take explicit stock of my role as an active participant in generating ethnographic knowledge; extending Van Maanen, neutrality was not available to me even in the form of an illusion.

Thinking reflexively about my research began with deciding a strategy of access and acknowledging forthrightly the different trade-offs each strategy was likely to carry (Feldman, Bell, and Berger 2003). Should I attempt access as an accredited researcher, writing a letter of inquiry to the relevant officials at various slaughterhouses requesting that they grant me participant-observation access to their plants? Should I attempt a kind of proxy access through conversational interviews with slaughterhouse workers, relying on their accounts to reconstruct a world I would not enter directly myself? Or should I attempt direct access as an entry-level worker, showing up in person to apply for work in a slaughterhouse?

Each of these strategies—formal access with plant management approval, proxy access through interviewing and surveys, and direct access through entry-level employment—would locate me in a radically different position and structure not only the information I gleaned from the research but also the very filter(s) through which I would interpret that information and give it meaning. A recognition of the second meaning of the political in political ethnography required that I make explicit how the mode of access would structure my line of vision in the ethnographic research setting. Would it be a vision from above? from below? from the outside looking in?

For a variety of reasons—primary among them the goal of encountering the slaughterhouse through the lived experiences of those who participated in its daily activities—I decided to attempt direct access by applying as an entry-level employee at several industrialized slaughterhouses in the central United States. After three mornings of returning to a crowded employment trailer outside one of the plants, I was hired to work on the kill floor. The hiring process itself quickly disabused me of any romanticized notions of unproblematic identification with the majority of slaughterhouse workers. I spoke fluent English. I had a valid U.S. driver's license and social security card, giving me a large advantage over many of the thirty or so others who milled around nervously with me in the plant's dingy employment trailer. At the same time, certain autobiographical aspects helped me to blend in. I had brown skin, I was born and raised in Southeast Asia and had immigrated to the United States as a young adult, I was a young male, and I had previous experience with manual labor in industrial settings. These autobiographical characteristics helped the management in charge of hiring to code me as typical entry-level slaughterhouse material.

Once inside the slaughterhouse as an active participant, I found myself inextricably caught up in what Burawoy (1998, 22) calls "relations of power" and what Van Maanen (1991, 40) refers to as "webs of local associations." Van Maanen in particular depicts the positioning of the ethnographer as a matter of choice. But once inside the slaughterhouse, the various webs of power in which I was positioned were largely chosen for me. My movement between and among different horizontal perspectives in the division of labor and different vertical levels in the hierarchies of power in the slaughterhouse profoundly structured what I learned, and yet the substance, timing, and direction of this movement were contingent and unforeseeable at the outset of my research, underscoring the importance of *bricolage* (Humphreys, Brown, and Hatch 2003) and improvisation (Yanow 2001) in fieldwork. Although I had made a conscious decision about where I would position myself initially within the *vertical* fractures separating layers of hierarchical authority in the slaughterhouse (entry-level production workers vs. line supervisors vs. managers vs. front office workers vs. owners), the minute division of labor within the slaughterhouse gave me little control over where I would be located in its vast network of *horizontal* fissures.

My time in the slaughterhouse can be divided into three distinct phases: liver hanger, chute worker, and quality-control personnel. In the first two of these phases, my position within the vertical hierarchy of power remained constant: I was an entry-level employee. Nonetheless, the shift from liver hanger to chute worker involved a dramatic relocation in horizontal space. In my movement from the chutes to quality control, my position within the vertical hierarchy of power changed radically, and I was freed from the constraint of restricting myself to a single location in horizontal space. In what follows, I offer an account of how movement through these horizontal and vertical locations impacted the lines of sight and power relationships that proved central to the larger ethnographic project.

Livers

For the first two months of my fieldwork, I worked in a vast cooler, technically an employee of the slaughter side of the plant, but geographically located in an ambiguous area positioned between the slaughter side, where the live cattle are killed, dehided, and eviscerated, and the fabrication side, where they are cut into pieces, boxed, and shipped.

As a vantage point, hanging livers in the 34-degree cooler as an entry-level worker proved highly limiting in some ways and expansive in others. On my first day, I was taken from the second-floor supply room to the first-floor cooler via the same entrance stairway I had used to access the building. On the first floor, I was led through several nondescript hallways ending at a door that opened into an alcove directly in front of the cooler. Each day, after donning my clothes in the locker room, I would travel via this same nondescript passageway, emerging on the inside of the slaughterhouse only at the exact point where I was needed. There I would stand for nine to ten hours a day less than three feet in front of a tall, dirty white wall, taking freshly eviscerated livers off a chain of sharp, moving hooks that traveled down to the cooler from the kill floor upstairs. Day after day, my experience of slaughterhouse work was restricted to watching the line of moving livers overhead and hearing the clanging of the metal trolley wheels that bore the swinging half-sides of cattle down to the cooler to be chilled.

It would be three weeks in the slaughterhouse before I saw a live animal, and this only because I accidentally discovered the pens where the live cattle were housed, while walking outside during a lunch break. It would be a month and a half before an extended breakdown of one of the machines on the line would give me the opportunity to walk upstairs and catch an all-too-brief glimpse of the kill floor itself. It occurred to me more than once during my two months hanging livers in the cooler that I might very well spend the entirety of my research located in this cramped vantage point, never learning how the cattle were killed or how the thousands of livers I hung each day were eviscerated. My coworkers and I worked completely divorced from any experiential understanding of the total process we actively contributed to. This perspective led me to stress the potential sterility of industrialized killing, the ways in which spatial partitioning and the division of labor allow large groups of people to directly contribute to a massive, repetitive killing process with minimal sensory involvement.

And yet, if the vantage point of the cooler was impoverished in terms of a horizontal knowledge that would have allowed me to map the terrain of the slaughterhouse, it proved rich in allowing me access to the relationships and rhythms of work in my particular location in the cooler. Liver work in the cooler was divided between two groups of people. One was a two-person team responsible for removing the livers from the line, hanging them on hooked carts to chill, pushing the carts over to a packing area farther inside the cooler, and cleaning the hooks on the moving line as well as on the carts. The second was a three-person team responsible for removing the chilled livers from the carts, wrapping them in plastic bags, and then packing them, two to a box, in heavy cardboard, before placing them on pallets that would eventually be moved to the freezer to await shipment for export.

As a member of the two-person team hanging livers on the carts, I got to know my fifty-nine-year-old partner extremely well. A native of Michoacán, Mexico, Ramon[5] had followed two of his sons to the Great Plains from California where he had worked in the construction industry. Both of Ramon's sons worked on the fabrication side of the slaughterhouse, where carcasses were cut into smaller pieces and boxed for shipment, and he and I started work on the same day. For a variety of reasons, not least the frigid temperatures in the cooler, hanging livers allows for much more independent collaboration between workers and entails much less direct supervision than other areas on the kill floor. In addition, a rivalry developed between the two groups of liver workers, with each viewing the other as having the "easier" set of tasks.

These conditions fostered a sense of solidarity between Ramon and me, and we soon discovered that we lived less than five minutes from each other. After a few weeks, we made arrangements to commute to work together and would often visit the bank, get haircuts, and go to the grocery store together after work. Even after we were both transferred away from hanging livers in the cooler, Ramon and I tried to eat lunch together in the cafeteria whenever our breaks coincided. The relatively unsupervised space of the cooler also gave me opportunities to develop relationships with other cooler workers, many of whom were employed by the fabrication side of the slaughterhouse but worked in the cooler near the liver hangers to organize the incoming half-carcasses on long rails where they were chilled overnight.

Chutes

After two months of hanging livers, Ramon and I were abruptly told by our supervisor that the "liver contract" had run out. Ramon was told to report to the "gut room," where he would use jets of water to flush ingesta out of eviscerated small intestines. I was told to report to the chutes. Although I remained an entry-level worker at the lowest level of the power hierarchy in the plant, I was told to turn in my white frock and trade my white hard hat for a gray one, signifying my relocation from the "clean" to the "dirty" side of the kill floor.

I quickly discovered that the hygiene-inflected discourse opposing "clean" to "dirty" was materially reproduced in the divisions of space and the partitioning of work experience on the kill floor. The kill floor boundary between the "dirty" and the "clean" side is marked by the point where the hides are stripped completely from the animals. Unlike the vast majority of "clean" side workers who only saw the cattle after they had been dehided, beheaded, bled, and to a large degree de-animalized, "dirty" side workers unloaded live animals from tractor-trailers; shot them in the head; cut their carotid arteries and jugular veins; made incisions directly into their hides; severed their legs, tails, ears, noses, and sexual organs; and saw, smelled, and in some cases stood directly in the blood that drizzled in a nonstop stream onto the floor below.

The partitioning between "clean" and "dirty" on the kill floor was materially reproduced not only by hard-hat colors worn by the workers themselves, but also by segregated bathroom and lunchroom facilities as well. Clean side workers used the "Clean Men's Lunch Room," the "Clean Men's Shower," and the "Clean Men's Bathroom"; dirty side workers used facilities labeled, literally, "Dirty Men's Lunch Room," "Dirty Men's Shower," and "Dirty Men's Bathroom."[6] While touted in the company's promotional literature as a way of avoiding bacterial cross-contamination, this strict separation also had the important effect of creating at least two broad classes of workers, each with radically differing experiences of the work of killing, and of preventing experiential cross-contamination from one class to another.

In the chutes, my specific job was to use plastic paddles, whips, and electric shockers to move live cattle from a circular squeeze pen up two narrow chutes into the "knocking box" where they were mechanically restrained and shot in the head with a 4-inch steel bolt released from a gun powered by compressed air. Unlike the sterile route I took to get from the locker room to the cooler, the route I took to get to the chutes now led me straight through the "dirty side" of the kill floor. On my way to the chutes each morning, I walked past shiny, gleaming equipment: large scissor-like machines that cut the front and back legs (shanks and hocks) off cattle with one snap; metal funnels attached to huge hoses used to suck hair and feces off cattle appendages; and robotic machines with massive clamps that ripped hide from flesh. By the end of each day, this same equipment was caked in layers of blood, feces, flesh, and hair.

Working in the chutes put me in constant, direct contact with live cattle. Yelling and using paddles, whips, and electric shockers, my fellow workers and I spent nine to ten hours each day driving thousands of cattle into the knocking box, and from where I worked I could see each animal being hoisted up by its hind leg—still kicking and jerking wildly—after it had been shot in the head. I could also hear the animals bellowing, and the impact of their hooves on the hard concrete regularly splattered feces and vomit up over the walls of the chute onto my shirt, my arms, and my face.

Work in the chutes was physically and emotionally stressful: the cutting smell of feces and vomit; the constant splattering; the bellowing of the cows when they were electrically shocked; the whites of their large eyes and their frothing mouths as they walked and ran by me. All were made unbearably potent by their sheer concentration and duration. If work in the cooler had been a daily struggle with the overwhelming monotony of the banal, work in the chutes became a daily struggle with the overwhelming monotony of suffering.

Further, unlike the relative freedom of the cooler, the supervisory regime in the chutes was constant and harsh. Because nothing inside the slaughterhouse could function at its determined speed without a steady supply of live animals, we were under constant pressure to drive the animals through the chutes and into the knocking box as quickly as possible, without delay or interruption. This meant, in practical terms, the constant, almost rote, use of the electric shockers to push the animals up on top of and against each other so that we could guarantee a steady supply of live cattle through the knocking box. If there were any delays in the stream of cattle, a supervisor would come out to the chutes to find out "what the problem was." Once, when there were several delays in a single day, both kill floor managers walked out to the chutes and forcefully threatened us with termination.

Unlike the sense of solidarity I shared with Ramon and the other cooler workers, my relationships with my fellow chute workers deteriorated rapidly over arguments about how much to use the electric shockers on the cattle. I worked with another man, Gilberto, near the entrance to the knocking box. Two other men, Fernando and Raul, worked farther down the chutes, near the circular squeeze pens. On my first day, I was horrified at how Gilberto shoved his electric shocker into the anuses of the cattle, making them bellow in pain, kick back with their hind legs, and then lunge forward into the cattle in front of them, ramming those animals farther into the knocking box in a sort of domino effect. I tried as much as possible to use only the plastic paddles, resorting to the electric shocker when it became clear the animal was not going to move otherwise.

Soon, Fernando and Raul were yelling at me to use the shocker all the time. When I refused, Fernando became especially furious, yelling, "They are all going to die anyway!" I looked to Gilberto, with whom I had exchanged conversation about family and hobbies, for support, but he merely shrugged and said that if we did not use the shockers, we would be fired. This conflict over how to keep the cattle moving up the chute lurked beneath the surface and would erupt whenever there was a delay in the line of cattle. After a few days in the chutes, I found myself using the electric shocker more and more because, without thinking about it consciously, I came to realize that it was indeed the easiest way to keep the cattle moving. Relying on the pain of electric shock to force the cattle forward, I worried less about where I positioned my body so that the cattle would not balk and stop. This meant less moving around, less expenditure of energy, and fewer visits from supervisors.

My vantage point in the chutes provided me with a critically important foil to my work hanging livers in the cooler. It exploded my experience of the sterilized compartmentalization involved in the work of killing and gave me a critically important point of triangulation. Having worked in entry-level positions on both the clean and the dirty sides of the kill floor helped me articulate the critical importance of the division of labor and space, even on the kill floor itself, as mechanisms that enabled the normalization and routinization of killing. Although I remained an entry-level worker at the bottom of the power hierarchy in the plant, the serendipitous horizontal relocation sparked by the termination of the "liver contract" dramatically expanded the kinds of insights I developed during my fieldwork.

Quality Control

Not long after starting work in the chutes, I was promoted to the semi-managerial position of quality control, where I would remain for my final three months in the slaughterhouse. As one of two quality-control personnel on the kill floor, my formal job description charged me with maintaining the cleanliness of the carcasses that were being sent from the kill floor to the cooler. I did this by arriving at the plant at 5:00 a.m.—two hours before kill floor operations started—in order to inspect equipment to make sure it had been cleaned properly; performing random hourly checks of the carcasses once kill floor operations had started; "monitoring" line workers to make sure they were complying with rules about sanitizing their equipment; and filling out documentation on a variety of forms dealing with temperature, acid concentration levels, and vacuum pressure. Informally, the kill floor managers made it clear that my primary task was to use diversion and redirection to keep the federal meat inspectors from noticing problems that would cause them to exercise their mandated authority to slow or stop production.

My promotion to quality control was sudden and unforeseen but not entirely surprising. The work required someone fluent in English, and when one of the two quality-control workers quit, my immediate supervisor and the plant managers saw me as a logical choice for the job. Once I became aware of the job opening, I pushed hard for it, stopping by the kill floor manager's office during the morning break to introduce myself and let him know I was interested in the job. The next day, he arranged an interview with the quality assurance manager and the vice president of the company, and I was offered the job on the spot.

Although I was still paid hourly, and therefore technically was not a supervisor, the move from line worker to quality control involved a clear shift in my location in the plant's vertical power hierarchy. I was given the green hard hat of the quality-control worker to replace the white and gray hard hats of the line workers. I wore a laundered uniform with my name monogrammed on it. I had a radio that gave me access to all the communication between the managers and supervisors on the plant floor. I had access to the slaughterhouse's paperwork and was responsible for filling out some of it. I was expected to move from place to place on the production floor, which meant, not insignificantly, that unlike the majority of workers tied to one repetitive function on the line, I could use the bathroom whenever I needed to. And ironically, like the upper-level management and outside visitors whose privileged perspective from above I had once mocked, part of my job now involved walking the catwalk high above the kill floor several times each day, secretly watching the white and gray hats to make sure they were sanitizing their knives and performing their jobs "correctly," and calling their red-hat supervisors on the radio when they were not.

The vision "from below" I had accessed as an entry-level worker in the cooler and the chutes contracted sharply, replaced by a very different kind of situated knowledge shaped by conversations and interactions with plant managers, kill floor supervisors, federal meat inspectors, and various personnel in the slaughterhouse's fabrication department and front office. This new vantage point allowed me to map the terrain of the slaughterhouse, gaining a sense not only of the kill floor as a whole, but of its relationship to the cooler, the fabrication department, and the front office. While work in the cooler and the chutes had severely restricted my movement in space, I now had the ability to move to any point on the kill floor more or less at will and, equally important, had access to a realm of radio and face-to-face communication between and among plant managers and supervisors that was previously opaque to me as a line worker.

This new line of vision allowed me to see that management and the federal meat inspectors were not the monolithic unity they had appeared to be from my vantage point as a line worker. Fractures, divisions, and ongoing debates existed, particularly between the kill floor and the front office and between the plant and the federal meat inspectors. Each of these groups had their own way of talking about the work of industrialized killing and of framing themselves and other workers in relationship to that work. The powerful have their hidden transcripts as well (Scott 1990), and my promotion to quality-control worker allowed me access to a backstage (Goffman 1959) I would never have been aware of had I remained an entry-level worker.

Although I made an effort to maintain the relationships with the white- and gray-hat workers that I had formed during my time as a liver hanger and chute worker, it was painfully clear that my move up the plant hierarchy imposed costs. People who knew me well, such as Ramon and a few of the other cooler workers, remained friendly and open, continuing to invite me to sit with them if our lunch breaks coincided. Even with them, however, a certain strangeness came between us. In part because of our now different schedules, Ramon and I stopped driving to work together. In the lunchroom, he stopped telling me how many carcasses he had seen fall on the cooler floor or how many wads of fat he had managed to chuck at another worker.

A veil of suspicion soon framed my interactions with other line workers who did not know me or who knew me only by sight. This was noticeable in the sudden lapses in conversation when I entered a room, the quick glances, and the exaggerated deferential behavior in the locker room and on the kill floor. At first, I tried hard to overcome this, to show by my refusal to eat lunch in the Quality Control Office and my friendly inattention on the catwalk that I really was "still on their side." But regardless of what I might say and do, it was as plain as the green hard hat on my head and the monogrammed blue uniform I now wore that, at least in my formal role, I was anything but on their side. The hidden transcripts (Scott 1990) once available to me as a fellow white hat or gray hat were quickly shut down, replaced by a scripted public transcript I myself had once followed in the presence of supervisors, managers, and federal meat inspectors. Having entered the slaughterhouse "from below," I was now actively enforcing and reproducing its regimes of surveillance and discipline.

Ultimately, the ethical dilemmas inherent in the work of quality control—both the diversion and redirection required in relating to federal meat inspectors and the surveillance and discipline I imposed on subordinate workers in the plant—became, in my judgment, untenable, and I resigned from my position and left the slaughterhouse in December 2004. I continued to stay in contact with Ramon and other workers from the plant, including federal meat inspectors, even as I shifted the locus of my research from fieldwork inside the slaughterhouse to participant observation and interviews with broad-based organizing groups, unions, cattle ranchers, federal meat inspectors, and small-scale (custom) slaughterhouse owners and operators.

Conclusion: The Double Meaning of the Political

This highly abbreviated account of the shifting perspectives and locations in networks of power that characterized my fieldwork on the kill floor underscores the intimate relationship between the two meanings of the political in political ethnography that I have sought to advance in this chapter. Reflexive attention to how I would access the slaughterhouse and to where I was situated—both physically and symbolically—once inside contributed directly to insights about how violence that is seen as both essential and repugnant to modern society is organized, disciplined, and regulated. In addition, this reflexivity generated intrinsic lessons of its own, four of which I highlight briefly by way of conclusion.

First, I quickly learned that whatever the attraction of "the subjugated," "the weak," or the "standpoint from below" in the abstract, such viewpoints simply do not exist in the material world as pure, uncontested categories of being. As a research method, political ethnography may be especially suited to uncovering the hidden transcripts of the subaltern, but in practice there is no "woman," no "worker," no "manager," no "immigrant" who does not also perform that identity at the intersection of many other possible identities, such as "mother," "husband," "Mexican, not Guatemalan," "Guatemalan, not Sudanese," "knife worker, not sanitation worker," and so on. This is not to deny that "woman," "worker," "manager," and "immigrant" provide a shorthand for identities that inhabit power structures that place very real limits on—and create very real opportunities for—the people who perform them, but it is to deny that such shorthand notation is ever capable of capturing any core "essence" of experience.

One form of silencing—and perhaps the most ironic form of all because of its underlying intention to give voice—is for the ethnographer to claim a viewpoint from below based on a certain characteristic or set of characteristics, and in doing so to close herself off to the multiplicities of belows, some of them in fierce contestation with each other, that might exist. The quest to *become* the subjugated, to achieve an ethnography from below in the sense of ingesting something essential about that shorthand of power, is both quixotic and dangerous.

And yet, as the changing relationships involved in my vertical movement from line worker to quality-control worker demonstrate, there are degrees of approximation that matter greatly and are well worth trying for. If I had never entered the slaughterhouse as a line worker, chances are I would have failed to notice the slight but portentous changes in behavior and speech that characterized my relationship with line workers once I became a quality-control worker. I noticed these changes and understood their meaning only because I myself had engaged in similar tactics toward my supervisors and the federal meat inspectors during my time as a line worker. Had I entered the slaughterhouse as a guest of management, the scope and acuity of my vision would have been even more restricted. There may be no essentialized viewpoint from below, but relationships of domination exist in every research site, and how one is positioned within them has tremendous impact on the kinds of ethnographic knowledge available, not only for reasons of access, but more profoundly because the specific position in relations of power changes *how* one sees and hears.

Second, there were the ways in which my being seen would affect how and what I saw. My self-presentation and the inscriptions of my cumulative life experiences on my own body, speech, and mannerisms—what Pierre Bourdieu (1991) refers to as *habitus*—combined to translate into certain interpretations that others formed of me. There were the markings of ascription: dark brown skin, black hair, and narrow, brown eyes. In the employment trailer, these markings helped me get hired. In the plant, they were often misread: many times my coworkers were incredulous to learn that I was not Mexican; still others persisted in referring to me only as "chino" even after learning my name. There were the markings of voice: my bilingual English and Thai, and the relative confidence, inscribed through years of formal education, with which I voiced opinions and asked questions. There was the fact that I was a male in a male-dominated workplace, making it extremely difficult to form relationships with the fifteen or so females who worked on the kill floor. All these factors and more affected how I was seen by others, and, consequently, how they presented themselves to me.

Third, there was the tension inherent in the dual role I played both as slaughterhouse worker and researcher. In many ways, when my ten-to-twelve-hour day at the slaughterhouse was over, my work as a researcher was just beginning. At the end of each day I struggled, often unsuccessfully, to sit at my desk and translate into words the experiences, impressions, and conversations of the day. No matter how strongly I identified with my fellow workers during the day, this forced time of writing and reflection served as a constant reminder of the boundary Burawoy (1998, 23) describes so forthrightly as the relations of domination that characterize the observer. Perhaps the most conscious reminder of this boundary, however, was the ever present option I had to exit the slaughterhouse, to quit and leave without the burden of feeling the world closing in on me, of an oppressive lack of other possibilities. I stayed in the slaughterhouse for five and a half months. Ramon stayed for fifteen and left only because the cold of the cooler and the ten hours of standing each day had affected his arthritis so badly he could hardly walk.

The fourth lesson lies in the future. When the finished research circulates back to the field, either as a complete written work or as a fragment of some other discourse, it may change what I described there in unpredictable ways. Perhaps these changes will be for the better, perhaps they will not. But worst of all is the possibility that my ethnographic voice will change nothing there at all, that it will remain a form of scholasticism (Bourdieu 2000) with currency only in the particular academic field in which it was produced. This, to me, would be a realization of Burawoy's (1998, 25) concept of normalization in the most awful possible way: the normalization of an academic political science that operates in a parallel world to, and yet has little or no effect on, the relationships of power, domination, and resistance it studies.

These lessons underscore the importance of attributing a double meaning to the political in political ethnography. Political ethnography is such not only because of its unique capacity to contribute to our knowledge about politics, but also because the embodied nature of the ethnographic research process is itself political.[7] In a way that would not have been visible to me had I maintained the illusion of being a neutral observer, my active complicity in the slaughterhouse's networks of power forced me to pay explicit attention to my own location and the inevitable partiality of sight that brought with it. This reflexive attention to my own location—both literal and metaphorical—in the field in turn helped to generate insights about how the divisions of labor and space in the slaughterhouse operated as mechanisms of power in the normalization and routinization of violence on the kill floor.

The word *partiality*, of course, is anathema to those who long for a social science of dispassionate, disengaged objectivity, a social science of the god-trick, which contemplates with fascination its own absence (Haraway 1991, 191). The second definition of the political in political ethnography, however, acknowledges that partiality *is* the starting point, the solid ground to thrust our feet against and cast off from, the foothold that enables the work of the imagination that makes sustained, empathic inquiry possible. Working as an entry-level worker in the cooler and chutes of the slaughterhouse did not mystically make me one with the subjugated, any more than my promotion to quality control automatically transformed me into an oppressor. My active participation in these roles did, however, provide the partiality that gave me the power to see, the power to make possible sustained, engaged, and situated dialogue with those worlds.

Emphasizing the double meaning of the political in political ethnography opens the discipline of political science to insights that come with practicing an ethnography that is self-conscious of the power dimensions inscribed in the relationships between the ethnographer and the research world(s). Political ethnography ought to give an account not only of how the ethnography informs knowledge about politics, but also of how the ethnographer navigates the specific political decisions that inevitably infuse the process of ethnographic research and writing itself. This "keen awareness of, and theorizing of, the role of the self in all phases of the research project" (Schwartz-Shea 2006) must be a central component in any ethnography that seeks transparency rather than obscurity about the central role played by the researcher in cogenerating knowledge. Far from being an unfortunate liability of ethnographic research, attention to the politics of embodiment is capable of generating insights about politics and power that might otherwise be missed. In this way, the first and the second meanings of the political in political ethnography are interrelated and, indeed, inseparable.

Notes

This chapter has benefited from feedback offered by audiences at a 2006 American Political Science Association panel on ethnography, an October 2006 workshop on Political Ethnography at the University of Toronto (both organized by Edward Schatz), and a May 2007 seminar on Power and Politics in Ethnographic Research at Vrije Universiteit in Amsterdam (organized by Dvora Yanow). Special thanks go to Dvora Yanow, James C. Scott, Sohini Guha, Sierk Ybema, and Edward Schatz for comments offered while playing the roles of discussants and chapter editor, and to James C. Scott and Steve Striffler for facilitating the fieldwork. My partner, Julie Jay, and our daughters, Parker and Mia Jay-Pachirat, moved thousands of miles, tolerated bloodstains and heinous odors, begrudged me my moustache (such as it was), and otherwise kept me (more or less) sane during my time on the kill floor.

1. I am indebted to Dvora Yanow's insightful comments in her role as discussant at the 2006 American Political Science Association meeting for foregrounding the double meaning of the political latent in my argument.

2. Shehata (2006) offers a compelling account of the relationship between researcher identity and ethnographic knowledge production in two textile factories in Egypt. There are significant areas of overlap between my argument and Shehata's; one important but complementary difference is that Shehata's reflexive account centers largely on identity and knowledge production, while the one I present here focuses largely on positionality and sight. More broadly, work on evaluative criteria in interpretive methods in political science is increasingly recognizing reflexivity as an important hallmark of trustworthy research and writing (Schwartz-Shea 2006; Yanow 2006b; Yanow, this volume).

3. See, for example, Flyvbjerg 2001; Bayard de Volo and Schatz 2004; Laitin 2003, 2006; Hopf 2006; Herrera 2006a.

4. In an otherwise laudable argument for the importance of ethnography in political science, Bayard de Volo and Schatz (2004) distance the kind of ethnography they recommend to the discipline from what they term "a more recent trend in anthropology" (268)—namely, ethnography "allowing for an ongoing dialogue ('reflexivity') between subject and object" (268). This trend, according to Bayard de Volo and

Schatz, "has become the defining feature of entire bodies of research," and "in its worst forms, this reflexivity can become a sort of transcendental principle that rivals any methodologically narrow navel-gazing practiced in other disciplines" (268). Although it is true that Bayard de Volo and Schatz only decry such reflexivity "in its worst forms," thereby leaving a hypothetical opening for better (best?) forms of reflexivity, they offer no references to—for that matter, no very clear definition of—reflexive ethnography, whether in its worst forms or otherwise. The imagination is left to run wild, conjuring all manner of navel-gazing social anthropologists intoxicated on transcendental principles.

5.   I have changed some names and locations to protect identities.
6.   The small number of women who worked on the kill floor used a separate, shared bathroom labeled, simply, "Women."
7.   For another understanding of the political role that ethnography plays, see Shdaimah, Stahl, and Schram, this volume.

PART THREE

Ethnography's Varied Contributions

Part 3 lays bare some of the varied contributions ethnography has already made, showing that politics at the micro-level has its own dynamic, which is not reducible to, or deducible from, social structures or public policies. Rather, it is a realm of political activity that requires sustained study on its own terms.

In chapter 7, Katherine Cramer Walsh takes on a venerable tradition of public-opinion research (especially as it concerns the study of the United States) that relies on large-scale surveys. Without denying the value of this tradition, she reveals the importance of using ethnographic immersion based on participant observation to examine the micro-level processes of opinion formation. As she shows, our understanding of public opinion is not simply made richer via ethnography; it may in fact be fundamentally changed in the process.

In chapter 8, Michael Schatzberg takes insider perspectives to heart. Arguing that we should not stop with recognizing that Africans believe in witchcraft, thus "othering" a value-system that is different from our own, we instead should attempt faithfully to represent the Congolese perspective by—at least for a moment—believing what Africans believe about witchcraft. Schatzberg thus makes the strongest possible case for accepting the *prima facie* validity of insider viewpoints and then shows how fundamentally altered our conceptions of the "political" realm and causality become as a result. His argument is informed by a strongly ethnographic sensibility, which, in turn, was generated by years of fieldwork-based immersion.

In chapter 9, Cédric Jourde examines the value an ethnographic sensibility brings to the study of Islamism and regime type in West Africa. Jourde argues that ethnography need not mean participant observation. Instead, a sensibility that seeks to discover empirical and theoretical "blind spots" brings us closer to an understanding of political dynamics in the region. His chapter highlights just how limited our initial state of knowledge may be; open-minded, inductive inquiry based on an ethnographic sensibility can better ground our understanding of key political phenomena and simultaneously challenge received wisdom about them.

In chapter 10, Lorraine Bayard de Volo reflects on how two extremely different ethnographic research projects she has undertaken encourage a reconceptualization of where "politics" takes place. In the case of social mobilization in Nicaragua, she highlights the crucial political function that emotional engagement plays. In the case of casino cocktail waitresses in Nevada, she demonstrates how outsiders' preconceptions about power and gender relations can be misleading. Her relationship to the two communities being studied could scarcely be more different; yet each proves fruitful in producing ethnographic insights of fundamental significance to diverse literatures.

SEVEN

Scholars as Citizens: Studying Public Opinion through Ethnography

KATHERINE CRAMER WALSH

Public opinion is a force in its own right. As democrats we know this, or at least hope that it is true; we expect democratic governments to respect and respond to the opinions of the public far more than would be the case under other forms of government. And even though we are aware that political actors craft and manipulate public opinion in democracies (Jacobs and Page 2005; Jacobs and Shapiro 2000; Lippmann 1922), we also know that they do so in wary anticipation of that same public opinion. In this way, public opinion exerts power over what messages politicians attempt to convey (Key 1961).

At the same time that public opinion is a powerful political force, so, too, is our study of it. We exert power over public opinion, and this has consequences for politics. In this chapter, I discuss the power that scholars exert over how the public and political leaders perceive public opinion. I argue that using ethnography can help us check this power by giving the people we study more agency over the research situation. I do so by drawing on lessons learned from two ethnography-based studies, as well as surveys and conversations with several groups of midwestern state and provincial legislators. Insights gleaned from these studies suggest that inserting a bit of ethnography into the study of public opinion can reveal how the method of polling influences the conclusions we reach and can enlarge understanding of public opinion. It can also perhaps improve the balance between the dual roles we play as both citizens and scholars.

Public-Opinion Scholars' Power over the Public

Political scientists who study public opinion often walk a blurry line between scholar and practitioner. Many belong to the American Association of Public Opinion Researchers, whose membership includes journalists and professional pollsters, as well as academics. Also, many of us conduct state-wide political polls through our university survey labs—polls that journalists ask us to interpret for public consumption. The survey results often become political objects, as campaigns attempt to spin the results. The results affect perceptions of candidate viability and therefore perhaps the outcome of elections (Bartels 1988).

When we choose which topics to include on these surveys, we are also exerting power by proclaiming which issues are most important and deserve the attention of policymakers. For example, in recent U.S. elections, conservative groups or state legislatures have successfully placed initiatives concerning same-sex marriage on the ballot in many states.[1] Some people allege that this is a tactic intended to mobilize conservative voters to the polls (Dao 2004). If this is the case, and we draw more attention to an issue by including related questions in our polls, we are helping to promote a particular political agenda. At the same time, if we choose *not* to ask about these issues, we are supporting yet a different agenda.

Our work also affects perceptions of the role the public plays in political processes. For example, if we delay asking questions about significant social movements until those movements are well under way, we may contribute to the perception that such movements are spurred by elites, rather than by insurgent members of the public (Lee 2002). Since we have little survey-based information on attitudes toward the civil rights movement until after national-level political elites had made public pronouncements on related legislation, we have little data to test the idea that it was African American community leaders, and not members of Congress or White House administrations, who mobilized mass support for civil rights legislation.[2]

Also, the way we construct our surveys influences the picture of public opinion that results.[3] Given the widespread perception that public opinion is That Which Polls Measure, poll responses are taken as facts, not as snapshots in time gathered in a particular context. But this overlooks the influence that question-wording and order can have on respondents. Sometimes we alter the interpretation of public opinion through the alternatives we offer as responses. For example, the 2004 U.S. general election exit poll asked respondents, "Which ONE issue mattered most in deciding how you voted for President?" People were allowed to choose from the following list: "moral values, economy/jobs, terrorism, Iraq, health care, taxes and education." Twenty-two percent opted for "moral values," which led journalists to conclude that President George W. Bush was reelected by a public that was preoccupied with morality and attracted to the Republican Party because of its alliance with conservative Christians. Careful analyses conducted with the luxury of time and additional data showed this to be erroneous (Burden 2004; Langer and Cohen 2005), but that initial impression likely persists for many.

Scholars of public opinion exert power over the public because we have a great deal of control over a major mechanism by which the public communicates its opinions to people in government: public-opinion polls. The decisions we make about the conditions and terms of this communication are amplified through mass media, shaping how the public as well as political decision makers view the public will.

Is Public Opinion That Which Polls Measure?

The choices public-opinion scholars make in fielding surveys can have negative consequences, but they can also contribute invaluably to policymakers, the public, and other scholars. Scientifically conducted public-opinion polls are the most efficient way of capturing what a large population of people think about public issues. Skepticism about the ability of polls to accurately characterize public opinion is often overblown. People who are skeptical that a sample of a thousand people can accurately describe the opinions of a state, province, or an entire nation ought to tell their doctor to take all their blood (rather than a sample) the next time they have a blood test.[4]

Public-opinion polls also have value because they are easily replicable. The same questions can be asked of similar populations and at different points in time to accurately compare groups or gauge longitudinal change. Polling houses can minimize the effect of the interviewers through carefully training them to avoid interjecting any biasing information while reading questions or answering respondents' requests for clarification. In addition, surveys gather information quickly.

Surveys are also desirable for democratic reasons. Random-sampling methods ensure that surveys capture the voice of people who are unlikely to express their opinion through other channels, such as contacting public officials or writing letters to editors (Verba 1996). The publication of poll results may also allow some members of the public to recognize that they are not alone in their concerns, perhaps fostering collective action.[5]

By designing survey instruments thoughtfully and minimizing bias through careful sampling methods, public-opinion scholars can respect the public trust. We can also do this, though, by recognizing the merits of alternative methods of investigating public opinion. Currently, the study of public opinion is synonymous with conducting polls. For example, Brady and Collier, in their introductory chapter to a book *dedicated to qualitative methods* (which we might expect to be more open to ethnographic approaches), assume the study of public opinion *is* the practice of polling. In their call for shared standards across a variety of methodologies, they offer the following:

> These shared standards can facilitate recognition of common criteria for good research among scholars who use different tools. . . . By tools we mean the specific research procedures and practices employed by qualitative and quantitative researchers. . . . Methods of data collection are also tools: for example, *public opinion research*, focus groups, participant observation, event scoring, archival research, content analysis, the construction of "unobtrusive measures," and the systematic compilation of secondary sources. (Brady and Collier 2004, 7–8; emphasis added)

Even among scholars who welcome qualitative methods, public-opinion research is equated with public-opinion polling.

But is it the case that public opinion is that which polls measure? Historically, this was not always the case, and for a time this question was hotly debated (Kinder 1998, 780–82). Before mass-sample scientific surveys were common and reputable, people judged public opinion through other means. The Greeks determined public opinion through debate; the American colonists gauged it through pamphlets and newspapers (Glynn et al. 2004, chap. 2). With surveys on the horizon, some scholars anticipated that they would become synonymous with public opinion. Sociologist Herbert Blumer vehemently contested equating surveys with opinion, arguing that if the thing we wish to understand is the force that moves policy, then poll results are not a good measure. Instead, to him, public opinion emerged through competition among interest groups, and could not be measured by individuals voicing their thoughts in isolation (Blumer 1948). V. O. Key was less hostile to polls but nevertheless defined public opinion as "that which governments find it prudent to heed," a definition that does not automatically equate opinion with public-opinion surveys (1961, 14).

Sidney Verba refreshed this debate in 1995 by focusing his presidential address to the American Political Science Association on the merits of mass-sample survey polls. In the current era, polls have become inputs to governance—government actors *do* heed them. And Verba argued that this is perhaps a good thing: polls are egalitarian. In Blumer's time, what governments heard was a function of who had the resources and the mobilization to make their opinions known. But now, polls communicate a view of the public will that weights each member's views equally, or at least provides a better assessment of the views of a cross-section of the public than any other means of citizen activity (Verba 1996).[6]

The Difference Ethnography Makes

Most scholars continue to assume that public opinion is poll results. Yet there are alternative ways to conceptualize and study public opinion. Public-opinion polls do not capture everything, and in particular they do not capture how respondents *interpret* the issues they are asked to express opinions about.

Perhaps the people who know this best are those who actually conduct the polls—the interviewers. Ask anyone who has ever administered a public-opinion survey by a phone or face-to-face interview what such a job is like, and you will most likely hear stories about the reluctance of respondents to slot themselves into the provided categories, their frequent attempts to qualify or explain their responses, and how the comments respondents make between questions are often more fascinating than their answers to the questions themselves.

My own experience with face-to-face interviewing in graduate school opened my eyes to these aspects of polling and alerted me to the possibilities of ethnography. I conducted interviews for Kent Jennings and Laura Stoker's political socialization study in places my Wisconsin upbringing had not exposed me to: rural areas of Arkansas, Mississippi, and Virginia.[7] I interviewed people in their homes or their workplaces. During each interview, I heeded my interviewer training and stuck to the questions. But when the interview was over and the laptop cover was down, people would often elaborate on their responses and place their ideas in context for me. It made perfect sense to several of them, for example, to vote faithfully for Democrats, even though their policy stances pointed clearly toward the Republican Party. In the postinterview conversations, I was able to ask people how they conceptualized the Democratic Party, and how they understood their own affiliation with it.

Opinion scholars have used creative tactics to study these types of thoughts through surveys. They have employed stop-and-think probes, such as "Still thinking about the question you just answered, I'd like you to tell me what ideas came to mind as you were answering that question.

Exactly what went through your mind?" (Zaller and Feldman 1992, 587). Others have embedded in-depth interviewing techniques into mass-sample surveys to observe how responses shift or take on new shades when people are alerted to additional considerations (Chong 1993). These studies have gone a long way toward revealing the ambivalence underlying individuals' political attitudes and the effect that bringing to mind additional considerations can have on the positions people are willing to support.

But what I valued most about my postinterview conversations was that during this part of my visit, neither I nor the authors of the survey were setting the agenda or framing the range of possible responses. I was at these times primarily a listener and a guest in a person's home and community. As my hosts, they were in command, and they explained themselves to me in their own words. They strung their thoughts together in packages and structures that had meaning to them, if not necessarily to researchers designing a nationwide survey. What they said was inspired in part by the topics of the survey and likely influenced somewhat by the realization that I was a stranger with the authority conferred by a university survey center badge. However, they had the power to relate their personal histories to contemporary events in the manner and order that resonated with their own identities and perspectives. Also, in those conversations, people made frequent reference to their local geographic and political context, something that did not arise during their responses to the survey questions. Listening to how they contextualized their stances within a complex web of understanding moved me closer to explaining, not just describing, those stances.

Researchers could structure surveys to gather more of this type of information. They could instruct interviewers to supplement the data with rich observations of the place in which respondents live (in addition to the notes that face-to-face interviewers are often instructed to make about the nature of the dwelling and the neighborhood), and could strive for longer interview sessions that encourage and allow time to record respondents' own interpretations.

Rather than continuing to center the study of public opinion exclusively on the method of mass surveys, however, we have much to gain by more regularly using ethnography. By ethnography, I mean the act of spending time with people, as unobtrusively as possible, to listen to what individuals say and how members of groups interact with one another, in the settings in which they normally meet, under the conditions they set for themselves. I tend to call this participant observation, and I think of the balance between the two roles implied by that term in the following way: In this method, the researcher is enough of a participant that she has access to the people she wishes to study and is allowed to remain in the setting in which they meet, but she is mainly an observer. The term *ethnography* has historically been used to refer to the method of spending time immersed in a particular culture, such as the life of a particular neighborhood or community. But with respect to the study of public opinion, I use it to refer to intensive observation of the conversations and behavior among a group of people who congregate of their own accord. It need not entail following one or more of these people into all aspects of their daily lives. Instead, ethnography can be used to observe opinion expression by listening to what people say to one another when they are speaking in their own terms, on their own turf.

When researchers spend long periods of time with the people whose opinions they wish to study, they can make detailed observations about what these people value through noticing the way they spend their time and the topics they talk about and with whom. The result is a type of understanding that is not matched through other methods. When researchers' primary methods of gathering data are listening and observing, rather than administering questionnaires (whether structured or unstructured, closed- or open-ended), what they get is a reflection of behavior that the people have chosen to display. It is a reflection not only of issue preferences, but of agendas and the frameworks or perspectives through which people understand these issues. In other words, when we use ethnography, the people we study are no longer respondents or people who have been enticed to reveal a part of themselves. They *are* themselves, the selves they choose to portray in the environments they choose to place themselves in.

When I had finished interviewing for the Jennings and Stoker project, I began my dissertation research, aimed at investigating the way people interpret current affairs through informal conversations. My plan was to learn as much as possible about this from existing research and then use a mass-sample survey to further my knowledge about the process. I found that existing research on the role of conversations in political understanding was fascinating, but left open a host of questions, such as how these processes work in groups people form themselves, in settings of their own choosing (compare Gamson 1992).[8] So I asked long-time residents of the city I lived in at the time, Ann Arbor, Michigan, if they knew of a coffee shop or similar place where a group of people met regularly to spend time together. I started observing the activity of patrons in a neighborhood corner store many people had suggested, and eventually asked a group of regulars—a group of retired, white, predominantly white-collar men—if I could join them. I ended up studying them, and several other groups, for three years.

I gained access slowly to this group. I spent time in the store for approximately a month, gradually mustering the courage to ask for their consent to sit with them. As I watched their interactions, I noticed that when their coffee cups began to run dry, one of them would go behind the counter, grab the regular and decaf urns, and pour everyone a round. After several days, some of the patrons started stopping by my table to introduce themselves to me, and I got up the nerve to serve a round of coffee. As I did so, I explained that I was a social scientist studying informal groups and asked for their permission to join them. They welcomed me, albeit with some amusement that a young female wanted to join their group.

For the next three years, I would arrive at the place several days a week about 8:00 a.m., sit in one of the seats, and listen to their conversations. I participated mainly through body language, avoiding as much as possible inserting my own opinions. Occasionally, they would ask questions of me, and I would answer to the greatest extent possible without revealing that I was particularly interested in their conversations about politics (until the last stage of the study). After several months, they treated me like a member in some respects, such as asking me to sign group cards to ailing members of the group. However, I was still the one "writing the book" who was only in Ann Arbor temporarily. My gender alone signaled that my group membership was unique.[9]

Through conducting participant observation of this group, I was able to watch how the regulars, who called themselves "the Old Timers," collectively interpreted politics. Their sense of themselves as individuals and particularly as people of a similar "type"—their social identities—were a main tool they used to talk about current events. For example, someone would mention a local referendum, and they would talk about whether "people like us should vote for this." They would similarly talk about candidates in terms of whether or not they were people who were "like us" or who reflected their values.

To illuminate what ethnography can reveal in comparison to polls, we can look to the way they made sense of women in public life. When I spent time with them, they were represented in Congress by a female Democrat, Lynn Rivers. Their mayor was also a woman. They called themselves Republicans, described themselves as moderates or conservatives, and expressed rather traditional views about the place of women in public life. Many of these views were revealed when their conversations turned to me. They regularly puzzled over my marital status (single, during most of my fieldwork), and would segue from this into conversations about their daughters' and granddaughters' life choices.

The following is an example of one of their conversations about the role of women in society. On a January morning in 1998, Baxter asked Orville about his recent trip out to Pasadena, California, to watch the University of Michigan football team play in the Rose Bowl, and about his relatives whom he had run into at the airport.[10] Then Baxter asked about another of Orville's relatives, a prominent woman in the community who had kept her maiden name as her middle name.

SAM: Which name comes first?

MIKE: Well, it depends on the situation—she switches them around to her advantage.

HAROLD: Gee, it sounds like you've had contact with her. Did she [do business with the company you own]?

MIKE: No. . . . I wanted to ask her which one she was divorced from!! [Laughs with everybody]

BAXTER: My daughter, she uses both, too. Sometimes she is Susan Smith and sometimes she is Susan Wilson. I have a hard time knowing what her name is.

MIKE [sarcastically, to me, and I roll my eyes and smile]: These women have too many privileges.

BAXTER: At the Rose Bowl, they had a program listing all the people that were there with the Michigan delegation. You should have seen some of those names. All these asexual names. . . . don't know whether they are a man or a woman. Have to ask. Like "Leslie" or "Kelly."

HAROLD: My daughter's name is Kelly.

ORVILLE [to Baxter]: Well, like Tracy [referring to a mutual acquaintance].

BAXTER: That's right. It was [a family name], very common to do that.

In this conversation, the Old Timers talked skeptically about the use of maiden names, and Baxter related this to the use of asexual names. It seems that both were a violation of their sense of appropriate behavior or gender norms. In the context of this group, women were expected to take their husband's last name upon marriage, and they were expected to have traditional, feminine names.

A common theme in the Old Timers' conversations was that many of society's current ills could be traced to the fact that gender roles had been muddied, that more women had begun working outside the home, and that more children did not have a mother staying at home full time. These attitudes were steeped in their perspectives as lifetime Ann Arborites who had fought in wars, lived a self-labeled middle-class life, lived through rapid twentieth-century changes, and had experienced a time when "life was more simple."

These perspectives had implications for their attitudes toward gender-related public policies, such as affirmative action, and also for the way they made sense of public women like their congresswoman, their mayor, and Hillary Clinton. For example, on one June morning in 1998, someone mentioned "politics" and then the following conversation ensued:

AL: I have a joke to tell. . . . So Bill Clinton and Billy Graham die on the same day. Bill Clinton gets sent up to Heaven, and the preacher goes to Hell. St. Peter notices the mistake and so the two get sent to opposite places. On the way down, Bill sees Billy Graham and says, so what do you think? And Billy Graham says, well, I always wanted to meet the Virgin Mary. And Bill says, "Well, you're too late."

[Laughter, a few people tell other jokes, then Al adds the following:]

AL: Bill Clinton dies and goes to Heaven and he says to God, "I'm Bill Clinton, the President of the United States of America." And God says, "Oh, well sit right here (at his right-hand side)." And then Al Gore dies, goes to heaven and says, "I'm the Vice President of the United States of America," and God says, "Oh well sit right here (on his left side)." And then here comes this blond woman, gorgeously dressed, walks up to God and says, "I'm Hillary Rodham Clinton and you're in my seat!"

[Huge laughter.]

AL: Since [Hillary's] in office . . .

TIM: But she's not in office. . . .

AL: Well . . .

JAKE: You know, I just don't think that's right. . . . You can have influence, but to have her hand in things the way she does. . . .

AL: She's a smart person. . . .

JAKE: You know I think that once they're out of office, she's gone.

AL: You think so?

TIM: I don't know.

JAKE: Oh yeah, she's gone. . . . That is all for show.

AL: Well, I think she knows what she's doing. You know, I think we will never un-
derstand—maybe Kathy here will—what that lifestyle is like, what kind of things those people go through. She knew what she was doing when she met him at Yale, she knew where he was headed. . . .

JAKE: Yeah, I think so . . .

These men perceived Hillary Rodham Clinton as a threat to their traditional values, as representative of a lifestyle they did not understand and did not want their family members to emulate. They made sense of public figures like her through the lens of their identity as people of a different, "middle American" lifestyle.

Standard survey questions can get at this, but not as well as ethnography. During my fieldwork, I gave the Old Timers a survey to fill out by hand and return to me. The questions included items about their reasons for spending time in the corner store, political leanings, recent vote choices, and demographics, as well as their attitudes on a few specific issues. I distributed thirty-two of these questionnaires to the Old Timers, and received twenty-six back (for a response rate of 81 percent). One of the items I included was the standard seven-point scale used in the American National Election Studies about the proper role for women:

> Recently there has been a lot of talk about women's rights. Some people feel that women should have an equal role with men in running business, industry and government. Others feel that women's place is in the home. And other people have opinions somewhere in between. [The questionnaire then displayed a picture of a seven-point scale with the ends labeled with these views.] If you haven't thought much about this issue, please check here ___ and go to [the next question]. If you have thought about it where would you place yourself on this scale?

The scale ranged from 1 to 7, where 7 was the most conservative response, "Women's place is in the home." The average response on this scale among the Old Timers was a 3.12 (st. dev. = 1.45), a response slightly on the *liberal* end of the scale. Not a single respondent marked 6 or 7, the most conservative responses,[11] although their responses to other policy questions conveyed a strong conservative tendency in the group.

Over time, the percentage of people in national samples giving the more conservative responses to this question has declined.[12] Nevertheless, if I were to try to characterize attitudes about women's roles among the members of this group using this standard measure, I would conclude that these men held fairly moderate views about the place of women in society. But their conversations and their behavior strongly suggested otherwise. They were folks with traditional social views who regularly struggled with balancing the values they had espoused and lived by throughout their lives and the changing norms around them. Ethnography demonstrates this; cross-sectional public-opinion polls obscure it. If I had used only surveys, I would not necessarily have noticed that these people actively tried to figure out what behavior is appropriate for women in contemporary society, and I most certainly would not have been able to draw conclusions about *how* they did so, together.

Using ethnography can do more than allow us to see the people we study differently. It enables us to investigate different questions. In the fall of 2000 I learned about a city government initiative in Madison, Wisconsin, where I had just moved, that brought racially diverse groups of volunteers together to talk about race over repeated sessions with the guidance of a facilitator. Since I had conducted my project on informal political conversation mainly among racially homogeneous groups of people, I wanted to examine the effects of conversations within racially diverse groups. I worked with our local Urban League, which had been hired to administer the discussions, to conduct a pre-post comparison group survey study of the effects of the program on participants' attitudes and behaviors. (I also conducted a similar study of participants in the Aurora, Illinois, Community Study Circles.) We measured racial tolerance, self-reports of racial interaction, and interest in engaging in further community involvement. We found very little change, which was not surprising given that the participants were a self-selected group of already highly participatory and relatively racially tolerant people.

However, while administering the surveys, I also conducted participant observation in one of the Madison groups. Although the survey study suggested that very little happened to people as a result of their participation, the actual discussions suggested otherwise: it seemed that something important was going on. Fortunately, I was able to conduct participant observation of similar groups in other cities over extended periods of time (Walsh 2007). The surveys had allowed me to gauge individual attitudinal and behavioral change, but the ethnography alerted me to a different set of concerns. What actually happens when people in diverse groups talk face-to-face about race? How do they balance the strong pull toward unity in our political culture and the simultaneous desire to have their cultural identity recognized and respected? How, collectively, do they get each other to pay attention to difference and yet not exacerbate racial divides? These were questions with equally important consequences for our understanding of the place of interpersonal communication in civic life and the future of race relations, but I would not have thought to ask them if I had not directly observed this communication. Also, the answers were not accessible to me through survey methodology.

Ethnography as a Reflection of Practical Public Opinion

Ethnography can help us move closer to an understanding of public opinion because listening to and observing the expression of public opinion is how many political actors measure it themselves. In local and state politics, representatives rarely have the chance to examine opinions among their constituents through public-opinion polls. Sometimes citywide or statewide data are available, but even then, the number of cases is usually too small to provide insight on attitudes in a particular district. Susan Herbst's analysis of policy making in the Illinois state legislature demonstrates that most officeholders and staffers gauge public opinion through mass media content, interest groups, and direct contacts with constituents. Even when issue polls are available, staffers tend not to find them useful because they perceive that such polls "are used so selectively by the parties for rhetorical purposes," are unable to capture public sentiment on complex and rapidly changing issues, and are a "lowly and manipulative" tactic when fielded by interest groups. They are also skeptical of the results, given potential methodological problems. In addition, polls have little utility for many staffers since the results are rarely broken down by district (1998, 48–52).

In recent years, I have had the opportunity to talk with a group of midwestern state legislators about the way they gauge public opinion. The University of Wisconsin–Madison's La Follette School of Public Affairs and the Midwestern Legislative Conference of the Council of State Governments hold the Bowhay Institute for Legislative Leadership Development each summer for a select group of legislators from state and provincial legislatures in the United States and Canada. I taught a seminar on public-opinion polling and voter opinion formation to the legislators who attended this institute from 2002 to 2005. To prepare, I sent out a questionnaire to the participants asking several basic questions about their thoughts on public opinion and their constituencies, including, "Who are your constituents?" and "How do you determine what your constituents think or feel?"[13]

Their responses are a striking contrast to the prevailing operationalization of public opinion in political science literature. These legislators do not equate public opinion with polls. Across the four years that I taught this seminar, 103 legislators returned the preseminar questionnaires (or 71 percent of all participants). In response to the question, "How do you determine what your constituents think or feel?" only 22 (or 21 percent of the respondents) mentioned polling through responses such as "surveys,"

"surveys I place in the newspaper or on email," "survey in district newsletter," and "sent a survey to every household in the district."[14] Notably, these mentions were typically referring to informal, nonscientific surveys.[15]

However, 87 (or 84 percent) wrote that they determined what their constituents think or feel through talking directly with their constituents. Many mentioned contacts such as emails, telephone calls, surface mail, and faxes. But in these questionnaires, as well as in our discussions during the seminars, the most common method of gauging public opinion was through *listening to people in person*. For example, common responses included "door knocking," "visiting with my constituents," and "when I am out in the community attending events." Perhaps one participant put it most eloquently by writing: "I do a lot of PBWA, polling by walking around."

During the seminar, one legislator said that she actually recruited several trusted staffers to eavesdrop in coffee shops each morning—one in a more liberal setting, another in a more conservative setting—and then immediately report back what they had overheard.

When I asked the legislators during the seminar why they preferred talking and listening to people as a way of reading public opinion, they did not mention the prohibitive cost of polls. Instead, they stated things such as their desire to listen to the way people explain their opinions, to get a sense of "where people are coming from," to probe their opinions further, and to give themselves a chance to respond to their constituents' concerns. Even those who reported that they used surveys typically remarked that face-to-face interaction was a more effective means of gauging what was on their constituents' minds. One participant described these sentiments in his pre-seminar survey:

> A substantial amount of my information flow comes from other [representatives] in my party. In addition, we gather information from polling as well as by analyzing media stories. . . . Perhaps, most of all, nothing replaces talking to as many people from as many walks of life as possible.

Polls are invaluable because they allow public officials to get a sense of what a large cross-section of the public is thinking, but a common sentiment among these legislators was that *talking with people* provides richer and more useful data.

In other words, ethnography is not just a tool that social scientists interested in meaning-making processes can use to study public opinion: it is actually a mainstay of current political practice.[16] It is a basic part of the process of representation at the state level, and it is quite likely even more indispensable at lower levels of government. This is particularly notable when taking into account that almost all the elected officials in the United States serve at these lower levels of government.[17] If so much of the public opinion that actually matters for governance is what is expressed in face-to-face conversation, we would do well to pay more attention to what it looks like in this form.

Using Methods That Give Our "Subjects" More Agency over Our Research

One of the most often cited critiques of ethnography is that researchers become too emotionally attached to their subjects. I would like to turn this allegation on its head. All social scientists should strive for rigor in the sense of constantly justifying how we know what we say we know (Manna 2000), and continuously asking ourselves to consider alternative explanations and conclusions. But why is it inherently preferential to opt for methods in which we have no emotional attachment to the people we study or, as is typically the case in the field of public opinion, no actual personal interaction with them at all? At the most charitable level, the premise of such claims is that we should have analytical distance from the people we study. But what does this really mean? Often these claims seem to convey that we should be "above" our subjects, that we know more than they do, and that if we actually interact with them, our observations will be biased toward sympathy with their views or concerns.

Such sentiments bring us back to the dual role that many public-opinion researchers play as pollsters as well as scholars. Commonly, public-opinion poll results released by research universities are accused of exhibiting a liberal bias. Given this state of affairs, it seems self-defeating to contribute to the perception that we are separate from, or worse yet, above the public. Why not acknowledge that we, too, are part of the public, and that we have much to gain from treating our "subjects" as the arbiters of knowledge, rather than starting from the premise that people are ignorant?

One concrete way in which participant observation and polling could be fruitfully combined would be to use observation to generate questions for subsequent polls. For example, pollsters commonly decide which public policy topics to ask about by taking account of issues at the top of the news agenda and asking public officials, staffers, and journalists for information on emerging topics. An alternative way to decide which issues to ask about is to physically visit communities across the geographic area we sample from and listen to the concerns people express in the course of their daily lives. Given that news media regularly cover poll results, and this news constrains what issues policymakers can avoid and what they must attend to, generating poll content in this manner would confer some agenda-setting power on members of the public.[18] Also, merging polling and observation in this manner simultaneously capitalizes on the unique capacity of the method of observation to uncover unrecognized concerns and the ability of polls to characterize stances across a population quickly.

If we spent some time as participant observers, we might find that the viewpoints through which people interpret the political world have merit. We lead ourselves toward a particular set of conclusions by assuming that people are less expert than we are. Why not start from the realization that we do not see the world through the same lens as many of the people we study, and *try* to develop sympathy for those perspectives? We might move closer to understanding, for example, a puzzle that is currently high on the agenda of political pundits and scholars: how people can seemingly vote against their own economic interests (Frank 2005; Bartels 2006). From the viewpoint of a political scientist with ready access to information about public officials' stances and about the likely beneficiaries of different policy platforms, we might conclude that people make ill-informed choices.[19] But if we listen to the way people understand their votes or policy preferences, we might conclude otherwise. Are they really not making sensible choices? Or are they just making choices that do not make sense through the perspectives that we assume are appropriate?

As scholars, we exert power over the rest of the public through the manner in which we study public opinion. We do this regardless of the methods we choose, at a minimum, through our choices about what is worthy of attention. But we are also fellow citizens, and can respect that role by occasionally turning to methods that partially reverse this hierarchy. There is wisdom in the public, in the ordinary person, and the ordinary community, and the arrogance in assuming otherwise interferes with the quest for knowledge we profess to have mastered.

Notes

My sincere thanks to Joe Soss and participants of the Political Ethnography workshop, especially Edward Schatz, Elisabeth King, and Marie-Joelle Zahar, for feedback on an earlier version of this paper.

1. For example, in the 2004 general election, voters in Arkansas, Georgia, Kentucky, Michigan, Mississippi, Montana, North Dakota, Ohio, Oklahoma, Oregon, and Utah voted to adopt amendments to their state constitution that effectively ban

same-sex marriage. Arizona, Colorado, Idaho, South Carolina, South Dakota, Tennessee, Virginia, and Wisconsin voters decided on similar measures in November 2006. All passed except the Arizona referendum. In November 2008, Arizona passed such a referendum, along with Florida and California.

2. See Lee (2002) for an innovative use of letters written to U.S. presidents as a way of circumventing this lack of data.

3. See, for example, Schuman and Presser (1981); Rasinski (1989); Lockerbie and Borrelli (1990); Jacoby (2000).

4. Thanks to Ken Goldstein for passing along this wisdom from CBS News to me.

5. My gratitude to Lisa Wedeen for making this point.

6. Verba granted that polls are not perfectly representative. An important example of this comes from recent work demonstrating that people with fewer resources are less likely to make their opinions known in surveys (Berinsky 2004) and less likely to be included in public-opinion polls in the first place (Brehm 1993).

7. In 1965 the study interviewed a nationally representative group of people who were high-school seniors at the time, as well as their parents. They were reinterviewed in 1973, 1982, and 1997. Their parents were reinterviewed in 1973 and 1982 as well. Spouses of the class of 1965 were interviewed in 1973, 1982, and 1997, and offspring were interviewed in 1997. See, for example, Stoker and Jennings (2005).

8. Focus groups cannot achieve the objectives I am striving for here. I am advocating research that investigates public opinion as it is expressed among people who meet of their own accord or in the settings of their everyday life (e.g., their workplaces), and it is expressed on their own time (not structured to fit the constraints of a two-hour focus group session).

9. See Walsh (2004) for full details of the study.

10. I use pseudonyms for the people in this study to protect their confidentiality.

11. Two of the respondents did not answer this question.

12. In 1972, 23 percent of the electorate gave one of these most conservative responses, but in 2004, only 7 percent did so. For full results see http://www.electionstudies .org/nesguide/toptable/tab4c_1.htm.

13. In 2002 I asked the second question using different wording: "When you have made a statement about what your constituents think or feel, what sources and types of information fed into that claim?"

14. It is possible that if this question were asked of people who represent larger constituencies (e.g., U.S. governors, senators, or members of the U.S. House of Representatives), the percentage stating that they rely on polls would be larger. Even at that level, however, representatives do not have the resources to conduct polls of their constituents on all issues on which they must decide.

15. By nonscientific, I mean surveys in which the respondents choose whether or not they are going to be a part of the sample (e.g., by choosing to send the newsletter), rather than a pollster sampling the respondents through a method in which each person in the target population has a known non-zero probability of being included in the poll.

16. The use of "PBWA" is most apparent at the state and local level, but the behavior documented in Fenno's *Homestyle* (1978) suggests it has been (and most likely still is) a staple of congressional governance as well.

17. According to the 1992 Census of Governments conducted by the U.S. Census Bureau, more than 96 percent of all elected officials serve at the local level (Macedo et al. 2005, 66).

18. In the summer of 2007, I began generating questions for the University of Wisconsin's statewide Badger Poll in this manner, through the generosity of an Ira and Ineva Reilly Baldwin Wisconsin Idea Endowment Grant.

19. Bartels (2006) demonstrates that the claims that working-class white voters have defected to the Republican Party are greatly overstated, if not largely mistaken. However, for additional evidence of the seeming dissonance between policy preferences and policy choices, see Bartels (2005).

EIGHT

Ethnography and Causality: Sorcery and Popular Culture in the Congo

MICHAEL G. SCHATZBERG

One advantage of an ethnographic sensibility is that it enables social scientists to glean insider perspectives and then take them seriously in constructing explanations. In so doing it also permits us to transcend some of the parochialism inherent in our ostensibly universal theories. Although this chapter is not itself based directly on participant-observation fieldwork, it is firmly anchored in the perspectives and orientations I have acquired by having done such work in the Congo (and also in Cameroon, Kenya, Senegal, and Uganda) over the past three decades.[1] Politics in the Democratic Republic of the Congo (DRC, formerly Zaïre) has always created difficulties for even the most robust theoretical frameworks. The Congo's size and diversity, and the complexity of its political life, have usually defied parsimonious explanation. Empirical complexity, however, is only one reason why our theories have not delivered on their promises. A second reason is even more germane. Put simply, most of the theoretical frameworks that Western social scientists have generated make implicit culturally based assumptions about causality and explanation, about the parameters of the political, and about the nature of power itself. And while these assumptions might make perfect sense in the cultural contexts in which they were originally derived, when confronted with Congolese realities, they are often either seriously incomplete or slightly out of focus. Moreover, this lack of theoretical acuity has obscured the empirical complexities and ambiguities of how people understand political causation in their daily lives.

Among the most pervasive of these culturally implicit assumptions is that all peoples share the same understandings of political causation. This chapter contends that this is wrong. Moreover, I also argue that one of the great advantages of an ethnographic sensibility is an awareness of how culture and context shape the perceptions of individuals as well as their orientations toward politics and political life. Unless we understand how the people whom we study interpret causal phenomena, we shall never be able to explore the wellspring of political behavior and the causal forces and calculations that drive individual political actors. The epistemological implications of this for Western social science theories, and especially for political science, are serious. Starkly put, scholars need to pay more attention than we have done to ascertaining whether there is a proper fit between our own theoretical assumptions about causation, on the one hand, and the alternative causal modes that the people they study actually employ, on the other. In a probabilistic world, the closer the fit, the more likely a theory will explain and perhaps even predict behaviors successfully. Various contemporary strands of social science theory thus need to accommodate, better than they have done thus far, the different alternative causalities that many individuals employ regularly.

Three Causal Modes

In Congo, as in much of the region I have called "Middle Africa" (which also includes Senegal, Côte d'Ivoire, Ghana, Nigeria, Cameroon, Kenya, and Tanzania), ordinary individuals, as well as sophisticated and powerful politicians, harbor complex and contextually sensitive mixtures of different modes of political causality. (A mode of causality is simply an implicit conceptual template that privileges a specific causal factor, such as the maximization of interests, divine intervention, sorcery, or, for those who may favor astrology, the location and movement of the heavenly bodies.) People display, in other words, several alternative understandings of the causal forces shaping political life. As we shall see, in this regard Congolese are no different from anyone else. For them, three modes of political causality seem particularly relevant.

First, there is the contemporary, modern, and scientific understanding of causality. During DRC's political liberalization of the early 1990s, for example, Bishop Monsengwo (1992, 5) addressed the reopening of the Sovereign National Conference in these terms: "On the contrary, we ourselves have not even yet begun, as a Sovereign National Conference, the serene self-criticism of our past, the reading of our history to discover the objective causes of the bankruptcy of our society so as to avoid them in the construction of our new political system."[2] Here we find implicit assumptions that there are "objective causes," that we may discover and then study them, and that such newly acquired knowledge can be used to construct solutions for the problems that have troubled society in the past. The rational relation of means to ends, the belief in the possibility of progress, and a notion of the validity of scientific or objective thought as a way to achieve this progress all undergird the bishop's remarks. So deeply entrenched in the very mission and procedures of the social sciences is this mode of causality that we rarely, if ever, question its fundamental assumptions. Like the air we breathe, it is simply part of the environment that we take for granted, without question, unless there is something so anomalous that we are forced to reevaluate our preconceptions. Furthermore, it is this contemporary scientific mode that most social science simply takes for granted and assumes, unthinkingly, to be universally applicable.

A second understanding of political causality is broadly spiritual and often pertains to the teachings and doctrines of the world's major religions. In some cases, believers express this in a manner so that political or economic actions and their consequences flow naturally from either sin or virtuous behavior. In January 1992 the Assembly of Kinshasa (Catholic) Abbés (Abbés Kinois 1992, 3) conveyed a message from the pulpit of the Cathedral of Notre-Dame. Part of it follows:

> How sad it is to have to ascertain that the political options taken by our society have been for a society without God. From whence [comes] the suppression of courses of religion, a bad conception of secularity, inversion of values, return to magical [*fétichistes*] practices, paganism, and the cult of personality. All that has thrust us into a material and mental underdevelopment such that the country has truly become a Zaïre victimized by disaster. Underdevelopment is always the expression of sin . . . [while] the project of the Creator by definition tends toward an improved condition, a superior condition.

In this vision the causal explanation of underdevelopment has less to do with comparative advantage, good governance, or another human-made, theoretically generated "objective" cause than it does with the violation of God's laws. In addition, when resorting to this mode of causal understanding, people will often invoke a vision of either the deity or the devil to explain a political phenomenon.

Sorcery, the darker side of power, is the third and final mode of causality, and will occupy most of our attention here. Many Congolese understand sorcery as a mode of causality because they are persuaded that it influences daily events and national politics. People in all spheres of activity, and at all levels of education and wealth, are sure that sorcerers and spirits play an important role in everyday life, influencing larger political outcomes and affecting individual life chances. A means of effecting certain outcomes in the material world by actively precipitating the intervention of the spirit world, sorcery might well be instrumental in finding a spouse, obtaining a promotion, or even winning the lottery. Like the second mode of causality, sorcery is also broadly spiritual in that it refers to the ability of certain individuals to harness powers that lie beyond the realm of material life. These spiritual forces also generally elude the doctrinal reach and effective competence of the world's great religions, whose adepts often dismiss them as mere superstition. Sorcery is a notoriously difficult term to define precisely, and I shall not spend much time doing it here.[3] Writing of witchcraft (I shall use the terms *witchcraft* and *sorcery* interchangeably), one Kenyan legal scholar (Mutungi 1977, 9) defined the concept and those who practice it as a "supernatural power" and "people who are possessed of, and practise such power," respectively. Sorcery is also about the spiritual aspects of pain and explanation—causing pain to others and explaining things to oneself. And, in some contexts, it is a means not only of causing pain but of protecting oneself and one's family from the pain and spiritual aggression of others. One initial example will suffice.[4] In the mid-1980s, an article in the sports section of a Kinshasa daily, *Elima*, noted that things in the city of Kisangani were getting out of hand. The article (Nsasse 1984,13) related that:

> Decidedly, it will not be soon that we shall see our football divorced from magical practices. In Afkis [the Kisangani football association], the open practice of [using] *gris-gris* [magical charms] has gone beyond the tolerable. [And] that in the view and in the knowledge of the referees and the directors of this association. . . . A recent case: Armed with great nerve, a director of a team began pouring more than a liter and a half of blood contained in a white plastic receptacle on the floor of the corridor of the locker rooms. Everyone who was to take his place on the platform of honor at Lumumba Stadium had to walk over it. . . . Evidently, the players of the opposing team had to walk over it, for the area is an obligatory passage to reach the field.

The intent, and the logic, appears to have been that if the opposing players trod through the blood, then the spell or magical properties of the blood would throw them off their game. The match ended in a one-one tie, and the journalist noted that the team that had resorted to the dark arts did not play particularly well. Nevertheless, the mode of causal understanding is clear: The match does not go to the team with the best players employing the latest training techniques and coaching strategies (the scientific mode); nor does it go to the team that seeks an invocation from a priest, pastor, or imam (the religious mode); rather it goes to the team that employs the most powerful sorcerer who is able to bewitch the members of the other side. As we shall see, although such beliefs and practices permeate virtually all spheres of activity, the sports pages—and especially the coverage of football—are important because sports is one of the few sociopolitical sites in Africa where one finds a relatively open and lively discussion of the occult.

To render these three alternative modes of causality more vivid, let us consider an election. The contemporary scientific understanding of political causality might proclaim that Joseph Kabila won Congo's 2006 presidential election because voters deemed that his party's platform and his personal attributes and demeanor offered the best chance of bringing peace and prosperity to the country. Or they might have decided to vote for Kabila because he was the candidate they thought would do the most for them personally. In either case, however, the causal logic is scientific in that voters know that certain actions and conditions have predictable consequences and that cause is easily related to effect. The religious mode of political causality would view the returns of this or any particular election as the direct result of God's will or intervention. And the third mode of understanding political causality would see, and explain, the election returns as a consequence of President Kabila enlisting enough of the most powerful sorcerers to have been decisive.

Congolese apply these three alternative modes of understanding causality to explain life's daily events as well as more remote instances of high politics. Furthermore, these alternative modes of explanation are certainly not mutually exclusive. There is a flexible ambiguity at work. People simultaneously hold complex, inconsistent, and often contradictory views on the nature of causality, weaving them together in a manner to emphasize different causal understandings in different contexts. In some circumstances they will see a political event as the result of a rational and predictable concatenation of events; in others, they will explain a political event as a consequence of divine intervention; in yet another, they will have no trouble accepting that the incantation of a powerful sorcerer caused a particular event. So it should not surprise us, to return briefly to one of the examples cited above, that Bishop Monsengwo could feel quite comfortable adopting a scientific understanding of political causality.

Congolese, in other words, choose from among these three modes of understanding and interpreting political causality. Their choice of a precise mode is usually a consequence of the specific political or economic context. At certain times, therefore, politicians will act on the basis of a scientific mode of causality—as, for example, when they are interacting with representatives of the World Bank. At other junctures they may act, and reason, on the basis of a religious mode of causality. It is God's will that Congolese remain impoverished because they have sinned. At still other moments they may resort to hiring sorcerers to enhance their hold on power. These three modes of political causality coexist and are not mutually exclusive. Depending on the context, one may come to the fore rather than another. In addition, and to make matters even more complex, these alternative modes of causality often blend into one another. Most of us do not even stop to think about this conceptual blending and switching, and we are usually unaware that we are doing it (Fauconnier and Turner 2002). Clearly, such alternative causalities and modes of causal understanding do not "fit" into the causal reckonings of most empirical social science. Yet equally clearly, people believe in them, act upon them, and both understand and explain their political world as being subject to their causal influences. The influence of these alternative causalities will simply be implicitly understood as commonsensical and intuitive.

Two caveats need attention. First, Congolese are not unique in this regard. If one looks closely enough, various alternative causalities may be found to coexist in virtually all societies, even those that pride themselves on being at the technological and scientific cutting edge. And second, although I have chosen to present these three alternative modes of causal understanding because of their political relevance for the Congo, one should not assume that these are the only three that exist either in this part of Africa or, for that matter, elsewhere. Two examples from the United States should suffice.

In the waning days of the Reagan administration (1981–89), Donald Regan—President Ronald Reagan's former secretary of the Treasury and White House chief of staff—was forced out of office. By his own admission somewhat bitter about his experiences in government service, this former chairman of the board and CEO of the financial conglomerate Merrill Lynch published a scathing memoir of his frustrations in the White House. In his own words (Regan 1988, 3–4):

> Virtually every major move and decision the Reagans made during my time as White House Chief of Staff was cleared in advance with a woman in San Francisco who drew up horoscopes to make certain that the planets were in favorable alignment for the enterprise. . . . Although I never met this seer— Mrs. Reagan passed along her prognostications to me after conferring with her on the telephone—she had become such a factor in my work, and in the highest affairs of the nation, that at one point I kept a color-coded cal-

endar on my desk (numerals highlighted in green ink for "good" days, red for "bad" days, yellow for "iffy" days) as an aid to remembering when it was propitious to move the President of the United States from one place to another, or schedule him to speak in public, or commence negotiations with a foreign power.

Former Secretary Regan (1988, 74) then suggested that this delegation of control over the president's calendar was critical because "the President's schedule is the single most potent tool in the White House, because it determines what the most powerful man in the world is going to do and when he is going to do it."

The second U.S. example occurred shortly after 11 September 2001, when Reverend Jerry Falwell appeared on Pat Robertson's Christian Broadcasting Network television program, *The 700 Club*. A partial transcript (Mann 2001, C8) of their remarks on 13 September 2001 follows:

FALWELL: I agree totally with you that the Lord has protected us so wonderfully these 225 years. . . . I fear . . . This is only the beginning. And with biological warfare available to these monsters . . . what we saw on Tuesday, as terrible as it is, could be minuscule if . . . God continues to lift the curtain and allow the enemies of America to give us probably what we deserve.

ROBERTSON: Jerry, that's my feeling.

FALWELL: The ACLU's got to take a lot of blame for this.

ROBERTSON: Well, yes.

FALWELL: And, I know that I'll hear from them for this. But, throwing God out successfully with the help of the federal court system, throwing God out of the public square, out of the schools—the abortionists have got to bear some burden for this because God will not be mocked. And when we destroy 40 million innocent babies, we make God mad. I really believe that the pagans and the abortionists and the feminists and the gays and lesbians who are actually trying to make that an alternative lifestyle, the ACLU, People for the American Way—all of them who have tried to secularize America—I point the finger in their face and say, "You helped this happen."

ROBERTSON: Well, I totally concur.

It can almost go without saying that each example displays an alternative understanding of political causality. The Reagans ran the White House with the aid of an astrologer; Reverends Falwell and Robertson believed the terrorist attacks had occurred because God had withdrawn his mantle of protection because of his displeasure with "alternative lifestyles."

Sorcery and Daily Life

Sorcery is ubiquitous and thus banal in the DRC. Daily life is filled with instances of people at all levels of the social, political, economic, and educational hierarchies resorting to these practices. One columnist (Mamounia 1984, 2) put it this way: "Sorcery is a universal phenomenon. Certain people possess, in effect, supernatural gifts, mysterious powers that they can put in the service of good or evil. Sorcery is spoken of when these powers are placed in the service of evil with the unique goal of hurting the entourage. That is why the population takes vengeance against the evil-doer when he is unmasked." Two of the pillars of popular culture in this part of the world, soccer and beer, illustrate admirably sorcery's centrality in daily life.

Soccer

On 14 June 1984 Bobutaka, the celebrated striker and high scorer of Congo's Vita Club, died in the middle of a match against Matonge when he was tackled by the goalkeeper just as he was about to score a goal. One of the subsequent commentaries in the press began with the headline query, "Who Killed Bobo?" To be sure, the press coverage explored why there was no ambulance on the field, why other medical facilities were lacking, why team authorities permitted Bobo to play even though he had been suffering from headaches for several days, and why the terrain was so uneven. It also mentioned the "mentality" of the players and the team officials, a veiled reference to occult forces. Despite the attention to these diverse factors, it is nonetheless significant that the headline query was not "Why did Bobo die?"; not "How did Bobo die?"; not "What caused Bobo's death?"; but "Who killed Bobo?" That the press would pose the question in this manner speaks to the salience of sorcery in the world of Congolese soccer (Monsa and Kitemona 1984, 8; Kitemona 1984, 16). In searching for the causes of Bobo's death, the headline may be read either to indicate a primary belief in malevolent agency rather than in a scientific understanding of disease, or a religious understanding of divine predestination and providence. Under the assumptions of either mode of causality, there is room for neither coincidence nor chance. In consequence, explanations emphasizing conspiracy also abound.

The influence of the occult on soccer has long been a subject of lively debate and concern throughout most of Africa. On one level, all governments subscribe to the international rules and standards that categorically prohibit such practices. On another level, however, especially when there are international championships at stake, high-ranking government officials either look the other way or cooperate actively in facilitating the presence of sorcerers in the game. This has occasioned much debate.

In virtually every African state, sorcery is strictly forbidden in the realm of sports. Various international governing bodies prohibit it; no state wishes to see its teams disqualified from international competitions because of it. Most states usually delegate the enforcement of these rules either to the Ministry of Sports or to the local football federation that organizes competition between clubs in the first division and is ultimately responsible for the selection of a national team to represent the country in international competitions. For example, the Congolese Ministry of Sports published the official rules of its football championships in 1980. They were unambiguous on the question of sorcery, and the banner headline read "Magical [*Fétichistes*] Practices are Prohibited!" Article 12 was formal on the subject: "Any club surprised in flagrante delicto of fetishistic practice as much on the field as in the sporting installations will lose the match by forfeit. Whoever observes a case of fetishistic practice on the field, in the sporting installations (halls, toilets, locker rooms, locales, etc.) or in the immediate vicinity of these must instantly inform the commissioner of the match who will proceed to the verification of the facts and will make note of them in his report" (Anonymous 1980, 15).

The Congolese measures were well in line with the international prohibitions of the day, but the ban was never really enforced, and this remains the situation today (Schatzberg 2006). If the rules and legislation prohibiting sorcery are clear, and they are, it is equally clear that they have usually been honored only in the breach. These practices mask a host of beliefs and social tensions that social scientists cannot dismiss lightly. In the 1970s and 1980s it was both well known and generally assumed that major football clubs sought the assistance of gifted sorcerers. One critical commentary from the early 1980s noted that belief in magical charms was widespread because there were "naive people" who put their faith in their "mysterious efficacity." The article lamented that among the believers in such matters were political cadres and even intellectuals, and that most clubs in Kinshasa had formed "research committees" to find individuals who, for a serious sum, could harness the occult to facilitate happy results for the club. Once the right person was found, the mysteries of the spirit world resided in the pockets of the players, in magic handkerchiefs, and in pots that were jealously guarded in the locker rooms. These things, the author lamented, rather than training and hard work, now dominated the Kinshasa football league (Mukaku 1983,10). Indeed, this trend survived the demise of the predatory Mobutu regime that lasted for more than thirty years (1965–97). In 1998, for example, the sports ministry urged its national soccer team to avoid magic charms and sorcerers in the competitions for the Africa Nations Cup. The cabinet director at the ministry, Emmanuel Mukaz, urged the team to respect the Ten Commandments, to perform honest work, and not to touch any fetish. He added, "There is plenty of proof that fetishes cannot help us win. For example, during the World Cup in 1974 a whole plane was sent filled with witch doctors and it created a lot of trouble" (Reuters 1998). Of course, such a statement would not have been necessary had the ministry official been confident that his team was uninvolved in such practices. Equally interesting was that the official's remarks alluded implicitly to the three modes of political causation: Ten Commandments (religious mode), honest work (scientific mode), and fetishes (sorcery).

In the DRC, as elsewhere in Africa, the discourse surrounding the role of sorcery in soccer is extensive, appearing regularly in the sports pages and, occasionally, in popular literature. Although there are variations, many of the discussions describe in scathing terms the activities of the sorcerers while deploring their substantial influence. In general, they are ashamed of the image this presents to the outside world, and argue for a more "scientific" or "rational" approach to the game. Although this discourse is invariably written from the perspective of those who would like to abolish sorcery and is thus not a genuine debate, it nevertheless both frames and distinguishes clearly two distinct alternative understandings of causality.

The same one-sided discourse deploring the influence of sorcery and the spirit world on the world of soccer is also present in many accounts of Congolese football, and popular literature often echoes the press. One of Zamenga's (1975, 20) novels, *Sept frères et une soeur* (Seven Brothers and a Sister), describes a football match in the following way:

The suspense was total with ten minutes left: the two teams were still tied. Who is going to win? In the two blocs thus formed, one noticed with surprise beings dressed strangely in raffia [a fiber of the palm tree]. They could be seen spitting mouthfuls of palm wine mixed with chewed kola nuts; at certain times, one could see a type of mud leaving their mouths that they spit in the direction of the players. It was whispered that these bizarre beings were the representatives of some very celebrated *nganga nkisi*, or fetishers. Thanks to their magic, the *nganga nkisi* made the legs of the players that they supported lighter, more supple, and also quicker than those of the others which got heavier, becoming incapable of scoring a goal.

The press blamed officials of the Kinshasa Football League (LIFKIN) for such sorry spectacles as the one Zamenga describes above. "Since instead of using its authority to block the road to the grave-diggers of our football who camouflage themselves behind chimerical practices, LIFKIN seems to act in connivance with them. We have for proof football matches played at the 20th of May Stadium during which the locker rooms are taken by the assault of armies of sorcerers" (N. K. 1983, 16). After reiterating that success in sports rests with serious training rather than with "charlatans," one commentary castigated a "dishonoring" display that occurred during the half-time of a major match between two of the dominant teams in the league (Vita and Imana). "The lawn momentarily liberated by the players was, in effect, invaded by imposters who paraded with an infernal rhythm, going out and then returning in turn, one with a goblet, one with a packet of fetishes that they ostentatiously dumped in the goals. Even the poor nets would have given in under the snout thrusts that these 'nganga' inflicted on them" (M'Vuma 1983, 8).

One Congolese football coach (Lusadusu 1984, 15) with a degree in physical education argued that fetishes and magical charms just were not going to do the trick when the country was confronting "technically evolved football." And according to this particular observer, the deep belief in the influence of sorcery was a cause for concern among those who possessed "a scientific vision" of the future of football. A Congolese social scientist (Koba 1985, 46), however, noted that those involved in the various facets of football may not actually perceive a dichotomous opposition between a belief in sorcery and a more scientific approach to the game. "Major sports teams see there [in sorcery] the key to their victory to the point that before an important sporting event, they will retire from the course of habitual life accompanied by a fetisher who completes, through mystical and spiritual training, the tactical and technical training which has already been accomplished."

Beer

Beer is intimately integrated into the Congo's political life and popular culture, in both rural and urban areas (Schatzberg 1981). At least in retrospect, therefore, it was not entirely surprising when beer attracted some attention during the period of political liberalization (1990–97) in the waning days of the Mobutu regime. This period of the DRC's history featured the birth of a relatively unfettered press, the introduction of limited multi-partyism, and the defection of many barons of the old political order. One of these defectors, Sakombi Inongo, had served the Mobutu regime loyally and faithfully for years, often at the pinnacle of power. Sakombi's defection took a religious turn in the early 1990s after he was visited by God. He then founded a church and devoted himself to a series of public testimonies to expose the old regime's excesses.

In April 1992, two years after the political opening, a newly penitent Sakombi came forward. At a "national day of repentance" organized by prayer groups and independent ministries of the city of Kinshasa, the former Mobutist baron and erstwhile defender of the old order bore witness to his involvement in the state's abuses, naming names and providing details of many of the regime's extraordinary practices. Such public confessions are not unique to Congo, and throughout the 1990s we witnessed similar phenomena in South Africa and other postauthoritarian societies. At an open-air gathering of roughly ten thousand people, Sakombi spoke of the political importance of sorcery at the highest levels of the Mobutu regime.

A contrite Sakombi (1992, 9) maintained that beginning around 1971, Mobutu had cast a series of satanic spells on the people of the Congo, which kept them politically quiescent, their loyalty to his regime unquestioned and assured. He testified that the regime had dumped tons of "mystical products" into the River Congo at its source in Katanga to achieve this political effect. Furthermore, according to the former minister, this scheme was why the regime had banned the importation of all foreign beers from 1976 to 1978. In this manner, even the wealthy, who could afford to buy imported beer, would be obliged to drink the local products and would thus be politically bound to Mobutu and incapable of posing a threat to his continued rule.

Political scientists rarely consider these sorts of data and generally assume a political world governed by a different set of causal forces. As a case in point, my own earlier fascination with the political economy of beer in the town of Lisala certainly operated in light of a different understanding of political causality. While I did note that "political legitimacy and stable beer prices would thus seem to go hand in hand," the explanatory causal connection emphasized that—in the words of a bureaucratic memorandum—the "stability of these [beer] prices ensures the confidence of the population in the Father of the Nation" and that political unrest might ensue if people did not have an assured supply of beer because important aspects of local social life, such as weddings (bridewealth), funerals, and just plain socializing, depended on it. If the beer did not flow, then people might become unhappy and blame the government. The causal link, in other words, was a political-economic one between an ample supply of cheaply priced beer and political quiescence (Schatzberg 1980, 86). But immediately after reading Sakombi's testimony, a plausible alternative hypothesis suddenly appeared, linking beer to both political quiescence and political legitimacy in a way that was entirely independent of the beer-and-circuses hypothesis. There were displayed, in other words, two entirely different explanations based on two alternative modes of understanding political causality.

Both my logic and my unstated and unexamined assumptions about causality were the same as far as the international dimension of the question was concerned. Although I wrote nothing directly about the ban on the importation of foreign beers, the following comment illustrates my thoughts at that time. "From a national perspective, beer-belly dependency poses a dilemma for the regime in power. Zaire cannot afford to spend $15 million per year on its beer industry [for imports of hops and malt] at a time of financial crisis. Such expenditures do nothing to end the crisis and contribute to a further evaporation of the state's precious supply of hard currency" (Schatzberg 1984, 297).

My analyses were not wrong, but they were incomplete, missing as they did a significant dimension of the politics of beer. Moreover, I would now also maintain that the reason they were incomplete was because the theoretical orientations I was immersed in (political economy, social class dynamics, bureaucratic politics, cultural pluralism) all shared a dual shortcoming. First, they simply did not consider the possibility that sorcery was important to understanding politics at the national level. Sorcery, after all, was beyond the parameters of the political as they were implicitly understood in most Western social science. And second, they failed to recognize, even as a hypothetical possibility, that Congolese political actors operated, at least part of the time, in a world with a substantially different understanding of causality and causal forces than most Western social and political scientists possess (Bockie 1993; Blier 1995). Once in the field, buried in Lisala's bars, I gradually learned the important effects of sorcery and spirits on local life (Schatzberg 1974–75, 72).[5] The prevailing scholarly paradigms, however, assumed a different universe of political causality— one that neither conceived of the possibility nor encouraged the application of this localized knowledge of sorcery to the realm of social-scientific explanation.[6] Had I been more attuned to the importance of sorcery as an alternative mode of causality, I might well have sought to explain—at least in part—the politics of the 1973 Zaïrianization of the economy in those terms. The local acquirers might have made use of the dark arts to ensure that they would be among those chosen to take over the European-owned commercial houses. They might also have explained their success, or failure, in those terms. But that hypothesis simply did not occur to me (Schatzberg 1980, 121–52). So "natural," so powerful, so hegemonic are the unstated assumptions of causality in the prevailing paradigms, that it never dawned on me that this was something worth questioning. Nor did it occur to me that there could be one or more alternative causalities.

Different Data, Other Analyses

Sakombi's testimony, and the entire thrust of this chapter emphasizing the banality of sorcery and its pervasiveness in Congolese life, raises several possible objections. First, some might object that this analysis, as well as any analysis based on an ethnographic sensibility, is too anecdotal. There are two lines of response to this criticism. Charles Jones (1989, 981–82) advances the first in a review essay dealing with some of the memoirs that emerged from the Reagan administration. Writing in the context of the United States, Jones argues that when they are done well, memoirs (such as Donald Regan's) can provide previously unknown details on important political events; they can illustrate the strategic thinking of an administration; they can show the interactions among high-ranking policymakers; and they can offer perspectives on the political elite that differ from those in the media. Although Jones deplores the specific problem of the "inside tidbit," such as the revelation of astrology in the White House, he still argues that memoirs should not be dismissed out of hand. His position is ultimately one of skeptical mistrust that requires verification, a stance whose scholarly caution I appreciate.

A second response to the charge of "anecdotalism" is simply to ask, "What are data?" Data, of course, do not exist independently of the theories that generate them and order them into meaningful theoretical and explanatory patterns. Our tendency, therefore, would be to dismiss Sakombi's testimony when it provides information that our usual theories of political behavior cannot account for or accommodate comfortably. But if our theoretical orientation recognizes the existence of alternative understandings of causality that people do act upon, then Donald Regan's revelations about astrology in the Reagan White House become data, as does Sakombi's testimony. The better our theories, in other words, the more likely it is that scholars will come to see that certain "insider tidbits" and "revelations" are data when seen through a conceptual lens that is able to infuse them with analytical meaning.

Another possible objection to the line of analysis in this chapter concerns veracity. Are Sakombi's accounts true, and how can we know this? Let us break this question down further. Did the Mobutu regime really dump tons of "mystical products" in the Congo River? And if so, what specifically were they and did they have any demonstrable effect—chemical, political, or other? Did Mobutu and others around him actually believe that this action would create ties of political loyalty between ruler and ruled, as people consumed beer brewed with the treated water? Even if the products were not placed in the river, was Sakombi nevertheless persuaded that this had happened, and was he, therefore, telling the truth to the best of his knowledge? Regardless of whether this or other comparable events actually occurred, is there a significant portion of the population who believe that such events are possible, occur frequently, and undertake their own political action in light of that knowledge?

Unfortunately, I cannot answer all of these questions. I do not know whether the authorities truly filled the river with "mystical products." If they did, I do not know what these were, or whether they had a demonstrable effect on people who were exposed to them. Nor can I say with any certainty whether Mobutu or members of his entourage actually believed that brewing beer with "treated" water would forge bonds of political loyalty between the president and his people. It is, however, reasonable to suspect that more than a few high-ranking officials entertained these or similar beliefs. To be candid, although it is a strong suspicion, I cannot be absolutely certain. Was Sakombi telling the truth about this and the other incidents he witnessed, at least in the sense that he was speaking openly and to the best of his knowledge? I think so. What would have been his motivation to lie? He claims to have undergone a religious conversion, and there is no reason to doubt his sincerity. To be sure, in the early 1990s he might have simply, and cynically, wished to distance himself from the obviously failing Mobutu regime. And while such an explanation is possible, other former political barons did this in more conventional ways by simply pointing to the regime's corruption and the pervasive economic regression that had occurred under Mobutu. Had this been Sakombi's desire, he could easily have done the same without the magical mystery tour. While there is obviously ample room for disagreement in this matter, I do believe that Sakombi's testimony had the ring of sincerity. But in a fundamental way the answer to the last question posed here, in many ways the easiest of the questions, renders moot all such speculation. Regardless of whether the incidents actually occurred, regardless of whether Mobutu actually believed in sorcery, regardless of whether Sakombi's testimony was sincere, it is absolutely certain that there are large numbers of Congolese who believe in sorcery and thus would have been prepared to accept explanations for familiar political phenomena (such as the tax on imported beers or the death of Bobutaka on the soccer pitch) that were rooted in the alternative causalities that they lived with every day and were thus accepted unthinkingly. Furthermore, at least in the Congolese case, Mobutu and his regime used these beliefs, and the fear they inspired, to promote political quiescence in the face of increasing repression and declining economic well-being.

The epistemological implications of this are large. Depending on the context, theoretical explanations need, at the least, to take into consideration a political world in which there are alternative notions of causality at play. Moreover, and in consequence, all causal theories will need to be examined for how well they cope with these alternative causalities. Critics might object that one problem with the alternative causalities I have elaborated is that they require that the political analyst actually get into the heads of the population under study to determine both whether and how they perceive cause and effect. This is certainly true. But is this requirement not true of all explanatory frameworks? Is not one of the great attractions of rational-choice perspectives that there are times and contexts in which many different peoples will behave like the proverbial *homo economicus* and understand causality as a function of the maximization of gains and the minimization of losses? Ordinary individuals tell us that this is so, and we believe them. We believe them, moreover, because they are consistent in expressing this and, significantly, because we are easily able to observe their behavior—some of which might reasonably be adduced to be consistent with this particular scientific understanding of causality. In addition, our explanatory frameworks need to flow not only from the specific subject matter at hand, but also from the particular, complex, and contextual understandings of causation that the people whose behavior is under scrutiny actually use. Unfortunately for the scholar, notions of political causality are not always articulated, often remaining tacit and subjacent. Theorists of whatever contemporary stripe might well find it enlightening, and perhaps more than occasionally troubling, to probe the relationship between their paradigm and the alternative causalities employed by the people whose behavior they are actually trying to explain.

Let me again be clear. We need not discard political and social-scientific theories derived from the West. I do not recommend this, for within their limits, they are useful analytical tools. In many areas of Congolese political life they capably provide us with valid, even compelling, explanations of political phenomena. Although I have been critical of my own previously published analyses, I am still prepared to defend them as competent, albeit partial, treatments of Congolese politics. But they are incomplete; their patterns of explanation are culturally specific; and they are perceptually limited. They are not, however, invalid, because there are many areas of overlap between the political realm of the West and the political realm as it is understood in the Congo. Furthermore, there are indeed times when Congolese will act politically on the basis of an understanding of causality that is quite consistent with the assumptions of certain political theories of Western origin.

When such congruence exists, there is no reason why a Western theoretical perspective cannot enlighten us concerning those aspects of Congolese politics. But the congruence between Western and Congolese visions of the frontiers of the political kingdom is imperfect. Similarly, there are often different, alternative understandings of causality that can, and do, come into play in any given society. When this occurs, theories generated with one set of causal assumptions in mind are unlikely to provide us with entirely satisfactory explanations of political phenomena and may actually impose the scholar's perceptions on other people. In such cases, however, we need theories and explanations that are flexible and subtle enough to incorporate other perceptions of political reality and alternative visions of causality and explanation. Political scientists, and all who would pretend to work on theory and explanation, need to pay much greater attention to other ways of knowing, both popular and endogenous. How might we do this?

Stated directly, we must listen carefully to what people say. If someone tells us that a certain political outcome is God's will, or the result of the intervention of the spirit world, or a consequence of some other form of alternative causality, we need to take them seriously whether or not we share their perceptions or beliefs. They may not necessarily be suffering either from a form of false consciousness or from a mystification by the hegemonic ideological order. Instead, they may simply be operating politically under an alternative understanding of causality, or a different perception of the parameters of the political, or a culturally specific and contextually immediate understanding of certain key political concepts. To unearth these factors, it is important that political scientists expand the range of primary source materials they invariably consult. The parameters of the political, as well as stunning examples of alternative causalities, may be found in the ordinary events and places of daily life: in the bars and on the soccer pitch. Popular culture, popular literature, popular religion have much to tell us about politics, as do proverbs, jokes, rumors, group discussions in various locales, and popular music. Finally, we need to include other perceptions of power, other understandings of causality, and other visions of the contours of the political realm in our theories of political behavior. I advance these suggestions not as a competing approach, but perhaps as a complementary, or parallel, theoretical and epistemological imagination which would enhance our understanding of the motivations behind certain manifestations of power and other political phenomena. In short, we need to understand better how all peoples, Congolese as well as ourselves, comprehend and interpret their political world. To achieve this, an ethnographic orientation and sensibility are necessary critical steps.

Notes

This chapter is a revised version of an analysis that originally appeared in Schatzberg (2001, 111–44). I am indebted to Edward Schatz, the group of scholars he assembled in Toronto to discuss insider perspectives on power, Richard Merleman, and two anonymous referees for their comments.

1. See Schatzberg (1979, 1980, 1981, 1986, 1988, 2001, 2006).
2. This and all subsequent translations are mine.
3. For the classic definition, see Evans-Pritchard (1937, 21); for an enlightening recent treatment see Ashforth (2005).
4. I begin with this example for illustrative purposes and because soccer is a critical part of popular culture in the DRC. Note, however, that sports are as political and as power-laden as any other sphere of life. Sorcery is omnipresent and thus pervades the realms of both the "low politics" of popular culture and the "high politics" of ministerial mischief. Other examples in this chapter will come from this latter realm.
5. A previous stint in Cameroon (1969–71; see Schatzberg 1979) had already sensitized me to the importance of this aspect of local life.
6. For an exception to the rule, see Scott (1998), who highlights the importance of local knowledge.

NINE

The Ethnographic Sensibility: Overlooked Authoritarian Dynamics and Islamic Ambivalences in West Africa

CÉDRIC JOURDE

What do particular subfields of political science stand to gain through broader use of ethnography? A general answer is that ethnographic methods allow political scientists to uncover what Denis-Constant Martin (2002) calls "UPOs," or "Unidentified Political Objects" (*objets politiques non-identifiés*). In other words, ethnography invites researchers to see and question political relations and political sites that are generally unseen, or "unidentified," by mainstream political science but which are nonetheless meaningful for local political actors. These unidentified objects include rituals and dramaturgical performances, as well as political struggles over the labeling of groups and the meanings of those labels. I will illustrate the contribution of an ethnographic sensibility by referring to two important research areas in political science: first, the survival and adaptation of neo-authoritarian regimes; second, the rise of Islamism or "political Islam." In the first instance, I will explain that ethnographic methods help analysts to be aware of the critical role of informal institutions and "meaning-making" practices (Wedeen 2002) in the survival of authoritarian regimes. In the second case, I argue that ethnographic methods reveal the extent to which the use and ascription of social labels such as "Islamists" are at the core of tense and complex political struggles, battles in which some political scientists take part, consciously or not, in the wake of the terrorist attacks of 11 September 2001. Research material from Mauritania and Senegal provide the material upon which this chapter is based.

What Political Ethnography?

It is important to explain at the onset that my research experiences are not based solely on ethnographic methods, if understood as being nothing less than full participant observation or long-term fieldwork (say, arbitrarily set at more than twenty-four successive months). However, my understanding of research that has at least an ethnographic sensibility includes Schatz's (2007, 2) definition: "approaches that rely centrally on person-to-person contact as a way to elicit insider perspectives and meanings." As Hopf (2006, 19) also argues, in addition to direct and sustained contacts with research participants, one may also undertake ethnographic research, at least in spirit, if we see ethnography as "the discovery of the intersubjective world of a community of interest." This is also what Read (2006, 10) has in mind when he puts forward the concept of "site-intensive methods," which he defines as "the collection of evidence from human subjects within their own contexts." In the West African countries where I do my fieldwork, Mauritania and Senegal, eliciting this "collection" of "insiders' perspective" is accomplished through intensive and recurring discussions with informants at their homes; life-history interviews; attendance at rituals such as the daily (Muslim) prayers and Thursday-evening prayer groups; and participation in other events, such as evening tea-drinking discussion groups among a town's factions of notables, sociocultural festivals, and zyâra (visits to saintly figures). But it may also include the reading of newspapers with an "ethnographic lens," as well as listening and watching audiotaped and videotaped political ceremonies and religious sermons (Hirschkind 2001). More generally, the ethnographic sensibility can only be acquired by interacting extensively with our research participants *and* their social world, and as Lecompte (2002, 296) says, "especially if we don't know much about those worlds or if we are operating on assumptions about, rather than real experience of them and their problems." In sum, this is the ethnographic sensibility that has guided my research.

Unidentified Political Objects (UPOs)

One major contribution of political ethnography is to bring into view Martin's (2002) UPOs. As Martin argues, political scientists too often restrict their investigations to a *limited repertoire of political objects*; seeing beyond this repertoire and expanding it is thus an important task. The notion of "unidentified" specifically refers here to political scientists' narrow field of vision—that is, "those practices and products that are not usually taken into account by political science" (Martin 2002, 16). But it also refers to objects that are more familiar to us but that ought to be looked at through an unusual perspective. Why can ethnography do that? Because through extensive fieldwork and its quest for "meaning-making practices" (Wedeen 2002) in open, one-on-one encounters, participant and nonparticipant observations, or more generally "site-intensive methods" (Read 2006), it encourages political scientists to reflect more extensively on questions they had not foreseen as important. To paraphrase Bourdieu (1981, 4), ethnography's main benefit is that it expands the realm of the "political scientifically thinkable." Hence, ethnography is useful for political scientists "when we do not even know the right kinds of questions to ask" (Stevenson 2005, 12). But even more, ethnography is useful *when political scientists (wrongly) think that they already know the right kinds of questions to ask.* Research programs that are "locked in" on a path often fail to identify new questions, as researchers involved in these programs believe that the main objects of inquiry have already been identified. In such cases, political scientists walk on their path, not realizing that they are surrounded by UPOs that could be, and often are, politically significant for the actors involved in them, if not more significant than the political objects researchers have already "identified." More generally, by soliciting "insiders' perspective," by deploying a deeper sensitivity to actors' subjectivity and to social intersubjectivity, one realizes not only the limits of his or her basic assumptions, but also the range of alternative questions and objects of inquiry.

Unidentified Political Sites in a Neo-Authoritarian Regime

In my research, a first application of this "ethnographic sensibility" relates to the study of neo-authoritarian regimes. In general, studies that investigate those contemporary regimes that keep a strong authoritarian core despite the "Third Wave" pressures to democratize (regimes called "electoral authoritarian," "competitive authoritarian," or "neo-authoritarian," for instance) tend to consider formal political institutions as the main loci of political legitimacy, hegemony, and opposition. As I have mentioned elsewhere (Jourde 2005), the repertoire of "autocratic methods aimed at keeping incumbents in power" (Levitsky and Way 2002, 59) does include a broad range of tactics that involve formal political institutions: engaging in censorship of formal media (newspapers, television, and radio); "making full use of its reserved domains" (Case 2006, 107); making "elections instruments of authoritarian rule" (Schedler 2006, 3); "keeping a tight grip on parliament" (Van de Walle 2002, 68); using physical repression to thwart democratic transitions (Levitsky and Way 2002, 57–58); as well as institutionalizing in the long term a ruling political party to manage conflicts among autocratic and opportunistic elites and prevent defection to the opposition (Brownlee 2007).

However, the study of this authoritarian repertoire must be enlarged: authoritarian elites also invest other sociopolitical realms to that end, realms that are generally "unidentified" by many political scientists, but are critical for the production of compliance, repression, or contestation. Since the literature on new authoritarian regimes is relatively recent, it is still easy to ask ourselves new questions—that is, to avoid entrapping ourselves in locked-in research programs in which our fundamental assumptions cannot be questioned. This endeavor is facilitated in part by those approaches that analyze representations, "definitions of reality," frames, and the discursive and symbolic relations upon which authoritarian regimes are founded, negotiated, and contested (Doty 1996; Thornton 2002; Wiktorowicz 2004; Bayat 2005; Schatz 2009; Jourde 2007). And those representations, frames, and discourses are often located in political sites not seen by most political scientists. But political ethnography provides the necessary cultural sensitivity to find these unidentified sites and to ask questions that were previously "unthinkable."

Authors such as Ellis (1999) and Richards (2005) remind us that "classical" phenomena in political science, like civil wars, cannot be properly understood if political scientists do not look at (what is for most of them) UPOs, such as witchcraft practices and beliefs. Similarly, the "Third Wave" authoritarian regimes must be analyzed through a different perspective, through political objects insufficiently identified by scholars, such as rituals. In that line of thought, some authors have put forward fascinating studies, based at least in part on ethnographic methods. Wedeen (1999), for instance, through her interactions with Syrians of various social backgrounds, listened to anecdotes and informal discussions, and treated written texts as performances, enabling her to explore new sites where Syria's authoritarian regime is established, accepted, and contested, such as cartoons or "dream-telling" stories. As well, she shows that what many political scientists may have considered to be phony "cults of personality" (under then president Hāfiz al-Asad) organized in Syria's football stadiums should rather be taken very seriously and be interpreted as sites where the political authorities display "disciplinary-symbolic power," essential in the construction of the regime. In the same vein, Hammoudi (1997) shows in his ethnographic research that the hierarchical and gendered rituals that structure relations between Sufi "masters" and disciples are replicated in larger, national organizations, notably within political parties and, even more, at the level of regime-subjects relations, thereby constituting a foundational pillar of Morocco's male-dominated authoritarian regime.

My fieldwork in Mauritania has also allowed me to recognize the significance of rituals and celebrations, which I had not "identified" before carrying out fieldwork there. At first I had no knowledge of their importance, as I was mostly interested in the regime's more "visible" strategies to weaken the timid democratic reforms it had promulgated in the early 1990s, such as the use of repression and electoral fraud. But after several months of intensive, sustained, and personalized discussions and social interactions with state elites and notables from the country's southern region (almost always at their homes, not at their workplaces), living in some of these elites' homes for several days in small rural towns and in the capital city, I began to realize that rituals and dramaturgical representations also constituted meaningful cultural practices that inform the process of authoritarian survival, as political actors attempt to communicate, negotiate, and impose their political interests and norms upon different audiences. So I inquired more specifically about local and national rituals and ceremonies, such as "presidential tours" that the head of state would carry out for days visiting the country's different regions, as well as Islamic Sufi "visits" (*zyâra*), and I linked these events to the larger process of authoritarian restoration (Jourde 2002, 2005).

Rituals such as presidential tours and *zyâra* had rarely been analyzed seriously despite a striking feature about them: high-ranking political leaders I had met invested vast amounts of money in them, organized countless "preparatory" meetings, mobilized thousands of people, and spent several days attending them. Clearly, these men's and women's assumptions of what constitutes *meaningful* political activities included that of participating, organizing, and financing such ceremonies. They conceived of these ceremonies as significant political battlefields, where the protagonists and antagonists include proregime elites and opposition groups, but also rival factions of the proregime elite. My reading of newspapers also began to change, as I came to realize that journalists' accounts of these events were not only extensive, amazing sources of information, but also were based on the assumption, previously hidden for me, that these rituals, and the numerous cultural performances that compose them, convey significant political ideas about relations among elites and between elites and masses in a neo-authoritarian context. In addition, intensive discussions with these elites and interaction in their social worlds also revealed the critical importance of rumor and gossip, an importance that easily matches that of "formal" media, and which played an important role in the unfolding of these rituals.

Among the political objects that are generally ignored ("unseen" by political scientists), one finds the multiple political battles that were played out during the organization of these rituals and their actual unfolding. For instance, during presidential visits to small rural towns, issues such as the choice of "bards" (*griots*) and poets who praise the visiting president, the donation or not of gifts to the president (and the type of gift), the language people use in their speeches, rumors about "witchcraft attacks," the choice of locations where the president meets with "local notables," the type of entry (alone or in group) under the presidential tent, and claims about who had brought the most spectators: all these issues appeared as meaningful performances in the construction of the authoritarian regime and the weakening of opposition groups in Mauritania. Similarly, what appeared to me at first as simply a religious ritual (*zyâra*) to honor what I thought was a *shaykh* was in fact *simultaneously* an event that helped the authoritarian regime to launch its first decisive attacks against prodemocracy opposition movements. As I looked more closely at which local political faction hosted the *shaykh*, how in his speech the holy man combined religious and political elements, how the *shaykh*'s matrimonial linkages extended deep into the town's family politics, how his charisma had a powerful mobilizing capacity that surpassed that of politicians, and the official prohibition of competing social events in this region, it became clear that this was a major political ritual to investigate the authoritarian regime's strike against the region's antiregime forces. In a nutshell, an ethnographic sensibility was useful to "see" that public accusations about the bewitching of a local official's son and the visit of a Sufi *shaykh* to a burial shrine were critical political moves—indeed, "political objects" worth studying in the context of an authoritarian regime's process of survival and adaptation.

The Politics of Labeling: Islamism, Sufism, and Politics

The contribution of ethnographic methods is also crucial in a second major research area: the politics of Islam. While analysts often externally impose their definition of "Islamism" when investigating Islam and politics, ethnography provides a sensibility that allows political scientists to "see" the large variation of meanings such a word can have across Muslim societies, as well as the complex political struggles that are fought over this word.

An entry point to my overall argument is provided by the few authors who have analyzed a similar case, that of the concepts of democracy and legitimacy. The ethnographic work of Schaffer (1998) and Karlstrom (1996), in Senegal and Uganda, respectively, offers an alternative to the numerous studies that put forward their *a priori* definition of democracy while ignoring (consciously or not) the important gap between their definition and the various meanings attributed to this concept in local communities. Both authors analyze how people "say" and conceive of democracy, showing that in countries like Senegal and Uganda, the term *democracy* belongs to a family of concepts and values that are subject to varying interpretations, many of which differ significantly from the common definitions found in political science. Similarly, Schatzberg (2001) and Bertrand (2002), studying middle Africa and Indonesia, respectively, argue that the notions of democracy and legitimacy are tightly connected to the "world of the invisible" and witchcraft. Schatzberg (2001, 108) sums up the problem nicely: "Western political scientists have assumed, incorrectly and largely without reflection, that the very parameters of politics that they implicitly understood constituted a conceptual template that they could apply elsewhere without qualification."

This implies that we need to identify people's various interpretations of the term *democracy* in their own languages and analyze how these different meanings become tied into power struggles, such as the preservation or contestation of unequal political orders. This is important for political scientists, first, because if we do not understand how insiders conceive of "democracy," we may misunderstand the political actions they perform, as well as those they do *not* enact. The theoretical framework we elaborate may mislead us. Second, we run the risk of missing critical pieces of the puzzle—that is, critical political actors and events that we cannot identify because of our own blindness. For instance, if Schatzberg and Bertrand are right that the "world of the invisible" is key to understanding democracy in different African and Southeast Asian countries, then our analysis will be mistaken when we fail to see the critical games that are played in these political sites, the role played by "sorcerers" and "occult advisers" in Indonesia, as well as political leaders' relationships with spirits and ancestors during phases of "democratization." These would remain UPOs to us.

In political contexts where, in both everyday and scholarly discourses, Islam has become a major issue, a concept like "Islamism" deserves as much attention as that of democracy. And ethnographic methods are particularly well suited here. In a research project on the politics of Islam in West Africa, I realized that a major issue at stake was precisely the meaning of my concepts. Simply put, my first encounters with the field forced me to ask simple yet fundamental questions: Who are the "Islamists" that seem so important in the politics of Islam? Are the "Islamists" those who themselves use that term? Are they the people who are labeled as such by the state or by journalists? Can I unilaterally decide who the Islamists are, even if those I label as such refuse that categorization? Where can I draw the line between those who are the Islamists and those who are not? Should I even draw such a line? As I will explain, most often researchers already have assumptions (hidden or not) about who the Islamists are. Yet, as I began to hold intensive and personalized interactions with field informants, the existence of a significant gap between the meaning "Islamism" generally has in political science and the meanings attributed by my informants became clear, as did the numerous ambiguities and contradictions inherent in informants' understandings of this concept, all of which had to be fully taken into account, rather than glossed over. And so do the tense political battles that are fought about the very meaning of this concept, battles about who should be labeled as an Islamist, what it means to be against or in favor of Islamists, and the very tangible, if not physical, consequences of labeling self and/or others as Islamists.

In scholarly studies of Islamism, especially in Africa, South Asia, and Southeast Asia, this concept is often defined in a dichotomous way, as a form of Islamic orthopraxy and orthodoxy that contrasts with another way of thinking about and practicing Islam, that "something else" being Sufism (*tasawwûf*), sometimes referred to as "popular Islam" (Rosander and Westerlund 1997; Gomez-Perez 2005, 10–12). Take the following definition found in the literature: "Islamist" qualifies people or groups that "see in Islam a guiding political doctrine that justifies and motivates collective action on behalf of that doctrine. . . . Islamists are Muslims who feel compelled to act on the belief that Islam demands social and political activism, either to establish an Islamic state, to proselytize to reinvigorate the faithful, or to create a separate union for Muslim communities" (Hafez 2003, 4–5). For its part, Sufism is generally defined as a mystical form of Islam, in which believers can evolve on a path to God via religious masters who are personally blessed by God (*Baraka*) through dreams or other divine revelations. These religious leaders and their disciples belong to larger, transnational "orders" (*turuq*, sing. *tarîqa*), whose privileged religious knowledge is transmitted from generation to generation in complex rituals (Vikor 2000, 441–42).

However, researchers who use site-intensive methods and rely on insiders' perspectives (Schatz 2007) are led to see things that such definitions fail to capture: the significant varieties and ambiguities of meanings and the power struggles that develop as actors use these concepts and their different meanings. As Bayat (2005, 899) says, "It is crucial to note that the term

'Islamism' is often taken to describe not the same but many different things in different national settings" (see also Rosander and Westerlund 1997).

On the one hand, scholars who have used ethnographic approaches did encounter informants who consider "Islamism" and "Sufism" to be very different forms of religious practice and ideas in various Muslim societies, though these scholars see reasons for this dichotomous perspective that others may not see. Informants sometimes use these two terms as opposites and invest strong negative and/or positive connotations in them. This contradiction and ambivalence must be taken as it is, and must not be discarded. As one man told me during my fieldwork in Mauritania, the "Muslim Brothers [the local branch of the Egypt-based *al-Ikhwân al-Muslimûn*] are bandits and renegades. Nobody will follow them in this country because 99 percent of us are *Tijani* [the largest Sufi *tarîqa* in the region]."[1] Another told me, "The few people who join these so-called 'reformists' [another word for "Islamists"] do it only because they are opportunists and because they are looking for their egoistic interests. . . . These people are trouble-makers for whom any Muslim who does not follow their path is not a real Muslim. . . . They just want to denigrate the religious heritage of our [Sufi] Fulani clerics."[2] In her fieldwork in the Gambia, where Sufi orders are also dominant, Janson (2005, 466) was told by an elderly person that the *Sunnidingolu*, or "Children of the Sunna" (a name given to those who criticize the Sufi orders) "do not have any respect for our parents. . . . The Prophet belongs to all of us and not only to the *Sunnidingolu*. . . . Let them go to the [Christian] Church. There they may find people whom they can convert."

Likewise, in his ethnographic study of political relations between different Muslim groups in a town in Chad, Seesemann (2005) found that leaders and disciples of Sufi *turuq* were outraged by local officials' decision to ban a major Sufi ritual, the celebration of the Prophet's birthday (*Al Mawlûd*), pointing at these local officials' affiliations with the *Ansâr as-Sunna* organization, which considers such a celebration as a deviation from the right path. Conversely, many people who define themselves as Islamist or Reformist decry "Sufists" in the very same negative language. For instance, Adrianna Piga (2002, 47) was told by her informants that Sufi *tarîqât* are "responsible for division and exploitation of the Muslim community." Loimeier (2000) similarly found that his interlocutors believed that Sufi leaders had brought Islam on a devious path, full of wrong innovations (*bid'a*). In opposition to the Sufi orders, they told him, true believers should rather preach a return to the true values of the first generation of pious Muslims (*Salaf*). If our interlocutors employ dichotomous understandings of their world, we cannot ignore their dichotomies.

On the other hand, ethnographic research simultaneously reveals that "Islamism" and "Sufism" are not always opposite ideas. Though he was looking at the case of Senegal, Fall's (1993, 203) argument would apply to many other Muslim countries: Islamism and Sufism are "sometimes mutually exclusive," but they "most often interlace and merge," and even mix literally through matrimonial relations. In effect, during discussions with informants in Mauritania, I realized that many members of Sufi orders would perfectly agree with the alleged uniquely "Islamist" idea that religion should be the standard against which political behavior is measured, that Islam should be "a guiding political doctrine that justifies and motivates collective action on behalf of that doctrine" (to use Hafez's definition above). In Senegal, Schafer's (1998) ethnographic study of the meaning of democracy among Senegal's Wolof-speakers demonstrates that political leaders and peasants alike, most of whom belong to Sufi orders, substantially draw on Islamic concepts and metaphors in their representations of an appropriate political order and of legitimate political relations between rulers and citizens. Villalón (2007, 163) similarly observes that the distinction between "traditional Sufi and Islamist groups" in Senegal is "blurred." An example of this is seen in the rise of the *Dahiratoul Moustarchidina wa al-Moustarchidaty* (DMM), a religious movement that shows strong overlaps between Sufism and Islamism.[3] Though the DMM has deep and solid ties with the most powerful Sufi order in Senegal (the *Tijaniyya*), its leaders and disciples are strongly opposed to the state's secular agenda, and they hold a discourse that combines classical Sufi elements and ideas associated with an "Islamist" discourse (Samson 2005, 348–49; Villalón 1995, 2007). Meanwhile, all Senegalese Sufi orders politically oppose the Senegalese state's *caractère laïc* (secular character), and many Sufi leaders and disciples have expressed their disapproval of state leaders when they tried to push secular reforms, like the secular "Family Code" that, in their view, violated fundamental Islamic precepts (Loimeier 2000, 183).

In the Gambia, as Janson (2005, note 54) observes, members of the largest "Islamist" movement, *Tablîgh*, perform a ritual (*dhikr*) that is central to any Sufi order, and also use a nomenclature from the Sufi orders. A similar pattern can be seen in Morocco, where one of the most popular religious movements (*Al-'Adl wal Ihsân*), which analysts label as "Islamist" (Cavatorta 2006), incorporates both in its discourses and practices several elements from Sufism. As Lauzière (2005, 244) explains about the movement's leader, 'Abd al-Salam Yasin, "By connecting mystical elements to Islamism, 'Abd al-Salam Yasin could aspire to transcend this hegemonic Salafi epistemology and reach out for the Sufi sensibilities of Moroccan masses." Even if actors often "publicly *proclaim*" fundamental (if not irreconcilable) differences between Islamism and Sufism, they may display in everyday reality a "*practical* flexibility" that blurs the rhetorical differences (Scheele 2007, 306; emphasis added). As Scheele (2007, 317) explains with respect to the Algerian region where she has conducted fieldwork, beyond the discourses held by the various actors, one simultaneously finds practical accommodation and flexibility: "The boundaries between these various traditions were and always had been rather flexible, and they allowed for—and were inherently dependent on—compromises on a day-to-day basis." This echoes a pattern observed in the largest Muslim country in the world, Indonesia, where "Sufism, then, is very much a part of the wider Islamic revival that heretofore has been characterized in Western scholarship largely in scripturalist [or 'Islamist'] terms" (Howell 2001, 722).

In sum, research conducted with an ethnographic sensibility at the local level enables us to see that beyond a concept like "Islamism," and the *a priori* definitions we use, unfolds a much more complex and ambiguous reality that we need to account for. It is important for political scientists to "see" this ambivalent reality, not simply for its own sake, but also because we would then be better equipped to identify important political struggles and power relations that we would otherwise not perceive.

For instance, looking at the meanings and debates surrounding the use of labels ("Islamists," "Sufi," "Popular Islam") helps us see critical struggles among local sociopolitical groups. In effect, although tensions over the labels "Islamists" and "Sufi" do involve religious notions, as when Sufi are accused of committing sins of "association" (*shirk*; when Sufi disciples consider their *shaykh* to be God's equals or "associates"), *bid'a* (devious "innovations"), and *taqlid* (blindly "imitating" their *shaykh*), ethnographic methods allow one to see that these religious disputes are simultaneously constituted by other local sociopolitical tensions. As Scheele (2007, 311) argues, the battle over the meanings of Islamism and Sufism is "intrinsically part of the local socio-political context."

To take an example from Mauritania, repeated interactions with local informants helped me to realize that the meaning of a comment like "Islamists" are "bandits" attacking our "Sufi Fulani clerics" is related to a struggle about and for "status" in the Pulaar-speaking community, between religious leaders of the "clerical" (*Toroobe*) status against those of the "pastoralist" (*Fulbe*) status. In effect, the emergence of the "Islamist" Al-Falah movement in Mauritania, Senegal, and Mali in the mid-twentieth century under the leadership Al Hâjj Mahmadou Ba Diowol, has its roots in the marginalization of *Fulbe* pastoralists in the Senegal River Valley region (at first in the Bossea area and then throughout and beyond the valley) by a small clique of ruling *Toroobe* clerics, who controlled the *Tijaniyya* Sufi order (Kane 1997; and personal discussions with informants, Nouakchott, June 2006). The *Al-Falah* movement's harsh discourse against Sufi orders (the movement strictly prohibits its members from being disciples of Sufi orders) must thus be understood simultaneously in terms of both its religious *and* its sociopolitical meanings.

Similarly, in her Gambian case study, Janson (2005, 453) makes an insightful observation about how, in a predominantly Sufi society, "Islamists" are often labeled as *Sunnidingolu* (Children of the Sunna). As she points out, the allusion to "children" is a direct indication that beyond the religious battle also lies a generational struggle between a Sufi elderly class that monopolizes power through its control over Islam, and younger religious scholars and disciples who want to bypass the elders' power. Calling these people "children" is a way to deny them the right to make any political or religious claim. The use of terms related to age and generations is also found in Tanzania, where Becker (2006, 583) conducted ethnographic research in a small village in which religious disputes erupted between the local Sufi leaders and their disciples, and an emerging "reformist" movement. The two groups fought over the proper ways to conduct rituals, such as burial ceremonies and daily prayers. Interestingly, the Sufi leaders called their new rivals the "Al Qaeda Boys," here again revealing the close relationship between religious tensions and an "underlying generation gap" between, on the one hand, Sufi elders, who enjoy close ties with Tanzania's ruling party (Chama Cha Mapinduzi, CCM), own the scarce land, and control the mosque committee, and, on the other hand, younger men, "boys" (there is a gender dimension in this conflict) under thirty, who feel excluded from the circles of power and wealth (Becker 2006, 587). LeBlanc's (1999, 500) ethnographic research in central Côte-d'Ivoire similarly uncovers a struggle that combines religious and generational elements, between Sufi elders and younger "Islamist" men and women, which she aptly refers to as "the stakes of gerontocracy."

A second type of political struggle about labels and their meanings is the one pitting state authorities against various social groups. The stakes are higher as governments play their part in the politics of labeling: categorizing certain groups as "Islamists" can be a prelude to a series of government policies that involve repression and exclusion. Ethnographic methods thus invite researchers to pay attention to who labels whom, and to what meanings are involved in this process of labeling.

An interesting case is that of one of Mauritania's (and West Africa's) largest religious movements, the *Da'awa wa Tablîgh* (hereafter *Tablîgh*).[4] Political scientists often pigeonhole this organization as "Islamist" or "Salafist" (Le Vine 2007, 92–93), thereby attributing a political meaning to it. Yet *Tablîgh's* leaders and members deny any political activism. *Tablîgh*, which was founded in colonial India in the 1920s and eventually reached almost every Muslim society including West Africa, preaches a strong reaffirmation of one's faith, a clearer obedience to sacred Muslim texts, and also the obligation to undertake travels or "missions" to propagate the Muslim faith (Kepel 1991, 56–59, 252–54; Janson 2005). But a major pillar of the *Tablîghî* doctrine is its "apolitical" stance. As Kepel (1991, 253) explains, *Tablîghî* have adopted a "policy of non-confrontation with government authorities" (see also Ould Ahmed Salem 1999). Their main concern is not "the state," but rather the (re-)Islamization of society from below, on each and every micro-behavior and thought that constitutes everyday life. As one member said to Janson (2005, 462), "We cannot expect from the government to introduce *shari'a* as this is a secular nation. All we can do is to integrate *shari'a* in our personal lives." Taken at their own words, *Tablîghî* do not fit the social-scientific definitions of Islamism because they clearly exclude any "political" dimension from their movement.

Thus ethnographic methods invite us to focus on how such groups define themselves and why they do so. In the specific case of the *Tablîghî*, we may try to understand why they reject vehemently defining themselves, and being defined by others, as political actors. Here, one needs to take into account the context in which neo-authoritarian regimes have used the label "Islamist" to oppress real or alleged opponents. In the Gambia, for instance, it may be that *Tablîghî's* strong denial of any political activism is a way to avoid the wrath of the state (Janson 2005, 453). This must be understood in a context in which, since the early 1990s (and more so since the terrorist attacks of 11 September 2001), many West and North African regimes have adroitly drawn on Western governments', and many scholars', simplistic and dichotomous meaning of "Islamism," "terrorism," "political instability," and the like, to obtain international support. In turn, that support is often used to weaken and, sometimes, crush opposition movements.

The Mauritanian regime is one of those regimes that, since the mid-1990s, has enacted a series of symbolic and discursive performances for its Western audiences, through which it represents itself as a bastion against threatening Islamist networks. These performances include the numerous waves of arrests of people it accused of being "Islamists" between 1994 and 2005, public accusations of coup attempts, and televised declarations by arrested alleged Islamists in which they confess their intention to threaten the "security of the state." The regime's defining of some individuals as "Islam-ists," in terms similar to those found in political science works, became a discursive tool that has made possible the arrest, imprisonment, and tor-ture of several people, self-proclaimed opponents or not, self-proclaimed "Islamists" or not (Jourde 2007). While I was doing some research in Mau-ritania in May and June 2006, the head of state and leader of the interim military junta undertook a presidential tour of the country's regional capi-tals, during which he told his audience that he would never allow "Islam-ists" to have their own political party in Mauritania, associating those who asked for the creation of such a political party with "Kalashnikov Islam." That this speech was pronounced in Arabic (the official language) *and* French is significant, as the latter is the *lingua franca* of Western diplomats in Nouakchott.

The categorization of opponents as "Islamists" and the attribution of a "destabilizing" nature to this essentializing concept was critical for the Mauritanian government, and for some other governments in West and North Africa. In effect, Mauritania was added to various regional and in-ternational geostrategic alliances, such as the major U.S. military assistance program called the Trans-Saharan Counter-Terrorism Initiative (TSCTI) (previously known as the Pan-Sahel Initiative), as well as the Mediterra-nean Dialogue (a NATO-related organization). Through these "initiatives," Mauritania and other countries of the Sahel and North Africa received ex-tensive financial and military support, such as the training of elite Maurita-nian military units by U.S. Special Forces. It is worth noting that these Mau-ritanian units (notably the Commando Parachutists) are in fact the coercive pillars of the authoritarian regime, and have contributed significantly to the regime's survival for the last fifteen years. Mauritanian officials adapted very well to Western interpretations of what Islamism means; they "spoke" the language of "Islamism" and "instability" fluently (Jourde 2007).

Accordingly, without deep and thick knowledge of the region, scholars cannot "identify," or "see," the complex struggles that actors play out in re-lation to labels such as "Islamism," and may easily buy into that discourse, thereby feeding and nurturing the representation that takes for granted the reality of a reified and threatening Islamism in the region. When scholars "objectively" depict Mauritania and West Africa with predetermined cate-gories like "Islamism," "terrorism," "instability," and the like (Stevenson 2003; Lyman and Morrison 2004), they play a part in the transformation of political reality. Scholars then become the producers of a *littérature de sur-veillance,* as Van Bruinessen (1998, 192) aptly calls it, a literature with "se-curity concerns" similar to those of the colonial administrators working for the "Muslim Affairs Bureau," who up until the 1960s monopolized the production of "scholarly" works on Islam in French West Africa and North Africa. Consequently, they participate in the reification and homogenization of "Islamism"; they play their part in power struggles fought through concepts. As Villalón (2007, 180) sums up with respect to the Senegalese case, with a resonance for other West African countries, "it is misleading and confusing to attempt to analyze such dynamics by distinguishing 'Islamists' from 'Sufis,' or 'radical' from 'moderate' Muslims—in an exercise reminiscent of the colonial efforts to sort out the 'good' from the 'bad' Muslim"—and, I would add, the "White" from the "Black" Islam, as colonial administrators also did in Mauritania and Senegal.

Sustained and intensive interactions with political actors, whether through frequent casual discussions, focus groups, or by living within families, endow researchers with the sensibility needed both to question their own assumptions about categories like "Islamism," "Sufism," or "Tablîghî," and to enable them to capture the richness, the complexity, and the unresolved (and unsolvable) inconsistencies of their informants' performances and enunciations. Without site-intensive methods, sophisticated theoretical structures aimed at explaining the behaviors of "Islamists" and "Sufi" quickly appear to be built on weak foundations, as they ignore or misconstrue insiders' perspectives and meanings. In addition, the sources and the extent of political struggles such as those involving, for instance, "Sufi" elders and "Islamist" youngsters in Côte d'Ivoire or "Sufi" clerics (*Toroobe*) and "Islamist" pastoralists (*Fulbe*) in one Mauritanian region, remain UPOs for political scientists if they are not cognizant of the struggles fought over the meanings of these terms.

Conclusion

For epistemological or practical reasons, such as the lack of time and financial resources, political scientists may decide not to carry out full ethnographic research. But if they at least work with an ethnographic sensibility, with site-intensive methods, their research can contribute significantly to research areas (such as those on authoritarianism and Islamism) that are severely bounded by unquestioned assumptions, that do not question dominant representations about how the political world works. Intensive, sustained, and open-ended interactions with social actors and the attempt to elicit their meanings of how the political world (or parts of it) functions can help political scientists to see what used to be Unidentified Political Objects and to measure the gap between their understanding of a given reality (the "reality" of Islamism and Sufism, for instance) and the complex, fluid, and contradictory understandings of their research participants. It is true, however, that the actual techniques to acquire this ethnographic sensibility are difficult to enumerate and specify.[5] There is an element of "learning by doing" as we try to identify the best ways to "elicit meanings" from individuals and from other social sources (newspapers, archival sources, audiotapes, ritualistic performances). But as practitioners of this type of research begin collectively to examine their common practices, we may arrive at a more accurate picture.

Notes

1. Nouakchott, May 2006.
2. Nouakchott, September 2005.
3. See Philippon's (2006) study of an organization very similar to DMM in Pakistan.
4. Other names are also used, such as *Jama'at Tablîgh, Tablîghî,* and *Da'awat.*
5. See Yanow, this volume, for an important enumeration of key principles of interpretive ethnography.

TEN

Participant Observation, Politics, and Power Relations: Nicaraguan Mothers and U.S. Casino Waitresses

LORRAINE BAYARD DE VOLO

Ethnography is far from a common method in political science. It has made few appearances in political science journals (Bayard de Volo and Schatz 2004). It is not standard fare in graduate methods courses (Schwartz-Shea 2003). Indeed, sociologists seem more engaged in political ethnography than are political scientists.[1] Ethnographic methods are particularly well suited to the study of certain political processes, yet in the discipline's slowness to adopt the method, we bar ourselves from accessing certain types of information, asking certain political questions, and gaining certain insights. Thus, political scientists are in danger of falling behind the cutting edge of political research, a danger that is readily apparent as one becomes familiar with the work of cultural anthropologists and sociologists who *do* employ ethnographic methods (see, for example, Lichterman 1998; Auyero 2006a).[2] If we are to be defined as political scientists by the subject that we study—politics—rather than by the methods that we employ, then we must be open to and educated about a broad array of methods, including ethnography.

With this aim in mind, here I explore insights and challenges that arose out of my own work: two very different ethnographic projects, one in U.S. casinos, the other in postwar Nicaragua. The exploration covers issues I have struggled with in ethnographic research, which I have divided into two sets of questions. First, what can ethnography bring to the study of politics? Here I argue that ethnography yields otherwise unobtainable and often unexpected insights, notably in terms of multilevel processes. Such insights, while valuable in and of themselves, also lay the groundwork for culturally sensitive future research, policies, and political action. Second, how should political science be challenged to better accommodate and appreciate ethnography, and in turn, how might we alter or clarify the ethnographic method for application to politics? I expand upon dominant understandings of both "politics" and "science" to make space for inductive research and the study of power relations outside of institutional politics. I also explore notions of sameness and difference between researcher and researched. Finally, I advocate for a better appreciation of emotions in research. Not only is it futile to attempt to scrub them from our research, but the attempt itself may be damaging.

What Can Ethnography Bring to the Study of Politics?

New Sources of Information

Ethnography presents a means of obtaining information and insights not accessible through other techniques (Agar 1980; Jorgensen 1989). To illustrate this point, I draw from my research into the meaning participants attach to collective action. My fieldwork with the Mothers of Heroes and Martyrs of Matagalpa, Nicaragua, stretched across roughly a year in 1992–93, with follow-up visits in 1994, 1998, and 1999. Nicaragua had gone through a series of rapid political shifts from the late 1970s through the early 1990s. The Sandinista-led insurrection overthrew the Somoza dictatorship in 1979. With the Sandinistas in power, U.S. funding of counter-revolutionaries led to the Contra War, which stretched through most of the 1980s. Then, in 1990, the Sandinista incumbent president Daniel Ortega lost to his conservative opponent, Violeta Chamorro, who brought an end to the war and implemented neoliberal austerity programs.

The Mothers of Heroes and Martyrs was a prominent Sandinista mass organization of women who had lost a son or daughter in the insurrection of the 1970s or the Contra War of the 1980s. I was interested in how and why the Sandinista state (1979–90) had mobilized women, and furthermore how members of this women's organization experienced that mobilization. That is, what meanings did members attach to their organization? Why did they participate, and how did they understand the effects of activism (Lichterman 1998)? Most of my fieldwork was spent participating in organizational activities and visiting members at home, the latter activity involving both recorded, semi-structured interviews and more informal discussion. I also pursued documentary sources of information, most notably in the state-run and the opposition newspapers, poetry, speeches, communiqués, and pamphlets from the Mothers' office archives, and U.S. State Department documents obtained through the Freedom of Information Act.

Judging by virtually all the documentary evidence, the Mothers' own public pronouncements, my interviews with Sandinista officials, and my initial interviews with members themselves, the Mothers' "reason for being" was political and involved carrying on the Sandinista struggle of the martyred children. That is, it existed as an organization to support the Sandinista party in order to honor the memory of the fallen children and ensure that the children's "blood had not been shed in vain." Sandinista memoranda also noted that the organization was a means by which the state could mobilize a sector of society—middle-aged and older women—into the Sandinista fold. This was particularly important for those women whose sons had died as draftees in the Contra War, as they were viewed as tending toward opposition to the state.

But moving off the written page and away from the official reasons, I became interested in what sustained members' activism on a daily basis. Years after the death of their children and the end of the war, and in an era when the Sandinistas were no longer in power and material resources within the organization were distributed based upon need rather than level of activism, why did these women continue to participate on a weekly if not daily basis? Is reference to long-range official organizational goals—carrying on the Sandinista struggle—a sufficient explanation for sustained participation on the part of individual members? Or did members perceive other benefits or goals to their activism?

Through participant observation, I noted that much of the interaction among members revolved around expressions of emotion linked to their activism. This generated new questions for me. When I first asked members why they had joined the organization, they tended to respond with the standard political and ideological reason of carrying on the Sandinista struggle. But I gained new insights once I began to discuss with them why they continued to participate on a weekly basis over so many years, long after the death of a child and even several years after the Sandinistas were voted out of office. In these discussions, many stressed their sense of obligation and affection for other members, the therapeutic benefits of collective action, and their own sense of personal growth and political empowerment through the process of organizing. For example, Doña Maria Elsa explained: "That was [something] I gained from the committee—having a friendship with each one, making intimate friends. I felt happy. I felt peaceful. I felt trusted because I love them, all of them." She went on to say: "I can remember so many times when I felt so proud solving some problem for a Mother. I feel content because I know that I have done something." These responses, then, differed from those in my initial interviews and the organizational rhetoric.

I have written about this as the public and private face of organizing, in which the latter involves long-term, nonmaterial benefits to collective action (Bayard de Volo 2001, 2006; see also Melucci 1989). Without ethnography, I would have had to rely upon the "public face" of the organization in determining why these women organized and what their goals were, and thus I would have missed much of the meaning they attributed to membership and their definition of benefits. The ethnographic approach generated new questions based upon my participant observation and interviews, guiding me to emic or insider understandings of the organization, a perspective too commonly absent from social-movement research.[3] Without an ethnographic approach, then, I would have missed much of these women's motivation in collective organizing. More generally, I would also have missed the broader social implications of a mobilized population. That is, activism may be good for the individual and also good for democratic society if it means a heightened sense of political empowerment and a greater affinity for collective benefits (Bayard de Volo 2006).

Ethnographic Surprises

As a second and related benefit, ethnography can yield unanticipated insights, uncovering the implicit meanings associated with activism, as in the example just given, or power struggles in the workplace. In my workplace ethnography of the casino floor—specifically, the work of cocktail waitresses—I set out to better understand the meanings such waitresses attached to their work. Their job was predominantly viewed from the outside as "sexualized," aimed at inviting the heterosexual male gaze. I was particularly interested in a diagnostics of power relations to identify instances of accommodation and resistance at the micro-level.

My fieldwork involved eighteen months of participant observation between 1988 and 1995, in which I worked as a cocktail waitress at three casinos in Reno, Nevada.[4] My observations relied primarily on those waitresses with whom I worked most regularly and had the best rapport—my "informants." The three casinos of this study represent the variety of casinos found in Reno—both corporate and privately owned casinos, which varied in terms of size and income-level of customers. Participant observation was supplemented by interviews with several ex-cocktail waitresses and labor activists, as well as exploration of documentary sources.

Because their uniforms of miniskirts or French-cut bodysuits suggest women's sexual subservience to men, gendered resistance on the part of casino cocktail waitresses can seem counterintuitive (Bayard de Volo 2003b). As women in the United States enter male-dominated professions in greater numbers, the casino cocktail waitress seems a holdover from an earlier, less enlightened era. As one activist newsletter put it in an article entitled "Sexploitation in Nevada's Casinos" (Alliance for Workers' Rights 1999), "Those of us . . . who have spent any time in a Nevada casino are aware of the exploitation of female casino workers, particularly in regards to the 'uniforms' worn by cocktail servers. [These] bring about . . . unwelcome remarks and the objectification of women."

I wondered: is the workplace politics of casino cocktail waitresses best understood in terms of "sexploitation," with the skimpy uniforms constituting the necessary evidence? It is tempting to focus on how these uniforms objectify and thus oppress women. They seem to "invite the male gaze, celebrate male leers, and pose women as objects, potential prizes to be won by the lucky (male) winners" (Bayard de Volo 2003b, 356). Through ethnography attuned to the meanings waitresses attached to their everyday work lives, however, it became evident that the waitresses did not experience their uniforms as oppressive. In my discussions with coworkers about the uniform, their critical responses referred to the physical integrity or comfort of the uniform—"The rhinestones are falling off," for example, or "The jacket is too hot." More often, they expressed some sort of satisfaction and pride in their uniform. Interestingly, many were unselfconscious wearing the uniform and even oblivious to how others might perceive them. That is, however self-conscious they may have felt at first, the uniform soon became "normalized," such that its revealing nature was not something they consciously reflected upon (Loe 1996). For example, even though it was against casino policy, Linda used to arrive at work already dressed in her uniform in order to save time. When a manager asked whether she was embarrassed to walk on the street from her car to the casino "that way," at first Linda did not understand the question.[5]

Throughout my research, no waitress expressed a desire for less revealing uniforms. Their preferences were clarified when one casino considered changing its cocktail uniforms and asked several waitresses to try out some new styles—one of which was a long, velvet dress. The waitresses themselves rejected the latter uniform, which resembled an evening gown and revealed much less than the current uniform. Of all the styles, the majority voiced their preference for the current, and most revealing, uniform. Eventually, management chose the "evening gown" style in an effort to present a "classier" image, yet as a compromise to the cocktail waitresses, the casino allowed them to choose between a short or a long skirt.

In sum, based upon one interpretation of feminism—or social conservatism—we might expect that the cocktail waitresses would associate their skimpy uniforms with sexual harassment and even objectification, and thus welcome a shift toward a more modest uniform. Participant observation, to my own surprise, revealed otherwise.

Combining Multiple Levels of Insight

A third contribution of ethnography is the unique insight it can bring to the study of multilevel processes. Political scientists employing ethnography may ask how power dynamics circulating at the micro-level connect with those occurring regionally, nationally, and globally. How do people *experience* politics in the form of laws, surveillance techniques, structural shifts, and political violence? What meanings do they attach to macro-level political processes, and how do they respond—accommodation, collective resistance, or more subtle nonconformity?

For my fieldwork with the Mothers of Heroes and Martyrs in Nicaragua, I charted processes unfolding at the national and international "macro-level" with those at the "micro-level" of the mothers' group. At the macro-level, I conducted discourse analysis of dominant representations of women, femininity, and motherhood by comparing pro- and anti-state newspapers, as well as other texts produced by the FSLN (Sandinista National Liberation Front), anti-Sandinista groups, and the U.S. government. This comparison allowed me to chart how the Sandinista state and anti-Sandinista groups represented and appealed to women, how this changed over time in relation to political and economic factors, and how this was linked at the micro-level of the Mothers' organization.

One example of the linking of macro- and micro-level processes through ethnography involves the Mothers' work in the early years of the Contra War, as the FSLN recruited these women to accompany the bodies of fallen soldiers home to the families. In addition to comforting the grieving mother, the Mothers' task was also to lessen the family's resentment toward the state and the new draft, as detailed in the Mothers' 1984 progress report to the FSLN: "Each time that there are fallen [Sandinistas], we accompany the new mother of this movement in this difficult moment, but we also prevent the enemies of the Revolution from taking advantage of the family's grief. We work to rescue all the mothers whom we find isolated or resentful until we convince them that we confront problems better united."[6] One mother explained the therapeutic reasons behind this difficult task:

> Wars are horrible. . . . [W]e knew how [the mother's] heart would stop as we told her, "The one that we bring is your child." . . . We went first to accompany her as other mothers. And also to talk with her. We cried as much as she did! The death hit her like it hit us because to deliver the dead child was like the delivery of our own dead child. And so we tried to make things easier on her.

Another member pointed to the political aims of the visit:

> [The mothers] would start to cry and they would ask how could it be that their children died. Some reacted badly. They would say . . . "It's the *Frente* [Sandinista]'s fault that my son fell." In this work we would say to them that it wasn't the *Frente* that was killing them. It was the Contra. If the Contra weren't in the mountains, [their children] wouldn't have died.

Through the linking of the macro-level processes of civil war, on the one hand, and the delivery of a body to the family, on the other hand, we gain insight into how death in war—so often expressed in the discipline in terms of statistics and their impact on foreign policy—is experienced at the ground level by those most profoundly affected, dead soldiers' loved ones. But we also better understand it as a process by which meaning is attached to this experience, whereby emotions are not only expressed and shared, but also (re)directed, channeled, and contained by a state at war. In this case, the Mothers of Heroes and Martyrs, a Sandinista mass organization, was a conduit through which the construction and dissemination of the meaning of death in war in a manner conducive to Sandinista victory was carried out. As such, it is also instructive in helping us to better understand the underappreciated psychological terrain of war—the battlefields that lie in people's hearts and minds.

Essential Information for Culturally Sensitive Research

As a fourth benefit, ethnography can produce information that is key to culturally sensitive future research, policies, or political action. In my casino fieldwork, for example, in addition to asking how cocktail waitresses see themselves in relation to their uniform and their workplace, I also explored how they experienced and responded to power relationships. Are casino cocktail waitresses best seen as subservient, even victimized, or do they maintain a sense of control and exercise agency in the workplace? What issues or relationships are most likely to produce collective resistance? Such questions point to a "diagnostics of power" in which the analysis reveals formerly hidden transcripts and magnifies micro-modes of resistance to help us better understand how power circulates (Abu-Lughod 1999; Scott 1985, 1990). Through analyzing the "infrapolitics" of the casino floor—micro-modes of resistance that are, by design, difficult to detect—we are better able to identify contexts in which cocktail waitresses might engage in collective resistance (Scott 1990). Infrapolitics, then, is not simply an alternative to collective action but also "a way to gauge the grievances of working people" (Kelley 1994, 230). Examinations of infrapolitics also teach us what people (in this case, cocktail waitresses) bring to organized movements.

As discussed earlier, waitresses were generally untroubled by their skimpy uniforms. Rather, the daily articulations of power as experienced by waitresses were more nuanced and varied than is captured by the concept of "sexploitation" and its attendant assumptions of catcalls and unwanted groping. In looking beyond "sexploitation" to a more complicated array of power relations, we can explore the transformative potential of infrapolitics. What do these micro-struggles suggest about the nature and potential of cocktail waitresses' collective action?

An insider perspective of casino cocktail waitresses reveals the entrepreneurial nature of the work. In my fieldwork, waitresses individually pursued tips from customers, which constituted the majority of their income; for them, their casino hourly wage was relatively insignificant. Waitresses, then, worked on a one-on-one basis with each gambling customer, providing good service to earn a tip, with very little oversight from management. Rather than being grateful, waitresses balked at management's preference for more modest uniforms, for the most part fearing a negative impact on tips.

Cocktail waitresses had an impressive arsenal of resistance techniques or "infrapolitics" that they employed against nontipping customers. One of the more common tip-training techniques was used with customers who did not acknowledge the waitress's presence, expecting her to simply set the drink down and walk away. As Donna coached me, "Just hold the drink out to them and make them take it. That way, they have to look at you." Ostensibly, this was easier for the waitress, who was busy holding a drink-laden tray; however, it also jolted some gamblers out of their "gambling trance" long enough to elicit a tip.

If this did not work, Donna instructed me to linger beside the customer and "look busy arranging drinks or your tips on the tray." This might apply enough pressure to squeeze some change out of the more determined non-tippers. If these tactics did not work, a nontipping customer's next drink might be "lost" or "forgotten," or the waitress might "accidentally" skip that customer's row the next time she took orders. In the rare cases when non-tippers complained to management about the service, the waitress could plausibly claim innocence or imply that the customer was drunk.

Most conflicts involved resistance through such infrapolitics and were primarily aimed at enhancing tips. More rarely, conflicts arose due to management scheduling that contradicted the seniority system and affected tip income. These conflicts offered glimpses into cocktail waitresses' common understanding of their interests and thus possibilities for collective resistance. Assignments to stations on the casino floor, which varied significantly in terms of tips, were to follow seniority, not managers' preferences. There was virtually no disagreement on the seniority system among cocktail waitresses. New managers soon learned that changes that bypassed seniority or were otherwise perceived to threaten tips would be quickly met with collective resistance.

Through my ethnographic work, then, it became apparent that management interventions in seniority and the entrepreneurial tipping relationship between cocktail waitress and customer had a high potential to be met with collective resistance. This theory was later borne out when management placed a refrigerator amid gambling tables to hold nonalcoholic drinks for gambling customers. Customers could simply help themselves rather than ordering from a waitress (thus avoiding the obligation to tip). This move by management—intervening in the tipping relationship between cocktail waitresses and customers—prompted the relatively rare response of organized resistance on the part of cocktail waitresses. They vigorously and successfully protested this move, arguing that it cut into their tip income.

Making Space for Ethnography:
Changing Definitions and Cautionary Notes

Given these advantages, how might political science be challenged to better accommodate and appreciate ethnography, and furthermore, how might we alter or clarify the ethnographic method for application to politics? What follows is not a comprehensive survey of challenges and clarifications. Rather, I have selected three issues that were particularly complex for me in conducting ethnography as a political scientist. First, I challenge "science" and "politics," advocating for inductive research and broader definitions to accommodate the study of power relations that are often of interest to ethnographers, specifically those outside of institutional or formal politics. Second, I explore the "delusions" of sameness and difference that ethnographers might confront in fieldwork, suggesting means of navigating the pitfalls of either extreme (Stacey 1991). Finally, I turn to emotions and challenge the axiom of "objectivity" in political science research. I argue against the possibility of research devoid of emotions, but also provide instances in which emotions can be essential to the success of fieldwork.

A Broader Understanding of "Politics" and "Science"

If ethnography is to be accepted as a method within the discipline, we must first reconsider what is meant by political "science." Because it challenges the "scientific pretensions of neutral observation or description," ethnography can seem a radical departure from mainstream political science (Stacey 1991, 115; see also Clifford 1986).[7] Anthropologist Bronislaw Malinowski, pioneer of the ethnographic method, posed the goal of the ethnographer to be to "grasp the native's point of view, his relation to life, to realise his vision of his world" (1961, 25). Ethnography, then, has traditionally been an inductive and open-ended mode of inquiry that does not aspire to scientific detachment. As such, the ethnographer commonly does not start with a concise and falsifiable thesis to test, but rather attempts to ascertain what processes and events the local population understands as important and then to study these "in their own terms." Furthermore, ethnographers acknowledge that, unlike a sterilized laboratory, the field setting is unavoidably altered by the ethnographer's presence. The task is not to remove the researcher's influence on the group being studied—not only is this an impossible task, but one might miss key insights in the effort. Rather, the researcher's task is to fold her presence into the study itself and even use it to draw out aspects of the group or site.[8]

Regrettably, ethnography employed in this way can present problems for the political scientist giving a job talk, submitting an article to a traditional political science journal, or applying for a National Science Foundation (NSF) grant.[9] These are contexts in which one is likely to encounter political scientists who are either skeptical or relatively ignorant about ethnographic studies. They will want to know, for example, about hypotheses. They might ask, "What is the thesis of this thesis?" with an expectation that lessons learned from fieldwork can be distilled into a one-sentence finding without losing much value. In deliberations over job candidates, supporters of the candidate who has conducted ethnography might be called on to defend the value of what detractors charge to be purely descriptive work. Political science reviewers can find ethnographic papers frustrating in their tendency to lapse into "storytelling" rather than following a format more familiar to proponents of deductive science. And lack of parsimony can be an unforgivable sin in political science.[10] While not the only solution, discussion and deliberation on the uses of ethnography (such as that found in this volume) will help to lay bare such methodological biases, as will pressures placed on funding agencies and graduate programs.

A related problem arises over the definition of *politics*. For those who apply ethnographic methods to study processes outside of formal institutional politics, one's work can even be challenged as "not really" political science but instead anthropology or sociology. In response, I have come to define *politics* as "the articulation of power relations," which thus encompasses not just issues from "high politics," such as the determinants of war, but the micro-level understandings of political violence—not just surveys of U.S. attitudes on casinos, but also the infrapolitics of the casino floor (Bayard de Volo 2003a, 93; Randall 1982, 7–8). Since power relations circulate within and across all social spheres, "politics" is not limited to what has traditionally been known as the public sphere or institutional politics (Okin 1998). This definition of politics within the discipline encourages attention to socially subordinate groups, such as women and racial/ethnic minorities—groups that traditionally have not been present or active in institutional politics (Bayard de Volo and Schatz 2004). More generally, the definition works to legitimize the study of social interactions outside of institutional channels. Notably, ethnography is a particularly appropriate method for studying precisely such groups and forms of politics—populations whose voices are not well represented in the dominant discourse and whose poverty, geographic location (remote rural areas or poor neighborhoods, for example), marginalized status (ethnic minorities, women), lack of education, or distrust of strangers or authority make them more difficult to access through other research methods (phone or door-to-door surveys, for example).

Sameness and Difference in the Field

In contrast to the dominant scientific method, whereby the hypothesis is developed *before* the evidence is analyzed, ethnography engages us to continuously ask "why" *throughout* research. The method is particularly effective in encouraging the researcher to ask "why" with regard to processes that the researcher or the local population has taken for granted as natural or "the way things have always been," or conversely, to make sense of otherwise bewildering, unimaginable, or seemingly irrational practices. As anthropologist James Clifford put it, ethnography "makes the familiar strange, the exotic quotidian" (Clifford 1986, 2). Yet those of us trained as distant, neutral (political) scientists might be particularly ill prepared to navigate the divide implied here between familiar and strange, sameness and difference, insider and outsider.

Asking "why" from the position of the "researcher as stranger" (or as Clifford put it, making the exotic quotidian) involves getting a handle on a foreign form of daily interaction and systems of meaning, coming to detect the subtle power plays within the group, and learning the status hierarchy—the order itself, but also the meanings that produce and are produced by the hierarchy, the system of inclusion and exclusion, and the repercussions of that system. In my Nicaraguan fieldwork, one of the most important forms of asking "why" as "researcher as stranger" involved what it means to be a mother who has lost a child in war. There were various aspects of the notion of stranger here—most obviously, I was not Nicaraguan, but also I was not a mother (and especially not a mother who had lost a child). Asking "why" from the position of "researcher as stranger" meant listening closely as the Mothers spoke about their loss and asking questions about the relationship between that loss, their grief, and their activism. I asked, for example, why the organization was composed only of mothers—why not mothers and fathers? This question often struck mothers as naïve or even silly—the answer being so very obvious. That is, fathers simply did not suffer this loss as mothers did; mothers' grief was unique. Nonetheless, they spelled out to me, the naïve nonmother, their causal link between pain at the birth of a child and pain at the death of a child. Doña Esperanza R. explained, "The child costs the mother [emotionally] more than the father [because] the fathers don't carry the child in the womb. The father doesn't feel the pain of childbirth. The father gives the money that he gives and goes off to work." Doña Rosaura put it simply: "Clearly a mother suffers more [at the death of a child] because the child was in the womb, and you felt the pain of mothers [giving birth]." Maternal labor, then, provided an exclusive form of knowledge about the cost of life, warranting an exclusive organization not only to address grief but also to provide a means through which these mothers might collectively speak to policymakers and the public, and make demands based upon their exclusive knowledge about casualties of war. In their constructed hierarchy of pain and suffering, not only fathers were excluded from such knowledge, but also war widows and even mothers whose children had "only" been wounded.

I came to this understanding of emotion and knowledge in large part through asking "why" about issues that members themselves thought obvious or natural. In this case, the obvious answer—for members of the Mothers organization—was that men and women are different, such that *all* mothers emotionally suffer the same pain, a pain that is unique to mothers and based upon the experience of giving birth. I did not come into the field with this question. It arose based upon my observations *in* the field. Furthermore, asking "why" throughout research, coming up with new questions along the way, was in this way facilitated by my position as stranger.

Ethnography can also make "the familiar strange," which again involves asking "why," but this time one of those called upon to respond is the researcher himself. As a "native" or "indigenous" ethnographer, the researcher is an insider studying his own culture, calling into question processes that have become naturalized, again shining a light on power relations, wondering at points of resistance (Moffatt 1992; see also Miner 1956). There is the advantage of native fluency in the language and a more refined attunement to cultural nuance. One can perhaps blend in more easily, establishing better rapport.

However, two cautions are in order for "native" ethnography. First, it is no small task to make "the familiar strange," to become aware of one's own cultural assumptions and tacit understandings. One does not have the same advantage here of exaggerated difference and contrast (the strange culture of fieldwork versus the familiar culture of home) to draw attention to, much less call into question, such understandings (Moffatt 1992, 206; Miner 1956).

Yet such a conception assumes a homogeneous culture, which leads to the second cautionary note: there are many differences within, and the ethnographer must take care not to exaggerate the familiarity. The researcher can never be fully familiar within what is considered her own culture. There are always "others" within, processes that we do not understand, strangers, exotic practices. One can still be a stranger even if doing fieldwork in one's own society and speaking one's native language. As Moffatt noted about native ethnographers, "Identifying with 'them' does not necessarily mean you are like them, or that they are all like one another, or that they all trust or identify with you, or that they want to be studied by you" (Moffatt 1992, 207). Sameness, then, is never complete (Aguilar 1981; Moffatt 1992).

Indeed, I was drawn to study casino cocktail waitresses because to me the line of work represented a women's world in my own culture that I did not understand very well. Why do women wear uniforms designed to invite the male gaze? How do they navigate (what I assumed to be) constant harassment on the part of male customers? What forms does their resistance take, if any? In retrospect, casino cocktail waitresses represented an Other to me, and I had hoped to close the gap I perceived between "women like me" and "women like them." Yet through my participant observation, I found that contrary to a popular (often feminist) concern with leering, lecherous male customers, the daily articulations of power that most troubled cocktail waitresses had little to do with sexual harassment on the part of customers; rather, they involved management interventions in the tipping relation with customers, bartender economic control mechanisms, uncomfortable shoes, and more mundane (not overtly sexual) conflicts with customers (Bayard de Volo 2003b).

A related ethnographic challenge for me was to navigate between what Judith Stacey refers to as the delusion of separateness and the delusion of alliance (Stacey 1991). Many ethnographers reject the position of the neutral scientist (in a figurative white lab coat) objectively collecting data from respondents as an alienating process reliant upon a hierarchy between researcher and researched. However, we should not lapse into the delusion that ethnography dissolves power relations, that we can become "one with the people" and still carry out research. The research process is never fully egalitarian, and one of the ethnographer's tasks is to strive for self-awareness with regard to power and the ethnographic setting, in part through an awareness of the shifting balance between alliance and separateness, sameness and difference between researcher and informants.

Among many possible examples, I will offer two to explore the dilemmas inherent in the power differentials arising in participant observation. As several ethnographers have recalled about their own fieldwork, in Nicaragua I found myself in the middle of several disagreements between members (Stacey 1991, 113; Stack 1996, 102). A key debate involved whether mothers of fallen Contras should be allowed to join this organization of Sandinista mothers (that is, should mothers of combatants on both sides of the war form an alliance?). In the postwar context, many members accepted Contra mothers in the name of national reconciliation and Christian forgiveness. Yet a vocal minority was opposed and sought me out as a potential ally. I strove to avoid even the appearance of taking sides—a difficult task indeed, as whom I visited or even sat next to at a meeting might imply a bias. Moreover, while striving to always demonstrate respect, I did not deny power differentials between myself and members, which were all too obvious, given geopolitics and members' extreme poverty; rather, I tried to be always mindful of them (as were members themselves). Such mindfulness was especially important when my opinion on a matter could be usefully exploited by one side or the other of the disagreement. Members were not only cognizant of the power differential that I introduced, but were politically astute enough to sometimes consider leveraging it for their own purposes. I referred to my outsider status to recuse myself from taking sides, explaining that I was there to learn from them, and thus was very interested in their views, but because I was not a member, I was not in a position to take sides. Notably, this is a form of neutrality, though embraced not in the name of scientific detachment but out of an ethical concern not to abuse power relations.

I propose, however, that the ethnographer *can* ethically participate in debates when one is also a participant on a relatively equal footing with others in the group observed and would be similarly affected by the outcome—for example, when the researcher is also a member of the organization or a coworker in the workplace. Indeed, I sometimes engaged in disagreements in my casino ethnography—for example, with bartenders and management—and in the process gained valuable insights into workplace hierarchies and power relations.

As this implies, my struggle with Stacey's twin delusions of alliance and separateness took a very different form in my casino fieldwork. My initial efforts to inform my respondents (that is, my fellow employees) about my research project were often met with patronizing disbelief ("Sure, that's what you're doing, hon"), indifference, and even some bristling due to a perception that I was positioning myself above the other workers, better than them. In refusing to take my fieldwork seriously, they refused the hierarchical relation between researcher and researched: I was a casino worker, just like them, even if I had delusions of grandeur and fancied myself as something more. In this case, my immediate ethical concern was whether they were fully informed if they did not take my project seriously.[11] But unlike the situation in my Nicaragua fieldwork, here my identity as a researcher did not introduce a power imbalance that my coworkers or I perceived as relevant.

My two ethnographic projects, then, presented different challenges in relation to the extremes of alliance and separateness. Some ethnographic projects present greater danger in the way of these extremes than others. There was little danger of my being confused for a Mother of Heroes and Martyrs, and ethically I had to be continually aware of the power differential between myself and members. However, there was the possibility of *political* alliance—being on the same side of an internal debate—that was important to avoid. For the casino work, the balance to strike was between ensuring respondents were informed of my work and at the same time not positioning myself as completely separate and thus creating animosity.

Emotions and Fieldwork

Attempts to achieve scientific neutrality and detachment can undermine fieldwork in other ways as well. Ethnography requires some degree of empathy, connection, and concern for one's research "subjects," and thus the attempt to appear scientifically neutral and unconnected is likely counterproductive, if not detrimental (Stacey 1991, 112). Indeed, in participant observation, it is hard to *participate* without having a social connection and some compassion for the problems of those observed.

In my casino ethnography, it would have been impossible to juggle my casino job with maintaining a scientific distance. The attempt would have required regular positioning of myself as a researcher rather than a worker in my interactions with management and customers, which would have lost me the job. An effort to keep my coworkers at arm's length in pursuit of a detached, objective position would have earned me ostracism—clearly counterproductive to any attempt to gain knowledge.

Two key forms of emotional interaction were critical to the success of my casino fieldwork. The first involved humor. There was an atmosphere of competitive banter, dominated by the senior cocktail waitresses and bartenders. Failure to engage in the ongoing joke slinging would indicate naïveté or, worse, "bitchiness." As a new waitress, I initially served as an appreciative audience for the senior waitresses and bartenders. Their bawdy jokes and stories offered valuable insights into the work, but they were also enjoyable in and of themselves. I began to participate more actively, offering a few of my own (hopefully) funny stories. Over time, senior waitresses warmed up to me through these interchanges, and a few took me "under their wing," to teach me the secrets of the trade, particularly as they related to making better tips, evading managerial control, and dealing with difficult customers.

For example, Elaine showed me how she drank alcohol on the job, her technique fine-tuned over two decades of cocktail waitressing. As she filled her customers' drink orders, she would include a drink for herself—a mixed drink containing alcohol that was visually indistinguishable from a non-alcoholic drink, such as a glass of soda or juice. After delivering the drinks, she would return to the waitress station with the extra drink, as if the customer who had ordered it had left. Then she would drink it while standing next to the garbage can. If she saw a manager approaching, she would drop the evidence, glass and all, into the garbage.

As this implies, Elaine had a serious drinking problem, which points to the second main form of emotional interaction in this project—compassion for the problems of coworkers. While Elaine's specific methods were unique, her problem was not. Indeed, cocktail waitresses and other beverage department employees with whom I worked closely suffered numerous problems: alcoholism, substance abuse, domestic violence, divorce, secret love affairs, ex-husbands refusing to pay child support, theft, gambling addictions, low self-esteem linked to body image, and lack of a high-school diploma. Many of my conversations during this fieldwork involved discussions of such personal problems. Compassion for the problems of coworkers was far from "scientific" neutrality, yet it was crucial to developing an insider perspective through *participating* as well as simply observing.

In Nicaragua there was even more at stake in terms of the place of emotions in research, and the emotions themselves were more intense—for both members and myself. In explaining their activism, the Nicaraguan Mothers spoke of their grief at the death of sons and daughters, often in very moving terms. Once, as I accompanied members on a trip deep into the countryside, we stopped at the site where one Mother's son had been killed defending a Sandinista agricultural cooperative several years earlier. A member of the cooperative joined us and gave details of the battle and this son's last moments: "The Contras attacked us from over that hill. [Your son] bravely defended our cooperative from over there until his final breath. He was shot and died right here. His last words were '*Patria libre o morir* [Free homeland or death].'" This was an emotionally trying moment for me, to say the least. Everyone else was relatively stoic; they had been emotionally processing violence and death in war for at least fifteen years, had heard such stories many times, and perhaps had witnessed far worse. But as a relative newcomer to violent death and war, I was shaken. The mother of this son sat next to me as we continued the journey, and *she* comforted *me*. As I sniffled, she explained how they had learned to respond to and bear their grief, counseling me on a more personal level rather than instructing me on operating procedures of the organization. In this interchange, I gained new insight into how the Mothers' organization functioned during the war as a Sandinista mass organization that both spread Sandinista ideology and was emotionally therapeutic. Furthermore, the members on this trip were noticeably more affectionate and familiar with me afterward, at least in part because my emotional response indicated to them that I cared.

The point, of course, is not that one should invent or exaggerate one's emotions to elicit better responses from informants. But spontaneous and culturally appropriate emotional responses to experiences in the field—not just sadness but also joy, humor, fear, relief, affection—can open doors to new levels of understanding. By the same token, people around will certainly notice and perhaps resent or respond negatively to an ethnographer who appears inappropriately unaffected (which is to say, "neutral").

Such expectations, however, are often gendered. As a woman in Nicaragua, I had higher expectations placed upon me to be demonstrative with my emotions, compared to what members of the organization would expect from a male ethnographer. A common theme among members in making gender comparisons involved the idea that fathers had less of an emotional bond with their children and, more generously, men are afraid to show their emotions. More generally, there was an understanding that women were naturally more emotional than men. Indeed, a common criticism of other women foreigners (especially non-Latinas) living in Nicaragua was that they were "cold," though I never heard this criticism directed against a man.

Conclusion

I have attempted in this chapter to create more space for ethnography in political science by suggesting what it might bring to one's own research and also to the study of politics more generally. Ethnography can produce otherwise unobtainable insights into politics, which can be counterintuitive to understandings developed without an insider perspective and which can allow us, in turn, to better understand macro-level political processes. I also addressed ethnographic challenges based upon dilemmas I encountered both in the field and in the discipline. First, because mainstream definitions of both *politics* and *science* can, in my experience, define many political ethnographers out of the discipline, I revised the definitions to be more inclusive. Then, I compared my two ethnographies—the "foreign" case of Nicaragua and the "familiar" case of the United States—to explore ethical dilemmas in ethnography that can arise in moving along a spectrum of sameness and difference. Finally, I discussed the researcher's emotions in the conduct of research—a topic practically absent from political science (except to imply that they do not belong), but unavoidable (and potentially beneficial) in ethnographic work.

There are many relevant topics that I have not addressed—among them, how parenthood can conflict with ethnographic fieldwork, frustrations with university internal review boards, career implications of participant observation in gendered low-status work (such as cocktail waitressing), the emotional and physical trials of ethnographic fieldwork, and the ethical implications of political ethnography employed by militaries. Along these lines, then, future work might address the gaps in the gendered, ethical, and practical considerations of political ethnography as both a method and a sensibility.

Notes

I would like to thank the anonymous reviewers, as well as Dvora Yanow, James Scott, Michael Schatzberg, Sohini Guha, and especially Edward Schatz, for their insightful comments.

1. See sociologist Javier Auyero (2006a), who documents that in the last decade of the *American Political Science Review* and the *American Journal of Political Science* (1996–2005), out of a total of 938 articles, only one employs ethnography as a data-production technique. As Auyero notes, sociologists too have been slow to adopt ethnographic methods.

2. Some of the most vigorous new advocates of political ethnography are in the U.S. military, as its scholars and strategists reflect upon failures in Iraq and Afghanistan. These advocates provide compelling examples of the policy confusion and tactical mistakes generated when ethnographic insights are not pursued (See, for example, Renzi 2006, 17). Critical discussion of the ethical and practical implications of this military trend has developed in anthropology but is thus far missing in political science (González 2007; Price 2007).

3. For exceptions and discussion, see Lichterman (1998); Gould (2003); and Auyero (2006a).

4. Fieldwork included work in three casinos during the summers of 1988 and 1989, April–May 1993, and September 1994–July 1995 (part-time, twenty to twenty-five hours per week). Because my graduate program's methods courses did not cover ethnography, I began the fieldwork early in graduate school with the aim of learning and practicing this technique. This initial research in 1988 and 1989 was preliminary and insufficient to produce published research. I returned to complete this casino ethnography as I was writing my dissertation based upon the Nicaragua fieldwork.

5. Names of fieldwork informants are pseudonyms.

6. "Information Sheet about the Movement of Mothers of Heroes and Martyrs" by the Office of the Mothers of Heroes and Martyrs of Matagalpa, 1984 (exact date unknown).

7. For a different view, see Allina-Pisano, this volume.

8. For more discussion, see Pachirat, this volume.

9. I single out National Science Foundation (NSF) grants both because many political science departments in U.S. research universities consider successful NSF proposals to be important to achieving tenure and because the grant-making process of the political science program of NSF is skewed toward relatively narrow understandings of methods appropriate to "science." The NSF Sociology Program, in contrast, has made notable strides toward methodological diversity, as evidenced by the NSF workshop report on qualitative methods by Ragin, Nagel and White (2004), which

includes ethnography. There *are* granting agencies that judge projects in terms of the research questions and research design without insisting upon a specific understanding of political *science*. Furthermore, in my experience, book publishers, including prominent university presses, are noticeably less concerned to uphold disciplinary boundaries, in part because an ethnographic study from a political scientist is likely to have cross-disciplinary appeal, translating into better sales.

10. There are some useful strategies to address such problems. Most generally, political ethnographers should try to anticipate such questions and preempt them early on in the talk or paper, avoid taking a defensive tone, and cite prominent ethnographies in the discipline. In addition to working to disarm skeptics, such an approach will also help arm reviewers or members of the hiring committee, giving them language with which to support the research. Furthermore, the typical political science audience does not have the patience for "letting the narrative unfold." The political ethnographer should summarize the analytical insights of the research early on, situating them within the literature and highlighting how they contribute something new to the discussion, *then* move on to the rich narrative. Those using ethnography from a rational-choice perspective or in conjunction with quantitative methods will be less likely to confront these problems as their approaches will bear greater similarities to dominant modes of scientific research design.

11. Despite the initial lack of interest, I continued to discuss my research project, and my key informants began to ask about it, eventually with some interest. Notably, I was a graduate student during this fieldwork. Ethnographers with a Ph.D., which would lend credibility to their project, would likely confront a different power dynamic.

PART FOUR

Placing Ethnography in the Discipline

The twin claims this volume makes—that ethnography adds value to the study of politics and that this value too often goes unrecognized—lead to questions about what place ethnography *might* occupy in professional political science.

In chapter 11, Enrique Desmond Arias sketches an ambitious research agenda for the study of Latin America. Highlighting how the informal use of violence characterizes Latin America's regimes—including its democratic ones—he shows what is missed when ethnographic approaches are underused and what might be gained by reversing the trend. His chapter provides an excellent example of how different an entire research area might look were political ethnography (understood as participant observation or a broader ethnographic sensibility) to become the central tool of inquiry.

In chapter 12, Corey Shdaimah, Roland Stahl, and Sanford Schram provide an alternative way forward. Cautioning against a desire to champion political ethnographic approaches (or any other approach, for that matter), they argue that a problem-driven study of politics should be agnostic about methods and methodology. Through an extended example of multiple-methods research that incorporates ethnographic elements, they argue that "participatory action research" better serves the people being studied than do other approaches, including ethnography.

In chapter 13, Dvora Yanow addresses both those who write ethnographic accounts and those who read them. Beginning with the premise that ethnographic work implies a sensibility and set of techniques unfamiliar to many social scientists, she details principles that constitute successful ethnographic work. Her goal—to build bridges between those working in ethnographic and nonethnographic traditions of political inquiry—emerges from a professional and methodological reflexivity that is in its own way "ethnographic."

ELEVEN

Ethnography and the Study of Latin American Politics: An Agenda for Research

ENRIQUE DESMOND ARIAS

For the last generation scholars have struggled to understand the success and ongoing limitations of democracy in Latin America. Despite tremendous advances since the early 1980s, the region's governments are far from problem-free, having experienced the growth of subnational authoritarianism in areas characterized by local strongmen and criminal groups, growing violent crime, official corruption, ineffectual political institutions, and high levels of inequality (O'Donnell 1993, 1355–69). Guillermo O'Donnell (1993) has argued that an adequate understanding of some of these phenomena requires the use of "transdisciplinary" methods, such as ethnography. Unfortunately, political science has largely abandoned these approaches in the study of Latin American politics. At the same time, scholars in other disciplines working on the region have opened up a new line of political studies that critically assess institutional and noninstitutional political structures and raise questions about the assumptions that underlie notions of "democracy" and "democratic institutions," which drive much of the debate about the politics of the region.

Ethnography has made important contributions to political science over the years. These include James Scott's (1977) analysis of peasant politics, revolution, and state practice; Jan Kubik's study of the rise of Solidarity in Poland (1994); Sonia Alvarez's (1989, 205–51) discussions of social movements in the transition to democracy in Brazil; and Elisabeth Jean Wood's (2003) analysis of peasant collective action in the Salvadoran civil war. These interventions in the wider political science literature provide crucial insights into changing, unstable, and often difficult-to-observe phenomena.

This chapter offers a "forward-looking" examination of the role of ethnography in Latin American politics by critically engaging with the state of the subfield today and its wider shortcomings. Building on the work of scholars looking broadly at the Hemisphere, I offer a research agenda in which political ethnography plays a central role in the study of the region.

Latin American Politics: The State of the Field

There is an assumption in the political science of Latin America that critical answers can be found by parsing out the formal dynamics that drive democratic institutions. Despite continuing human rights abuse and rising crime, as well as persistent corruption in many countries in the region, the discipline's journals have published relatively little on the question of violence or the informal relationships that characterize the operation of democratic institutions. Among the most visible disciplinary journals (*American Political Science Review, American Journal of Political Science,* and *Journal of Politics*), only one article published between 2002 and 2006 even mentions violence in Latin America in its title, and this piece offers a historical analysis of the impact of guerrilla violence on public opinion in Peru (Arce 2003, 572–83). A partial exception to this trend may be found in Susan Stokes's (2005) piece on machine politics in Argentina. While this article is based on formal modeling and survey techniques, it does draw on her own past qualitative research on clientelism in Peru and more ethnographic work on Argentine clientelism (Stokes 2005). Journal articles over the past five years have instead focused on decentralization, union activities, presidentialism vs. parliamentarism, and the dynamics of legislatures and elections. The content of *Comparative Political Studies* is similarly biased toward institutional analyses, frequently with a large-n orientation. Even this analysis of institutions is limited by a lack of in-depth knowledge about the underlying dynamics that drive those institutions. More often than not pieces focus on the formal institutional dynamics that lead to specific political outcomes, such as the passage of a law or the result of an election, without a nuanced understanding of how individuals working in those institutions operate.[1]

The challenges facing contemporary political science, however, go beyond this. The field today is focused in a basic way on analyzing the visible outcomes of political processes in democratic institutions. These institutions, however, often fail to live up to the liberal or social democratic ideals that many political scientists see in contemporary North America and Western Europe. This has pushed the literature in two directions. The first is a cottage industry that has developed around adjectivally modifying the term *democracy* to reflect the deficiencies authors perceive in political institutions in the region. Thus, we learn of such things as illiberal, low-intensity, and formal democracy, as well as low-intensity citizenship (Collier and Levitsky 1997, 430–31; Carothers 2002, 6; Brinks 2003; Paley 2001). The second is a growing literature on the "quality of democracy," which, as Marc Plattner puts it, "deal[s] with countries whose basic claims to being democratic are not in question, even if they may have significant deficiencies in democratic governance. The great virtue of studies of the quality of democracy is that they offer an approach that can bridge the sometimes artificially inflated gap between new and established democracies. After all, it is hard to find any democracy that is not in need of improvement" (Plattner 2005, 6). In general, writing in this school focuses on general expectations of democracy and why the formal institutions of some countries fail to live up to these expectations as a result of problems in institutional design (Diamond and Morlino 2005; for a critique of this approach, see Brinks 2008, 256).

In this context, scholarship has shifted away from small-n studies based on interviews, historical methods, and ethnographies, and toward larger-n quantitative comparative studies (Collier 1999, 1–6). As O'Donnell and Schmitter (1986, 4) put it, "When studying an established political regime, one can rely on relatively stable economic, social, cultural, and partisan categories to identify, analyze, and evaluate the identities and strategies of those defending the status quo and those struggling to reform or transform it. We believe that this 'normal science methodology' is inappropriate in rapidly changing situations, where those very parameters of political action are in flux." While this was the general framework for democratization studies in the 1980s and earlier 1990s, today many scholars conclude that much of Latin America is stable enough to merit a narrower set of methodologies.

There are two negative implications to the use of "normal science" as the primary mode of studying political institutions in Latin America. The first is that inevitably the institutions do not measure up to what scholars experience on an everyday basis in developed democracies. The result is, despite the protestations of scholars, an emerging teleology in which imperfect developing democracies are set on a continuum defined by the types of regimes that exist in North America and Western Europe. The second is that political scientists, by prioritizing the study of democratic institutions, accept claims implicit in the political projects of national leaders that these regimes are, indeed, basically similar to the democratic regimes that govern other parts of the world and that can be fixed with limited institutional reforms. This ignores important critical assessments offered in other fields suggesting that the structure of existing regimes in Latin America may limit their capacity to change in the ways preferred and that the apparent imperfections in these regimes may be more than minor flaws; they may be fundamental regime functions and necessary compromises to stabilize those systems (Arias and Goldstein, forthcoming).

This is especially the case with the pervasive violence affecting the region. Guillermo O'Donnell (1993, 1361–64) has argued that Latin America faces a problem with emerging "brown areas" of subnational authoritarianism set off from the democratic processes that governed national-level politics. As these problems grew, O'Donnell (1999, 314–15) lamented our lack of knowledge about "brown areas," writing:

> It is difficult to avoid concluding that the circumstance I have . . . described must . . . affect the . . . workings of these polyarchies, including its institutions at the center of national politics. Admittedly, however, this conclusion is based on a sketchy description of complex issues. . . . due in part to space limitations and in part to the fact that the phenomena . . . have been documented by some anthropologists, sociologists, and novelists, but with few exceptions, they have not received attention from political scientists. . . . I believe that knowledge about the phenomena and practices I have sketched above is also important, both *per se* and because they may be surmised to have significant consequences upon the ways in which those regime institutions actually work and are likely to change.

O'Donnell (1999, 333–34) continues in an endnote:

> Political scientists are not trained to observe the latter [the institutional breakdown and forms of order characterized by "brown areas"]. And the usually highly disaggregated and qualitative kind of data (often of an ethnographic character) they tend to generate is of difficult interpretation. . . . In settings where career and promotion patterns place a prize on working on mainstream topics and approaches, the transdisciplinary skills required by these phenomena and . . . the difficulties in translating findings into solid and comparable data sets are a discouraging factor for this type of research.

Some will argue that it is simply a division of labor to have political scientists focus primarily on institutions, while anthropologists and sociologists look more intently at nonstate actors, but this division reifies often arbitrary distinctions between formal political institutions and social organizations. It provides us with little help in understanding the complex informal dynamics that govern day-to-day politics, legislative functions, and elections. It also deprives political scientists of a nuanced and rigorously political understanding of the often violent and informal groups that seek to influence and re-create political institutions and the wider political and social distribution of power within a country and on the international stage in the democratic context. Only with the precise set of tools offered by ethnography can we get at the depth of these issues, understand the political implications of these groups, and grasp the effect they have on the political system.

The Value Added by Political Ethnography

Political ethnographers from a variety of disciplines working on the region have conducted studies in recent years that have provided important insights into the limitations of the region's regimes—limitations that require new analytic directions. Perhaps the most interesting of these assessments is offered by Julia Paley (2001), who, in her analysis of activists in poor communities in neoliberal Chile, suggests that calls for civic mobilization and community participation as a component of contemporary democracy have a demobilizing effect on large segments of activists. Asking groups in poor areas to take responsibility for soup kitchens and other programs to benefit the population, in the absence of wider state initiatives to deal with inequality and address popular needs, has the effect of exhausting local activists; since they are busy providing for individuals' basic needs, they cannot make demands that the government take on these efforts (Paley 2001).

The questions Paley raises about the type of democracy that exists dovetail neatly with some criticisms of writing in political science on democracy and democratization. On one level Paley suggests that democratic regimes conceived under certain circumstances will tend to follow certain paths toward sustained inequality. Thus, the highly unequal regimes in Latin America tend to reinforce levels of inequality and systems of exclusion, not just rendering their regimes different from regimes in North America and Western Europe but also creating conditions that make it extremely difficult for those Latin American regimes to conduct the types of reforms and improvements in quality that would make them like the more idealized developed regimes (Arias and Goldstein, forthcoming). Similarly, Thomas Carothers (2002) argues that not all circumstances of transition necessarily lend themselves equally well to building the expected types of democracies.

Ethnographic approaches provide us with the tools necessary to understand not just the political outcomes of formal institutions but also the informal processes by which those outcomes are achieved. The current literature has a tendency to work backward from political outcomes to explain how the result was achieved via formal rules. Fernando Coronil's (1997) work on pre-Chavez-era Venezuelan politics provides a striking example of the role that ethnography can play in shining a light on the complex processes that produce political outcomes. In *The Magical State* (1997) Coronil writes about the administration of Carlos Andres Perez in the 1970s and makes clear the role of informal channels in facilitating political outcomes. Here he looks at the complex interlocking social circles around the Perez administration and the ways they interacted in the context of bureaucratic power, oil production, intimate personal relations, and electoral pressures to understand the underlying informal political processes that drove the formal dynamics of parties and elected institutions (Coronil 1997, 329–60).

Many of the insights that Coronil provides about Venezuela in the 1970s are absent from contemporary analyses of politics in Latin America or are simply categorized as forms of corruption that constrain formal institutions rather than, possibly, the dynamics that drive forward those institutions. This is particularly notable in the context of the corruption scandals that rocked the first administration of Luiz Inácio Lula da Silva (Lula) in Brazil but which had only a minimal effect on the government, its electoral prospects, or, over the course of his second term, how state decisions were made. Indeed, in early 2008 Lula appeared to strongly support the efforts of one cabinet minister deeply implicated in a corruption scandal in her efforts to obtain the Worker's Party nomination for the presidency in 2010.

Another substantial failing of the existing literature is to treat today's democracies as a complete break with their authoritarian predecessors, when many political processes and relationships survive from one regime to the next. Ethnography, however, through close extended observation, can help to understand how current political practices, relationships, and ideologies have emerged out of previous sets of relationships, the importance of those historical relationships in structuring existing regimes, and the role they play in making those regimes function. Coronil (1997), for example, shows that the trope of oil continues to play a role in constructing a national myth of political and economic development; in Venezuela it transcends both authoritarian and democratic regimes. Javier Auyero, a sociologist, similarly shows the importance of historical myths in constructing contemporary political practice in local-level organizing in Argentina. Building on his analysis of clientelist practices in Argentine shantytowns, he has also shown how relationships among party leaders, political brokers, and police contributed to riots that eventually brought down the government of President

Fernando de la Rua in 2001, an issue that has received scant treatment in major political science journals (Auyero 2001; Auyero 2006b, 241–65).

Elisabeth Wood, a political scientist, in her study of peasant insurgents in El Salvador, makes clear the importance of ethnography in studying politics in Latin America today.[2] In this project, she uses ethnography because there are few written records maintained by the government of its response to the insurgency and because there are no accurate surveys of the peasant population during this period. Further, standard political science survey techniques would have been very difficult to carry out under such conditions. Even if they had been carried out, there would be serious questions about the accuracy of results (Wood 2003, 31–32)—questions that could only be resolved through a close ethnographic work that would facilitate their analysis. The conditions that Wood outlines are all too common in much of Latin America, but they are hardly the only justifications for using ethnographic methods.

There are few accurate criminal justice statistics, and those that exist are usually not comparable across countries. In Brazil, it is difficult to build a valid comparison even between subnational states, since each uses a different crime report. For example, in Rio de Janeiro, murders committed by police in the line of duty are separated from other homicides. In some states homicides committed during a robbery are categorized differently from homicides in general. In Colombia, one-half of all recorded homicides are unresolved.[3] Finally, crime statistics are among the more politicized statistics any government issues (Moore and Fields 1996, 24–25).

It is hard to imagine how this complexity could be effectively captured by standard political science methods. Those political scientists driven by methods have therefore restricted themselves to studying discrete political institutions. The result is, in the context of violence, a limited attention of the field on human rights and policing, and very little attention to the complex dynamics and practices that underlie problems with the police.

Ethnography offers an opportunity for political scientists to gain extended and profound access to particular places to learn about the lives of people living in those communities and to develop a deeper understanding of politics and power. Ongoing, engaged presence in an area building trust and working to understand social relations can help to dispel the notion that the researcher is affiliated with government agencies, a frequent fear of the residents of high-violence locales. The following sections of this chapter will demonstrate the importance of ethnography, not just in contexts where data are difficult to obtain but also more generally in making our understanding of politics in the region more nuanced and sophisticated.

The Role of Ethnography in Latin American Politics Today: A Research Agenda

In this context of violence, corruption, and multiple and varied informal modes of politics inside and outside of government institutions, researchers need a subtle and diverse collection of methods to understand the complex flows of violence, order, and state administration. The remainder of this section describes how ethnographic approaches would develop political science research in three key areas of Latin American politics.

Corruption

In 2006 Brazil went through a serious political scandal as it became increasingly apparent that the incumbent president had grossly violated campaign finance laws and laundered money to pay off members of opposition parties to vote for his legislative agenda (Rohter 2006). Today, Brazilian papers regularly reference massive levels of corruption, yet very few articles in political science journals touch this issue. Nevertheless, corruption is one of the most important and persistent complaints about the region's regimes and, historically, a common justification for authoritarian coups of democratic governments.

One reason for this scanty attention is that corruption is a complex, clandestine practice undertaken at all levels of the state. The data on corruption are quite limited and often merely skim the surface of the political practices of any particular country. Corruption also operates within cultural contexts that are not easily translatable or analyzable via the types of quantitative data that drive political science today. Further, corruption is simply (and unfortunately) not a big issue in the analysis of U.S. politics. In an environment where the methods for studying Latin American politics are often driven by trends in the study of U.S. politics, this leads to an incomplete study of corruption in the region.

There are a variety of ways in which researchers could approach this subject using ethnography. A political scientist, for example, could study businesses involved in government contracting and observe how that process operates. Extensive interviews with those involved with contracting and real estate would probably get at some of this, since business owners often are unhappy with the bribes required to win contracts.[4] Alternatively, taking a page from an exceptional study of American politics, a researcher could engage in an analysis of legislators' service to constituents, as Richard Fenno (1978) did in *HomeStyle*. During one brief period of participant observation

I conducted with a candidate for city council in Rio, I was able to see how he approached and negotiated with a drug dealer for access to a shanty-town (*favela*). A more extensive period of participant observation would no doubt yield much more useful information on a variety of political topics, but would also get researchers closer to understanding the issue of political corruption.

Violence

At the heart of the concerns that I laid out earlier was a lack of attention to violence in the region and its impact on politics. To date, most political analyses of these questions have focused on the problems generated by po-lice and efforts to improve police strategy. A solid understanding of vio-lence in the region, however, will only come from ethnographic studies of police and other armed actors.

Due to rising crime rates and the paradox of growing human rights abuse under democratic regimes, policing has become an important re-search focus for scholars of Latin America. Several good studies have been published on the role of different police practices and institutional factors that tend to lead to higher levels of abuse and a failure to control crime in many parts of Latin America (see Brinks 2003, 6–7; Pereira 2000, 217–35; Ahnen 2007; Dammert and Malone 2006). In the end, though, our under-standing of the politics of policing is very limited. We understand almost nothing of internal police politics in Latin America, or of the complexities of the relationship between police and elected officials. A deeper knowl-edge will only come through spending extended time among police in the region; that will help to illuminate the interior structures of policing agen-cies, why they resist change, and how they may shift over time.

Without ethnographic intervention, our understanding of Latin Ameri-can policing will remain limited. Police are a complex institution. Mem-bers change over time and have shifting interactions with the government and with other policing agencies. Snapshots of their activities, opinions ob-tained through surveys, or even detailed interviews cannot reflect the struc-ture of the relationships and informal practices that drive these institutions. While direct participant observation of police units probably carries exces-sive risks for most researchers, scholars can conduct ethnographic research about the police in various other ways. For example, a researcher could engage in in-depth interviews (similar in character to those described by Wood, this volume). This could then turn into longer periods of time ob-serving a station house. While some policing agencies are hostile to outsiders, this is not universally the case, and within most forces are reformist elements that might welcome the presence of a political scientist.

Presence in policing operations would provide us with important insights into the politics of violence and corruption in Latin America. Once you get police talking, few types of informants are more forthcoming. This type of approach, although it would likely fall short of a pure ethnography, could yield important information on the practice of police violence, how police perceive their relationship with the wider state, the role and activities of criminal gangs in the neighborhoods the police work in, and patterns of police corruption.

A principal problem with this type of research is the potential risk to the observer. I certainly would not suggest that political scientists select particularly risky opportunities for research. Scholars should attempt to conduct this research in the relatively safe settings of police stations or patrols in calmer neighborhoods. Moreover, faculty advisers who counsel students interested in such issues face ethical issues that cannot be treated lightly.

Nonetheless, understanding policing is essential for appreciating the nuances of current and future Latin American politics. Policing that succeeds in controlling crime and protecting citizens is the backbone of human rights, which democratic regimes have not succeeded in delivering to their citizens (Pereira 2000, 217).

We also need to know about the impact of violence and crime on politics. Though a number of anthropologists and sociologists have addressed the politics of criminal organizations, few political scientists have considered the impact of these groups on political questions (Davis and Pereira 2003; Gay 1994; Goldstein 2003, 22–43; Rogers 2006, 267–92; Arias 2006, 293–325; Bailey and Godson 2000, 217–24). A good deal of basic ethnographic and qualitative research needs to be done on the operation of nonstate violent actors and how they position themselves in the political system in non–civil war contexts. O'Donnell's "brown areas" have not, to date, received the sustained attention they deserve.

Work on these issues must address the question of persistent armed violent groups. While political scientists have long studied insurgencies (Scott 1977; Gurr 1971), these groups are much more rarely analyzed when they operate within seemingly stable political systems. Nevertheless, without a concrete political goal that would lead to a direct assault on the state, gangs and other armed groups have many political avenues open to them, including building alliances with state actors.

Understanding the political activities of these organizations depends on close ethnographic analysis of their operations. Ethnography is particularly important in conceptualizing how persistent nonstate violent actors, especially long-ignored criminal groups, operate within the political system. Even if we can get to a place where we can begin to conduct a more quantitative study, that ongoing work would only make sense if we were to continue to conduct that analysis in the context of in-depth ethnographies.

In my experience, the best way to study violence is to work around the edges, looking either at violent groups that are in the process of changing into something less violent—such as organizations in the process of demobilization or a short time after a conflict has ended (as may currently be the case with paramilitaries in Colombia)—or working with people who live around the edges of these groups but who are not directly involved with them, such as dissidents in communities run by drug traffickers (Gay 2005).

Political Institutions

Ethnographic research methods could also offer a tremendous amount of information on other types of political institutions, including legislatures, political campaigns, nongovernmental organizations, social movements, and unions. While we know a great deal about the outcomes these institutions produce, we have a much less clear idea of what actually goes on inside them.

Studies of social movements in Latin America and of political institutions in the United States can provide an important model for these efforts. We need to know much more about how political parties and electoral processes function. For example, we have many articles written today about how the Brazilian congress operates, who the veto players are in legislatures, and the impact of the institutional executive power on legislative outcomes. We have very little idea, however, of what actually goes on in the daily life of the Latin American legislatures—such as how members conceptualize their work, how they spend their time, or how the actual process of vote negotiation proceeds.

Developing this knowledge would not be exceptionally difficult. Each election year offers numerous opportunities to follow political campaigns. Very often dissident politicians who disagree with the overall direction of the political system are happy to talk to researchers and to provide access. Alternatively, in nonelection years incumbent politicians will likely provide researchers with access to their offices for observation. Similar contacts may also help to develop a deeper understanding of unions or other civic organizations.

The courts are another area of institutional research. In recent years we have learned much about the career trajectories of judges, how they affect policy making, and how local-level regime issues shape the composition of courts (Bill Chavez 2004, 451–78; Perez-Liñan, Ames, and Seligson 2006, 284–95; Taylor 2006). While we are beginning to develop a strong notion of how courts function and interact with other elements of the political system, we know less about the day-to-day operations of courts and what implications this has for the political system. In Latin America I have heard few individuals express confidence in the courts as a forum for either seeking justice or resolving grievances. While we know that politics sometimes influences judicial decisions, we have little idea of how this process works in practice inside a courthouse.

Understanding the operation and arc of democratic systems in Latin America necessitates an ethnographic engagement with the courts. Close observation of the legal profession, its interaction with the court system, and an examination of the experience of the accused as they move through the judicial system could provide invaluable insights about where courts function within democratic norms and where they do not. In turn, this knowledge can illuminate the path to appropriate judicial reform. Finally, ethnographic observation of court activities may provide insights into the nature of corruption within the judiciary and possible remedies for this problem.

This work could be done in a variety of ways. One possibility is to observe the work of a criminal defense attorney. By going to court and attending meetings in offices, scholars could gain important insights about the criminal process. Another possibility is for scholars simply to attend trials. Watching different court proceedings, examining argumentation styles, and interviewing judges and attorneys would provide important insights into how courts work and the challenges they face.

Ethnography: Problems and Solutions

One of the big challenges facing ethnographers is the question of generalizability. I have received comments in peer reviews of articles comparing three parts of Rio urging me not to generalize to other neighborhoods in the city. Clearly, however, we can and must use ethnography to make wider arguments. Anthropologists generalize all the time. The difference is that anthropologists conceptualize the relationship between case observation and theory very differently, tending to focus on what can be generalized from a single set of close observations, rather than looking at multiple complex but related cases and linking these cases through meso-level analyses of particular states or groups of states to general theory. As a result, political scientists tend to seek a larger number of cases, compare their similarities and differences, and extrapolate their insights to wider, country-level institutions. This complicates the use of ethnographic data.

While ethnography is essential to studying the issues that I have described here, it imposes the substantial limitation of forcing the scholar to focus on fewer cases, since doing ethnography involves devoting a considerable period of time to living in a particular place. As a result, ethnographers have a great deal of trouble actually engaging in substantive comparative empirical analysis.

Comparativists should work to lay out guidelines for ethnographic research and analysis. What are our primary concerns when looking at ethnographic data, and what particular types of data or data points do we think are necessary to accurately answer comparative questions (that is, questions that are relevant to ask across country contexts)? Since research is being conducted by different people across countries, a set of guidelines would structure ethnographic research and help immensely in obtaining comparable data. Quantitatively oriented researchers already do this by vetting questionnaires prior to research. It may make sense for political ethnographers to begin to informally publish research practice working papers where they explicitly discuss interview processes and question structures and strategies. Asking at least some similar questions across cases would generate the opportunity to compare the results, while not inordinately constraining the ethnographer. Some of this work could be done through online bulletin boards or a political ethnography conference that took place at regular intervals. These efforts could eventually result in pooling certain types of questions that ethnographers would work together to ask at different research sites, the answers to which we could share in research projects.

A final way to overcome some of these difficulties is for ethnographers to develop strategies for wider and more explicit cross-national collaborations. With some effort, teams of ethnographers could develop projects together that would have comparative value. For example, we could learn much about policing in Latin America if four different ethnographers spent six months studying four different police forces. These ethnographers would have certain questions in mind that they would pursue in conversations, and they would have to maintain contact with each other to update questions and push forward new lines of inquiry. The result could potentially be powerful cross-national analysis with a strong ethnographic component.[5]

I have already alluded to the major challenge presented by the research agenda laid out here—the risks that a scholar studying violence faces—but it deserves further attention. It is not easy to get information about illegal activities, and asking questions about criminal activities can draw the attention of violent actors to the research. Any research design should incorporate provisions that will enable the scholar to complete a useful study even if research on a specific illegal activity or a specific place becomes impossible to accomplish. Thus, scholars should have ideas about backup research sites and questions. To do this, scholars need to maintain a broad array of local contacts that can help them to build alternative contacts to gain access to specific places and groups. Local contacts are also important in providing protection for researchers against potentially violent groups. For example, while a scholar may want to study police corruption, it may be useful to frame at least a substantial part of the study around legal police practices, so that if information on corruption is hard to come by, the study will still prove fruitful. Whatever information we gain about criminal activities is better than having no information at all.

A second major challenge to this type of study is the institutional complications of securing funding and Institutional Review Board (IRB) approval. Scholars beginning work inevitably face greater challenges in obtaining startup funds than other, similarly ranked scholars working in less risky areas. This problem can only be resolved through careful preliminary research and contact building. Scholars who are beginning research in these areas should do their best during preliminary research to obtain written institutional contacts not just from universities but also from civic groups they might work with during their studies. Thus, a letter from a community organization or a state agency they may work with during the project is often essential to securing support. IRBs also will have legitimate questions about these projects. Scholars should, as necessary, work with IRBs to build acceptable protocols to reflect IRB concerns and the concerns of research participants. These are substantial barriers, but the work done to respond to the concerns of senior colleagues, support agencies, and IRBs will generally improve the study.

In short, ethnographers need to find ways to collaborate. The intensive nature of our work often isolates us from others in our discipline and in the academy. If we are able to more carefully define our agenda and the theoretical strategies we use, we could work together to produce empirically well-grounded comparative data that would bring into sharper focus the crucial, though understudied, informal dynamics that drive politics in Latin America, and, very likely, in other world regions, as well.

Notes

1. *Comparative Politics* is the exception to the rule. As a journal it reflects wider methodologies, and this has led to the publication of several articles and review essays in recent years on violence and human rights issues in Latin America.
2. See also Wood, this volume.
3. Author's analysis of Colombian government homicide data.
4. Clearly, the researcher would have to provide anonymity and other types of protection to her interviewees to make this both possible and ethical.
5. For a view that suggests the difficulty of conducting such coordinated efforts, see Schatz's conclusion to this volume.

TWELVE

When You Can See the Sky through Your Roof: Policy Analysis from the Bottom Up

COREY SHDAIMAH, ROLAND STAHL, AND SANFORD F. SCHRAM

Critics have noted that public policy analysis too often is narrated in a top-down discourse that fails to account for how people affected by policy experience it (Fraser 1990; Stone 2001; Fischer 2003). Political ethnography is an important corrective to decontextualized and universalizing approaches to public policy analysis (see Aronoff, this volume). Interpretive approaches to political ethnography can highlight the embedded perspectives of those being studied, whether they are people affected by particular public policies, street-level bureaucrats, or policymakers. We agree with the other authors of this volume that interpretive ethnography that involves data collection via participant observation or in-depth interviewing is valuable, but we are skeptical that any one method or perspective ensures that research reflects the concerns of the people being studied (Schram 1995). In what follows, we suggest that there are reasons to think that multiple-methods approaches, when implemented in collaboration with the people being studied, can be more faithful to their concerns than interpretive approaches, such as participant observation or in-depth interviewing, alone. We argue for an approach that emphasizes that regardless of the methods of data collection, research should be done in a way that ensures it is aligned with the people on the bottom so that their concerns and experiences can better inform public policy making. We use this chapter to introduce a note of caution about the limits to interpretive ethnographic work.

At least four problems emerge if we assume that the interpretive approach of political ethnography necessarily answers all the concerns raised by critics of top-down policy analysis:

1. Interpretive political ethnography is not as bottom-up as it appears to be. Much interpretive analysis is theory-driven, as opposed to problem-driven, and as a result, uses client understandings to answer theoretical questions rather than to address problems clients experience with public policy (Shapiro 2005).

2. While political ethnography tries to capture the perspectives of those being studied, it does not necessarily do so in consultation with them. The failure to engage those being studied sets limits on the extent to which people affected can "talk back." Thus, in important ways conventional political ethnography remains etic (Brewer 2005; for an alternative view, see Schatzberg, this volume).

3. Political ethnographers, in failing to engage those affected, may fail to consider the implications of their research in the policy arena, particularly for marginalized groups (Naples 2003).

4. Unlike some other versions of ethnography, such as those used by anthropologists who define ethnography as a study of a people or place, political ethnography too often is limited to interpretive assessments of people's subjective perspectives and frequently devalues quantitative methods that could prove fruitful for understanding policy and those affected by policy (Schram 1995).

To illustrate our theoretical argument, we offer an example from a participatory-action research project that constituted a problem-driven, mixed-method study on low-income home repair problems and policies in Philadelphia.

Bottom-Up, Participatory Policy Analysis

Our approach has affinities with the critical assessment of mainstream policy analysis, including those of political ethnography (Fischer 2003). Too often, policy analysis mimics the public policy-making process by following a top-down approach (Yanow 2003; Fischer 2003). What James Scott (1998) calls "seeing like a state" fails to apprehend the way policies play out for people affected by those policies. This is, in part, because much top-down policy analysis seeks general explanations and solutions (Flyvbjerg 2001) and thereby misses the effects of policies on people in particular contexts. Also, top-down research and policy making are exclusionary, rather than deliberative; dialogue with those directly affected by policy is too often missing (Fischer 2003).

Bottom-up studies call for including perspectives of those affected by policy. Yet bottom-up studies remain top-down when they are studies of subordinated groups as *subjects* rather than as *authors* or *collaborators*. They remain top-down in that the researcher, as outside arbiter of subjects' experiences, retains power (Brewer 2005). Insofar as political ethnography does not fully engage the people being studied, it is an insufficient correction to mainstream policy analysis (Schram 1995). Nancy Naples (2003), for example, has argued for "everyday world policy analysis" that grows out of work with the people most directly affected. Everyday world policy analysis looks at public policy from the perspective of those affected in collaboration with them and remains open to using a variety of data-collection methods to highlight their experiences. Our Philadelphia home-repair study was conceived of as participatory-action research with this goal in mind (Shdaimah and Stahl 2006; Stahl and Shdaimah 2008).

Political ethnographers—especially those working in the realist tradition (see chapter 1)—often distinguish their approach from participatory-action research on the grounds that political ethnography maintains scholarly detachment so as to achieve objectivity and resist the analysis being seen as partisan. Yet whether social scientists acknowledge it or not, they can never fully achieve the detachment they seek. Simply refusing to adopt the perspectives of the people they are studying does not mean their work is based on what Thomas Nagel (1989) calls "the view from nowhere." All research is, consciously or unconsciously, grounded in some perspective; all human knowledge about human behavior is tied to some particular context (Smith 2002). Moreover, researchers' work always has effects, since it can be used to legitimize, stigmatize, and privilege some people, practices, and understandings over others (Sandoval 2000; McCoyd and Shdaimah 2007).

Dialogical engagement with those affected by research enhances, rather than undermines, the scholarly integrity of political ethnography. Researchers engaged in work of relevance to policy analysis must forego the pretension that they stand outside their subject matter. Those who pretend they are not involved may suffer the consequences of such neglect, as when researchers end up producing information that helps control rather than empower.[1] The choice for researchers is not *whether* to be involved, but *how*. Researchers should consciously decide how to structure their relationship with those affected by their research, especially regarding the power dimensions of the researcher/research participant relationship. The choice to work *with* the people being studied may not always be appropriate, as in the case of hate groups, people who exploit others, or those who actively abuse power. Yet choosing to work with the people being studied is a choice to affect power relationships from the bottom up in order to help overcome marginalization or lessen oppression. It is a choice to ensure that the research empowers the people being studied, rather than let it serve whoever has the most access to it. As part of that process of empowerment, dialogue keeps critical political ethnography honest, helping it to remain true to its originating spirit to understand people on their own terms so that knowledge can help them live their lives better.

Bottom-up policy analysts, therefore, should consider more inclusive approaches, such as participatory-action research (PAR). PAR researchers collaborate with the people being studied to help frame, constitute, and interpret the facts that the research produces (see discussion in Stahl and Shdaimah 2008). Such research not only is politically engaged, but it also offers accountability that can improve the research itself, since researchers open their work to be checked against the understandings of the people on the bottom of the policy process. Dialogical relationships that involve conflict as much as consensus enhance the integrity of the research because they invite multiple perspectives that otherwise might be absent. The policy process is itself made more democratic because it includes the voices of those traditionally left out of that process.

The Philadelphia Home Repair Collaboration: A Mixed Methodology of the Oppressed

In 2003 we were recruited by the Women's Community Revitalization Project (WCRP) to collaborate on a campaign to get the city of Philadelphia to do more to enable low-income homeowners to stay in their homes. A small, grassroots, self-help organization, WCRP over time built a successful, multipurpose social welfare agency and became a developer and manager of housing. WCRP joined two other advocacy groups, Philadelphia ACORN (Association of Community Organizations for Reform NOW) and United Communities of Southeast Philadelphia, to organize low-income homeowners in three very low-income city neighborhoods with high rates of homeownership—Fairhill, South Philadelphia, and Strawberry Mansion.

Our collaboration was financed by a grant to WCRP from the William Penn Foundation to investigate home repair and home maintenance problems faced by low-income homeowners. WCRP hired the authors expressly to work as collaborators in a research process, expecting researchers and advocates to jointly develop research strategies and refine the analysis in a dialogical process (for a detailed picture of the collaboration, see Shdaimah and Stahl 2006).

Here we present an overview of our findings from this collaboration.

Once-popular assets-based approaches promote homeownership among low-income families as a solution for their poverty (Sherraden 2005). PAR revealed a more complex picture. Our findings suggest that while low-income families may benefit in some ways from owning a home, they are much less likely to own homes that they can convert into appreciable assets than are their middle-class counterparts (Shdaimah and Stahl 2005; see also Harkness and Newman 2002). For many low-income families, homeownership may be more liability than asset, something that has become much more apparent since the implosion of the U.S. low-income home mortgage market in 2007–8. When low-income families acquire cheap but old and poorly maintained homes, they may be overwhelmed by maintenance and repair costs. In Philadelphia, most low-income families own homes of very limited value; some are barely habitable. When low-income homeowners look from the bottom up, they may literally "see the sky through the roof."

This is an important caveat to recent developments in low-income housing policy, which are predicated on the idea that homeownership will automatically place low-income homeowners on a path to the middle class (Schram 2006; Reid 2004; Retsinas and Belsky 2002). Looking at homeownership from the bottom up suggests that abstract concepts of homeownership have little meaning. It makes a difference which home is owned, what resources the homeowner has, and in which community the home and the homeowner are situated. This is not surprising; in fact, most who have a desire to scratch below the surface could easily figure this out.

Our PAR project brings an added twist. Although our research revealed a host of problems that low-income homeowners encounter, our findings also made it difficult to simply argue *against* low-income home owning. Listening to low-income homeowners who live in particular communities, we learned that there are few viable alternatives to owning a home. An embedded understanding shaped our interpretation of the data, which showed the need for increased support for low-income families that are already homeowners to help repair and maintain their homes. Through this lens, the strategy of supporting home repair specifically can be seen as part of a broader strategy to increase the stock of affordable housing (rented and owned), while preventing housing abandonment and homelessness.

Deciding on Methods

Paulo Freire (1970) articulated a "pedagogy of the oppressed," whereby oppressed people could educate themselves to see their shared plight as systematic effects of structures that marginalized them rather than as isolated acts of personal irresponsibility. Freire called this process "conscientization." Chela Sandoval (2000) has written of a "methodology of the oppressed," whereby oppressed people interrogate the dominant discourses that narrate their marginalized condition in ways that make resistance less likely. While we were interested in the voices of low-income homeowners and solicited their input in our research, WCRP is one step removed from homeowners (Stahl and Shdaimah 2008). WCRP is a grassroots organization housed in the community it serves, but our work was largely with its staff of paid professionals and included little direct contact with homeowners. This limitation was mitigated by the fact that our study's focus on homeownership was directly informed by what WCRP heard from its constituents and the centrality that we gave to the homeowner interviews and walk-throughs described below.

Bottom-up research inevitably raises issues of perspective, position, and discourse that are related to questions of power (Schram 1995; Naples 2003; Sandoval 2000). As Nelson's (2005) work on national and international policy discourses of aid and assistance has demonstrated, the interpretive resources of bottom-up research need not be limited to discourse analysis. Interpretive fieldwork, most often based on in-depth field interviews with informants, can also provide the basis for a bottom-up interrogation of dominant structures of power (Nelson 2005; Lindhorst and Padgett 2005; Strier 2005; Tickamyer et al. 2000; Curtis 1999). Interpretive resources for a bottom-up interrogation of a policy discourse can also extend beyond qualitative methods.

A PAR bottom-up perspective demands that research methods be decided in collaboration with research partners. From the outset, we were open to the methods that would be most amenable to answering the questions most important to our collaborators. This is an example of what Ian Shapiro (2005) has called "problem-driven" research, which he contrasts to "theory-driven" or "method-driven" research. Method-driven research is preoccupied with the value of a particular way of studying a topic. As a result, it often eschews all but the chosen method of data collection to help understand the social problem under study. Theory-driven research aims to test a particular theory, rather than being open to alternative explanations or allowing theory to emerge from the data. Problem-driven research, however, employs the methods and theories best suited to explore and interpret the problem under study. Together with our research partners, we made methodological decisions that were informed by the goals of the study.

Our study partners were interested in the circumstances of low-income homeowners in Philadelphia. They wanted information about the scope of the home repair and home maintenance problems citywide. Further, they were interested in understanding how Philadelphia compared to similar cities on these measures. Most important, they were interested in pinpointing a dollar amount required for Philadelphia to solve its home repair problems. These questions lent themselves to the study of quantitative data. Descriptive statistics alone could not provide all the desired information. Available statistical data did not capture all the problems that homeowners considered worthy of repair. We needed to understand the constellation of city programs, politics, and players, and how each of them viewed the problem. Understanding the adequacy and availability of programs encompassed whether people actually use such programs, and what processes and procedures are most accessible. These questions were amenable to qualitative analysis that solicited perspectives of a broad range of stakeholders and featured an everyday world policy analysis. A problem-driven methodology led us to a mixed-methods approach that goes beyond in-depth interviewing and participant observation and provides an in-depth perspective from the bottom up on low-income homeownership in Philadelphia.

Data Collection and Analysis

Quantitative data were derived from four sources: the U.S. Census, the American Housing Survey (AHS), the Philadelphia Neighborhood Information System (NIS), and administrative data from the city's major home repair program, the Basic Systems Repair Program (BSRP). U.S. Census data provided us with a broad overview of the population of Philadelphia for key variables, such as race/ethnicity, age, and income level. It further allowed us to compare homeownership levels in Philadelphia with those of other U.S. cities. We examined data from the 1999 AHS to develop an in-depth portrait of low-income homeowners and their critical repair and maintenance problems. We used an index available in the AHS that captures multidimensional standards of housing quality to estimate the number of low-income households that met the BSRP income cutoffs (150 percent of the official U.S. poverty line) *and* had repair problems similar to those addressed by BSRP.

We complemented statistical research with interviews with forty-three informants and an extensive review of relevant city documents and publications. Informants were drawn from city council staff, high-ranking and mid-level city program officials, and a broad range of nonprofit organizations, including community development organizations working at the city and the state level. We reinterviewed five informants as the study progressed. Most interviews were conducted in person; eight initial and all five follow-up interviews were conducted over the phone. We exchanged follow-up emails with program officials for clarification or further information. These exchanges helped us access documents needed for developing a detailed understanding of how the city's public policies affect the ability of low-income homeowners to address their home repair problems.

While the lack of assistance for low-income homeowners has been a major problem in Philadelphia, the way that available assistance has been structured and provided is an additional problem. Together with our study partners, we determined that to understand this better, we needed to study existing programs from the perspective of homeowners. Our analysis was informed by efforts of our community partners, who knocked on doors throughout three neighborhoods and talked to 107 homeowners about their home repair and maintenance problems. Based on these initial conversations, we conducted in-depth interviews with four homeowners from the three target neighborhoods. Three interviews were conducted in respondents' homes so we could see their home repair problems firsthand. For comparison purposes, we also examined data from four in-depth interviews with other city homeowners. The second component involved constructing a step-by-step "walk-through" of BSRP to sensitize us to the difficulties that low-income homeowners face as they attempt to maintain and repair their homes.

The State of Homes in Philadelphia

To put this Philadelphia story in perspective, we first turned to the 2000 Census to compare estimates of the housing situation in Philadelphia to those of other cities. Table 1 compares Philadelphia to thirteen other large and mid-sized cities on the East Coast and in the Midwest. Philadelphia's poverty rate for 2000 at 23 percent was not unusual. The city has a relatively old housing stock, with 58 percent of its housing built before 1950. The median value of owner-occupied homes in Philadelphia is relatively low at $61,000. This might help explain why homeownership rates among the poor are higher in Philadelphia than in any of our comparison cities—38 percent compared to a range from 8 percent in Newark to 33 percent in Detroit. In spite of a relatively high homeownership rate, Philadelphia has the highest rate of all our cities for housing units without a mortgage (44 percent).

Unmonitored and unmortgaged, many low-income homeowners in Philadelphia are able to forego expenses that other low-income families have trouble shouldering, such as rent or mortgage payment. Less recog-

Table 1. Fourteen-City Statistical Comparison on Housing-Related Indicators, 2000 U.S. Census

	Philadelphia	Washington, D.C.	Miami	Atlanta	Chicago	Baltimore	Boston	Detroit	St. Louis	Newark	New York	Cleveland	Pittsburgh	New Haven
Total Population	1,468,404	541,657	352,916	392,406	2,839,038	626,051	558,707	932,512	339,323	261,451	7,854,530	466,305	313,383	113,320
Percent below poverty level	23%	20%	28%	24%	20%	23%	20%	26%	25%	28%	21%	26%	20%	24%
Total Housing Units	661,958	274,845	148,554	186,998	1,152,871	300,477	251,935	375,096	176,354	100,141	3,200,912	215,844	163,366	52,941
Percent built before 1950	58%	51%	25%	27%	52%	55%	63%	56%	65%	45%	51%	66%	64%	49%
Median Dollar Value of Owner-Occupied Homes	61,000	153,500	116,400	144,100	144,300	69,900	210,100	62,800	63,500	132,800	221,200	71,100	60,700	104,300
Percent of owner-occupied units	59%	41%	35%	44%	44%	50%	32%	55%	47%	24%	30%	49%	52%	30%
Total Poor Renters and Owners	129,563	42,965	40,123	34,899	188,878	56,925	45,097	82,041	32,621	26,623	601,183	47,157	29,053	11,039
Percent poor owning homes	38%	16%	16%	18%	18%	23%	9%	33%	22%	8%	11%	22%	22%	9%
Percent owned housing units without mortgage	44%	28%	37%	27%	31%	32%	30%	37%	37%	27%	32%	32%	42%	28%

Source: U.S. Census (2000).

nized is that low-income homeowners, even when they do not carry mortgages, are also likely to be burdened with higher expenses, both in proportion to their income and in absolute terms. Low-income homeowners spend a much larger percentage of already tight incomes on homes, a phenomenon the city acknowledges.[2] From the AHS, we estimate that 64 percent of homeowners in Philadelphia with incomes under $20,000 pay 30 percent or more of their income for housing, an indicator of housing instability. Seventy percent of those poor households, in fact, pay 50 percent or more for housing. There are at least 30,000 fewer affordable housing units in Philadelphia than are needed for rental households with incomes below $20,000 (Hillier and Culhane 2003).

Homes that are "affordable" to low-income residents are costlier than their market value suggests. Philadelphia's "wealth" of old, poorly maintained homes chiefly comprises nineteenth- and early twentieth-century, two- and three-story row homes. These homes are often in poor condition and require costlier maintenance and repairs. They have more interrelated problems (for example, a leaky roof can lead to damage to the electrical system), and they incur larger related costs (for example, poorly sealed windows result in inefficient heating and increased gas or oil expenses), compared to their higher income counterparts.

Given that a focus of our research was the extent to which the underfunded but critical home repair program, the Basic Systems Repair Program (BSRP), should be expanded, a statistical portrait of the potential users of the BSRP was useful. Using data from the 1999 American Housing Survey, we determined that an estimated 33 percent of home-owning households meet BSRP income eligibility criteria of 150 percent of the federal poverty line. To estimate the number of homeowners who were BSRP income-eligible *and* had repair problems severe enough to be considered for BSRP services, we calculated how many of these households had homes that the AHS rated as "inadequate." While other homes might also require BSRP services, the information in the AHS was not sufficiently detailed to determine that with confidence; thus, we opted for a conservative estimate that considered only the most serious cases in what we call the "BSRP target population." We used an index available in the AHS that is based on a number of internal and external factors for determining housing quality, rating them as adequate, moderately inadequate, and severely inadequate. We combined the second and the third levels of the index because the repair problems captured by the "moderately" and "severely" inadequate levels indicate that these homes had problems severe enough to be eligible for BSRP services.[3] In our analysis, we estimated that 11 percent of Philadel-

Table 2. Profile of BSRP Eligible Population Owners with Homes Moderately or Severely Inadequate and Incomes < 150% of Poverty Line

	BSRP Target Population		All Homeowners in City of Philadelphia	
	Percent	Total	Percent	Total
Race				
White	14.6	2,012	48.3	183,903
Black	56.4	7,771	43	163,930
American Indian, Aleut, or Eskimo			0.5	2,046
Asian or Pacific Islander	7.0	963	4.9	18,511
Other Race	22.0	3,022	3.3	12,589
Spanish Origin	22.0	3,023	6.2	23,597
Age				
< 26	4.2	577	4.1	15,925
26–35	11.8	1,618	17	64,563
36–45	35.1	4,836	20.5	78,180
46–55	17.6	2,423	18.1	69,058
56–65	—	—	13.1	49,830
66+	31.3	4,313	27.2	103,424
Sex				
Male	36.8	5,071	42.5	162,050
Female	63.2	8,699	57.5	218,929
Received SSI, AFDC or PA				
Yes	28.5	3,928	5	1,8912
No	71.5	9,841	95	362,067

Source: American Housing Survey (2001).

phia households in 1999 were BSRP income-eligible *and* had moderately or severely inadequate homes.

Table 2 compares the demographic characteristics of all the city's homeowners with those whose incomes were below the BSRP cutoffs and who lived in houses rated moderately or severely inadequate by the AHS. Table 3 adds additional statistics on the age and values of the homes. The BSRP target population is more likely than the general population to be nonwhite, slightly more likely to have female heads of household, and much more likely to be on public assistance. They also live in homes of significantly lower market value. The average annual family income of the target population was also strikingly low, even for a population with incomes below 150 percent of the poverty line: $7,294 compared to $41,665 for home-owning families overall. These data indicate that the BSRP serves an

Table 3. Owned Homes in Philadelphia

	BSRP Population	Total Population
Year Unit Bought (mean)	1984	1979
Year Built	1925	1934
Current Market Value of Unit (mean/$)	30,203	73,865
Household Income (mean/$)	7,294	41,665

extremely marginal population. The BSRP is potentially an important factor in staving off homelessness; one city official referred to BSRP as "the biggest homeless prevention plan."[4] However, even with these conservative estimates of the number of low-income homeowners in need of home repair assistance, the severely underfunded BSRP serves only a fraction of income-eligible families with qualifying types of home repairs.

Home Repair Programs for Low-Income Homeowners: Too Little, Too Late

In Philadelphia, programs supporting the repair needs of low-income homeowners fall into two general categories: grant programs and loan programs. Nearly all have income eligibility guidelines and require that applicants be documented homeowners occupying the residence for which assistance is requested. Nearly all our informants indicated that most low-income homeowners could not take advantage of the city's loan programs because of credit problems or a lack of funds to pay off loans. Most borrowers have incomes that are well above the BSRP income cutoff, indicating that it is not the BSRP income-eligible populations who do (or can) take advantage of loan programs, but rather people in higher income brackets. This means that the most viable programs available to low-income Philadelphia homeowners are grant programs (*Repairing Houses, Preserving Homes* 2005). For this reason, our research focused on the city's main grant program.[5]

BSRP addresses only certain types of repairs that the city prioritizes (for example, electrical and plumbing), and it addresses those only on an emergency basis (for example, for roof repairs BSRP will open a file only if the applicant can literally see the sky through her roof).[6] BSRP is also limited by income criteria based on family size (for example, the income threshold for a family of four is $2,263 per month). In interviews, city officials attributed program limitations to resource constraints, acknowledging that a much larger pool of city residents needs and deserves the assistance that BSRP provides.

WCRP asked us for a rough estimate of the funding needed to provide BSRP sufficient resources for all the homes in Philadelphia that are in need of critical repairs. Because WCRP is confronted in its daily work with families in need of home repairs, ascertaining this number was a crucial part of the group's policy strategy. We found that if the existing average level of BSRP repair service of $5,298 per property[7] were extended to each of the 13,770 homes in need, the total cost would be about $72,953,460 a year. This would require a BSRP funding increase of about eight- to tenfold if it were to extend the average amount of home repair services just to the most critical cases. This is, therefore, a conservative estimate, since many other low-income homes in Philadelphia in need of critical repairs may be rated as adequate by the AHS.

Lack of resources also has an impact on access. Our comparison of the demographic breakdown of program beneficiaries provided by the BSRP with our AHS profile of the BSRP target population reveals that some populations do not use these services. While there are some difficulties in making these comparisons, due to the different categories employed, it is clear that African Americans make up a larger proportion of program participants (81 percent) than their proportion of the eligible population (56 percent), and all other categories are underrepresented. Persons of Spanish origin (so identified in the AHS) or Hispanics (as defined by BSRP) are underrepresented in the BSRP program compared to the population we estimate to be eligible and in need of services—10 percent vs. 22 percent. Asians are also severely underrepresented among BSRP participants (7 percent of the estimated eligible population versus less than 1 percent of BSRP participants). Senior citizens make up 31 percent of the estimated eligible population and are similarly 28 percent of the BSRP participants. Female heads of households are overrepresented, making up 83 percent, as compared to 63 percent of the eligible population.

Differences between the BSRP target population and program users raise concerns about access. Inaction likely influences levels of participation. BSRP does not advertise because funds are insufficient to accept all applicants. While BSRP prints pamphlets in English and Spanish, it does not generate written information in other languages. Last, because there is no outreach for BSRP and knowledge of the program is spread largely through word of mouth, districts where community organizations actively steer residents to the program tend to have higher levels of participation. Lack of outreach also means that the need for program services is much larger than indicated by applications. Although BSRP is viewed favorably by most, it is clearly insufficient. It is notorious for long waiting lists. Activists, community organizers, and homeowners told us that this deters low-income individuals from applying, also contributing to an underestimation of the need for services.

The shortest wait period—for major heating repairs and priority situations, such as water shutoffs and problems directly related to disability needs—is estimated at 55 days between client call and assignment to contractor. The longest wait time is for extensive "general" repairs, estimated at 440 days between client call and assignment to contractor. These estimates are only until contractor assignment and do not include the additional time for the contractor to begin and ultimately complete the approved work. Thus, the time to completion is often much longer. Participants who drop out or refrain from applying in the first place often find alternative means of addressing their home repair problems. Alternatives are largely improvisational, usually carried out informally by relatives, friends, or neighbors, who may be unlicensed, uninsured, or lack the requisite expertise. Therefore, they may solve the problems only temporarily and, in some cases, may exacerbate them.

City council staff, program administrators, activists, and homeowners noted additional hurdles, such as a lack of coordination among the various city agencies. One city council staff member told of a constituent who required and received BSRP services for damages from water leaking into his home from an adjacent abandoned property. His home was repaired, but the source of the problem was not addressed because BSRP does not repair homes that are not occupied by homeowners. As expected, the problem recurred, resulting in another repair that was also carried out by BSRP. Problems in the adjacent property were addressed only after the homeowner initiated the intervention of a city council member. Cooperation between BSRP and the city's Department of Licensing and Inspection would have conserved BSRP money and prevented aggravation and property damage suffered by the homeowner.

Walking through Programs as a Client

Until now, we have provided a perspective of the state of low-income Philadelphia home repair problems from the outside looking in, largely based on the reports of program officers, city officials, documents, and statistics. However, this does not tell the whole story. Our advocacy partners asked us to conduct research that would walk readers through the programs we studied so that people could "see like a client." Their expressed wish for a "walk through" parallels Naples's idea of "everyday world policy analysis" (2003). How does a homeowner seeking home repair assistance from the city experience the programs that we reviewed? One homeowner, whom we call Cecilia Simpson, had this to say:[8]

> I had got [this house] off my brother for little, for nothing. That's why I say "be careful what you ask for if you get it for nothing." If I had to do it all over again, I don't know if I would have. I put so much money into that house, trying to get it together. It wasn't even livable. . . . I had to do the floors, we had no kitchen . . . no cover to the vent, having to cover the kitchen 'cause of the draft coming out of there.

Ms. Simpson entered into a predatory loan to repair her house because she and her children could not weather another freezing winter. This depleted her other assets and put her at risk of losing her home; at the time of the interview she was fighting a foreclosure.

Much like what political ethnography advocates, Ms. Simpson's situation suggests that understanding how low-income homeownership plays out "on the ground" requires not only that we "walk through" the programs as a thought experiment, but that we literally *walk* across sinking floorboards and underneath dangling wires. If policies are to be effective and helpful, they must take into account the contextualized realities of those they are designed to serve. We were only visitors; what we saw and felt in our visits was only the barest sense of what is experienced daily by many low-income homeowners. Their stories provide a glimpse of what policy analysts and policymakers should see but often do not. Constructing walk-throughs from the interviews and program data helped us understand why these programs are underutilized and inefficient for low-income homeowners. They also helped us understand how profoundly inadequate they are, even when people seek them out and are granted assistance. They provided an informed basis for rethinking how these programs should be run in Philadelphia.

Veronica Barrow's failed application process is a good example of a policy conceived without regard for how people will experience it. She lives in a house inherited from her mother. Ms. Barrows moved in to discover extensive damage, particularly to the upstairs, which is currently stripped of dividing walls or drywall. The extensively damaged ceiling reveals exposed wires; the upstairs bathroom is in extreme disrepair. In the living room ceiling, a crack over 1 foot in length leaks intermittently, apparently from the upstairs bathroom. Water leaks constantly from the kitchen ceiling, a leak that Ms. Barrows catches in a bucket. A third leak in a large pipe located in the basement she has unsuccessfully stemmed with rags.

Ms. Barrows turned to the city's Weatherization Program while unemployed. Program representatives inspected her home and referred her to BSRP due to her home's extensive structural damage. She attended a group forum at BSRP's offices, where she was informed that she qualified by income and by her description of the problems. "A couple of months" after returning to BSRP with the deed to the house, she had a home inspection. She was subsequently notified in a form letter that her "application for repair assistance, through the BSRP has been canceled due to the following reason(s)." The reasons checked off on the form were "the required repairs exceed the cost limit of the BSRP" and "other." Under the category of "other" there was no further explanation, though the form contains a space for this information. No information was provided about possible alternative programs. The form indicated that while she could reapply, her application would be considered new and would enter the queue accordingly. Ms. Barrows did not challenge the decision, because she feared that her house would be condemned. By the time of the interview she had secured employment, placing her income just above the BSRP eligibility criteria. Even if she reapplies and undertakes some repairs on her own to make her property eligible, she is currently financially ineligible for the program.

Martha Grant's story corroborates that low-income homeownership in Philadelphia may at best be a mixed blessing, policy pronouncements notwithstanding. Her story also demonstrates that low-income homeowners who succeed in obtaining the help of BSRP will not necessarily be able to solve their repair problems permanently. Ms. Grant has been in her home for thirty-two years. Home owning is costly because everything that goes wrong is "on you," and it is important to "hurry up and fix it or it gets worse." She needed roof repairs; by the time the city responded, she needed extensive repairs to the room below. Ms. Grant knows the houses are old, but this is where she lives: "We're in them." When her windows and doors became too drafty, a friend referred her to "1234 Market Street" (the offices of BSRP and other city programs). The whole process of having her home repaired took about three years and included windows (done under the Weatherization Program), back doors, electrical rewiring, yard, roofing, and plumbing.

Ms. Grant was grateful that the city replaced all her windows and her door. However, she has had trouble with the plumbing and electrical work.

When BSRP contractors rewired under the floors, they put back the old floorboards. About a year later, she felt the floor weakening, and to this day her first and second floors are sinking. After new pipes were installed, the insulation came loose and they burst downstairs. Ms. Grant believes they were not repaired correctly, as it had only been three years. Although all the work was approved, no one told her what to do or who to call if something went wrong.[9] She mused that the house is old; maybe this is just the way it is.

Ms. Grant did not call BSRP or try to contact the contractor directly. Although she was given some papers, it was too much of a hassle to pursue. Instead, she took out a bank loan, using her home for collateral, to cover repairs of the upstairs floors and bathroom. Her son-in-law repaired the floors, and her brother painted. She paid for the sheetrock and other materials, and borrowed equipment. However, repairing the first-floor bathroom floors would entail lifting the supporting beams under the floor, which requires special equipment and training. The floor of the downstairs bathroom sinks so severely that it separated from the bottom of the tub, leaving a gap about two feet long and a few inches deep between the floor and the tub. This sinking slope can be felt in the hallway.

Ms. Grant's brother and husband are disabled and cannot help. Getting to BSRP is difficult; according to Ms. Grant, "you can be dead and gone by the time you get there." She contacted the Philadelphia Corporation for the Aged, which completes small repairs for disability-related problems, but it does not handle sinking floors. She paid off her loan and does not want to take out additional loans to fix the downstairs hall and bathroom floors because she fears going into debt on a fixed income; she is saving to pay for repairs. Ms. Grant thinks the city ought to do more to help people, particularly those with a low or fixed income.

The experiences we have portrayed are not intended to suggest that all low-income homeowners have homes that are unlikely to be assets. But they do show how, despite the best efforts of homeowners, many encounter problems that policymakers do not expect: they fall on the wrong side of arbitrary income cutoffs, fear contacting agencies, and experience problems caused by contractors chosen by the BSRP. The people profiled here have actively sought help, but still live in homes that are not the assets that top-down policymakers assume they are. While homeownership might be a strategy that works for *some* low-income homeowners in *some* neighborhoods, for many other low-income families, owning a home is not a realistic way to acquire assets, as much as it is a way to be burdened with additional liabilities.

Value-Added, Bottom-Up Participatory Action Research

The description of our home repair research highlights how policy analysts working in collaboration with advocates can counteract the biases of
top-down policy analysis by offering a bottom-up perspective on public
policies (Schram 1995). Such collaborations should not be limited to an
interpretive approach to political ethnography. Problem-driven, participatory action research like ours better counteracts the deficiencies of mainstream analysis because it enables researchers to work in alliance with the
people being studied, not just to better understand their point of view but
to contribute usable knowledge that addresses problems they confront. We
needed qualitative data to make an "everyday world policy analysis" of how
clients experienced the implementation of home repair policies. Our advocates knew that this would need to be combined with the broader perspective and scientific legitimacy that quantitative data provide in order to
convince policymakers of the scope of the problem (Stahl and Shdaimah
2008).

Complexities of low-income housing policy in Philadelphia are reflected
in the strategic considerations of our activist collaborators. Although WCRP
builds rental housing, the insufficient supply and actual state of most rental
housing requires an advocacy strategy that argues for repair programs to assist homeowners so that those units can continue to add to the stock of liv-
able housing in the city. The advocates were interested in low-income home
repair as part of WCRP's affordable housing campaign, even though they
do not buy into the asset-building approach that is increasingly popular in
Philadelphia and at the national level. Instead, they were interested in helping low-income homeowners stay in the homes they already own. Dialogue
with our advocate partners on the bottom provided us with a better understanding of why WCRP advocates favor repair programs for low-income
homeowners and how their understanding of the issues differs from what
might otherwise seem to buttress the asset-building approach. Given Philadelphia's housing stock and the economic difficulties faced by many homeowners, helping low-income homeowners was an essential strategy in trying to ensure that each and every resident has a decent place to live. Our
advocate partners (and many city officials) view this more as a homeless
prevention program than as an asset-building strategy.

Collaboration led us to make different decisions about data collection,
methods, interpretation of the data, and how to use the information. Based
solely on interviews with frustrated homeowners, a political ethnographic

approach might have led us to emphasize the homeownership critique with little understanding of how this might play out in the policy arena and what the implications would be for low-income homeowners. Ongoing dialogue with our community partners throughout the research process, including our data analysis, informed our emergent understanding; despite the difficulties faced by homeowners and the dubious contribution to assets that homeownership entailed, people wanted to stay in their homes and communities. They also pushed us to see homeownership within the context of the Philadelphia reality; although homeowners are in a tough situation, renters fare even worse. While it may be convenient for policymakers (and policy analysts) to ignore what happens to homeowners on the bottom, this will not make the problems of low-income homeownership and the lack of affordable low-income housing disappear. Collaborative, bottom-up policy analysis such as PAR is more likely to demand that the considerations of those on the bottom be part of the political dialogue.

Conclusion

Mainstream policy analysis must be countered with alternatives that can better inform the policy process (Schram 1995). Good scholarship and good politics are promoted when policy analysis is done in dialogue with the people affected by the policy. This is especially true when researchers address policy issues that affect people who have few resources to participate in the regular policy-making process. Once we entered into dialogue with our advocate partners, we challenged each other and cross-checked our findings against their experiences (Shdaimah and Stahl 2006). This dialogue shaped the ongoing choices of data sources, questions, methods, analysis, interpretations, and use of the research, leaving its mark on all of these phases. The contentious and lively nature of these debates challenged our thinking and our research throughout and led to changes in the choices that we made at each of these points.

Participant-informed, mixed-methods research resulted in a fuller, more complex story of the low-income home repair policies and problems than what could have been gained from a method- or theory-driven project, determined and implemented by researchers alone. A more robust objectivity in service of democracy is achieved when we do not just represent the subjective experiences of the people at the bottom of the policy process— as pure ethnography might—but when we conduct policy analysis in dialogue with them so that their voices are included. To have more science and democracy in policy analysis, we must move not just beyond mainstream policy analysis but beyond political ethnography as well.

Notes

1. For an example of this particular problem, see O'Connor (2001), discussing Oscar Lewis's work on the "culture of poverty"; for a more recent critique of ethnography of low-income immigrants, see Marchevsky and Theoharis (2006).
2. See Philadelphia Office of Housing and Community Development (2003, 11).
3. The AHS rates a housing unit to be severely inadequate if it has no plumbing facilities, has major heating equipment problems, or lacks electricity. A housing unit can also be severely inadequate if a combination of less severe problems exists, such as outside water leaks, inside water leaks, holes in the floor, cracks in the walls wider than a dime, areas of peeling paint or plaster larger than 8½ × 11 inches, or if rodents are seen in the unit. Moderately inadequate units are described by the AHS as "non-severely inadequate" (that is, inadequate, but not severely inadequate) if some of the following conditions exist: the unit lacks complete kitchen facilities, there were three or more toilet breakdowns lasting six hours or more in the last ninety days, or an unvented room heater is the main heating equipment.
4. For evidence supporting Philadelphia's Basic Systems Repair Program as effective in preventing homelessness and abandonment, see Research for Democracy (2001, 31).
5. Some programs (such as the Senior Housing Assistance Repair Program) serve specific populations, particularly the elderly, or meet specific housing needs, such as the Weatherization and Adaptive Modification Programs.
6. Designation of repairs as "emergency repairs" also allows the city to waive federal lead-abatement requirements. Although this is an acknowledged concern, addressing it would further squeeze the budget and further reduce the city's ability to make even the home repairs BSRP currently provides.
7. The best estimate of the average BSRP cost per home repair comes from the BSRP's own records, which are not very systematic. For estimating the costs per home, the best available BSRP data are in an unpublished chart entitled "Costs per Property, as seen from May 2001 through April of 2002, Basic Systems Repair Program." This chart indicates that during the 2001–2 period there were 1,400 closed properties. Using these figures, we estimate that repairs to these 1,400 properties cost on average $5,298. This figure is very close to the estimated cost per property referred to by the BSRP of $5,160, cited in the Consolidated Plan.
8. All names are pseudonyms in order to protect confidentiality.
9. All work is guaranteed for a year, except for roof repairs, which are guaranteed for five years. According to BSRP, clients are told to resolve problems with contractors directly and, if a resolution cannot be reached, BSRP will act as a mediator. Approximately 25 percent of all complaints end up referred back to BSRP for mediation.

THIRTEEN

Dear Author, Dear Reader:
The Third Hermeneutic in Writing
and Reviewing Ethnography

DVORA YANOW

Researchers . . . produce *claims* in which the author figures more as a claimant than judge. That is, each scientific article functions as a judgment passed on claims made by colleagues.

—Bruno Latour (2004, 78)

The scholarly enterprise is built on the exercise of judgment. Whether it is assessing a dissertation, evaluating a manuscript in the peer review process, or judging a research proposal for funding, scholars sit in judgment of others and, likewise, submit their own scholarship to such judgment. There are consequences of these judgments: some proportion of graduate students fails to receive degrees, some manuscripts are never published, and many research proposals go unfunded.

—Peregrine Schwartz-Shea (2006, 91)

What prior knowledge do readers bring with them to their readings of ethnographic (and other interpretive) manuscripts? Peregrine Schwartz-Shea vividly describes the *habitus* of the "traditionally trained political scientist, steeped in what might be called the 'variables gestalt,' which encompasses, among other things, a commitment to measurement, hypothesis testing, and causal analysis." Addressing this scholar, she writes: "when you sit down to read an empirical study, you bring with you a set of standard expectations about the logic of research, as well as a developed, discipline-directed set of critical reading skills honed through training in your field" (2006, 90). As Schwartz-Shea notes, a "particular reading experience results from these expectations and practices" (2006, 90): the reader looks for independent and dependent variables, causal reasoning and perhaps a causal model, and statistical analysis of some form, including its tabular presentation; and he or she anticipates assessing the operationalization and logic of all of these. Over time, reading and evaluating the scientific quality of such a manuscript becomes quite natural—routinized, we might say—for such a scholar (Schwartz-Shea 2006, 90–91).

Imagine, as Schwartz-Shea invites us to do, that a journal editor has asked this scholar to review a manuscript that has radically different constitutive elements: it compares two government agencies based on what are, arguably, aspects of a political ethnography—twelve months of participant observation, numerous in-depth, conversational interviews (ethnographic or phenomenological [Spradley 1979; Kvale 1983]), and the analysis of documents. She addresses the reviewing reader:

> The manuscript offers a radically different reading experience: None of the variables have been operationalized in the ways to which you are accustomed—in fact, what the variables *are* is not even clear, let alone which ones are dependent and which are independent; no causal model is offered; there are no tables reporting statistical analyses; there is no discussion of generalizability. (Schwartz-Shea 2006, 90)

And she concludes:

> In short, given your customary reading experience, this study is unrecognizable as a piece of scientific research: It does not fit your sense of what rigorous, objective research looks like. Your standard set of evaluative criteria simply does not apply, and you question whether such research qualifies as social science. What sort of evaluation can you, would you, send to the journal editor or to the author? (91)

As an epistemic-practitioner community, we who engage ethnographic and other interpretive methods have, with rare exceptions, not done as good a job as we might in educating members of other epistemic communities such that they could answer Schwartz-Shea's question using the scientific criteria that obtain for these kinds of research. In this, we have also not fulfilled our responsibility toward new members of our own communities of practice. Resulting manuscripts—including published ones—have not always clearly laid out what such work entails. Nor have methods textbooks, by and large, helped fill these gaps (Schwartz-Shea and Yanow 2002). This lack of clarity and transparency has led, in turn, to a mystification of such research processes, on the one hand, and, on the other, a sense among those proficient in other forms of research that these methods have no system—that they are impressionistic, rather than systematic (or "rigorous").[1]

Some characteristics particular to political ethnography—to our own *habitus*, if you will—contribute to this state of affairs. Most political scientists doing ethnographic research were not formally trained in social or cultural anthropology; we have learned our methods as we go along.[2] Anthropology departments themselves typically train ethnographic researchers through a kind of inductive apprenticeship, rather than through explicit textbook teaching. Anthropologists have not written methods texts, on the whole, "refus[ing] to specify method" (Lewin and Leap 1996, 1), relying instead on extensive reading of ethnographic texts, both classic and contemporary; conference talk, both at panel sessions and in corridor and bar conversations; and trial-and-error immersion in the field, all of which tend to develop a wealth of tacit knowledge about how ethnographic research is done and written. But, as Polanyi (1966, 4) remarked about tacit knowledge, we "know much more than we can tell." So students of political science, public policy, public administration, organizational studies, and planning who choose to do political or policy ethnography are often sent to other departments, such as anthropology, sociology or education, for methods coursework, where they take one or perhaps two courses plucked from their curricular and extra-curricular context (what Snyder [1973], in a different context, called "the hidden curriculum"), thereby often missing a considerable part of that tacit knowledge development; or they are left to learn their methods from research textbooks, themselves short on information, if not actually misinformed, about what this research entails. The methods themselves are largely known tacitly, and making them explicit is achieved, therefore, even—or perhaps especially—by seasoned researchers, with great difficulty.

It is becoming increasingly common in interpretive research, ethnography in particular, to consider writing as a method of generating knowledge (see, for example, Richardson 1994), and thereby as a "way of world-making" (Goodman 1978). This move has developed over the last twenty years out of a growing awareness that "theorizing is not a 'neutral' activity, but one guided by strong interests and values that need to be explicated" (Perrow 1986, 146; see also Brown 1976; Gusfield 1976). Understanding that researchers' perceptions are shaped by their lenses, frames, paradigms, or *weltanschauungen* is in keeping with a phenomenological perspective which argues that present understanding is informed by prior knowledge drawn from experience, education, personal background, and so on, as well as with a hermeneutic perspective that sees specific interpretations and interpretive practices as developing within epistemic communities. Both these perspectives emphasize the intersubjectivity of knowing, leading to a greater appreciation for the relational character of such research. This emphasis has also led to a growing call for explicit reflexivity on the part of researchers, not only during the research process, but also in their written work, on the ways in which their positionality—demographic characteristics, family and community background, and so on—might shape the research process, and thereby their "truth claims," through spatial and social locationing that enables access to some persons, areas, experiences, and ideas while blocking access to others (see, for example, Pachirat, this volume; Shehata 2006; Wilkinson 2008; Zirakzadeh, this volume).

Out of this enhanced sensitivity to the intersubjective character of meaning co-constructed between researcher and researched, a heightened awareness has developed of the ways in which not just fieldwork, but deskwork and textwork—the working out of ideas in, while, and through writing—also construct the social realities articulated in a research report (see, for example, in anthropology, Clifford and Marcus 1986; Geertz 1988; and Van Maanen 1988; in organizational theory, Golden-Biddle and Locke 1993, 1997; and Yanow et al. 1995; see also Brower, Abolafia, and Carr 2000; and McCloskey 1985).[3] This fits an understanding of "ethnography" as being a particular form of writing, in addition to being a set of methods and a "sensibility" (Pader 2006). Such a focus encourages writers of ethnographic texts to attend more explicitly to an interpretive phase in the research process that occurs after the double hermeneutic (Giddens 1984; see also Jackson 2006). The latter itself unfolds over three interpretive "moments," beginning during fieldwork. The first hermeneutic belongs to those we are studying—the so-called actors in the situation: their interpretations of their firsthand experiences. This is the initial interpretive moment. The second hermeneutic is the researcher's: the interpretations we make of situational actors' interpretations as we participate with them, talk with them, interact with and observe them, and read (literally or figuratively) their documents and other research-relevant artifacts. Collectively, these make up the second interpretive moment.[4] The third interpretive moment also belongs to the researcher's hermeneutic but takes place at a remove from fieldwork activity, during the deskwork phase, as she reads and rereads field notes and analyzes them, and during the textwork phase when crafting a narrative that presents both fieldwork and analysis.

This research process, however, entails not just a double hermeneutic,

Table 1. Meaning-Making in Ethnographic (and Other Interpretive) Research

Phase of Research*	Agent	Interpretive Moment	Hermeneutic
Fieldwork	Situational member	1. Experience	1st
	Researcher	2. Interpretation of 1, via interviews/talk, written records of events, and own observations and experience	2nd
Deskwork and Textwork (Writing)	Researcher	3. Analyzing fieldnotes & writing	2nd
Textwork (Dissemination)	Reader (audience)	4. Reading (hearing)	3rd

*Phases are not as distinct or as linear in practice as this table makes them appear: analysis takes place before and during fieldwork, for instance, and during textwork; and the researcher may return to fieldwork (depending on opportunity, distance, cost, and time) during either or both of those two phases.

but at least a triple one. The latter plays out over an additional interpretive "moment" in the course of the research and writing *and reading* process, when a reader (or a listener, in the case of an oral report) interprets the researcher's words. Here is the third hermeneutic: the reader's (table 1).[5] To the extent that researchers-writers can anticipate the third hermeneutic—reflect on possible readings of their texts, imagine responses, *and write for them*—it makes sense to consider reading, along with writing, as a method of discovery.

Seeing Like a Reader

Reading an increasing number of manuscripts as a reviewer, colleague, or external examiner, all of them purporting to do ethnographic (or some other form of interpretive) research, has sensitized my readerly antennae to the elements of such writing which serve as signals that a reader is in the presence of an ethnographic or other interpretive research project. It has become increasingly clear to me that there is a set of elements—dare I say, the *sine qua non* of this sort of writing—that shape a reader's experience of a manuscript and establish its procedural and presuppositional contours. Reading is not only a matter of interpretation; it entails a particular kind of sense-making, especially in an academic context, that involves making evaluative judgments. Specifically, the presence—or, in the event, absence—of these elements affects the extent to which a reader will be persuaded by the evidentiary character of the truth claims advanced in the analysis.[6]

I explore here both reading and writing, two facets of a textual encounter, and the extent to which reading itself might usefully be considered a way of knowing. For if science seeks to persuade, if methods are one way in which researchers convince others of the trustworthiness of their analyses, and if writing—word choice, phrasing, the overall structure of a report, and so forth—is the way through which methods and findings are communicated, it makes sense to consider not only writing as method, but reading as method. In this view, writing elements are inseparable from the content of an argument; persuasive discourse involves both writing and reading (on this point, see Ankersmit 1996, 265).

Both facets explored here concern the creation of meaning as might be done by two rather different imagined readers of ethnographic or other interpretive work. On the one hand, I engage readers coming from other epistemic communities regarding the criteria or evaluative standards that make this research good science—of an interpretive sort. Qualitative methodologists have anticipated such a focus on readers in developing arguments for "member checks" and "peer debriefing" as ways in which researchers can enhance the trustworthiness of their research (Erlandson et al. 1993; see discussion in Schwartz-Shea 2006). Here, I am addressing not members of the setting under study or peers reading to ascertain the "accuracy," "veracity," or adequacy of the writing, but those reading for other evaluative purposes—reviewers, editors, grantmakers, and such—who may be more or less familiar with what constitutes interpretive research, including ethnography. What components should such a reader look for in a text whose overall presence would signal that the text meets the scientific standards of this research community?

On the other hand, I write to those conducting ethnographic and other interpretive research, including researchers who may be learning how to write up such research, about ways to signal these criteria in their writing. Knowing how to answer the preceding question more explicitly may not only help those readers in their evaluations, but also may help writers produce texts whose truth claims are more compelling. Much has been written about the ontological and epistemological hallmarks of ethnographic and other interpretive methods, and how these translate into practice. If that constitutes a kind of top-down methodology, what I am engaged in here is a grounded, bottom-up approach that begins with written texts.

My conceit in this chapter, then, is to arrogate for myself the role of a participant-observer ethnographer studying the practices of writing and reading political ethnographies. My field setting, as it were, is the discipline of political science and more specifically, the epistemic community of interpretive researchers, and especially political ethnographers, within it. The particular event that I am trying to make sense of is the reading and reviewing of article-length manuscripts submitted to journals (although my "findings" bear on book-length manuscripts as well). My data are manuscripts and articles purporting to be ethnographic that crossed my desk between June 2005 and August 2006. In a kind of science studies approach to the creation and maintenance of an academic discipline, my research question is: What do readers need to find in a manuscript to convince them that it meets the criteria of this epistemic community for doing and being good scientific work?

I present my findings in two sections. The first, addressed to authors, represents a report on absences: reading the writings that constitute the (documentary) data sources for this study, I found myself asking at times not "Does this qualify as science?" but "What's missing from this manuscript that would make it an adequate work of interpretive science?" This line of inquiry led me to focus on the characteristics that, as a member of this community of practice, I have learned to anticipate—those criteria for interpretive scientific writing that help a manuscript meet the readerly expectations of ethnographers and other interpretive researchers. The first section is a compendium of items that, when absent from a written work, diminish the persuasiveness of its truth claims.

In the second section, I speak to reviewers, editors, grantmakers, and other readers I assume to be members of other epistemic communities. Here, I report on the presence of those elements characteristic of ethnographic (and other interpretive) writing that may appear, to readers less familiar with the scientific standards of this epistemic community, actually to be unscientific. Although they may not be customary in other epistemic communities within the political science discipline, these characteristics are commonplace, and even *de rigueur*, within this scientific community. Manuscripts with these features should not be disparaged because of the presence of these elements; rather, they should be regarded as meeting the highest scientific standards of the (interpretive) ethnographic epistemic community.

If I were true to what I argue here, I would document my analysis with quotes from my sources. I do not do this for two reasons. First, many of my data sources came to me via the peer-review manuscript system, and, as I do not know the authors' identities, I cannot secure permission to quote their writings. Second, what I report on in the first section are those absent elements that contribute to "failed writing" (Golden-Biddle and Locke 1993)—manuscripts that have not been published. Although I agree with Golden-Biddle and Locke that it would be useful to document the reasons for such failures, detailing the missing elements that undermine a reading requires much more space than I have available. Additionally, the absence of such "data details," together with the first-person voice I use throughout, may imply that I have ensconced myself as a despotic arbiter of things methodological, which is neither my self-image nor my intent. My conceit fails me, then, in these key respects. I hope I compensate for that, however, through other forms of textual density, including references to other methodological works that support these claims.

I have been referring to ethnography so far in its broader, more encompassing sense, as a set of research methods, a mode of writing, and a sensibility that informs the researcher's approach to framing research questions and design, implementing these through methods in the field setting, and writing up the research. Henceforth, I refer to ethnography as writing (and much of what I outline holds for other types of interpretive research writing, as well). Discussions of research criteria are typically written from the perspective of someone designing a research project. It is much less common to find such discussions taking the vantage point of someone writing a research report. What follows does just that, addressing first authors and then readers at the textwork phase of research.

Dear Author: Being There

The elements discussed in this section—place, time, exposure, positionality, access narratives, and data details—are commonly part of a research design, and you have most likely attended to them in planning your work. They also belong, however, in one way or another, in your manuscript. They typically figure in methods narratives, but they also come through less directly in the descriptive presentations of data and their analytic discussion.

It can be helpful to think about writing from the perspective of an imagined reader whom you want to persuade of the character and quality of your work—although such persuasion, and even the desire to do so, are often not conscious and explicit, but tacitly known and subtly achieved. The presence and elaboration of these elements give your reader a fuller understanding of what you have done in your research. They serve as signaling devices, helping that reader assess the believability of what you claim to have seen and/or heard and/or read, all of which serves to establish the trustworthiness of the truth claims of your analysis. Conversely, their absence weakens your claims to have "insider" knowledge of or evidence from the setting or event and/or people and/or documents under study, which may undermine the strength of your analytic claims. Ethnographic methods require making choices, including in the field when faced with field realities; and the more fully you explain the choices made—why you did some things and not others—the better able your reader will be to assess the analysis you present.

Place/Space: Research Settings

Ethnographic research is characterized by attention to "place-ness," as well as to the actors peopling those places and what they said, thought, and did, with what, and why, as reported by them and in written materials as well as through observations. The central feature of much ethnographic writing that perhaps distinguishes it from other forms of interpretive research is the extensive description of this place-ness—the setting(s) in which the research was carried out—not for stage-setting alone, but out of an awareness of the ways in which the particulars of the location provide shaping context for the research issue being analyzed.

Ethnographers make crucial choices concerning place or space; political ethnographers' settings are distinctive. What kind of polity or organization is likely to provide illustrations of the political or policy issues under investigation? What is the best neighborhood or community, region or state within which to explore the research question? Which level of government, which agency, which section, which department within an organization or set of organizations within an interorganizational field? The presence in the written report of deliberations concerning the selection of settings and the rationales behind the choices made help situate the analysis.[7]

Attention to settings extends to the choice of locations for "accidental" encounters with people for casual conversations, as well as of persons for formal interviews.[8] Here, "space" connotes the organizational level or the departmental location within the organization's structure or the political or communal role of the person being interviewed, aside from the physical place itself. For example, is this person likely to be more comfortable talking with me if we meet away from her workplace or his regular "hangout"? Will I get different information if we meet in a club setting where I might also be eligible for membership (see, for example, Wilkinson 2008)? Will my choice of setting enable access to some sources or some kinds of information but block others (see, e.g., Zirakzadeh, this volume)?[9] For documentary aspects of an ethnographic project, "space" refers more to the location and choice of archives, in terms of availability of certain materials, access to particular files, and lack of access to others.

Providing rationales for choices of setting(s) contextualizes the reader's sense-making of the text. This, in turn, adds plausibility to the account being offered, since a reader knows that data are gathered in particular settings at particular times by particular individuals ensconced in particular relationships.

Time

TIMING: DDT. Ethnographic research engages not only space but time—the "DDT," or timing, of a project. Over what *dates* or times of year was it conducted, which *days* of the week, and what *times* of day? "Bush anthropology" was designed to follow, at minimum, a full agricultural cycle. A year or more in the field may or may not be appropriate for political ethnographies, which have their own timing rationales: decision-making processes in legislatures, for example, whose normal sessions take place during business hours on weekdays with time off for summer and holidays. Spending time on location in August or December, on non-work days of the week, or at 5:00 a.m. or 11:00 p.m. would likely produce different understandings than research conducted at other dates, days, and times. Considering DDT focuses attention on the cyclical nature of timing in shaping the kinds and character of data that participant observation generates. Which among its three components is significant, and in what ways, depends on the research question.

For documentary (archival, newspaper morgue, library, or other source) aspects of a political ethnography, DDT is likely to be less important in one sense: the character of the documents or of the sources is unlikely to be affected by calendrical differences in the researcher's presence.[10] Differences in historical timing are, of course, central to that work, something those trained in historical methods are commonly highly attuned to and take into account in research design and analysis.

In interview components of research, DDT might conceivably have some bearing on truth claims (such as chronological distance from the event discussed or interview timing in relation to other relevant events), depending on aspects of the research question. I would expect an author to include this, if relevant.

DURATION. How long a researcher was present in the field, with what periodicity, can also bear on the character and trustworthiness of presented

evidence. Knowledge claims based on ten days' total immersion in the research field—say, one eight-hour day a week spread across ten weeks (8
hours × 10 days = 80 hours)—appear differently than those based on daily
encounter over the same time period (that is, 8 hours × 7 days × 10 weeks =
70 days, 560 hours), let alone for six months or a year (with whatever periodicity); and they appear differently than ten four-hour days over the same
period. Many methods reports do not make clear what constitutes "a day"
in the field. Was this 9:00 a.m. to 5:00 p.m., Monday through Friday, and
then the researcher went home? Or did research continue at the corner bar,
over dinner, at a meeting, at weekend gatherings? These deliberations are
typically (or should be) entertained in designing the research project. But
a reader expects clear statements of the duration of the research along with
an explanation of why that made sense for the specific study as context for
an article's truth claims.

Time and Space Together: Exposure

Exposure to the variety of perspectives on a research topic also supports
truth claims (and requirements of exposure often drive duration of time in
field, archival, or interview settings). Textbooks often present "prolonged
exposure" over time as one of the hallmarks of interpretive research. What
is missing, however, is the understanding that in a field setting, "prolonged"
exposure can refer to space as well as time. The two interact in interesting
ways in this kind of research.

Readers want to know that settings have been sufficiently "mapped."
In a governance research project, for example, this can mean covering all
(research-relevant) occupational roles; all possible perspectives within a
department; all departments in an organization (or a horizontal slice or
regional branch of one); or some combination of vertical and horizontal
swathes, much as an archaeologist might cut multiple trenches in various
locations within a single excavation site. In a community or policy study,
one might map one's territory by interest groups or race/ethnic or class or
gender or age groupings, or some combination of these, or something else
entirely, depending on the research question.[11]

In interviewing, exposure is achieved through what is commonly referred to as "purposive sampling" or "snowball sampling," or a combination of the two, leading to "saturation" as one begins to hear the same
information in response to substantive questions or the same names in response to the question, "With whom else should I be speaking?" A phenomenological position that interpretation and ensuing action reflect situ-

ated, lived experience and/or a hermeneutic position that interpretation and action reflect the unspoken, commonsense, tacitly known, everyday "rules" at work in various communities of meaning suggest(s) that conversational interviewing should be used to map the terrain of the research topic, as noted above, seeking to garner viewpoints across the spectrum of opinion, experience, expertise, and so forth about the topic.[12] Documentary research treats exposure in a similar fashion, seeking to garner views from various orientations toward the topic of study.

But a note of caution is in order concerning the language of sampling. Neither purposive choice nor snowball inquiry is a sample, or sampling, in the statistics-based sense of "a set of elements drawn from and analyzed to estimate the characteristics of a population."[13] Ethnographic (and other interpretive) research is not involved with estimates, nor is the logic of probabilities the basis for its evidentiary claims. These are grounded, instead, on lived experience and situated knowledge and knowers, including researchers and our positionality (see Hawkesworth 2006 for the parallel argumentation from feminist inquiry). As both of these tools signal a mapping of terrain over time, perhaps it would be more appropriate to call them *purposive* or *snowball exposure*.

These several methods build on the ontological presupposition that we live in a world of multiple possible experiences, and hence situated interpretations, of social realities, and also on the epistemological presupposition that the researcher's situational understanding will develop and deepen through exposure to a variety of perspectives or points of view, reflecting different lived experiences deriving from the various sources of these different experiences and interpretations. This is the advantage of the outsider's position: one is loosed from those societal strictures that immerse one in a single position and keep one there; and it is this stranger-ness that one seeks to preserve at the same time as one develops enough situated, local knowledge that enables one to understand members' acts and their reasoning about those acts. Readers assess researchers' truth claims against discussions of these issues, together with the deliberations and choices that led to the development of exposure, including those improvised along the way as the research design was altered (a point to which I return below).

Silences

Much harder to identify and access are those positions and views that have been silenced or are perhaps silent by choice. Snowball exposure, for example, builds on relational networks, and networks, by definition, do not include everyone. Given the various manifestations of power, oppositional voices may be more easily discoverable than voices not even on the "mattering map" (Goldstein 1983) of those most vocally involved in the issue under study. As a reader, I want to know that the researcher has thought about whether there might be silent, and silenced, voices and, if so, what efforts have been made to identify and include them.

Researcher's Role: Positionality and Prior Knowledge

Where are *you*, Dear Author, in this research project? In reading documents and in interviewing topic-relevant actors, you are—we assume—acting out of your role as researcher. But in field research that is participatory as well as observational, you may have adopted a situation-specific role in addition to your researcher-role (see Gans 1976), acting in keeping with the demands of the former when necessary. This dual role is central to ethnographic research, and it raises some of the more challenging, and methodologically interesting, issues for research ethics and truth claims. The more readers know about researchers' roles, the circumstances under which they chose or acquired or developed them, and any advantages or problems presented by a situational role (for example, role conflicts), the better able readers are to evaluate evidence and truth claims.

One particular feature of ethnographic research, as with interpretive research more broadly, is the extent to which choices of setting and role build on the researcher's prior experience and knowledge. Researchers often choose their settings because they worked or lived there previously, have family ties to that place, speak the local language or a related one, and/or have some personal connection to the activity they are studying. There is no reason to hide this. Within the ontological and epistemological presuppositions underlying interpretive research, "objectivity"—the ability of the researcher to stand outside the subject of study—is not conceptually possible (meaning, also, that it is not possible to avoid "interviewer effects"; on objectivity see Bernstein 1983; Hawkesworth 2006; Yanow 2006b). Aside from that, efforts to hide the practical or personal reasons for choosing a research setting often lend research narratives a sense of inauthenticity, thereby weakening the trustworthiness of the analysis. It is not that difficult to infer that someone with a Hungarian family name studying in a university in Ireland writing a dissertation comparing cases in Budapest and Belfast has made those choices of setting for reasons of personal background. The more explicit and transparent the explication of role and setting choices, the more trustworthy the research is likely to be—or at least, the less it will appear as if the researcher is trying to deceive. I take up other issues concerning positionality and reflexivity in the second section of this chapter.

Access: Getting In and Maintaining Relationships

How do researchers connect with the settings in which they conduct field research, with the people they speak with, or with the archive(s) in which they track down documentary sources? "Access" is not a matter of merely getting a foot in a door; it is about establishing relationships and maintaining them (see Feldman, Bell, and Berger 2003). Readers want to know how this was achieved—for example, if bribes were paid to keep information flowing (just kidding, Dear Author!—unless you consider treating "informants" to coffee or beer, or babysitting the kids, as methodological bribery, a potentially instrumental objectification of others that dogs ethnographic fieldwork, something to discuss as part of research ethics).[14]

Data Details

It has become increasingly common for researchers to claim "thick description" as their method, referencing Clifford Geertz (1973). This is an interesting acknowledgment that writing—here, the dense layering of material from field, interview, and/or archival notes—is itself a method of knowledge creation about the topic of study. But much like usages of Glaser and Strauss's grounded theory (see Locke 1996), thick description is often invoked in manuscripts as a signaling device alone, nodding toward desired membership in a particular epistemic community but without writing practices that give substance to the signal. What a reader wants to see is the layering of situational detail *that contextualizes action and nuances it*, so that, to take Ryle's example discussed by Geertz, the reader can discern whether the muscle movement in an actor's eye is involuntary twitching or intentional winking. Detail alone is not enough.

Representation

Interpretive researchers cannot use graphs and tables for presenting data analyses to the extent that quantitative researchers can: words—the central, traditional data of field research—do not lend themselves to such condensed summarizing. For readers, this means "consuming" more words than one typically encounters in quantitative writing. But other visual representations can be used effectively (such as maps, photographs, diagrams, organizational charts, flow charts, or descriptive statistics graphs, such as bar and pie charts), and writers might think creatively about ways to present, in comprehensive fashion, "reams" of word data (see, e.g., Tufte 1990; Dougherty and Kunda 1990). Writers also need to recognize that such visual representations do not speak for themselves. Graphics need titles, and the writer needs to explicate their significant elements in the text, noting what textual arguments are illuminated by a specific representation, how each one links and contributes to the argument at hand, and so forth.[15]

From a reader's perspective, there is a subtext to the provision of these sorts of information that goes beyond the substantive purpose of elucidating situated meaning. These elements convey the sense of "being there" that is so crucial in contextualizing the truth claims of an ethnographic report. The presence of details about these several elements, when included in a manuscript, contributes to conveying that you, Dear Author, really were where you claim to have been, saw what you claim to have seen, heard what you claim to have heard, talked to the people you claim to have spoken with, read what you claim to have read, and so on. Observation-based writing achieves this through myriad descriptive details of place and person, of events, acts, and interactions (who said or did what, to or with whom, when, where, with what, and how). Interview- and document-based writing accomplishes such layering through the details of direct quotations of key phrases, full sentences, and lengthier excerpts, along with paraphrased and summarized passages. These various details correspond to the where, when, who, what, and how of the situational narrative suggested by theater-based theories of human action (e.g., the pentad of Burke 1969/1945; Goffman 1959; see also Burke 1989). Drawing in reader-response theory (for example, Iser 1989) brings into the analogy the theater's "fourth wall," on the other side of which sits the audience—here, readers of the research manuscript, to whom I now turn.

Dear Reader: Reviewing Ethnographic Manuscripts

Writing as a way of world-making has drawn relatively little attention in policy or political ethnography, let alone other areas of political science. Some aspects of ethnographic writing that achieve this may appear, then, to a reader from a different epistemic community unaware of their status as hallmarks of such writing, to be misplaced or even unscientific. I turn to

these parts of the craft, including reasons why they are increasingly considered *de rigueur* in such writing today.

I-Writing

Schoolchildren and undergraduates are taught not to write in the first-
person singular. Single authors of French scientific reports write as *nous*, the
first-person plural. The rationale rests on accepting the possibility of objectivity: the absent "I" distances the subject matter, positioning the author outside the work. At least, this is the promise held out. Henry David Thoreau,
writing *Walden* in 1854, already addressed the limitations of such writing:

> In most books, the I, or first person, is omitted; in this it will be retained. . . .
> We commonly do not remember that it is, after all, always the first person
> that is speaking. . . . Moreover, I, on my side, require of every writer, first or
> last, a simple and sincere account of his own life . . . some such account as he
> would send to his kindred from a distant land; for if he has lived sincerely, it
> must have been in a distant land to me. (Thoreau, 1854, chap. 1)

The ultimate in this objectivizing strategy is the use of the passive voice,
which denies agency altogether, assigning responsibility for action to some
invisible force acting upon the object in question.

Interpretive researchers argue that objectivity is not possible (see
Hawkesworth 1988, 2006; Yanow 1996, 2006a). That is the heart of a
hermeneutic phenomenology that presupposes that the meanings of social realities are intersubjectively constructed and that understandings of
them derive from prior knowledge. This prior knowledge, in turn, is both
personal (coming, as it does, out of the knower's contextualized experience,
education, and so on) and collective (the rules for sense-making having
standing within epistemic communities—communities of meaning, of interpretation, of discourse, of practice; in short, paradigmatic communities
indwelling in shared, paradigmatic, experience-based hermeneutic circles).
If knowledge is situated knowledge, produced by situated knowers, "I" is
the most normal and natural voice for the researcher to use. Such use is ut-
terly in keeping with interpretive scientific writing.

Reflexivity

The personal "I" puts the researcher-author into the picture where he or she
belongs. But it does not tell us anything about that person's experience with

the research, not so much concerning the elements itemized in the first sec-tion of this chapter, but rather with respect to how that person's presence—aspects of personality, clothing and tone of voice, class and/or race-ethnic and/or religious identity, gender, birthplace and/or national identity, and so on—shaped the research and the data generated. Samer Shehata (2006), for example, details how being a male, Muslim, Alexandria-born, U.K.- and U.S.-educated, Egyptian-American researcher both enabled his access to some kinds and sources of information about shop-floor work and work-ers, and blocked his access to others. Timothy Pachirat (this volume) notes how his own physical features (and possession of a driver's license) made him appear a "natural" candidate for physical labor in the slaughterhouse and, later, how his command of English made him a leading candidate for promotion to quality control manager, as well as how both of these physical locations within the plant led to different sights and insights.

Reflexive writing, then, advances the objectivity argument one step fur-ther. Not only is objectivity in social research not possible; intersubjectiv-ity *requires* the involved presence of the researcher in cogenerating knowl-edge, interactively, with those in the setting being studied, with whom one participates in whatever degree, whom one interviews, whose documents one reads. The double hermeneutic at play in research settings—the inter-pretations made by the researcher of others' interpretations—takes place also in analyzing documents, whether historical or contemporary (see Jack-son 2006). Not only is there room for the "I" in interpretive writing (al-though it is not required, and different writers are comfortable using it in different degrees), but methodologists increasingly emphasize the need for a reflective consideration of how the person—the "positionality"—of the researcher (might have) shaped the research process. For that, we need not just a first-person speaker or firsthand details of the sort called for in the first section of this chapter; we need a considered exploration of the possible impacts or effects of those details in shaping research findings or knowledge- and truth-claims.

This does not mean that having made "biases" explicit, the researcher can get on about research and analysis in an objective fashion. Hawkes-worth (1988) demolished the logic underlying that conceptual move, ad-vanced in public policy analysis and planning theories in the 1970s, by showing that it is a logical impossibility on its own terms. It presumes that researchers can, in effect, stand outside of themselves and the key cogni-tions, experiences, and so on that constitute them as the persons they are. The impulse toward explicit reflexivity increasingly called for in ethno-graphic and other interpretive research and writing accepts that positionality shapes perception and interpretation. Rather than try to hide it, contemporary writing seeks to engage the contours of that shaping.

The move toward increased reflexivity has led some researchers to undertake auto-ethnographic research, using their own experiences with the subject of study—often *as* the subject of study—as a lens through which to understand how others might experience the same situations or processes. So, for example, Michael Humphreys (2005) used his own experience of a career change to illuminate others' taken-for-granted understandings of the organizational worlds he was studying. For some, such self-explorations are excessive. Different people have different comfort levels with personal disclosures—not only with disclosing aspects of their own lives, whether "factual" or emotional, but also with reading the open disclosures made by others. As with determining an appropriate level of detail to recount, the degree of self-disclosure should relate to how it supports the research and its truth claims. Yet even within such parameters, there is room for choice, and researchers need to find their own comfort levels. At the same time, although auto-ethnography is a form of reflexivity, reflexivity need not mean the conduct of an auto-ethnographic study. It would be a tremendous misunderstanding of what reflexivity promises methodologically to dismiss this important concept by reducing it to "hyper-personal" writing.

The Improvisational Character of Interpretive Research

Ethnographic and other interpretive research requires improvising. The best research design can only sketch out the broadest parameters of the project (such as setting, overall time period, some idea of the types of people the researcher intends to try to talk to, and other elements discussed in the first section of this chapter). As such research engages human beings, it is not possible to know ahead of time precisely how they will act or react—or how the researcher will be called upon to respond. This is one of the difficulties many Institutional Review Board protocols pose for field researchers (Yanow and Schwartz-Shea 2008). In observing (with whatever degree of participating), the researcher often needs to take on-the-spot action that he did not, and could not, foresee. In talking with people (whether in formal interviews or in curbside chats), the researcher needs to engage what she has just been told. Even document analysis can evoke an improvisational response, as one phrase points to an unanticipated source, a cache of letters in a distant archive or an individual to locate in another country.

But "improvisational" does not mean impressionistic. There is systematicity to improvisation, whether in performance or in interpretive methods (Yanow 2001); it is a misunderstanding to think of it as being entirely made up on the spot. Whether in jazz, in Renaissance-era early music, or in theater, improvisation builds on a repertoire of "moves" learned through extended practice and preparation, solo, but also with others. One may not know ahead of time what one will do in the moment, but one draws *in that moment* on the repertoire one has practiced with one's band- or troupe-mates. And improvisation requires *being* "in the moment": an intense focus on the matter at hand and on those with whom one is interacting. It requires a "yes, and" attitude: a willingness to build on what one has just been told, on an invitation or challenge just extended, on an unexpected word just encountered, rather than "blocking" (negating) it.[16]

So it is that ethnographers and other interpretive researchers practice their craft, learning how to observe or converse with "in the moment" focus to remember the details afterward; how to enact "yes, and" in a conversation to keep it focused on the research topic. As with all practices, the repertoire of observational and conversational "moves" builds with experience. Starting a conversation with strangers gets easier the more practiced one is, as does remembering an hour-long conversation without benefit of a tape recorder. (And yes, it is easy to fall out of practice.)

Those who do not practice improvisational music-making or theater tend to misunderstand it—to construe improvising as entirely invented on the spot, without any method, rather than as a practiced craft. This may be one of the reasons that ethnographic and other interpretive research methods are denigrated: they are seen as something that "anyone" can do, without preparation or practice; they are perceived as unskilled, make-it-up-out-of-your-head commonplaces rather than as skill-based, "advanced" research tools. Methodological improvising is not a scientific failure of research design or execution, Dear Reader—especially you who are evaluating research proposals for funding. Given the character of human interaction and meaning-making in ethnographic-interpretive research, a methods section in a proposal that is less programmatic than its quantitative cousin regarding anticipated findings or even some of the elements discussed earlier in this chapter is not only common, but necessary.

"Alternative" Writing Styles

I had a long fight with my dissertation adviser. Wanting my writing to re-trace my own sense-making in the field as the research unfolded, I began my draft with the case-study story, leading from that to the theoretical frame. She argued that without that frame, there was nothing to guide the reading of the story; the theoretical material needed to come first. I gave in. And I have come to see that she was right, in many ways.

That said, it is, I think, possible to find a middle path, in which the manuscript begins with some amount of case narrative before turning to the theoretical frame. The immediacy of dialogue or quoted text or event description can draw a reader in, setting the stage on which to ground the theorizing that follows. As a literary device, the subsequent turn to theory can parallel the omniscient narrator in fiction turning back in historical time, breaking with a present-day narrative and recounting the background that will lead readers up to current events. More postmodernist scholars might attempt writing that has no narrative thread, enacting their theoretical argument.[17] Alternative forms of writing, a developing area in interpretive research, are often intentional efforts to express epistemological alternatives, rather than signs of unscientific or ill-prepared work. At the same time, this should not be read as an excuse for bad (illegible, illogical, ungrammatical, etc.) writing that interferes with communication. One writes to communicate with one's readers, and journals and their fields have accepted styles. If experimentation—say, presenting research in theatrical, dialogical, diary or novelistic style (e.g., Ellis 2004)—causes one to lose one's readers, it would be better, it seems to me, to find another genre.

Writing Like a Reader: Writing "Being There" into the Narrative

Doing field research systematically is a complex process. It may focus on single cases, thereby qualifying terminologically as a "single-n" or single-site study.[18] But single-n cases typically entail multiple observational areas within their geographic, organizational, or political settings; multiple interviews and chats; multiple events observed; multiple passages read in documents. Shehata (2006) studied workers on the shop floor, the manager in his office, the riders on the bus going to work, male coworkers at gathering places away from work; Pachirat (2008) enumerated over 120 different occupational roles on the slaughterhouse floor, plus several other administrative roles—all in the same "single site" research. Field complexities also render writing complex.

Still, writing can be learned. Would-be fiction and poetry writers are told to read widely. Anthropology has long taught methods this way, inductively, through the reading of ethnographies. Political and other social scientists writing ethnographic and other interpretive texts can follow suit.

My point of departure in this chapter presumes a political dimension to scientific research and writing, in the Aristotelian sense: that written reports are designed to persuade. They draw on the rhetorical devices accepted within their epistemic communities to convince readers of the trustworthiness of their evidence and their claims to knowledge. Although many of the elements I have discussed here are commonly considered in designing interpretive research, when included in the writing up of that research they also take on the rhetorical character of signaling devices (including signaling membership in a particular epistemic community). When they are absent, the believability of the research evidence can suffer, thereby diminishing the strength of research truth claims.

Research methods courses are typically taught without attention to underlying ontological and epistemological presuppositions; Statistics 101 courses, for example, usually dive right into descriptive statistics rather than beginning with a more philosophical treatment of the concept of probability and Popperian (or other) arguments concerning the possibility of certain knowledge. Perhaps for this reason, many scholars from noninterpretive epistemic communities are unaware that "reliability" and "validity," while standard indices for variables research, are inappropriate measures for ethnographic and other forms of interpretive research, methodologically speaking, where "trustworthiness" is the increasingly accepted evaluative criterion (see Schwartz-Shea 2006). The discussion in this chapter could help such readers of field research in their various roles—as reviewers, editors, grant-makers. As they look for and fail to find measures more familiar to them, these colleagues might instead discover the methodological elements and modes of writing discussed here; those "missing" measures notwithstanding, they might recognize, nonetheless, the trustworthiness (rather than reliability or validity) these elements (are intended to) engender. These are commonplaces within the canons of interpretive science, establishing the kind of systematicity that is particular to ethnographic methods. Knowing this might enable such readers to perceive the manuscript as a bit less strange or even unscientific. But that can only happen if researchers writing up their field research consider reading as an interpretive moment, engage it as a method of sense-making, and write from a reader's perspective, anticipating the contextualizing evidence a reader is or should be looking for and writing accordingly.

Editors who invite submissions of interpretive research should not be holding those manuscripts to the same methodological criteria that apply to non-interpretive approaches; these methodologies enact their considerably different ontological and epistemological groundings in different modes of writing. Each plays, as it were, by different rules; neither can ever meet the standards of the other; and both editors and reviewers, knowing that such differences exist, need to hold different types of research to their respective criteria for scientific standing. Moreover, it would be unfair to expect interpretive researchers to rehearse these methodological arguments in every manuscript submitted for publication: they typically do not have the page-length space to flesh out these arguments in addition to presenting the substance of their research; they may themselves not be schooled in methodological argumentation; and they should not be singled out to do so when, after all, we do not expect researchers using regression analyses and other statistical tools to detail the philosophical grounding for those methods every time they use them.

Some aspects of interpretive research manuscripts should be clearer in light of the foregoing. Authors are not just whining when they complain about the difficulties of condensing interpretive research reports into journal page-length restrictions of twenty-some double-spaced pages. "Being there" not only takes time; it takes page-length space to convey the data details necessary to support an argument. Data cannot always be concentrated in tables; photographs and sketches have their own spatial requirements; audio excerpts from recordings cannot be published in traditional outlets (bracketing ethical concerns for the moment). Reflexive writing takes even more space. These and other matters are issues not confronted by survey researchers and regression analysts, and to the extent that such work serves as the model for journal publishing, interpretive writing is trouble, and troubled. Equivalent issues arise in grant-making.

Reading back from writing-focused criteria to the prosecution of research in the field highlights the central aspect that distinguishes ethnography from some other forms of interpretive research—the feeling of "being there," developed by the researcher in the midst of doing and writing the research *and* by the reader in the midst of reading the research account. The elements discussed herein constitute some of the ways in which the researcher writes "being there" into the narrative, having been *there*—in extended space as well as time—in the field: in order to write "thick description" texts, the researcher needs to have conducted research "thickly" and written "thick" fieldnotes.

"Ethnography," as noted previously, refers to methods, writing, and a characteristic sensibility that informs the entire enterprise. One can use ethnographic methods—observing, with whatever degree of participating; talking, with whatever degree of formality and advance scheduling; closely reading research-relevant documents—without producing an ethnographic account. Data so generated can be treated using other sorts of interpretive (or other) analytic tools (for example, semiotics, conversation analysis); the research can be written up in non-ethnographic form; the sensibility can be absent altogether. Because of the centrality of place-ness to this research, a collection of formal interviews alone does not an ethnographic research project make—even if talking to people is an ethnographic tool. Neither does documentary research on its own (although metaphorically, "textual ethnography" could mean treating texts as if they were fieldnotes on contemporaneous observations and interviews, with appropriate argumentation for such usage and attention to historical setting; see Warren 2007). One is certainly "there" when one conducts an interview; but observing the outer office and its workings before the interview and interacting with the assistant on one's way out the door does not add up to the sense of twitches and winks and the differences and similarities between them that contextualizes the sense-making reported and analyzed, that brings "being" into existence.

This is what leads me to exclude from consideration one usage of "ethnography" in some recent political science research: that based on interviews alone (an argument also advanced by growing numbers of methodologists; see, e.g., Herbert 2000, 551, 552–53). Its claim for standing as ethnographic research may be explained in part by contemporary research developments and challenges. In political and some other social sciences, the term *qualitative methods* has become synonymous with *ethnography*, perhaps because ethnographic research is one of the better known of these methods, leading authors of more inclusive methods textbooks to focus on it in their brief treatments of qualitative research. Given their limitations (Schwartz-Shea and Yanow 2002), these treatments may suggest to newer researchers, who know that "interviewing" is "clearly" a qualitative method, that interviewing is ethnographic research. Another possibility turns on the settings of political ethnographies, which increasingly take place not in the bush, but in the boardroom or city council chamber, where formal interviews have a legitimate place. Yet whatever challenges we may have in defining political ethnography—is it a particular genre of ethnographic research? is it an ethnography of a political situation or event? do anthropologists and political scientists do it the same way?—it entails more than a set of interviews (even when the researcher "observes" the office setting throughout the interview). Part of political ethnography's distinctiveness relative to a generic "anthropological" ethnography is the role played by documentary sources; but we would never equate archival research with ethnographic research. In assessing ethnographic writing, readers look for evidence of the "being there" quality that enacts the "ethnographic sensibility" (Pader 2006) that is a central hallmark of ethnographic research—and this requires more than just interview-generated data.

The new ethnographer looking for methodological advice will not find in this chapter anything about theorizing—how to get from field data or field notes to a theoretically informed text. Ethnographers live in two worlds—that of the setting they study and that of their epistemic community—and many of us want to contribute to both. Theorizing is the way in which we engage what is of import to the academic community of which we are members. More needs to be said about the iterative movement between theoretical framing and field data in the crafting of such writing.

My plea for greater transparency and explicit rendering of methods may appear to some to be excessive. For those trained formally in ethnographic or participant-observer methods, the elements I have discussed here are probably second nature. With ever more researchers coming to these methods without such background, however, these elements increasingly need spelling out. My intention is not to encourage writers to write boring texts (something discussed by Doty 2004 and Sand-Jensen 2007)—on the contrary! I *am* concerned that foregrounding tacit knowledge about writing practices risks turning their subtleties into infelicitous heavy-handedness. There *can* be too much detail, or detail of the wrong sort: a level of detail unnecessary for or irrelevant to supporting the argument one is trying to make. Methods entail making choices; writers, and not just readers, also make choices, evaluative judgments with respect to what to include, what to omit. At the same time, the contemporary "evidence based" movement (in medicine, psychological counseling, and public policy analysis) has taken a very narrow and largely unspoken, unreflective, and uncritical view of what constitutes "evidence," and I hate to think that calling for a more explicit accounting of the elements of interpretive research practices would be taken as part of this movement. Nonetheless, in my readings of manuscripts in the last few years, I have been unconvinced by many of the narratives—and I am a sympathetic, informed reader. If I am unconvinced, how much more so a reader who is less well informed!

The need for this degree of explicitness is perhaps timebound for a second reason. As long as we write for one another within the epistemic and practice bounds of a community of political ethnographers (or interpretive researchers more broadly), we can assume a shared understanding of the prosecution of such research. The more we cross the boundaries that demarcate epistemic-practitioner communities, however, the more explicit we need to be, as writing and reading practices, along with evaluative criteria—

those things that make science "science"—are particular to specific communities and their work practices.[19] To the extent that scholars are judging work that follows scientific criteria of epistemic communities other than the ones of which they are members, methods need to be spelled out to a greater rather than lesser degree. That is the responsibility of writers. The responsibility of such readers is to inform themselves as to what these "other" criteria might be, so that they can judge work on its own terms rather than in terms of an epistemic community to which the research does not belong. Although some might argue on behalf of "the virtues of closet qualitative research" (Sutton 1997), I would strenuously resist such a move. Treating reading as method and writing from a reader's perspective is one path toward resistance.

Notes

Earlier versions of this chapter were presented at the 2006 American Political Science Association annual meeting and the University of Toronto workshop "Political Ethnography: What Insider Perspectives Contribute to the Study of Power" (26–28 October 2006). My thanks to participants in those sessions, especially Cecelia Lynch, Lee Ann Fujii, Timothy Pachirat, and Edward Schatz, who, along with Marleen van der Haar, Merlijn van Hulst, Lorraine Nencel, and Peregrine Schwartz-Shea, commented on those versions. I also thank Timothy Pachirat for help with the table, Merlijn van Hulst for continuing to bring to my attention other social scientists' writings on writing, and Edward Schatz for helpful editorial challenges.

1. The term rigorous appears in quotation marks because interpretive methods do not enact rigor in the ways that quantitative methods do (see Yanow 2006b for an extended discussion).

2. Salemink (2003) notes that ethnographic methods have never been the sole province of anthropology, whose roots trace to colonial administrative practices, themselves developed in the professional practice of community organization ("community development work" in England, *l'animation* in France; see Yanow 1976).

3. Parallel arguments have been advanced concerning museum exhibits (e.g., Karp and Lavine 1991). There is a cottage industry of advice on writing good academic prose: classic texts by Becker (1986) and Mills (1959), but also Forester (1984/1999, 2005) and Wildavsky (1971, 1993); see also Francine Prose's *Reading like a Writer: A Guide for People Who Love Books and for Those Who Want to Write Them*, a review of which (Barton 2006) I came upon while revising this chapter. After it was written, I found Hammersley's (1990) excellent, methodologically informed discussion of reading ethnographic texts; see also Gay y Blasco and Wardle (2007). Earlier versions of this chapter included my own compilation of notes for writers, omitted here for reasons of space but available at www.fsw.vu.nl/yanow.

4. I have in mind here not only acts as "text-analogues" (Taylor 1971), but built spaces and other physical artifacts that might be used in the field setting and key to understanding it, such as the color of a worker's hat (Pachirat, this volume) or the kind of shoe one wears (Shehata 2006); see also Yanow (2006b). The argument holds for those doing interview-based research, as well as for those doing document-based re-

search as a kind of "textual ethnography," reading legal, historical, or other kinds of texts to elicit their authors', or others', values, beliefs, worldviews—in short, their meanings (see, e.g., Brandwein 2007; Jackson 2006; Novkov 2007; this is what characterizes Zemon Davis's [1983] and Darnton's [1984, 2003] social and cultural history).

The distinction between first and second hermeneutics roughly parallels Geertz's (1973) between experience-near and experience-distant analyses, itself a gloss on the older emic-etic distinction. Interpretations of both are problematic in several ways, among them not accounting well for the participant observer's interpretations of his/her own firsthand experience of field events. When researchers are actively participating, the distinction between the first and second hermeneutic is collapsed—but not eliminated. Although the researcher's self (body and mind) is, in participant observation, the primary instrument of research, these interpretations are provisional, to be corroborated or refuted through subsequent interviews and/or observations. This renders the researcher's first-hand experience a second-level interpretation: it may be "experience-near" and also etic. Here is where questions enter concerning the weight to be accorded to the researcher-as-stranger's view, which, informed by prior theoretical reading and/or information from other interview, observational, and/or documentary sources, may generate insights that situational members might themselves not produce (Nencel and Yanow 2008).

5. This draws in the history of literary theories of textual meaning and interpretation, which over the second half of the twentieth century moved from locating sources of textual meaning in the author's intentions, to finding them in the text itself (see, e.g., Ciardi 1959; leading some to proclaim the death of the author), to locating them in the reader. The last of these, known as "reader-response theory" (see, e.g., Iser 1989), quite in keeping with a phenomenological hermeneutics, understands that textual meaning is created by readers through the lenses—the prior knowledge and lived experience—they themselves bring to the reading (or through some combination of all three sources).

6. One might well argue that this is common to all forms of writing and reading, not just academic ones. I concur. At the same time, there are distinctive writing and thinking practices that demarcate between humanities and social science scholarships; and academic careers are marked by different judgments and trajectories than those of journalists, novelists, and essayists.

7. There is a danger, in discussing the selection of "best" settings, interview participants, and the like, that new researchers, discovering the unavailability of their intended settings and participants, will feel they have failed. This is hardly the case: field research needs to accommodate to field "realities," and this is one of them. Hence, the improvisational character of such research and some of the problems that arise in considering access issues, both of which are discussed below.

8. Anthropologists have always talked at length to people in the field—about kinship, tools, language, and so on. They rarely, if ever, called it "interviewing." The need to designate such talk with that word seems to have been driven by other social scientists working at the survey end of the "talk" continuum who needed, or felt they needed, to locate what they were doing more firmly in "scientific" space. In political ethnography, the policymakers we want to talk to are often sitting in their offices rather than hanging out on street corners or in pool halls, and they have a different sense of the limits or flow of time than townspeople meeting in a coffee shop, which

means, typically, that we have to set up appointments to meet them. Hence, these talks become designated "interviews." My thanks to Merlijn van Hulst for helping me clarify this formulation of the point.

9. My experience, corroborated by others, has been that I learn more when talking to decision-makers in informal settings. But Peter Biegelbauer (personal conversation, 27 June 2007) notes that his interviews with policymakers have been more informative when he has met them on their own turf—in their own offices. This may, then, vary across political cultures.

10. Although one might read with greater attention in the morning than in the late afternoon, but this is not, typically, the sort of variability we attend to in methods statements, trusting researchers to monitor their own wakefulness.

11. I have drawn elsewhere on Murphy's (1980) analogy with wagon trains in the U.S. "old West" circling the campfire at night or on cubist portraiture such as Picasso's to illustrate taking multiple perspectives on the subject of study (e.g., Yanow 2000). I now understand that these imply, to some, the possibility of complete knowledge of the topic, much as some art critics see cubism as depicting more realistic views of its models by circling them (Hatch and Yanow 2008). Yet such an understanding of the wagon train analogy ignores the gaps and areas of darkness between the wagons and beyond the circle, or the features omitted in cubist portraits, such that complete knowledge is never possible (see the section on silences, below). Either analogy might also be taken to imply that positioned knowledge is external—that is, objective. This is close to a critical realist position that claims the possibility of objective knowledge of a constructed reality. It is a perspective enabled if one does not focus on the meaning(s) of the campfire or model to its observers, including those beyond the circle: as Maarten van Alstein (personal communication, 15 August 2006) points out, historically, the circling of the wagons was intended to keep certain people out of the center. Making meaning central puts analysis perforce in the realm of subjectivity and intersubjective and incomplete knowledge—the sense in which I envisioned the wagon train and Picasso analogies.

12. See the discussions in Yanow and Schwartz-Shea (2006). The main exception would be research based on a single person's experience, such as shadowing a prime minister; see, e.g., Behar (1993) or Rudolph and Rudolph (2000), although each of these studies draws on more sources of data than provided by engaging just one person or one diary.

13. Definition 2, *American Heritage Dictionary of the English Language,* 4th ed. (New York: Houghton Mifflin, 2000), accessed online: http://dictionary.reference.com/browse/sample (accessed 11 July 2006).

14. Kidding aside, there is an aspect of instrumentality, captured in the problematic terms *informant* and *going native* and in common notions of "access" characterizing the relationship between researcher and situational actors, that is still not widely engaged, despite awareness of the colonial heritage of ethnography and the state's role in much social research. Seeing access as relational is a modest step toward addressing this instrumentality. The American Anthropological Association (2002) states that research should only be conducted when it addresses a problem identified by situational members and the research is codesigned by researcher and participants; but even (participatory) action research does not always eliminate power relationships in the field—nor is power in the sole possession of the researcher. These concerns arise also in research regulation policies (e.g., U.S. Institutional Review Board

policies and programs) that are intended to address potential abuses of researcher power; but conceived in light of an experimental model, they are not appropriate for field research (Yanow and Schwartz-Shea 2008).

15. For that matter, the use of representations in science and other practices is itself increasingly a subject for research; see, e.g., Ewenstein and Whyte (2007); Latour (1999); Lynch and Woolgar (1990).

16. This should not be read as meaning that all invitations should be accepted. A researcher in the field might be invited to partake in illegal, immoral, or dangerous activity, something I have no intention of encouraging. One might well consider unexpected openings, but not at unexamined risk to one's personal safety: judgment must be exercised, including about others' views of outsiders. My thanks to Lee Ann Fujii for bringing to my attention this possible interpretation of following "yes, and."

17. My personal take on this is akin to my adviser's absolute "Don't! It doesn't work." But perhaps I just haven't yet read the right article.

18. Anthropology tends to treat the single-site study as the unmarked norm, as Røryvik (2006) observed; the marking of "multi-site" fieldwork renders it the exception.

19. For a similar perspective, see Schatz's conclusion to this volume.

CONCLUSION

What Kind(s) of Ethnography Does Political Science Need?

EDWARD SCHATZ

The best protective device against being taken in by one particular language is to be brought up bilingually or trilingually.

—Paul Feyerabend

When Feyerabend wrote about protecting oneself against being "taken in" by one particular language, he sounded a concern that resonates in the contributions to this volume.[1] No field of social inquiry should be metaphorically monolingual; to allow a pragmatic and intellectually open exchange between people working in different traditions, researchers should be conversant in several research "languages." Of course, to be bilingual or trilingual is not to abandon structures of grammar and representation that make for coherence. One who speaks both Spanish and English is able to communicate more ably and widely than one who speaks only "Spanglish."

In this conclusion, I address a series of issues related to a core question: What kind(s) of ethnography should be "spoken" in political science? After suggesting a way to think about the value of political ethnographic approaches offered by this volume's contributors, I ask what is distinctive about ethnography as it is used to study politics. In other words, why do we deploy the phrase "*political* ethnography"? I then consider two kinds of political ethnography and what their promotion would entail in the current intellectual and professional climate in political science. The first is a kind of ethnography that is used in multiple-methods research projects. The second is a kind of ethnography that stands alone. A third possibility— that nothing short of a hegemony of political ethnographic methods and sensibilities would suffice—is something that I leave to the polemicists uninterested in the kinds of pluralism that Feyerabend sought to create.

Overall, I suggest that stand-alone ethnography is crucial. I attempt to make the *hard* case that *even* neopositivist, causality-oriented theorists intent on generating decontextualized knowledge have good reason to protect space for stand-alone political ethnography. Moreover, they should embrace *even* that kind of political ethnography that distances itself from the project of producing causal theories. Because of the variety of sometimes conflicting ideas about ethnography and its value (many of which are covered in the preceding chapters), I think of the arguments in this conclusion as contributing to an ongoing discussion about, rather than as an attempt to offer the "final word" on, political ethnography.

When Political Ethnography?

Under what conditions and given what research questions is ethnography useful?[2] Could we identify specific, real-world conditions that recommend ethnography? Lorraine Bayard de Volo and I once contended that ethnography is particularly valuable *inter alia* "in cases where government statistics are suspect, media outlets are controlled by political interests, and poverty, lack of infrastructure, illiteracy, or political violence impede survey research" (Bayard de Volo and Schatz 2004, 269). While ethnography may be the only viable technique in some circumstances, it does not logically follow that in other circumstances ethnography is less useful. To the contrary, as the preceding chapters make clear, ethnography is crucial across a wide range of research circumstances. Walsh's chapter makes the point elegantly: even in the advanced industrial United States, with its abundance of government statistics, armies of pollsters, impressive media freedom, and relative infrequency of political violence, participant observation is crucial to our understanding of how public opinion is formed.

Putting research *conditions* to the side, do some research *problems* inherently lend themselves to ethnographic inquiry? Could it be that various aspects of micro-politics—quiet forms of deliberation, resistance, and mobilization; enactments of power relations that occur in the "private" domain; novel and contextual recombinations of social and political factors that generate unanticipated dynamics, and so on—to a degree *require* ethnographic approaches?

Following Shapiro (2005), I am convinced that "problem-driven research" is preferable to its "methods-driven" alternative. Yet the call for problem-driven research implies that "problems" are timeless abstractions. Are they? I view them as situated in particular flows of knowledge in particular disciplines at particular times. Or, if one prefers a less fluid metaphor, "problems" are embedded phenomena—embedded in the bedrock of disciplinary knowledge formed from the accumulated sediment of many-layered debates and practices, both inside and outside the academy.

Take a seemingly timeless "problem"—the relationship between banks and the state in advanced industrial economies. In 2004 one might reasonably have studied this relationship using quantitative measures of financial flows. By late 2008, when an intricate web of financial networks and dubious lending practices had become exposed, an ethnographic approach to reveal the interrelationships among key actors would have been invaluable.[3] In the abstract, the "problem" (banks and the state) had not changed, yet fundamentally different aspects of this relationship seemed to "deserve" study in 2004 than in 2008. The crucial point is this: methods—whether ethnography or others—do not flow seamlessly from particular questions taken as timeless abstractions (Schatz 2007).

Whether ethnography is recommended depends, I argue, less on the topic being studied and more on how the topic has been studied to date. That is, if ethnography is suited to uncover processes, discourses, and behaviors that generate a political dynamic that is important but scarcely visible (Scott 1990), then what is invisible depends on where our spotlight shines. Like the proverbial drunk who searches in vain for his keys only in the light of the streetlamp, we must search beyond what is currently illuminated.

The issue is principally epistemological. If micro-politics are hidden, it is largely because analysts have not (yet) gotten near enough to their inner dynamics.

Why *Political* Ethnography? Stepping Away from Holism

Why use the word *political* to describe what we do? Imagine a book on "political statistics" and the strangeness of the modifier becomes apparent. We emphasize that our work focuses on *politics*, because ethnography (unmodified and unmarked) has become so closely associated with the study of culture and society.

Our project represents a distancing from the attempts to represent *holistically* a culture, society, group, or locale that earlier generations of ethnographers offered.[4] Consistent with the postmodern condition, we do not claim complete knowledge or aspire to a full representation of social reality. Recognizing that, as Verdery (1996, 204) puts it, "What we can understand of something depends on how we think our way into it in the first place," we know that our accounts are delimited by our *a priori* assumptions. Our analytics are therefore partial; we study politics—the exercise of power in its varying manifestations.

Still, political ethnography is also about ethnography, and the ethnographer does not seek prematurely to hive off the political realm before learning where its boundaries might reasonably be viewed to lie.[5] Few political ethnographers pretend to holism, but we attend to concatenations of contextual factors more than nonethnographers do. In other words, we typically map the part (politics) in relation to the whole (the sociopolitical context, both in its temporal and locational sense).[6] And we are likely to view a wider range of objects—sorcery, coffee-shop talk, slaughterhouse work, waitress uniforms, rural road signs, home repair problems—as inherently, and sometimes deeply, political than would most nonethnographers. We happily scour the seemingly less political realm for evidence of power relations at play.

Taken together, the two parts of the term *political ethnography* thus imply a creative tension. *Ethnography* suggests a particularizing impulse, a desire to avoid premature empirical generalization, and a preference for inductive thinking. It implies attention to detail, to contextual factors, and to configurational thinking.[7] *Political* suggests a willingness to bracket aspects of what we see, to simplify for analytic coherence, and to seek to produce generalizations. It implies attention to cross-case comparisons, to broadly occurring factors, and to the power of deductive logic. The phrase thus contains the potential for each impulse to perform a check on the other, in the process producing empirically grounded and theoretically stimulating research.

Broadening how we understand the political realm is crucial to what a political ethnographer does. This does not, however, mean that everything is equally power-laden or that the manifestations of power relations are everywhere of equal importance. When an ethnographer studies politics, he is examining something vertical, often unspoken, and, therefore, potentially hard to reach. Inevitably, questions of access emerge. Can an ethnographer gain access to the truly powerful actors of "high politics"?

This is a particularly thorny question in the subfield of international relations (IR), where—the argument often goes—the level of analysis encumbers attempts at ethnographic inquiry. It is true that the constructivist IR scholarship that emerged in the 1990s proceeded from a core ethnographic sensibility—from a desire to probe the plural "inner logics" that govern the behavior of states (thus problematizing the commonplace assumption that states are homogeneous and essentially similar units). But is

IR limited by its core, field-defining research problems, such that ethnography as participant observation is unlikely?

The question is a valid one: are many of the interesting topics about the exercise of power simply beyond the reach of the participant observer? The answer has to be yes, but this yes should be qualified. First, many of the access problems that participant observers face have little to do with whether one studies "high" or "low" politics. Conducting ethnographic immersion about matrimonial relations between spouses might be no more possible than conducting a similar study about the causes of war. Challenges of scale and secrecy are real, but they are not confined to high politics. Moreover, the requirements for access can be formidable even in the most mundane affairs; think about the linguistic and cultural fluency, as well as the trust of interlocutors, that is the *sine qua non* of access for any participant observation. If one lets relative accessibility dictate the terms of research engagement, many fundamental questions about politics will go unaddressed.

It would be folly to deny that the National Security Council of the United States, for example, is unlikely to welcome a participant observer in its ranks; to expect access—whatever one's background characteristics, skills, and trust gained from interlocutors—would in this case be naïve. But access is a sliding scale, not a binary. The remote village, hermetically sealed from the outside world, no longer exists (and probably never did, except in the early ethnographic imagination); it is no longer useful (if it ever really was) to view the ethnographer as either "in" the village or "outside" it. The political ethnographer strives for the *nearest possible vantage point* to study a given problem. Interviews that fall short of participant observation, or participant observation in a site that falls short of the ideal location, are the stuff of real-world research compromises. Nonetheless, the political ethnographer will make every effort to achieve proximity and intimacy as a route to knowledge. To the extent that she falls short, she provides reasons why.

The principle of striving for the nearest possible vantage point indicates new possibilities for social-scientific work. Indeed, cultural anthropologists have begun to move beyond fetishizing the ethnographic method to embrace the study of increasingly complex global flows. As Comaroff and Comaroff (2003, 156–57) reflect:

> It is only by broadening our frames of reference that we may address some of the awkward questions that have come to confront us about our methodology: can we be sure, for example, that "the particular" we seek to study, or

the cultural worlds we presume to exist, may actually be *empirically* bounded? Is "the local" not the constantly refashioned *product* of forces well beyond itself (Appadurai, 1996; also 1997)? Does it not exist only as part of a socio-political geography of multiple scales and coordinates (Ortner, 1997)? Is it not true that the singularity of places, just like the singularity of "traditions," "customs," and "cultures," is being fashioned ever more in response to the market? Surely, neat antinomies between the local and the global, between field and context, between ethnography and metanarrative, beg the very questions that we should be asking.

Whatever difficulties exist for the ethnographer to access high politics, we have examples of successful ethnographic work in IR. Séverine Autesserre (2006) conducted ethnographic interviews (Spradley 1979) with "peacebuilders" in the eastern Democratic Republic of Congo to see how they understood violence. Michael Barnett (2003) reflected on his ground-level experience at the U.S. mission to the United Nations to understand how powerful actors could permit genocide to develop in Rwanda in 1994. Catherine Weaver (2008) used insider knowledge of the World Bank to argue that organizational culture weighs heavily on what the bank does. Though neither uses participant observation, Vincent Pouliot (2007b) employs a Bourdieu-inspired ethnographic sensibility to chart how diplomacy itself helps to constitute a security community,[8] and Ted Hopf (2002) deploys a core ethnographic sensibility to redescribe the contours of Russian foreign policy.

In short, when we consider these problems of access, we should weigh the extent to which they emerge from the topics being studied, on the one hand, and, on the other, the extent to which how a subfield imagines itself places artificial constraints on its possibilities. Admitting that access problems are real should not serve as an invitation to scholars to abjure the proximity that is the hallmark of ethnographic work.

What Kind(s) of Political Ethnography?

Should every student of politics become in part a political ethnographer? Metaphors that liken methods to "tools" in a "toolbox" (Bayard de Volo and Schatz 2004; Anderson 2005) imply that a capable researcher—who would be equally trained in Bayesian statistics, participant observation, interview techniques, discourse analysis, and so on—would simply reach for the tool appropriate for her current research problem. And, while some simple household chores could be completed with the aid of a single implement, most complex tasks would require the use of a variety of tools. Ethnography, in this view, is most useful when combined with other tools of inquiry.

With proponents of the toolbox metaphor, I agree that ethnographic approaches may be combined usefully with other methods, but multiple-methods research contains limits. Consider first some practical limits. Becoming trained in and employing any method takes time and involves sunk costs. The typical political ethnographer must learn the complexities of a context—the language, the cultural assumptions, and the history—before beginning firsthand research. While nonethnographers may also learn some of these complexities, the ethnographer faces particularly significant time commitments that preclude or at least postpone the development of other analytic skills. The trade-offs continue with fieldwork. The researcher usually invests months, if not years, developing relationships of trust with interlocutors and refining his knowledge of the research context. Given these practical realities, most scholars build entire careers on their graduate school training.[9]

Other limits are epistemological. To develop research skills is also to create sunk *intellectual* costs; put differently, research styles are habit-forming. Few scholars move effortlessly between the rigors of, for example, postmodernism and those of neopositivist social science; the logics, styles of inquiry, requirements, attributed meanings, and rewards vary too widely. The claims to knowledge embedded in ethnography can be reconciled easily with some methods, less easily with others.

What Happens to Ethnography in Multiple-Methods Projects

Multiple-methods work by Ashutosh Varshney (2002) illustrates the challenges of combining ethnographic and nonethnographic methods.[10]

Like David Laitin (1998), Varshney offers a serious attempt to harness the power of multiple-methods approaches. Varshney begins with a question: What produces interethnic peace in some Indian cities, while other Indian cities spiral into interethnic violence?[11] Arguing that attention to the micro-level is required to tease out an answer, he uses ground-level techniques (principally interviews, though some oral histories as well) among his methods to test an explanation for why ethnic violence became endemic in Aligarh, Hyderabad, and Ahmenabad, while remaining uncommon in Calicut, Lucknow, and Surat. He concludes that certain types of civic engagement are likely to maintain peace among ethnic groups, while other types are less likely to do so. Couched in familiar, abstract categories like "ethnicity" and "civic engagement," this argument easily "travels" to contexts far beyond the subcontinent—something that makes it a first-rate book in comparative politics.

This research design has rightfully been lauded for its willingness to attend to micro-political factors (King 2004), but it is worth asking what effect the design has on his research conclusions. On one hand, the *targeted* use of ground-level techniques helps Varshney to distinguish between superficially similar cases and explain outcomes that otherwise would be paradoxical. It helps him to accomplish a "process tracing" that links his independent variables (types of civic engagement) and dependent variables (ethnic peace or violence). Without this, there would be an enormous empirical gap.

On the other hand, several things occur to the subjects under study with such a targeted use of ground-level techniques.[12] First, the study's focus begins narrow and remains narrow; he is interested in what drives the production of interethnic violence or the maintenance of interethnic peace. He proceeds by first constructing an event-history dataset of violence in India to pinpoint which cases to use for ground-level study. Then he examines the secondary literature (archival records, newspaper and other periodical accounts) about these cases. Finally, he conducts fieldwork that involves human subjects (elite interviews, semi-structured interviews with a sample of ordinary people). In no way is Varshney insensitive to the tragedy that is ethnic conflict, but once he has contact with his research subjects, they are essentially useful as founts of information to test his variables.[13] Ground-level techniques here are in the service of a narrowly defined theoretical agenda; they are not used to pursue knowledge inductively. And even if induction plays an actual role, presenting one's work as deductive has come to be the preferred rhetoric.[14]

Second, the people being studied—when they appear—do so in a "flattened" way. Varshney claims that his sampling technique for interviews— using illiteracy to guide the sample—allows him to "hear the voices of the subaltern" (2002, 20). But, while these voices may have informed Varshney's background thinking, they are scarcely heard. Oral histories (as opposed to more structured interviews) are not cited individually (though they are cited as a group [344n10, 352n5]), and when evidence from interviews with ordinary people is used, what makes it to print are the responses to quantifiable (that is, closed-ended) questions (for example, 126–27).

Nothing is wrong with this; Varshney has made reasonable choices.[15] His goal—to contribute to decontextualized knowledge about ethnic conflict as a route to its prevention—simply runs up against the goal of letting individuals speak.[16] Indeed, Varshney contrasts his task with that of the ethnographer: "Having been trained as [a social scientist], I thought my comparative advantage lay in social science, not in constructing ethnographies or writing fiction" (xiv).[17]

In this sort of multiple-methods research, insider meanings cannot be given adequate expression. To attend to insider meanings, Varshney would have had to do at least some of the following: (1) let his subjects identify what being a Muslim or Hindu means, what violence and peace mean, and what civic engagement means—rather than positing their significance *a priori*; (2) let his subjects identify reasons for ethnic conflict and mine these reasons for valid information; and (3) let his subjects identify the conditions under which ethnic conflict is a salient topic and what related social facts his interlocutors associate with the topic. While the outsider with a research agenda is understandably determined to elicit responses on a particular subject, ordinary people typically have a complex array of associations and considerations.[18] A purer ethnographic account would give pride of place to interlocutors' worldviews, but when ethnography is subsumed by a very different logic, such an account is not possible.

Well-executed research such as Varshney's adds empirical flesh to theoretical relationships and offers opportunities to perform "process tracing" about empirical situations. But the limits are also clear: larger epistemological-ontological commitments subsume ethnography. Typically, such commitments reduce ethnography to ground-level data-gathering techniques that hold little space for insider meanings and concatenations of contextual factors.[19] A disciplinary atmosphere with an overriding commitment to neopositivist causal theory building refracts ethnography in decidedly nonethnographic directions—unless that ethnography stands alone.

Stand-Alone, Extrinsic-Value Political Ethnography

Imagine a continuum of stand-alone, political ethnographic work.[20] At one end is political ethnography whose *raison d'être* is external: it exists to produce evidence for decontextualized knowledge.[21] To the extent that ethnographic material gathered contributes to discussions based on empirical generalizations, it is considered valuable; whatever does not contribute to such debates is considered extraneous. This is *extrinsic-value* political ethnography.

Whatever potential the extrinsic-value political ethnographer has for contributing to decontextualized knowledge, her contribution may be underappreciated for several reasons. Consider what would happen, for example, if she offered an account that was in essence *consistent* with existing, decontextualized accounts. In the standard neopositivist narrative of science of cumulative knowledge, her study would be welcomed as increasing confidence of a theory's validity—a successful "test" of that theory. But the narrative and the reality diverge. In real-world professional contexts, such a study would often be dismissed as "merely another case of something we already knew" from the general theoretical account. If only for this practical reason, political ethnography is better positioned to problematize existing decontextualized accounts than to offer support for them.

If a political ethnographer offers an account *inconsistent* with existing decontextualized theory, her work might serve as a corrective. Consider Allina-Pisano (2004). Based on ground-level familiarity with agricultural reform in post-Soviet Ukraine, fluency in the region's languages, and carefully cultivated trust of her interlocutors, Allina-Pisano demonstrates that local authorities in the 1990s resisted neoliberal economic reforms for reasons that the theoretical literature overlooks. They sought not to protect their "rents" but rather to preserve Soviet-era rural institutions, which "served as socioeconomic anchors for their communities, providing employment, social services, inputs for household production, and food for urban populations" (557). The implications for the entire postcommunist region are important: to be successful, market-oriented reforms must pay attention to both local leaders and ordinary people. This study posits a different way of thinking about the value-rationality of postcommunist elites. That they are self-serving, even corrupt, individuals is one possibility; Allina-Pisano's work suggests an alternative.

Such political ethnography keeps those bent on abstract, decontextualized theorizing in check, forcing them to consider alternative renderings of empirical reality (Shapiro 2004), asking them to interrogate assumed causal relationships, and raising the possibility that what passes for knowledge can be based on specious conclusions. Such work potentially generates new directions for decontextualized research.

Unfortunately, however, extrinsic-value ethnography is unlikely to be more than a corrective; practical professional realities militate against it. Unless the political ethnography can be constructed as a "critical case study" (Eckstein 1975), findings that are anomalous are too often dismissed as "outliers." Indeed, the deck is stacked *against* ethnographically generated, cross-contextual, empirical generalization, since such generalization would require that entire teams of ethnographers conduct a coordinated, simultaneous project on a variety of contexts. How many trained political ethnographers are available and willing to conduct a study that would apply Allina-Pisano's insights to Moldova and Kazakhstan, let alone to Mauritania and Cuba? And if their findings confirmed the validity of her insights, would the value of any single political ethnographic account be adequately recognized?[22]

If a study like Allina-Pisano's generates enough intellectual traction and attention—and this depends on any number of professional and intellectual trends that would take us far afield—it could serve as a seminal idea for additional research. But again, to the extent that data for such research projects can *only* be produced via intensive research (her findings, after all, depend on proximity to local elites that is sufficient to discern their intentions, something that does not come easily), the deck is stacked against broad, decontextualized theorizing based on ethnographically generated insights. Moreover, the difference between a seminal and a still-born idea too seldom emerges from the idea's inherent qualities.

If the potential, extrinsic-value political ethnographer is thinking strategically, he might choose a different research direction. Recognizing that an empirically grounded, confirmatory study is undervalued, he might shift his approach at the outset to increase the number of "cases."[23] The growing number of cases in turn increases the chances that his study would be published and recognized, whether it confirms or questions existing theoretical accounts. At the same time, he drifts from political ethnography, since more cases compromise his ability to conduct immersion. Like Varshney, he might opt for a targeted use of ethnography, even if the potential for ethnographically generated insights remains unrealized.

Stand-Alone, Intrinsic-Value Political Ethnography

At the other end of the continuum is political ethnography whose *raison d'être* is internal. Its value inheres in the research process itself. By *intrinsic-value political ethnography*, I do not have in mind work that completely lacks connections to issues outside the empirical context from which it is drawn; whether or not it is desirable, no such work is possible. I am convinced that scholarship necessarily treats normative concerns, deploys analytic concepts, and employs empirical reference-points that are *tout court* nonindigenous.

Stand-alone political ethnography maximizes its potential when relieved of the chore of doing work it cannot reasonably be expected to do. It cannot and should not aspire to establish broad empirical generalizations. It cannot and should not seek to establish causality, understood as the probability that a decontextualized factor X leads to decontextualized factor Y. It cannot and should not purport to generate data that can be easily and meaningfully converted into quantities that might be subjected to statistical tests.

Relieved of these tasks, political ethnography can do much more. Instead of aiming to offer empirical generalizations, establish probabilistic causal relationships, or contribute a data-point for statistical analysis, it can produce conceptual innovation. Flyvbjerg (2001) adroitly shows that in the natural sciences, space for such conceptual innovation is crucial. Imagine what would occur if this space went unprotected in the social sciences. If Scott (1985) had been preoccupied with generalizing the empirical extent, frequency, and intensity of hidden forms of resistance—such as foot-dragging, gossip, and sabotage—he would have had to deploy a series of nonethnographic tools that likely would have hampered his ability to discover these forms of resistance in the first place. If Walsh (2004) had developed an overriding concern with finding a "representative" group of U.S. citizens for ethnographic immersion, we would know much less about how political opinions are formed. If Wedeen (1999) had set out statistically to "test" the causal impact of official discourses in authoritarian contexts, we would have been deprived of her crucial insights about the relationship of ordinary people to the state discourse in Hāfiz al-Asad's Syria. I strongly suspect that quite a few potentially valuable political ethnographies are never written because researchers feel motivated to pursue other objectives.

Political ethnographers are, of course, correct to reflect seriously on issues of empirical scope and causality. "How common is what I have identified?" and "How compelling is the evidence for the causal claims I am making?" should be natural questions for any scholar. But if a scholar *begins* inquiry with these questions, he or she is likely to focus only on those aspects of social or political life whose salience makes them easily visible and whose clarity makes them easy to trace. Political ethnographic work reminds us that the most visible and clear factors are not necessarily the most important ones.

Students of politics need not share the motivations of the intrinsic-value political ethnographer to see the importance of promoting such work, *even if it is disengaged from the preoccupying logic of neopositivist causal social science.* We know that insider viewpoints are a crucial part of human communities and social and political processes, but we also know that the central preoccupation with causal theorizing makes it difficult to consider them. As Wood (2007, 125–26) puts it:

An important category of data unavailable except through observation or face-to-face interaction with subjects is the preferences and beliefs of political actors as varied as union members (Lipset 1956), local elites (Dahl 1963), parliamentarians (Fenno 1978), and lobbyists and activists (Graetz and Shapiro 2005). How actors understand their identities and interests is often best approached through interviews, observation, and surveys designed specifically for that purpose. General public opinion surveys may be useful for some questions but often do not ask the right questions or do not ask them such that the results are relevant for scholarly analysis. In particular, how political actors perceive their strategic interactions with other actors in real settings—what choices they confronted, their beliefs concerning the likely consequences of different choices, their analysis of paths not taken—is often unavailable except through face-to-face interaction with the actors themselves, that is, through field research.

Let me put it more crudely: insider meanings and complex contextuality cannot be plugged into a regression equation, so one must either marginalize them (the current disciplinary solution) or create a space for research that attends to them (a more productive row to hoe, in my view). When intrinsic-value work flourishes, it provides a rich starting point for those interested in empirical generalization. Ultimately, it is far richer than the thinned empirical accounts that are encouraged when political ethnographers are asked to orient themselves to extrinsic goals.

Beyond conceptual innovation, the value of intrinsic-value political ethnography may simply be that to conduct ethnographic research on human beings is to grant legitimacy to their predicaments and concerns. It is typically to bypass top-down, often state-driven imperatives. To publish ethnographic work, in turn, is potentially to let the people being studied "speak," an exercise that gives voice to the powerless, the subaltern, and the understudied; it is therefore an inversion of the usual relationship between researcher and researched.[24] In turn, letting the subject speak may have implications for policy. When welfare recipients, victims of shantytown violence, or women who have lost children in civil wars are heard, their predicaments are brought to light, where they otherwise would remain in shadow.[25] The value of such research thus inheres in a combination of normative commitments and empirical focus.

All of this implies a need to advance intrinsic-value ethnography. Ethnography should not be *the single* goal of political science research, but it should be *among the goals* of political science research.[26] I imagine a professional political science that "speaks" a variety of ethnographic (not to mention nonethnographic) "dialects"—both intrinsic-value and extrinsic-value. This is a call for an ethnographic shift at the discipline-wide level, as a way to counter what Schram (2004, 417) calls a "scientistic drift." This shift would not reduce ethnography to ground-level techniques of data-gathering. Rather, it would centrally consider insider meanings and complex contextuality—and I repeat—even if this meant distancing the project from questions of causality.

The risk, of course, is that stand-alone, intrinsic-value ethnography could be marginalized by those in the discipline who categorically deny its potential value. The risk is real, and it implies responsibilities. Political ethnographers face the responsibility to make their research both intelligible and relevant to nonethnographers. They need not assume neopositivist logic or adopt its vocabulary, but they should address abiding questions about political and social life whose relevance is recognizable.

At the same time, nonethnographers face the responsibility to read widely and to consider ways of using stand-alone ethnographic research to inform their own (nonethnographic) studies of politics. Moreover, they must recognize that allowing space for ethnographic work in the institutional settings of universities demands, for example, that Institutional Review Boards (IRBs) sensitize their reviewers to the unusual requirements and challenges of ethnographic work.[27] Simultaneously, nonethnographers must resist the temptation to view stand-alone ethnography as "merely" exploratory research, as "simple" hypothesis-generation, and therefore as somehow inferior. Thus, any ethnographic shift will require a broad shift in sensibility across the discipline.

Political ethnographers and nonethnographers must find ways to build bridges across an eclectic and broad political science (Sil and Katzenstein 2005; Yanow, this volume). Substantive and methodological specialization is desirable (Morrow 2003), but only if the discipline simultaneously encourages much boundary-crossing (Drezner 2006) or, at a bare minimum, a recognition of the artificiality of boundaries.[28] I sense that students of politics are up to the task.

Notes

1. Feyerabend (1979, 91), as quoted in Deising (1991, 50).
2. Thanks to an anonymous reviewer for stimulating this line of thought.
3. For an insightful ethnographic account of Wall Street investment bankers, see Ho (2005).
4. Most of cultural and social anthropology has also abandoned attempts to holism, as Kubik details in chapter 1.

5. Kubik in chapter 1 describes neoclassical economists as having performed a "hiving off" by isolating the formal aspects of the economy assumed to be universal and ignoring the ways in which economic systems are themselves deeply embedded in specific cultural logics. See also Day (2005).
6. Thanks to a reviewer for encouraging this phrasing.
7. On configurational thinking, see Ragin (2000).
8. The essence of Pouliot's argument thus recalls Wedeen's emphasis on "performative practices" offered in chapter 3.
9. David Laitin is among the exceptions, having changed both geographic (from Africa to the former Soviet Union) and methodological (from ethnography and narrative to greater emphasis on game theory and statistics) focus. See Qualitative Methods (2006).
10. Thanks to Varshney (private communication) for his comments on Schatz (2007), which inform this discussion. For a similar argument about Laitin's work, see Hopf (2006).
11. *Ethnic* is Varshney's term to distinguish Hindus from Muslims in India.
12. My own work (Schatz 2004) likewise suffers from at least some of the shortcomings that I identify here.
13. Varshney might respond that testing such variables helps to tease out explanations that, ultimately, could guide conflict-prevention programs in the future.
14. In a spirited defense of his work, Laitin (2006, 31–32) contends that the central insight for his 1998 book—namely, that a new identity of "Russian-speakers" was emerging in ex-Soviet states—came directly from (inductive) fieldwork. If this is the case, then it is a puzzle why the book is couched in the rhetoric of *a priori* deductive theorizing. Laitin (private communication) has pointed out that all social science involves both deduction and induction. This is surely true, but it says nothing about the role, sequencing, or proportions of inductive versus deductive thinking. On these latter issues, see Pouliot (2007a).
15. See Varshney (2006) on basic trade-offs involved in the design and execution of any research project.
16. While Varshney proposes to steer a middle course between "stylized facts" and "thick description" (2002, 21), his is a causal story about independent and dependent variables, rather than a narrative about particular people in particular places at particular times. Whatever its theoretical contribution, Varshney's account holds little room for the human beings who dot the analytic landscape.
17. The implication that ethnography is opposed to, rather than a type of, social science is one that should be questioned.
18. When I described Varshney's book to my (educated, nonspecialist) neighbors in Toronto who are originally from Calicut, they insisted that most people rarely think about ethnic violence and peace; they are more concerned with getting their next meal. The contours of an ethnography need not be dictated by the interlocutors' point of reference, but they ought to carve out space for it.
19. Flyvbjerg (2001) argues that predictive theories are impossible in the social sciences not because of their inability to capture "subjective" factors, but because of their inability to attend to context, which is essential to the human experience.
20. By "stand-alone," I mean ethnography that is published separately from nonethnography. Most political ethnography is conducted in the gray area between the ideal types I identify here.
21. One way to understand ethnography's position is to consider Aristotle's distinction

between *phronesis* (contextualized knowledge) and *episteme* (abstract knowledge). Most ethnographers would agree with Flyvbjerg (2001) that while both *phronesis* and *episteme* are valuable, social science's great strength lies in the former rather than the latter. That is, they find much value in producing contextualized rather than decontextualized knowledge. For a debate on the applicability of Flyvbjerg's distinction to political science, see Schram (2004) and Laitin (2003).

22. The political ethnographer himself might be skeptical of the validity of cross-contextual empirical generalizations, given what he knows about his unique in-field conversations, the role of in-field contingencies, and an improvisational (in Yanow's sense from chapter 13) approach to research. Even ethnographic accounts of the same geographic context can vary widely. See Heider (1988).

23. Ragin and Becker (1992) usefully draw attention to the variety of ways of thinking about what constitutes a "case."

24. This is, of course, one possibility among many. Ethnographers and ethnographic knowledge were part and parcel of the European colonial enterprise (Said 1979) and the development of the Soviet state (Hirsch 2005). To this day, states employ ethnographers to "discover" (often construct) traditions that serve to legitimate an elite's authority (Schatz 2004). Large corporations now hire researchers who use ethnographic techniques to learn the behavior of ordinary people—as a way to improve marketing appeals. (Thanks to Dorian Warren and Dvora Yanow for revealing this interesting development on the Interpretation and Methods Listserv.) As Bayard de Volo mentions in chapter 10, the U.S. military has also begun to employ ethnographers.

25. On welfare recipients, see Soss (2000). On shantytown violence in Brazil, see Arias (2004). On mothers who lost children in Nicaragua, see Bayard de Volo (2001). The intrinsic-value ethnographer must convince those without an inherent interest in the subject that his subject deserves attention. Even if one studies violence or poverty—issues with a normative dimension that should speak for itself—it may still not be clear why a study of violence or poverty of one group deserves more attention than a similar study of another group.

26. It may be appropriate for some research to put insider meanings into the background. Most research in political economy, for example, would likely eschew such considerations, even given central insights of work that is fundamentally meaning-oriented (Herrera 2006b; Mwangi 2002). See Herrera (2006a) for a brief argument similar to what I present here.

27. For an exploration of the role that IRBs play in political science, see the special issue of *PS: Political Science & Politics* (41 [2008]), especially Yanow and Schwartz-Shea (2008).

28. Thanks to Patrick Thaddeus Jackson (personal communication) for this latter point.

WORKS CITED

Abbés Kinois. 1992. "Bâtir la nation, une tâche pour tous les chrétiens." CEDAF, Brussels. Dossier sur les évènements récents au Zaïre (janvier–février 1992). 2358 III 1992. 5 February.

Abbott, Andrew. 2001a. *Chaos of Disciplines*. Chicago: University of Chicago Press.

———. 2001b. *Time Matters: On Theory and Method*. Chicago: University of Chicago Press.

Abélès, Marc. 1992. *La vie quotidienne au Parlement européen*. Paris: Hachette.

———. 1997. "Political Anthropology: New Challenges, New Aims." Blackwell/UNESCO, September.

———. 2004. "Identity and Borders: An Anthropological Approach to EU Institutions." Twenty-First Century Papers: On-Line Working Papers from the Center for 21st Century Studies, University of Wisconsin–Milwaukee.

Abu-Lughod, Lila, 1986. *Veiled Sentiments: Honor and Poetry in a Bedouin Society*. Berkeley: University of California Press.

———. 1990. "The Romance of Resistance: Tracing Transformations of Power through Bedouin Women." *American Ethnologist* 17, no. 1:41–55.

———. 1999. "Comment on 'Writing for Culture.'" *Current Anthropology* 40:13–15. Special supplement on "Culture—A Second Chance?"

Ackelsberg, Martha A. 1991. *Free Women of Spain: Anarchism and the Struggle for the Emancipation of Women*. Bloomington: Indiana University Press.

Adler, Emanuel. 2002. "Constructivism and International Relations." In *Handbook of International Relations*, ed. W. Carlsnaes, T. Risse, and B. A. Simmons, 95–118. London: Sage.

Adler, Glenn. 1992. "The Politics of Research during a Liberation Struggle: Interviewing Black Workers in South Africa." In *International Annual of Oral History, 1990: Subjectivity and Multiculturalism in Oral History*, ed. Ronald J. Grele, 229–45. New York: Greenwood Press.

Agar, Michael H. 1980. *The Professional Stranger*. New York: Academic Press.

Aguilar, J. 1981. "On Anthropology 'at Home.'" In *Anthropologists at Home in North America*, ed. D. Messerschmidt, 15–28. Cambridge: Cambridge University Press.

Ahnen, Ronald E. 2007. "The Politics of Violence in Democratic Brazil." *Latin American Politics and Society* 49, no. 1:141–64.

Alliance for Workers' Rights. 1999. "Sexploitation in Nevada's Casinos." April newsletter.

Allina-Pisano, Jessica. 2004. "Sub Rosa Resistance and the Politics of Economic Reform: Land Redistribution in Ukraine." *World Politics* 56, no. 4:554–81.

———. 2008. *The Post-Soviet Potemkin Village: Politics and Property Rights in the Black Earth.* Cambridge: Cambridge University Press.

Almond, Gabriel. 1990. *A Discipline Divided: Schools and Sects in Political Science.* Newbury Park, Calif.: Sage Publications.

Alvarez, Sonia. 1989. "Politicizing Gender and Engendering Democracy." In *Democratizing Brazil: Problems of Transition and Consolidation,* ed. Alfred Stepan, 205–51. Oxford: Oxford University Press.

Alvesson, Mats, and Kaj Sköldberg. 2000. *Reflexive Methodology: New Vistas for Qualitative Research.* Thousand Oaks, Calif.: Sage.

Amadae, S. M. 2003. *Rationalizing Capitalist Democracy: The Cold War Origins of Rational Choice Liberalism.* Chicago: University of Chicago Press.

American Anthropological Association. 2002. *El Dorado Task Force Papers.* Vol. 1. Submitted to Executive Board as final report, 18 May.

American Housing Survey for the Philadelphia Metropolitan Area 1999: Current Housing Reports. 2001. H170/99–33. Washington, D.C. March. Appendix *D, Table X2, p. D-10. Available online: www.census.gov/prod/2001pubs/h170-99-33.pdf.

Americas Watch. 1986. *Settling into Routine: Human Rights Abuses in Duarte's Second Year.* New York: Americas Watch.

———. 1991. *El Salvador's Decade of Terror: Human Rights since the Assassination of Archbishop Romero.* New Haven, Conn.: Yale University Press.

Amigo, Angel. 1978. *Pertur: ETA 71–76.* Donostia: Hordago.

Anderson, Benedict R. 1983. *Imagined Communities: Reflections on the Origin and Spread of Nationalism.* London: Verso.

Anderson, Leslie. 2005. "Graduate Education in a Pluralist Context: The Metaphor of a Tool Box." In *Perestroika! The Raucous Revolution in Political Science,* ed. Kristen Renwick Monroe, 403–20. New Haven, Conn.: Yale University Press.

Ankersmit, Frank. 1996. "Politics and Metaphor." In Ankersmit, *Aesthetic Politics: Political Philosophy beyond Fact and Value,* 254–93. Stanford, Calif.: Stanford University Press.

Anonymous. 1980. "Les pratiques fétichistes sont prohibées!" *Elima,* 7 January, 15.

Appadurai, Arjun. 1990. "Disjuncture and Difference in the Global Cultural Economy." *Public Culture* 2, no. 2:1–24.

Apter, David E. 1973. *Political Change: Collected Essays.* London: F. Cass.

Arce, Moisés. 2003. "Political Violence and Presidential Approval in Peru." *Journal of Politics* 65, no. 2:572–83.

Arendt, Hannah. 1958. *The Human Condition.* Chicago: University of Chicago Press.

———. 1994. *Eichmann in Jerusalem: A Report on the Banality of Evil.* New York: Penguin.

Arias, Enrique Desmond. 2004. "Faith in Our Neighbors: Networks and Social Order in Three Brazilian Favelas." *Latin American Politics and Society* 46, no. 1:1–38.

———. 2006. "The Dynamics of Criminal Governance: Networks and Social Order in Rio de Janeiro." *Journal of Latin American Studies* 38, no. 2:293–325.

Arias, Enrique Desmond, and Daniel Goldstein. Forthcoming. "Violent Pluralism: Understanding the "New Democracies" of Latin America." In *Violent Democracies of Latin America,* ed. Enrique Desmond Arias and Daniel Goldstein. Durham, N.C.: Duke University Press.

Aronoff, Myron J. 1974. *Frontiertown: The Politics of Community Building in Israel.* Manchester: Manchester University Press.

———. 1989. *Israeli Visions and Divisions: Cultural Change and Political Conflict.* New Brunswick, N.J.: Transaction.

———. 1993. *Power and Ritual in the Israel Labor Party.* Revised and expanded edition. New York: M. E. Sharpe.

———. 2002. "Political Culture." In *The International Encyclopedia of Social and Behavioral Sciences,* ed. Neil J. Smelser and Paul B. Bates. Oxford: Elsevier.

———. 2006. "Forty Years as a Political Ethnographer." *Ab Imperio* 4:1–15.

Asad, Talal. 2003. *Formations of the Secular: Christianity, Islam, Modernity.* Palo Alto, Calif.: Stanford University Press.

———, ed. 1973. *Anthropology and the Colonial Encounter.* New York: Humanities Press.

Ashforth, Adam. 2005. *Witchcraft, Violence, and Democracy in South Africa.* Chicago: University of Chicago Press.

Austin, J. L. 1961. *Philosophical Papers.* Oxford: Clarendon Press.

———. 1965. *How to Do Things with Words.* Ed. J. O. Urmson. New York: Oxford University Press.

Autesserre, Séverine. 2006. "Local Violence, International Indifference? Post-conflict 'Settlement' in the Eastern D.R. Congo (2003–2006)." Ph.D. diss., New York University.

Auyero, Javier. 1999. "Re-membering Peronism: An Ethnographic Account of the Relational Character of Political Memory," *Qualitative Sociology* 22:331–51.

———. 2001. *Poor People's Politics: Peronist Networks and the Legacy of Evita.* Durham, N.C.: Duke University Press.

———. 2006a. "Introductory Note to Politics under the Microscope: Special Issue on Political Ethnography I." *Qualitative Sociology* 29, no. 3:257–59.

———. 2006b. "The Political Makings of the 2001 Lootings in Argentina." *Journal of Latin American Studies* 38, no. 2:241–65.

Bailey, F. G. 1983. *The Tactical Uses of Passion: An Essay on Power, Reason, and Reality.* Ithaca, N.Y.: Cornell University Press.

Bailey, John, and Roy Godson. 2000. "Conclusion." In *Organized Crime and Democratic Governability: Mexico and the U.S.–Mexican Borderlands,* ed. John Bailey and Roy Godson, 217–24. Pittsburgh: University of Pittsburgh Press.

Bambach, Charles R. 1995. *Heidegger, Dilthey, and the Crisis of Historicism.* Ithaca, N.Y.: Cornell University Press.

Barnard, Alan. 2000. *History and Theory in Anthropology.* Cambridge: Cambridge University Press.

Barnett, Michael N. 2003. *Eyewitness to a Genocide: The United Nations and Rwanda.* Ithaca, N.Y.: Cornell University Press.

Bartels, Larry M. 1988. *Presidential Primaries and the Dynamics of Public Choice.* Princeton: Princeton University Press.

———. 2005. "Homer Gets a Tax Cut: Inequality and Public Policy in the American Mind." *Perspectives on Politics* 3, no. 1:15–31.

———. 2006. "What's the Matter with *What's the Matter with Kansas?*" *Quarterly Journal of Political Science* 1:201–26.

Barth, Fredrik, Andre Gingrich, Robert Parkin, and Sydel Silverman. 2005. *One Discipline, Four Ways: British, German, French, and American Anthropology.* The Halle Lectures, with a foreword by Chris Hann. Chicago: University of Chicago Press.

Barton, Emily. 2006. "Brush Up Your Chekhov." Review of *Reading like a Writer: A Guide for People Who Love Books and for Those Who Want to Write Them,* by Francine Prose. *New York Times Book Review,* 27 August.

Bates, Robert H., Avner Greif, Margaret Levi, Jean-Laurent Rosenthal, and Barry R. Weingast,. 1998. *Analytic Narratives.* Princeton, N.J.: Princeton University Press.

Bayard de Volo, Lorraine. 2001. *Mothers of Heroes and Martyrs: Gender Identity Politics in Nicaragua, 1979–1999.* Baltimore: Johns Hopkins University Press.

———. 2003a. "Analyzing Politics and Change in Women's Organizations: Nicaraguan Mothers' Voice and Identity." *International Feminist Journal of Politics* 5, no. 1:92–115.

———. 2003b. "Service and Surveillance: Infrapolitics at Work among Casino Cocktail Waitresses." *Social Politics: International Studies in Gender, State, and Society* 10, no. 3:346–76.

———. 2006. "The Nonmaterial Long-Term Benefits of Collective Action: Empowerment and Social Capital in a Nicaraguan Women's Organization." *Comparative Politics* 38, no. 2: 149–67.

Bayard de Volo, Lorraine, and Edward Schatz. 2004. "From the Inside Out: Ethnographic Methods in Political Research." *PS: Political Science and Politics* 37, no. 2 (April): 267–71.

Bayat, Asef. 2005. "Islamism and Social Movement Theory." *Third World Quarterly* 26, no. 6:891–908.

Becker, Felicitas. 2006. "Rural Islamism during the 'War on Terror': A Tanzanian Case Study." *African Affairs* 105, no. 421:583–603.

Becker, Howard S. 1986. *Writing for Social Scientists: How to Start and Finish Your Thesis, Book, or Article.* Chicago: University of Chicago Press.

Behar, Ruth. 1993. *Translated Woman.* Boston: Beacon Press.

Benford, Robert D. 1997. "An Insider's Critique of the Social Movement Framing Perspective." *Sociological Inquiry* 67:409–30.

Bereciartu, Gurutz Jáuregui. 1981. *Ideología and estrategia política de ETA: Análisis de su evolución entre 1959 y 1968.* Madrid: Siglo Veintiuno.

Berger, Peter, and Thomas Luckmann. 1967. *The Social Construction of Reality: A Treatise in the Sociology of Knowledge.* New York: Anchor.

Berinsky, Adam J. 2004. *Silent Voices: Public Opinion and Political Participation in America.* Princeton, N.J.: Princeton University Press.

Berliner, Joseph. 1999. *The Economics of the Good Society.* Malden, Mass.: Blackwell.

Bermeo, Nancy Gina. 1986. *The Revolution within the Revolution: Workers' Control in Rural Portugal.* Princeton, N.J.: Princeton University Press.

Bernstein, Richard J. 1983. *Beyond Objectivism and Relativism.* Philadelphia: University of Pennsylvania Press.

Bertrand, Romain. 2002. *Indonésie: La démocratie invisible.* Paris: Karthala.

Biggs, Michael. 1999. "Putting the State on the Map: Cartography, Territory, and European State Formation." *Comparative Studies in Society and History* 41, no. 2:374–405.

Bill Chavez, Rebecca. 2004. "The Evolution of Judicial Autonomy in Argentina: Establishing the Rule of Law in an Ultrapresidential System." *Journal of Latin American Studies* 36, no. 3:451–78.

Binford, Leigh. 1996. *The El Mozote Massacre: Anthropology and Human Rights.* Tucson: University of Arizona Press.

———. 2002. "Priests, Catechists, and Revolutionaries: Organic Intellectuals in the Salvadoran Revolution." In "Community, Politics, and the Nation-State in Twentieth-Century El Salvador," ed. Leigh Binford and Aldo Lauria-Santiago. Unpublished book manuscript.

Black, Jeremy. 1997. *Maps and Politics*. Chicago: University of Chicago Press.

Blee, Kathleen M., and Ashley Currier. 2006. "How Local Social Movement Groups Handle a Presidential Election." *Qualitative Sociology* 29:261–80.

Bleicher, Josef. 1980. *Contemporary Hermeneutics: Hermeneutics as Method, Philosophy and Critique*. London: Routledge & Kegan Paul.

Blier, Suzanne Preston. 1995. *African Vodun: Art, Psychology, and Power*. Chicago: University of Chicago Press.

Blumer, Herbert. 1948. "Public Opinion and Public Opinion Polling." *American Sociological Review* 13:542–49.

Blyth, Mark. 2002. *Great Transformations: Economic Ideas and Institutional Change in the Twentieth Century*. Cambridge: Cambridge University Press.

Bockie, Simon. 1993. *Death and the Invisible Powers: The World of Kongo Belief*. Bloomington: Indiana University Press.

Bohannan, Paul J. 1967. "Introduction." In *Beyond the Frontier: Social Process and Cultural Change*, ed. Paul Bohannan and Fred Plog, i–xviii. New York: Natural History Press.

Bonnell, Victoria E. 1997. *Iconography of Power: Soviet Political Posters under Lenin and Stalin*. Berkeley: University of California Press.

Bookchin, Murray. 1977. *The Spanish Anarchists: The Heroic Years, 1868–1936*. New York: Harper & Row.

Bornstein, Brian H., Lesley M. Liebel, and Nikki C. Scarberry. 1998. "Repeated Testing in Eyewitness Memory: A Means to Improve Recall of a Negative Emotional Event." *Applied Cognitive Psychology* 12:119–31.

Bourdieu, Pierre. 1977. *Outline of a Theory of Practice*. Trans. R. Nice. Palo Alto, Calif.: Stanford University Press.

———. 1981. "La représentation politique : Eléments pour une théorie du champ politique." *Actes de la recherche en sciences sociales* 36–37:3–24.

———. 1991. *Language and Symbolic Power*. Cambridge, Mass.: Harvard University Press.

———. 2000. *Pascalian Meditations*. Cambridge: Polity.

Bowen, John R., and Roger Petersen. 1999. "Introduction: Critical Comparisons." In *Critical Comparisons in Politics and Culture*, ed. John R. Bowen and Roger Petersen, 1–20. Cambridge: Cambridge University Press.

Bradley, Margaret M. 1994. "Emotional Memory: A Dimensional Analysis." In *Emotions: Essays on Emotion Theory*, ed. Stephanie H. M. van Goozen, Nanne E. Van de Poll, and Joseph A. Sergeant, 97–134. Hillsdale, N.J.: Lawrence Erlbaum Associates.

Brady, Henry. 1995. "Doing Good and Doing Better." *The Political Methodologist* 6:11–19.

Brady, Henry E., and David Collier, eds. 2004. *Rethinking Social Inquiry: Diverse Tools, Shared Standards*. Oxford: Rowman & Littlefield.

Brandwein, Pamela. 2007. "A Judicial Abandonment of Blacks? Rethinking the 'State Action' Cases of the Waite Court." *Law & Society Review* 41:343–86.

Brehm, John. 1993. *The Phantom Respondents: Opinion Surveys and Political Representation*. Ann Arbor: University of Michigan Press.

Brewer, Rose M. 2005. "Response to Michael Burawoy's Commentary: The Critical Turn to Public Sociology." *Critical Sociology* 31, no. 3:353–59.

Brewer, William F., and Bruce L. Lambert. 2001. "The Theory-Ladenness of Observation and the Theory-Ladenness of the Rest of the Scientific Process." *Philosophy of Science* 68, no. 3: S176–86.

Brinkley, Alan. 1982. *Voices of Protest: Huey Long, Father Coughlin, and the Great Depression*. New York: Alfred A. Knopf.

Brinks, Daniel. 2003. "Informal Institutions and the Rule of Law: The Judicial Response to State Killings in Buenos Aires and São Paulo in the 1990s." *Comparative Politics* 36, no. 1: 1–19.

———. 2008. *The Judicial Response to Police Killings in Latin America: Inequality and the Rule of Law.* New York: Cambridge University Press.

Brody, Hugh. 1982. *Maps and Dreams.* New York: Pantheon.

Brower, Ralph S., Mitchel Y. Abolafia, and Jered B. Carr. 2000. "On Improving Qualitative Methods in Public Administration Research." *Administration and Society* 32:363–97.

Brown, Richard Harvey. 1976. "Social Theory as Metaphor." *Theory and Society* 3:169–97.

Brownlee, Jason. 2007. *Authoritarianism in an Age of Democratization.* Cambridge: Cambridge University Press.

Brubaker, Rogers. 2004. *Ethnicity without Groups.* Cambridge, Mass.: Harvard University Press.

Brubaker, Rogers, and Frederick Cooper. 2000. "Beyond 'Identity.'" *Theory and Society* 29:1–47.

Buchowski, Michal. 1997. *Reluctant Capitalists: Class and Culture in a Local Community in Western Poland.* Berlin: Centre Marc Bloch.

Burawoy, Michael. 1998. "Extended Case Study Method." *Sociological Theory* 16:4–33.

———. 2000. "Introduction: Reaching for the Global." In Burawoy et al., *Global Ethnography: Forces, Connections, and Imaginations in a Postmodern World,* 1–40. Berkeley: University of California Press.

Burawoy, Michael, Joseph A. Blum, Sheba George, Zsuszsa Gille, Teresa Gowan, Lynne Haney, Maren Klawiter, Steven H. Lopez, Sean O Riain, and Millie Thayer. 2000. *Global Ethnography: Forces, Connections, and Imaginations in a Postmodern World.* Berkeley: University of California Press.

Burawoy, Michael, and Katherine Verdery. 1999. *Uncertain Transition: Ethnographies of Change in the Postsocialist World.* Lanham, Md.: Rowman & Littlefield.

Burden, Barry C. 2004. "An Alternative Account of the 2004 Presidential Election." *Forum* 2, no. 4: article 2. Available online: http://www.bepress.com/forum/vol2/iss4/art2.

Burke, Kenneth. 1969 [1945]. *A Grammar of Motives.* Berkeley: University of California Press.

———. 1989. *On Symbols and Society.* Ed. Joseph R. Gusfield. Chicago: University of Chicago Press.

Butler, Judith. 1993. *Bodies That Matter: On the Discursive Limits of "Sex."* New York: Routledge.

———. 1997. *Excitable Speech: A Politics of the Performative.* New York: Routledge.

Carothers, Thomas. 2002. "The End of the Transition Paradigm." *Journal of Democracy* 13, no. 1:5–21.

Case, William. 2006. "Manipulative Skills: How Do Rulers Control the Electoral Arena?" In *Electoral Authoritarianism: The Dynamics of Unfree Competition,* ed. Andreas Schedler, 95–112. Boulder, Colo.: Lynne Rienner.

Castells, Manuel. 1996. *The Rise of the Network Society.* Oxford: Blackwell.

Caton, Steve. 2007. "History As It Happens." Public lecture delivered at the Middle East History and Theory Conference, University of Chicago, 12 May.

Cavatorta, Francesco. 2006. "Civil Society, Islamism and Democratisation: The Case of Morocco." *Journal of Modern African Studies* 44, no. 2:203–22.

Chabal, Patrick, and Jean-Pascal Daloz. 2006. *Culture Troubles: Politics and the Interpretation of Meaning.* Chicago: University of Chicago Press.

Chambers, Iain. 1986. *Popular Culture: The Metropolitan Experience.* London: Methuen.

Chomsky, Noam. 1967. "Objectivity and Liberal Scholarship." In Chomsky, *American Power and the New Mandarins: Historical and Political Essays*, 23–158. New York: Random House.

Chong, Dennis. 1993. "How People Think, Reason, and Feel about Rights and Liberties." *American Journal of Political Science* 37, no. 3:867–99.

Ciardi, John. 1959. *How Does a Poem Mean?* Boston: Houghton-Mifflin.

Clark, Robert P. 1984. *The Basque Insurgents: ETA, 1952–1980.* Madison: University of Wisconsin Press.

Clifford, James. 1986. "Introduction: Partial Truths." In *Writing Culture*, ed. James Clifford and George E. Marcus, 1–27. Berkeley: University of California Press.

Clifford, James, and George E. Marcus, eds. 1986. *Writing Culture: The Poetics and Politics of Ethnography.* Berkeley: University of California Press.

Cohen, Abner. 1974. *Two-Dimensional Man: An Essay on the Anthropology of Power and Symbolism in Complex Society.* Berkeley: University of California Press.

The Colbert Report. 2005. Comedy Central cable television. www.wikiality.com/Truthiness.

Cole, John W. 1977. "Anthropology Comes Part-way Home: Community Studies in Europe." *Annual Review of Anthropology* 6:349–78.

Collier, David. 1993. "The Comparative Method." In *Political Science: The State of the Discipline II*, ed. Ada W. Finifer, 105–19. Washington, D.C.: American Political Science Association.

———. 1999. "Letter from the President: Data, Field Work and Extracting New Ideas at Close Range." *Newsletter of the American Political Science Association Organized Section in Comparative Politics* 10, no. 1:1–6.

Collier, David, and Steven Levitsky. 1997. "Democracy with Adjectives: Conceptual Innovation in Comparative Research." *World Politics* 49, no. 3: 430–51.

Collins, Kathleen. 2006. *Clan Politics and the Transformation of Regimes in Central Asia.* New York: Cambridge University Press.

Comaroff, Jean. 1985. *Body of Power, Spirit of Resistance: The Culture and History of a South African People.* Chicago: University of Chicago Press.

Comaroff, Jean, and John Comaroff. 1991. *Of Revelation and Revolution. Vol. 1: Christianity, Colonialism, and Consciousness in South Africa.* Chicago: University of Chicago Press.

———. 1992. *Ethnography and the Historical Imagination.* Boulder, Colo.: Westview Press.

———. 1995. *Of Revelation and Revolution. Vol. 2: The Dialectics of Modernity on a South African Frontier.* Chicago: University of Chicago Press.

———. 2003. "Ethnography on an Awkward Scale: Postcolonial Anthropology and the Violence of Abstraction." *Ethnography* 4, no. 2:147–79.

Coronil, Fernando. 1997. *The Magical State: Nature, Money, and Modernity in Venezuela.* Chicago: University of Chicago Press.

Crapanzano, Vincent. 1986. "Hermes' Dilemma: The Masking of Subversion in Ethnographic Description." In *Writing Culture: The Poetics and Politics of Ethnography*, ed. James Clifford and George E. Marcus, 51–76. Berkeley: University of California Press.

Creed, Gerald. 1995. "The Politics of Agriculture: Identity and Socialist Sentiment in Bulgaria." *Slavic Review* 54. no. 4:843–68.

Curtis, Karen A. 1999. "'Bottom-Up' Poverty and Welfare Policy Discourse: Ethnography to the Rescue?" *Urban Anthropology* 28, no. 2:103–4.

Dammert, Lucia, and Mary Fran T. Malone. 2006. "Does It Take a Village? Policing Strategies and Fear of Crime in Latin America." *Latin American Politics and Society* 48, no. 4:27–51.

Dao, James. 2004. "Same-Sex Marriage Issue Key to Some G.O.P. Races." *New York Times*, 4 November, 4.

Darnton, Robert. 1984. *The Great Cat Massacre and Other Episodes in French Cultural History.* New York: Basic Books.

———. 2003. *George Washington's False Teeth: An Unconventional Guide to the Eighteenth Century.* New York: W. W. Norton.

Das, Veena. 1990. "Our Work to Cry: Your Work to Listen." In *Mirrors of Violence: Communities, Riots and Survivors in South Asia,* ed. Veena Das, 345–98. New York: Oxford University Press.

Daston, Lorraine, and Peter Galison. 2007. *Objectivity.* Brooklyn: Zone Books.

Davis, Diane, and Anthony Pereira, eds. 2003. *Irregular Armed Forces and Their Role in Politics and State Formation.* Cambridge: Cambridge University Press.

Davis, Eric. 2005. *Memories of State: Politics, History, and Collective Identity in Modern Iraq.* Berkeley: University of California Press.

Day, Richard B. 2005. "Globalization, Markets, and Ethics." *Perspectives on Global Development and Technology* 4, nos. 3–4:251–303.

Deising, Paul. 1991. *How Does Social Science Work? Reflections on Practice.* Pittsburgh: University of Pittsburgh Press.

Derrida, Jacques. 1976 [1967]. *Of Grammatology.* Trans. A. Bass. London: Routledge.

———. 1988. "Signature Event Context." In *Limited Inc.* Evanston, Ill.: Northwestern University Press.

Diamond, Larry J., and Leonardo Morlino. 2005. "Introduction." In *Assessing the Quality of Democracy,* ed. Larry Diamond and Leonardo Morlino, ix–xliii. Baltimore: Johns Hopkins University Press.

Dilthey, Willhelm. 1976. *Selected Writings.* Trans. and ed. H. P. Rickman. Cambridge: Cambridge University Press.

Dirks, Nicholas B., Geoff Eley, and Sherry B. Ortner. 1994. "Introduction." In *Culture/Power/History: A Reader in Contemporary Social Theory,* ed. Nicholas B. Dirks, Geoff Eley, and Sherry B. Ortner, 3–45. Princeton, N.J.: Princeton University Press.

Doty, Roxanne Lynn. 1996. *Imperial Encounters: The Politics of Representation in North-South Relations.* Minneapolis: University of Minnesota Press.

———. 2004. "Maladies of Our Souls: Identity and Voice in the Writing of Academic International Relations." *Cambridge Review of International Affairs* 17, no. 2:371–92.

Dougherty, Deborah, and Gideon Kunda. 1990. "Photograph Analysis: A Method to Capture Organisational Belief Systems." In *Symbols and Artifacts: Views of the Corporate Landscape,* ed. Pasquale Gagliardi, 185–206. Berlin: De Gruyter.

Drezner, Daniel W. 2006. "Notes from a Generalist." In "Symposium: Alexander L. George and Andrew Bennett's *Case Studies and Theory Development in the Social Sciences.*" *Qualitative Methods,* Newsletter of the APSA Organized Section on Qualitative Methods 4, no. 1: 34–36.

Eckstein, Harry. 1975. "Case Study and Theory in Political Science." In *Handbook of Political Science, Vol. 7: Political Science: Scope and Theory,* ed. Fred I. Greenstein and Nelson W. Polsby, 79–138. Reading, Mass.: Addison-Wesley.

Edles, Laura Desfor. 1998. *Symbol and Ritual in the New Spain: The Transition to Democracy after Franco.* Cambridge: Cambridge University Press.

Ekiert, Grzegorz, and Steven E. Hanson, eds. 2003. *Capitalism and Democracy in Central and Eastern Europe: Assessing the Legacy of Communist Rule.* Cambridge: Cambridge University Press.

Ellis, Carolyn. 2004. *The Ethnographic I: A Methodological Novel about Autoethnography.* Walnut Creek, Calif.: AltaMira Press.

Ellis, Stephen. 1999. *The Mask of Anarchy: The Destruction of Liberia and the Religious Dimension of an African Civil War.* New York: New York University Press.

Elster, Jon. 1985. *Making Sense of Marx.* Cambridge: Cambridge University Press.

Emparanza, José Luis Alvarez [political pseudonym "Txillardgi"]. 1980. "Testimonios personales de la crisis teórico política que motive mi salida de ETA." *Cuaderno de formación de IPES* 1:37-44.

Encyclopedia of American Social Movements. Vol. 3. Ed. Immanuel Ness. Armonk, N.Y.: M. E. Sharpe.

Erlandson, David A., Edward L. Harris, Barbara L. Skipper, and Steve D. Allen. 1993. *Doing Naturalistic Inquiry.* Newbury Park, Calif.: Sage.

Evans, Sara. 1978. *Personal Politics: The Roots of Women's Liberation in the Civil Rights Movement and the New Left.* New York: Alfred A. Knopf.

Evans-Pritchard, E. E. 1937. *Witchcraft, Oracles and Magic among the Azande.* Oxford: Clarendon Press.

Ewenstein, Boris, and Jennifer Whyte. 2007. "Beyond Words: Aesthetic Knowledge and Knowing in Organizations." *Organization Studies* 28:689-708.

Fabian, Johannes. 1983. *Time and the Other: How Anthropology Makes Its Objects.* New York: Columbia University Press.

Fall, Mar. 1993. "Les arabisants au Sénégal: Courtisans ou courtiers." In *Le radicalisme islamique au sud du Sahara,* ed. René Otayek, 197-212. Paris: Karthala.

Fauconnier, Gilles, and Mark Turner. 2002. *The Way We Think: Conceptual Blending and the Mind's Hidden Complexities.* New York: Basic Books.

Fay, Brian. 1996. *Contemporary Philosophy of Social Science. A Multicultural Approach.* Malden, Mass.: Blackwell.

Fearon, James D., and David D. Laitin. 1996. "Explaining Interethnic Cooperation." *American Political Science Review* 90, no. 4:715-35.

Feldman, Martha S., Jeannine Bell, and Michele Tracy Berger. 2003. *Gaining Access: A Practical and Theoretical Guide for Qualitative Researchers.* Walnut Creek, Calif.: AltaMira Press.

Fenno, Richard. 1978. *HomeStyle: House Members and Their Districts.* New York: Little Brown.
———. 1990. *Watching Politicians: Essays on Participant Observation.* Berkeley: Institute of Governmental Studies, University of California.

Fernandes, Leela. 1997. *Producing Workers: The Politics of Gender, Class, and Culture in the Calcutta Jute Mills.* Philadelphia: University of Pennsylvania Press.

Fetterman, David M. 1989. *Ethnography: Step by Step.* Thousand Oaks, Calif.: Sage.

Feyerabend, Paul. 1979. "Dialog on Method." In *The Structure and Development of Science,* ed. Gerard Radnitzky and Gunnar Anderson, 63-132. Dordrecht: Reidel.

Firth, Raymond. 1951. *Elements of Social Organization.* Boston: Beacon Press.

Fischer, Frank. 2003. "Beyond Empiricism: Policy Analysis as Deliberative Practice." In *Deliberative Policy Analysis: Understanding Governance in the Network Society,* ed. Maarten A. Hajer and Hendrik Wagenaar, 209-27. Cambridge: Cambridge University Press.

Flyvbjerg, Bent. 2001. *Making Social Science Matter: Why Social Inquiry Fails and How It Can Succeed Again.* Cambridge: Cambridge University Press.

Forester, John. 1984/1999. "Learning the Craft of Academic Writing: Notes on Writing in and after Graduate School." Unpublished ms. available online: http://people.cornell.edu/pages/jff1/learningacadwrtg.htm.

———. 2005. *Notes on Writing for the Cornell Urban Scholars Program: On Craft, Structure, and Your Readers.* Unpublished ms. 8 March. Available online: http://www.people.cornell.edu/pages/jff1/NotesonWritingforMastersStudents.htm.

Fortes, Meyer. 1945. *The Dynamics of Clanship among the Tallensi, Being the First Part of an Analysis of the Social Structure of a Trans-Volta Tribe.* London: Oxford University Press.

———. 1949. *The Web of Kinship among the Tallensi: The Second Part of an Analysis of the Social Structure of a Trans-Volta Tribe.* London: Oxford University Press.

Fortes, Meyer, and E. E. Evans-Pritchard, eds. 1940. *The African Political Systems.* London: Oxford University Press.

Foucault, Michel. 1980. *Power/Knowledge: Selected Interviews and Other Writings, 1972–1977.* Ed. Colin Gordon. Trans. C. Gordon, L. Marshall, J. Mepham, K. Soper. New York: Pantheon.

Frank, Andre Gunder. 1969. *Capitalism and Underdevelopment in Latin America: Historical Studies of Chile and Brazil.* New York: Monthly Review Press.

Frank, Thomas. 2005. *What's the Matter with Kansas? How Conservatives Won the Heart of America.* New York: Henry Holt.

Fraser, Nancy. 1990. *Unruly Practices: Power, Discourse and Gender in Contemporary Social Theory.* Minneapolis: University of Minnesota Press.

Freire, Paulo. 1999 [1970]. *Pedagogy of the Oppressed.* New York: Continuum.

Fujii, Lee Ann. 2007. "The Truth in Lies: Evaluating Testimonies of War and Genocide in Rwanda." Paper presented at the Annual Meeting of the American Political Science Association, Chicago, 29 August–2 September.

Gagnon, Philip V. 2004. *The Myth of Ethnic War: Serbia and Croatia in the 1990s.* Ithaca, N.Y.: Cornell University Press.

Gamson, William A. 1992. *Talking Politics.* New York: Cambridge.

Gans, Herbert. 1976. "Personal Journal: B. On the Methods Used in This Study." In *The Research Experience,* ed. M. Patricia Golden, 49–59. Itasca, Ill.: F. E. Peacock.

Garailde, J. [political pseudonym "Erreka"]. 1980. "VII Asamblea y el nacionminto de E.I.A. Una estrategia para el socialismo en Euskadi." *Cuaderno de formación de IPES* 1:31–36.

Garfinkel, Harold. 1984 [1967]. *Studies in Ethnomethodology.* Malden, Mass.: Polity Press/Blackwell.

Garmendia, José Mari. 1980. *Historia de ETA.* San Sebastián, Basque Country, Spain: L. Haranburu.

Garton Ash, Timothy. 1991. *The Polish Revolution: Solidarity.* Revised and updated edition. London: Granta Books.

Gaventa, John. 1980. *Power and Powerlessness. Quiescence and Rebellion in an Appalachian Valley.* Urbana: University of Illinois Press.

Gay, Robert. 1994. *Popular Organization and Democracy in Rio de Janeiro: A Tale of Two Favelas.* Philadelphia: Temple University Press.

———. 2005. *Lucia: Testimonies of a Brazilian Drugs Dealer's Woman.* Philadelphia: Temple University Press.

Gay y Blasco, Paloma, and Huon Wardle. 2007. *How to Read Ethnography.* London: Routledge.

Geddes, Barbara. 2003. *Paradigms and Sand Castles: Theory Building and Research Design in Comparative Politics.* Ann Arbor: University of Michigan Press.

Geertz, Clifford. 1973. *The Interpretation of Cultures.* New York: Basic Books.

———. 1980. *Negara: The Theatre State in Nineteenth-Century Bali.* Princeton: Princeton University Press.

———. 1988. *Works and Lives: The Anthropologist as Author.* Stanford, Calif.: Stanford University Press.

Gerlach, Luther P. 1971. "Movements of Revolutionary Change: Some Structural Characteristics." *American Behavioral Scientist* 14:812–36.

Gerring, John. 2001. *Social Science Methodology: A Criterial Framework.* Cambridge: Cambridge University Press.

Gewin, Victoria. 2005. "Scientists Attack Bush over Intelligent Design." *Nature* 436 (11 August). Available at: www.nature.com/nature/journal/v436/n7052/full/436761a.html.

Giddens, Anthony. 1976. *New Rules of Sociological Method.* London: Hutchinson.

———. 1984. *The Constitution of Society.* Berkeley: University of California Press.

Gitlin, Todd. 1980. *The Whole World Is Watching: Mass Media in the Making and Unmaking of the New Left.* Berkeley: University of California Press.

Glaser, James M. 1996. "The Challenge of Campaign Watching: Seven Lessons of Participant-Observation Research." *PS: Political Science and Politics* 29, no. 3:33–37.

Gledhill, John. 2000. *Power and Its Disguises: Anthropological Perspectives on Politics.* 2d ed. London: Pluto.

Glynn, Carol, Susan Herbst, Garrett J. O'Keefe, Robert Y. Shapiro, and Mark Lindeman. 2004. *Public Opinion.* 2d ed. Boulder, Colo.: Westview Press.

Goffman, Erving. 1959. *The Presentation of Self in Everyday Life.* Garden City, N.Y.: Doubleday.

Golden-Biddle, Karen, and Karen Locke. 1993. "Appealing Work: An Investigation in How Ethnographic Texts Convince." *Organization Science* 4:595–616.

———. 1997. *Composing Qualitative Research.* Thousand Oaks, Calif.: Sage.

Goldstein, Daniel. 2003. "'In Our Own Hands': Lynching, Justice, and the Law in Bolivia." *American Ethnologist* 30:22–43.

Goldstein, Rebecca. 1983. *The Mind-Body Problem.* New York: Random House.

Gomez-Perez, Muriel, ed. 2005. *L'Islam politique au sud du Sahara.* Paris: Karthala.

González, Roberto J. 2007. "Towards Mercenary Anthropology? The New US Army Counterinsurgency Manual FM 3-24 and the Military-Anthropology Complex." *Anthropology Today* 23, no. 3:14–19.

Gooding, Robert, and Hans-Dieter Klingemann, eds. 1996. *A New Handbook of Political Science.* Oxford: Oxford University Press.

Goodman, Nelson. 1978. *Ways of World-Making.* Indianapolis: Hackett.

Goodwin, Jeff, and James M. Jasper. 2004. *Rethinking Social Movements: Structure, Meaning, and Emotion.* Lanham, Md.: Rowman & Littlefield.

Goodwyn, Lawrence. 1978. *The Populist Moment: A Short History of the Agrarian Revolt in America.* Oxford: Oxford University Press.

Gough, Kathleen. 1968. "Anthropology and Imperialism." *Monthly Review* (April): 12–27.

Gould, Deborah. 2003. "Passionate Political Processes: Bringing Emotions Back into the Study of Social Movements." In *Rethinking Social Movements: Structure, Meaning, and Emotion,* ed. Jeff Goodwin and James M. Jasper, 155–75. Lanham, Md.: Rowman & Littlefield.

Grass, Günter. 2006. *Beim Haüten der Zwiebel.* Göttingen: Steidl.

Green, Donald, and Ian Shapiro. 1996. *Pathologies of Rational Choice Theory: A Critique of Applications in Political Science.* New Haven, Conn.: Yale University Press.

Green, Linda. 1995. "Living in a State of Fear." In *Fieldwork under Fire: Contemporary Studies of Violence and Survival,* ed. Carolyn Nordstrom and Antonius C. G. M. Robben, 105–27. Berkeley: University of California Press.

———. 1999. *Fear as a Way of Life: Mayan Widows in Rural Guatemala*. New York: Columbia University Press.

Greif, Avner. 1994. "Cultural Beliefs and the Organization of Society: A Historical and Theoretical Reflection on Collectivist and Individualist Societies." *Journal of Political Economy* 102, no. 5:912–50.

Gudeman, Stephen. 2001. *The Anthropology of Economy: Community, Market, and Culture*. Oxford: Blackwell.

Guha, Ranajit, 1983. *Elementary Aspects of Peasant Insurgency in Colonial India*. Delhi: Oxford University Press.

Gupta, Akhil, and James Ferguson. 1997. *Anthropological Locations: Boundaries and Grounds of a Field Science*. Berkeley: University of California Press.

Gurr, Ted R. 1971. *Why Men Rebel*. Princeton, N.J.: Princeton University Press.

Gusfield, Joseph R. 1976. "The Literary Rhetoric of Science." *American Sociological Review* 41:16–34.

Hafez, Mohamed M. 2003. *Why Muslims Rebel: Repression and Resistance in the Muslim World*. Boulder, Colo.: Lynne Rienner.

Halbwachs, Maurice. 1992. *On Collective Memory*. Ed. and trans. Lewis A. Coser. Chicago: University of Chicago Press.

Halebsky, Sandor. 1976. *Mass Society and Political Conflict: Towards a Reconstruction of Theory*. Cambridge: Cambridge University Press.

Hall, Peter A. 2003. "Aligning Ontology and Methodology in Comparative Research." In *Comparative Historical Analysis in the Social Sciences*, ed. James Mahoney and Dietrich Rueschemeyer, 373–404. Cambridge: Cambridge University Press.

Hammersley, Martyn. 1990. *Reading Ethnographic Research*. London: Longman.

Hammoudi, Abdellah. 1997. *Master and Disciple: The Cultural Foundations of Moroccan Authoritarianism*. Chicago: University of Chicago Press.

Haraway, Donna Jeanne. 1991. *Simians, Cyborgs, and Women: The Reinvention of Nature*. London: Free Association Books.

Harkness, Joseph, and Sandra J. Newman. 2002. "Home Ownership for the Poor in Distressed Neighborhoods: Does This Make Sense?" *Housing Policy Debate* 13, no. 3:597–630.

Harley, J. Brian. 1988. "Maps, Knowledge and Power." In *The Iconography of Landscape: Essays on the Symbolic Representation, Design and Use of Past Environments*, ed. Denis Cosgrove and Stephen Daniels, 277–312. Cambridge: Cambridge University Press.

———. 1992. "Rereading the Maps of the Columbian Encounter." *Annals of the Association of American Geographers* 82, no. 3:522–42.

Harrison, Lawrence E., and Samuel P. Huntington, eds. 2000. *Culture Matters: How Values Shape Human Progress*. New York: Basic Books.

Hatch, Mary Jo, and Dvora Yanow. 2008. "Methodology by Metaphor: Ways of Seeing in Painting and Research." *Organization Studies* 29:23–44.

Hawkesworth, Mary E. 1988. *Theoretical Issues in Policy Analysis*. Albany, N.Y.: SUNY Press.

———. 2006. *Feminist Inquiry: From Political Conviction to Methodological Innovation*. New Brunswick, N.J.: Rutgers University Press.

Hayden, Dolores. 1995. *The Power of Place: Urban Landscapes as Public History*. Cambridge, Mass.: MIT Press.

Hebdige, Dick. 1979. *Subculture: The Meaning of Style*. London: Routledge.

Heider, Karl G. 1988. "The Rashomon Effect: When Ethnographers Disagree." *American Anthropologist* 90, no. 1 (March):73–81.

Henderson, David K. 1993. *Interpretation and Explanation in the Human Sciences.* New York: SUNY Press.

Herbert, Steve. 2000. "For Ethnography." *Progress in Human Geography* 24, no. 4: 550–68.

Herbst, Susan. 1998. "Policy Experts Think about Public Opinion, Media, and Legislative Process." In Herbst, *Reading Public Opinion: How Political Actors View the Democratic Process,* 46–88. Chicago: University of Chicago Press.

Herrera, Yoshiko M. 2006a. "Theory, Data, and Formalization: The Unusual Case of David Laitin." *Qualitative Methods,* Newsletter of the APSA Organized Section on Qualitative Methods 4, no. 1:2–5.

———. 2006b. *Imagined Economies: The Sources of Russian Regionalism.* Cambridge: Cambridge University Press.

Herzfeld, Michael. 1997. *Cultural Intimacy: Social Poetics in the Nation-State.* New York: Routledge.

———. 2001. *Anthropology: Theoretical Practice in Culture and Society.* Oxford: Blackwell.

Hillier, Amy, and Dennis Culhane. 2003. *Closing the GAP: Housing (Un)Affordability in Philadelphia.* Philadelphia: Cartographic Modeling Laboratory, University of Pennsylvania.

Hirschkind, Charles. 2001. "The Ethics of Listening: Cassette-Sermon Audition in Contemporary Egypt." *American Ethnologist* 28, no. 3:623–49.

Ho, Karen. 2005. "Situating Global Capitalisms: A View from Wall Street Investment Banks." *Cultural Anthropology* 20, no. 1:68–96.

Holmes, Douglas R., and George E. Marcus. 2006. "Fast-Capitalism: Para-ethnography and the Rise of the Symbolic Analyst." In *Frontiers of Capital: Ethnographic Reflections on the New Economy,* ed. Melissa Fisher and Greg Downey, 33–57. Durham, N.C.: Duke University Press.

Holy, Ladislav. 1987. "Introduction: Description, Generalization and Comparison: Two Paradigms." In *Comparative Anthropology,* ed. Holy, 1–21. Oxford: Basil Blackwell.

Hopf, Ted. 2002. *Social Construction of International Politics: Identities and Foreign Policies, Moscow 1955 and 1999.* Ithaca, N.Y.: Cornell University Press.

———. 2006. "Ethnography and Rational Choice in David Laitin: From Equality to Subordination to Absence." *Qualitative Methods,* Newsletter of the APSA Organized Section on Qualitative Methods 4, no. 1:17–20.

Howell, Julia Day. 2001. "Sufism and the Indonesian Islamic Revival." *Journal of Asian Studies* 60, no. 3:701–29.

Humphrey, Caroline. 2001. *Marx Went Away but Karl Stayed Behind.* Ann Arbor: University of Michigan Press.

———. 2002. *The Unmaking of Soviet Life: Everyday Economies after Socialism.* Ithaca, N.Y.: Cornell University Press.

Humphreys, Michael. 2005. "Getting Personal: Reflexivity and Autoethnographic Vignettes." *Qualitative Inquiry* 11:840–60.

Humphreys, Michael, Andrew D. Brown, and Mary Jo Hatch. 2003. "Is Ethnography Jazz?" *Organization* 10, no. 1:5–31.

Hunt, Lynn, and Victoria Bonnell, eds. 1999. *Beyond the Cultural Turn: New Directions in the Study of Society and Culture.* Berkeley: University of California Press.

Hymes, Dell, ed. 1972. *Reinventing Anthropology.* New York: Random House.

Ignatiev, Noel. 1996. *How the Irish Became White.* New York: Routledge.

Iriarte, José Maria [political pseudonym "Bikila"]. 1980. "La crisis ideológica en 1980: El Proceso de Burgos: Aportaciones del Marxismo revolucionario ante el problema nacional." *Cuaderno de formación de IPES* 1:24–30, 54–56.

Iser, Wolfgang. 1989. *Prospecting: From Reader Response to Literary Anthropology.* Baltimore: Johns Hopkins University Press.

Iturrioz, Patxi. 1980. "ETA en al año 1966: Divergencias internas que lleva a la aparición de ETA-berri: Algunas aportaciones teórico-políticas a la causa revolucionaria vasca." *Cuaderno de formación de IPES* 1:3–9.

Jackson, Patrick Thaddeus. 2006. "Making Sense of Making Sense: Configurational Analysis and the Double Hermeneutic." In *Interpretation and Method: Empirical Research Methods and the Interpretive Turn,* ed. Dvora Yanow and Peregrine Schwartz-Shea, 264–80. Armonk, N.Y.: M. E. Sharpe.

———. 2008. "Foregrounding Ontology: Dualism, Monism and IR Theory." *Review of International Studies* 34:129–53.

Jacobs, Lawrence R., and Benjamin I. Page. 2005. "Who Influences U.S. Foreign Policy?" *American Political Science Review* 99, no. 1:1–17.

Jacobs, Lawrence R., and Robert Y. Shapiro. 2000. *Politicians Don't Pander: Political Manipulation and the Loss of Democratic Responsiveness.* Chicago: University of Chicago Press.

Jacoby, William G. 2000. "Issue Framing and Public Opinion on Government Spending." *American Journal of Political Science* 44, no. 4:750–67.

Janson, Marloes. 2005. "Roaming about for God's Sake: The Upsurge of the *Tablīgh Jama'at* in the Gambia." *Journal of Religion in Africa* 35, no. 4:450–81.

Jelin, Elizabeth. 1996. "Citizenship Revisited: Solidarity, Responsibility, and Rights." In *Constructing Democracy: Human Rights, Citizenship, and Society in Latin America,* ed. Elizabeth Jelin and Eric Hershberg, 101–19. Boulder, Colo.: Westview Press.

Jing, Jun. 1996. *The Temple of Memories: History, Power, and Morality in a Chinese Village.* Stanford, Calif.: Stanford University Press.

Johnson, James. 2003. "Conceptual Problems as Obstacles to Progress in Political Science: Four Decades of Political Culture Research." *Journal of Theoretical Politics* 15, no. 1:87–115.

———. 2006. "Consequences of Positivism: A Pragmatist Assessment." *Comparative Political Studies* 39, no. 2:224–52.

Jones, Charles O. 1989. "Mistrust But Verify: Memoirs of the Reagan Era." *American Political Science Review* 83, no. 3:981–88.

Jorgensen, Danny L. 1989. *Participant Observation: A Methodology for Human Studies.* Thousand Oaks, Calif.: Sage.

Jourde, Cédric. 2002. "Dramas of Ethnic Elites Accommodation: The Authoritarian Restoration in Mauritania." Ph.D. diss., University of Wisconsin–Madison.

———. 2005. "'The President Is Coming to Visit!': Dramas and the Hijack of Democratization in the Islamic Republic of Mauritania." *Comparative Politics* 37, no. 4:421–40.

———. 2007. "The International Relations of Small Neoauthoritarian States: Islamism, Warlordism, and the Framing of Stability." *International Studies Quarterly* 51, no. 2: 481–503.

Kain, Roger J. P., and Elizabeth Baigent. 1992. *The Cadastral Map in the Service of the State: A History of Property Mapping.* Chicago: University of Chicago Press.

Kane, Mouhamed Moustapha. 1997. "La vie et l'oeuvre d'Al-Hajj Mahmoud Ba Diowol (1905–1978) : Du pâtre au patron de la 'Révolution Al-Falah.'" In *Le temps des marabouts: Itinéraires et stratégies islamiques en Afrique occidentale française, v. 1880–1960,* ed. David Robinson and Jean-Louis Triaud, 431–65. Paris: Karthala.

Kapferer, Bruce. 1972. *Strategy and Transaction in an African Factory: African Workers and Indian Management in a Zambian Town.* Manchester: Manchester University Press.

Kaplan, Temma. 1977. *Anarchists of Andalusia, 1868–1903*. Princeton, N.J.: Princeton University Press.

Karlstrom, Mikael. 1996. "Imagining Democracy: Political Culture and Democratisation in Buganda." *Africa* 66, no. 6:485–505.

Karp, Ivan, and Steven D. Lavine, eds. 1991. *Exhibiting Cultures: The Poetics and Politics of Museum Display*. Washington, D.C.: Smithsonian Institution Press.

Kasza, Gregory. 2001. "Perestroika: For an Ecumenical Science of Politics." *PS: Political Science and Politics* 34, no. 3:597–600.

"Keeping Religion Out of Science Class." 2005. *Nature* 436 (11 August). Available at: www .nature.com/nature/journal/v436/n7052/full/436753a.html.

Keeter, Scott. 2006. "The Impact of Cell Phone Noncoverage Bias on Polling in the 2004 Presidential Election." *Public Opinion Quarterly* 70, no. 1:88–98.

Kelley, Robin. 1990. *Hammer and Hoe: Alabama Communists during the Great Depression*. Chapel Hill: University of North Carolina Press.

———. 1994. *Race Rebels: Culture, Politics, and the Black Working Class*. New York: Free Press.

Kepel, Gilles. 1991. *La revanche de Dieu: Chrétiens, Juifs et Musulmans à la reconquête du monde*. Paris : Editions du Seuil.

Kertzer, David I. 1996. *Politics and Symbols: The Italian Communist Party and the Fall of Communism*. New Haven, Conn.: Yale University Press.

Key, V. O. 1961. *Public Opinion and American Democracy*. New York: Alfred A. Knopf.

Kimmel, Michael S. 1990. *Revolution: A Sociological Interpretation*. Philadelphia: Temple University Press.

Kinder, Donald R. 1998. "Opinion and Action in the Realm of Politics." In *Handbook of Social Psychology*, ed. Daniel Gilbert, Susan Fiske, and Gardner Lindzey, 778–867. New York: McGraw Hill.

King, Charles. 2004. "The Micropolitics of Social Violence." *World Politics* 56, no. 3:431–55.

King, Gary. 1989. *Unifying Political Methodology: The Likelihood Theory of Statistical Inference*. New York: Cambridge University Press.

King, Gary, Robert Keohane, and Sidney Verba. 1994. *Designing Social Inquiry: Scientific Inference in Qualitative Research*. Princeton, N.J.: Princeton University Press.

Kitemona N'Silu. 1984. "Bobutaka, le célèbre buteur de Vita Club, meurt en plein match contre Matonge!" *Elima*, 15 June, 16.

Klotz, Audie, and Cecelia Lynch. 2007. *Strategies of Research in Constructivist International Relations*. Armonk, N.Y.: M. E. Sharpe.

Koba Bashibirira M. 1985. "Incidences magico-religieuses sur le pouvoir africain." *Cahiers des religions africaines* 19, no. 37:39–51.

Krige, Eileen Jensen, and Jacob Daniel Krige. 1943. *The Realm of a Rain-Queen: A Study of the Pattern of Lovedu Society*. London: Oxford University Press.

Kriger, Nora. 1992. *Zimbabwe's Guerrilla War: Peasant Voices*. Cambridge: Cambridge University Press.

Kubik, Jan. 1994. *The Power of Symbols against the Symbols of Power: The Rise of Solidarity and the Fall of State Socialism in Poland*. University Park: Pennsylvania State University Press.

Kuhn, Thomas. 1962. *The Structure of Scientific Revolutions*. Chicago: University of Chicago Press.

Kuklick, Henrika. 1997. "After Ishmael: The Fieldwork Tradition and Its Future." In *An-*

thropological Locations: Boundaries and Grounds of a Field Science, ed. Akhil Gupta and James Ferguson, 47–65. Berkeley: University of California Press.

Kundera, Milan. 1979. *Le livre du rire et de l'oubli*. Poitiers: Gallimard.

Kuran, Timur. 1995. *Private Truths, Public Lies: The Social Consequences of Preference Falsification*. Cambridge, Mass.: Harvard University Press.

Kvale, Steiner. 1983. "The Qualitative Research Interview: A Phenomenological and a Hermeneutical Mode of Understanding." *Journal of Phenomenological Psychology* 14: 171–96.

Kwon, Heonik. 2006. *After the Massacre: Commemoration and Consolidation in Ha My and My Lai*. Berkeley: University of California Press.

Laitin, David D. 1998. *Identity in Formation: The Russian Speaking Population in the Near Abroad*. Ithaca, N.Y.: Cornell University Press.

———. 2003. "The Perestroikan Challenge to Political Science." *Politics and Society* 31, no. 1:163–84.

———. 2004. "Comparative Politics: The State of the Subdiscipline." In *The State of the Discipline 3*, ed. Helen Milner and Ira Katznelson, 630–59. Washington, D.C.: American Political Science Association.

———. 2006. "Ethnography and/or Rational Choice: A Response from David Laitin." *Qualitative Methods*, Newsletter of the APSA Organized Section on Qualitative Methods 4, no. 1:26–33.

Langer, Gary, and Jon Cohen. 2005. "Voters and Values in the 2004 Election." *Public Opinion Quarterly* 69, no. 5:744–59.

Latour, Bruno. 1999. *Pandora's Hope*. Cambridge, Mass.: Harvard University Press.

———. 2004. "Scientific Objects and Legal Objectivity." In *Law, Anthropology, and the Constitution of the Social: Making Persons and Things*, ed. Alain Pottage and Marta Mundy, 73–115. New York: Cambridge University Press.

Lauzière, Henri. 2005. "Post-Islamism and the Religious Discourse of 'Abd Al-Salam Yasin." *International Journal of Middle East Studies* 37:241–61.

Leach, Edmund. 1976. *Culture and Communication*. Cambridge: Cambridge University Press.

LeBlanc, Marie Nathalie. 1999. "The Production of Islamic Identities through Knowledge Claims in Bouake, Côte d'Ivoire." *African Affairs* 98, no. 393:485–508.

Lecompte, Margaret. 2002. "The Transformation of Ethnographic Practice: Past and Current Challenges." *Qualitative Research* 2, no. 3:283–99.

Ledeneva, Alena. 2006. *How Russia Really Works: The Informal Practices That Shaped Post-Soviet Politics and Business*. Ithaca, N.Y.: Cornell University Press.

———. 2008. "Telephone Justice in Russia." *Post-Soviet Affairs* 24, no. 4:324–50.

Lee, Taeku. 2002. *Mobilizing Public Opinion: Black Insurgency and Racial Attitudes in the Civil Rights Era*. Chicago: University of Chicago Press.

Letamendia, Francisco. 1977. *Historia de Euskadi: El nacionalism vasco y ETA*. Barcelona: Ruedo Ibérico.

Le Vine, Victor. 2007. "Mali: Accommodation or Coexistence?" In *Political Islam in West Africa: State-Society Relations Transformed*, ed. William F. S. Miles, 73–99. Boulder, Colo.: Lynne Rienner.

Levitsky, Steven, and Lucan A. Way. 2002. "The Rise of Competitive Authoritarianism." *Journal of Democracy* 13, no. 2:51–65.

Lewin, Ellen, and William L. Leap, eds. 1996. "Introduction." In *Out in the Field*, 1–28. Urbana: University of Illinois Press.

Lewis, Oscar. 1961. *The Children of Sanchez: Autobiography of a Mexican Family.* New York: Random House.

Lichbach, Mark Irving, and Alan S. Zuckerman, eds. 2000. *Comparative Politics: Rationality, Culture and Structure.* Cambridge: Cambridge University Press.

Lichterman, Paul. 1998. "What Do Movements Mean? The Value of Participant-Observation." *Qualitative Sociology* 21, no. 4:401–18.

Lievens, Karin. 1988. *El quinto piso de la alegría: Tres años con la guerrilla: El Salvador.* N.p.: Ediciones Sistema Radio Venceremos.

Lindhorst, Taryn, and Julianna D. Padgett. 2005. "Disjunctures for Women and Front-line Workers: Implementation of the Family Violence Option." *Social Service Review* 79, no. 3:405–29.

Linz, Juan J. 1973. "Early State-Building and Late Peripheral Nationalisms against the State: The Case of Spain." In *Building States and Nations: Models, Analyses, and Data across Three Worlds,* ed. S. N. Eisenstadt and Stein Rokkan, 32–116. Beverly Hills, Calif.: Sage.

———. 1980. "The Basques in Spain: Nationalism and Political Conflict in a New Democracy." In *Resolving Nationality Conflicts: The Role of Public Opinion Research,* ed. W. Phillips Davison and Leo Gordenker, 11–52. New York: Praeger.

Lippmann, Walter. 1922. *Public Opinion.* New York: Free Press.

Little, Daniel. 1998. *Microfoundations, Method, and Causation.* New Brunswick, N.J.: Transaction.

Little, David. 1991. *Varieties of Social Explanation: An Introduction to the Philosophy of Social Science.* Boulder, Colo.: Westview.

Locke, Karen. 1996. "Rewriting the Discovery of Grounded Theory after 25 Years?" *Journal of Management Inquiry* 5:239–45.

Lockerbie, Brad, and Stephen A. Borrelli. 1990. "Question Wording and Public Support for Contra Aid, 1983–1986." *Public Opinion Quarterly* 54, no. 2:195–208.

Loe, Meika. 1996. "Working for Men—At the Intersection of Power, Gender, and Sexuality." *Sociological Inquiry* 66, no. 4:399–421.

Loimeier, Roman. 2000. "L'Islam ne se vend plus: The Islamic Reform Movement and the State in Senegal." *Journal of Religion in Africa* 30, no. 2:168–90.

Lukes, Steven. 1974. *Power: A Radical View.* London: Macmillan.

Lusadusu Basilwa. 1984. "Réflexion: Quel avenir pour le football zaïrois?" *Elima,* 2 August, 15.

Lyman, Princeton N., and J. Stephen Morrison. 2004. "The Terrorist Threat in Africa." *Foreign Affairs* 3:75–86.

Lynch, Michael, and Steve Woolgar, eds. 1990. *Representation in Scientific Practice.* Cambridge, Mass.: MIT Press.

MacDonald, Sharon. 2001. "British Social Anthropology." In *Handbook of Ethnography,* ed. P. Atkinson, 60–79. London: SAGE.

Macedo, Stephen, Yvette M. Alex-Assensoh, Jeffrey M. Berry et al. 2005. *Democracy at Risk: How Political Choices Have Undermined Citizenship, and What We Can Do about It.* A Report of the American Political Science Association's Standing Committee on Civic Education and Engagement. Washington, D.C.: Brookings Institution.

MacIntyre, Alasdair. 1978. "Is a Science of Comparative Politics Possible?" In *Against the Self-Images of the Age: Essays on Ideology and Philosophy,* 260–79. Notre Dame, Ind.: University of Notre Dame Press.

Mahmood, Saba. 2005. *Politics of Piety: The Islamic Revival and the Feminist Subject.* Princeton, N.J.: Princeton University Press.

Mahoney, James, and Dietrich Rueschemeyer, eds. 2003. *Comparative Historical Analysis and Social Sciences.* Cambridge: Cambridge University Press.

Malinowski, Bronislaw. 1961 [1922]. *Argonauts of the Western Pacific.* New York: Dutton.

Mamounia Ngyambila. 1984. "Fait du jour—La sorcellerie: Une source de conflits." *Elima,* 4 September, 2.

Mann, Judy. 2001. "Falwell's Insult Compounds Nation's Injury." *Washington Post,* 21 September, final edition, C8.

Manna, Paul F. 2000. "How Do I Know What I Say I Know? Thinking about Slim's Table and Qualitative Methods." *Endarch: Journal of Black Political Research* (Spring): 19–29.

March, James G., and Johan P. Olsen. 1989. *Rediscovering Institutions: The Organizational Basis of Politics.* New York: Free Press.

Marchevsky, Alejandra, and Jeanne Theoharis. 2006. *Not Working: Latina Immigrants, Low-Wage Jobs, and the Failure of Welfare Reform.* New York: New York University Press.

Marcus, George E. 1998. *Ethnography through Thick and Thin.* Princeton, N.J.: Princeton University Press.

Marcus, George E., and Michael M. J. Fischer. 1999. *Anthropology as Cultural Critique: An Experimental Moment in the Human Sciences.* 2d ed. Chicago: University of Chicago Press.

Markell, Patchen. 2003. *Bound by Recognition.* Princeton, N.J.: Princeton University Press.

Markoff, John. 1996. *The Abolition of Feudalism: Peasants, Lords and Legislators in the French Revolution.* University Park: Pennsylvania State University Press.

Markovits, Andrei S., and Philip S. Gorski. 1993. *The German Left: Red, Green, and Beyond.* Oxford: Oxford University Press.

Markus, Gregory B. 1986. "Stability and Change in Political Attitudes: Observed, Recalled, and 'Explained.'" *Political Behavior* 8, no. 1:21–44.

Martin, Denis-Constant. 2002. *A la recherche des OPNI.* Paris: Karthala.

Martín-Baró, Ignacio. 1988. "La violencia en Centroamérica: Una visión psicosocial." *Revista Costarricense de psicología* 12, no. 13:21–34. Reprinted as "Violence in Central America: A Social Psychological Perspective." In *Towards a Society That Serves Its People: The Intellectual Contributions of El Salvador's Murdered Jesuits,* ed. John Hassett and Hugh Lacey, 333–46. Washington, D.C.: Georgetown University Press, 1991.

Mazie, Steven V., and Patricia J. Woods. 2003. "Prayer, Contentious Politics, and the Women of the Wall: The Benefits of Participant Observation in Intense, Multifocal Events." *Field Methods* 15, no. 1:25–50.

Mazzarella, William. 2003. *Shoveling Smoke: Advertising and Globalization in Contemporary India.* Durham, N.C.: Duke University Press.

McCloskey, Donald N. 1985. *The Rhetoric of Economics.* Madison: University of Wisconsin Press.

McCoyd, Judith L. M., and Corey S. Shdaimah. 2007. "Revisiting the Benefits Debate: Salubrious Effects of Qualitative Social Work Research?" *Social Work* 52, no. 4:340–49.

McKeown, Timothy. 2004. "Case Studies and the Limits of the Quantitative Worldview." In *Rethinking Social Inquiry: Diverse Tools, Shared Standards,* ed. Henry E. Brady and David Collier, 139–67. Lanham, Md.: Rowman & Littlefield.

Medhurst, Ken. 1982. "Basques and Basque Nationalism." In *National Separatism,* ed. Colin H. Williams, 235–61. Cardiff: University of Wales Press.

Melucci, Alberto. 1989. *Nomads of the Present: Social Movements and Individual Needs in Contemporary Society.* Philadelphia: Temple University Press.

Messick, Brinkley. 1993. *The Calligraphic State: Textual Domination and History in a Muslim Society.* Comparative Studies on Muslim Societies 16. Berkeley: University of California Press.

Miller, Daniel. 1997. *Capitalism: An Ethnographic Approach, Explorations in Anthropology.* Oxford: Berg.

Miller, Richard W. 1987. *Fact and Method: Explanation, Confirmation and Reality in the Natural and Social Sciences.* Princeton, N.J.: Princeton University Press.

Mills, C. Wright. 1959. "On Intellectual Craftsmanship." In Mills, *The Sociological Imagination,* 195–226. New York: Oxford University Press.

Miner, Horace. 1956. "Body Ritual among the Nacirema." *American Anthropologist* 58, no. 3:503–7.

Mitchell, Timothy. 1990. "Everyday Metaphors of Power." *Theory and Society* 19, no. 5: 545–77.

Moffatt, Michael. 1992. "Ethnographic Writing about American Culture." *American Review of Anthropology* 21:205–29.

Monroe, Kristin, ed. 2005. *Perestroika! The Raucous Rebellion in Political Science.* New Haven, Conn.: Yale University Press.

Monsa and Kitemona. 1984. "Qui a tué Bobo?" *Elima,* 16–17 June, 8.

Monsengwo, Mgr. 1992. "Discours de Mgr. Monsengwo, reprise solennelle des travaux de la CNS." Mimeographed text. CEDAF [Brussels], Zaïre: Documents relatifs à la Conférence Nationale. 2343 III, 1991. 6 April.

Moore, Richter H., Jr., and Charles B. Fields. 1996. "Comparative Criminal Justice: Why Study?" In *Comparative Criminal Justice: Traditional and Nontraditional Systems of Law and Control,* ed. Charles B. Fields and Richter H. Moore, Jr. Prospect Heights, Ill.: Waveland Press.

Morris, Aldon D., and Carol McClurg Mueller. 1992. *Frontiers in Social Movement Theory.* New Haven, Conn.: Yale University Press.

Morris, Rosalind C. 2007. "Legacies of Derrida: Anthropology." *Annual Review of Anthropology* 36:355–89.

Morrow, James D. 1994. *Game Theory for Political Scientists.* Princeton, N.J.: Princeton University Press.

———. 2003. "Diversity through Specialization." *PS: Political Science and Politics* (July): 91–93.

Mukaku Lalabi-Muke. 1983. "Ces pratiques fétichistes qui avalisent le sport." *Elima,* 12 August, 10.

Murphy, Jerome T. 1980. *Getting the Facts.* Santa Monica, Calif.: Goodyear.

Mutungi, O. K. 1977. *The Legal Aspects of Witchcraft in East Africa, with Particular Reference to Kenya.* Nairobi: East African Literature Bureau, Kenya.

M'Vuma Nkanga. 1983. "Les fétiches battus par le football." *Elima,* 4 June, 8.

Mwangi, Wambui. 2002. "The Lion, the Native and the Coffee Plant: Political Imagery and the Ambiguous Art of Currency." *Geopolitics* 7, no. 1:31–62.

N. K. 1983. "Ces pratiques fétichistes qui 'tuent' le football kinois! Qu'attend la Lifkin pour réprimer les auteurs?" *Elima,* 6 October, 16.

Nagel, Thomas. 1989. *The View from Nowhere.* New York: Oxford University Press.

Naples, Nancy. 2003. *Feminism and Method: Ethnography, Discourse Analysis, and Activist Research.* New York: Routledge.

Narotzky, Susanna. 1997. *New Directions in Economic Anthropology.* London: Pluto Press.

Nelson, Nancy. 2005. "Ideologies of Aid, Practices of Power: Lessons for Medicaid Managed Care." *Medical Anthropology Quarterly* 19, no. 1:103–22.

Nencel, Lorraine, and Dvora Yanow. 2008. "On Methodological Relics: Etic Outsiders, Emic Insiders, and Fieldwork Relationships." Prepared for presentation at the European Association of Social Anthropologists, Ljubljana, 26–29 August.

Nordstrom, Carolyn. 1997. *A Different Kind of War Story.* Philadelphia: University of Pennsylvania Press.

North, Douglass. 1990. *Institutions, Institutional Change and Economic Performance.* Cambridge: Cambridge University Press.

———. 1997. "Understanding Economic Change." In *Transforming Post-Communist Political Economies,* ed. Joan M. Nelson, Charles Tilly, and Lee Walker, 11–18. Washington, D.C.: National Academy Press.

Norton, Anne. 2004. *95 Theses on Politics, Culture, and Method.* New Haven, Conn.: Yale University Press.

Novkov, Julie. 2007. "Legal Archaeology." Handout for The Methods Café, Western Political Science Association Annual Meeting, Las Vegas, 8–10 March.

Nsasse Ramazani. 1984. "Le fétichisme à l'honneur: De sang humain au stade Lumumba." *Elima,* 7 September, 13.

Nugent, David, and Joan Vincent, eds. 2004. *A Companion to the Anthropology of Politics.* Blackwell Companions to Anthropology. London: Blackwell.

O'Brien, Flann. 1996. *The Poor Mouth: A Bad Story about the Hard Life.* Normal, Ill.: Dalkey Archive Press. Originally published as Myles na Gopaleen. 1941. *An Béal Bocht.* Dublin: National Press.

O'Connor, Alice. 2001. *Poverty Knowledge: Social Science, Social Policy, and the Poor in Twentieth-Century U.S. History.* Princeton, N.J.: Princeton University Press.

O'Donnell, Guillermo. 1993. "On the State, Democratization and Some Conceptual Problems: A Latin American View with Glances at Some Postcommunist Countries." *World Development* 21:1355–69.

———. 1999. "Polyarchies and the (Un)Rule of Law in Latin America: A Partial Conclusion." In *The (Un)Rule of Law and the Underprivileged in Latin America,* ed. Juan E. Méndez, Guillermo O'Donnell, and Paulo Sérgio Pinheiro, 303–38. Notre Dame, Ind.: University of Notre Dame Press.

O'Donnell, Guillermo, and Philippe C. Schmitter. 1986. *Transitions from Authoritarian Rule: Tentative Conclusions about Uncertain Democracies.* Baltimore: Johns Hopkins University Press.

Okin, Susan Moller. 1998. "Gender, the Public, and the Private." In *Feminism and Politics,* ed. Anne Phillips, 116–41. Oxford: Oxford University Press.

Olick, Jeffrey K., and Joyce Robbins. 1998. "Social Memory Studies: From 'Collective Memory' to the Historical Sociology of Mnemonic Practices." *Annual Review of Sociology* 24:105–40.

Oliver, Pamela E., Jorge Cadena-Roa, and Kelley D. Strawn. 2003. "Emerging Trends in the Study of Protest and Social Movements." In *Research in Political Sociology: Political Sociology for the 21st Century* 12, ed. Betty A. Dobratz, Timothy Buzzell, and Lisa K. Waldner. 38(4) JAI Press.

O'Neill, Barry. 1999. *Honor, Symbols, War.* Ann Arbor: University of Michigan Press.

Orlove, Benjamin. 1991. "Mapping Reeds and Reading Maps: The Politics of Representation in Lake Titicaca." *American Ethnologist* 181:3–37.

———. 1993. "The Ethnography of Maps: The Cultural and Social Contexts of Cartographic Representation in Peru." *Cartographica* 30, no. 1:29–46.

Ortner, Sherry B. 1995. "Resistance and the Politics of Ethnographic Refusal." *Comparative Studies in Society and History* 37, no. 1:173–93.

Orwell, George. 1952. *Homage to Catalonia.* New York: Harcourt, Brace & World.

Ould Ahmed Salem, Zekeria. 1999. "Prêcher dans le désert: L'univers du Cheikh Sidi

Yahya et l'évolution de l'islamisme mauritanien," *Islam et sociétés au sud du Sahara* 14–15:5–40.

Pachirat, Timothy S. 2008. "Repugnance and Confinement: Dividing Space, Labor, and Bodies on the Kill Floor of an Industrialized Slaughterhouse." Ph.D. diss., Yale University.

Pader, Ellen. 2006. "Seeing with an Ethnographic Sensibility." In *Interpretation and Method: Empirical Research Methods and the Interpretive Turn*, ed. D. Yanow and P. Schwartz-Shea, 161–75. Armonk, N.Y.: M. E. Sharpe.

Paley, Julia. 2001. *Marketing Democracy: Power and Social Movements in Post-Dictatorship Chile*. Berkeley: University of California Press.

———. 2002. "Toward an Anthropology of Democracy." *Annual Review of Anthropology* 31:469–96.

Palmer, Richard E. 1969. *Hermeneutics*. Evanston, Ill.: Northwestern University Press.

Passerini, Luisa. 1980. "Italian Working Class Culture between the Wars: Consensus to Fascism and Work Ideology." *International Journal of Oral History* 1, no. 1:4–27.

———. 1992. "Introduction." In *Memory and Totalitarianism*, 1–19. International Yearbook of Oral History and Life Stories 1. Oxford: Oxford University Press.

Patterson, Molly, and Kristen Renwick Monroe. 1998. "Narrative in Political Science." *Annual Review of Political Science* 1:315–31.

Payerhin, Marek, and Cyrus Ernesto Zirakzadeh. 2006. "On Movement Frames and Negotiated Identities: The Case of Poland's First Solidarity Congress." *Social Movement Studies* 5, no. 2:91–115.

Payne, Stanley G. 1976. "Regional Nationalism: The Basque and the Catalans." In *Spain in the 1970s: Economics, Social Structure, Foreign Policy*, ed. William Salisbury and James D. Theberge, 76–102. New York: Praeger.

———. 1979. "Terrorism and Democratic Stability in Spain." *Current History* 77, no. 451:167–71, 182–83.

Pearce, Jenny. 1986. *Promised Land: Peasant Rebellion in Chalatenango, El Salvador*. London: Latin American Review.

Pereira, Anthony. 2000. "An Ugly Democracy: State Violence and the Rule of Law in Postauthoritarian Brazil." In *Democratic Brazil: Actors Institutions and Processes*, ed. Peter R. Kingstone and Timothy J. Power, 217–35. Pittsburgh: University of Pittsburgh Press.

Perez-Liñan, Aníbal, Barry Ames, and Mitchell Seligson. 2006. "Strategies, Careers, and Judicial Decisions: Lessons from the Bolivian Courts." *Journal of Politics* 68, no. 2: 284–95.

Perrow, Charles. 1986. *Complex Organizations: A Critical Essay*. 3d ed. New York: Random House.

Petersen, Roger. 2001. *Resistance and Rebellion: Lessons from Eastern Europe*. Cambridge: Cambridge University Press.

———. N.d. "Emotion, Individual Memory and Community-based Narrative: Reconstructing Life in Violent Eras." Typescript. St. Louis: Washington University.

Philadelphia Office of Housing and Community Development. 2003. *Year 29 Consolidated Plan, Fiscal Year 2004*. Philadelphia.

Philippon, Alix. 2006. "Bridging Sufism and Islamism." *ISIS Review* 17:16–17.

Pierson, Paul. 2004. *Politics in Time: History, Institutions, Social Analysis*. Princeton, N.J.: Princeton University Press.

Piga, Adriana. 2002. "Neo-Traditionalist Islamic Associations and the Islamist Press in

Contemporary Senegal." In *Islam in Africa*, ed. T. Bierschenk and G. Stauth, 43–67. Münster: Lit.

Pitkin, Hanna Fenichel. 1993 [1972]. *Wittgenstein and Justice: On the Significance of Ludwig Wittgenstein for Social and Political Thought.* Berkeley: University of California Press.

Platner, Marc F. 2005. "Introduction." *Journal of Democracy* 16, no. 1:5–8.

Plattner, Stuart, ed. 1989. *Economic Anthropology.* Stanford, Calif.: Stanford University Press.

Polanyi, Karl. 1957. "The Economy as Instituted Process." In *Trade and Market in the Early Empires: Economies in History and Theory*, ed. K. Polanyi, Conrad M. Arensberg, and Harry W. Pearson, 243–70. Glencoe, Ill.: Free Press.

Polanyi, Michael. 1966. *The Tacit Dimension.* New York: Doubleday.

Polletta, Francesca. 1998a. "Contending Stories: Narrative in Social Movements." *Qualitative Sociology* 21, no. 4:419–46.

———. 1998b. "'It Was Like a Fever . . . ': Narrative and Identity in Social Protest." *Social Problems* 45, no. 2:137–59.

———. 1999. "'Free Spaces' in Collective Action." *Theory and Society* 28, no. 1:1–38.

Poovey, Mary. 1998. *A History of the Modern Fact: Problems of Knowledge in the Sciences of Wealth and Society.* Chicago: University of Chicago Press.

Portelli, Alessandro. 1985. *Biografia di una città: Storia e racconto: Terni 1830–1985.* Turin: Einaudi.

———. 1991. *The Death of Luigi Trastulli and Other Stories: Form and Meaning in Oral History.* Albany: SUNY Press.

———. 1997. *The Battle of Valle Giulia: Oral History and the Art of Dialogue.* Madison: University of Wisconsin Press.

Pouliot, Vincent. 2007a. "'Sobjectivism': Towards a Constructivist Methodology." *International Studies Quarterly* 51, no. 2:359–84.

———. 2007b. "Pacification without Collective Identification: Russia and the Transatlantic Security Community in the Post–Cold War Era." *Journal of Peace Research* 44, no. 5:605–22.

———. 2008. "The Logic of Practicality: A Theory of Practice of Security Communities." *International Organization* 62 (Spring): 257–88.

Price, David. 2007. "Buying a Piece of Anthropology Part 1: Human Ecology and Unwitting Anthropological Research for the CIA." *Anthropology Today* 23, no. 3:8–13.

Proceedings of the Sixth International Conference on Social Movements: Alternative Futures and Political Protest, vol. 2, ed. Colin Barker and Mike Tyldesley, 1–13. Manchester: Manchester Metropolitan University.

Przeworski, Adam, Michael E. Alvarez, José Antonio Cheibub, and Fernando Limongi. 2000. *Democracy and Development: Political Institutions and Well-Being in the World 1950–1990.* Cambridge: Cambridge University Press.

Qualitative Methods. 2006. "Symposium: Ethnography Meets Rational Choice: David Laitin, for Example." *Qualitative Methods*, Newsletter of the American Political Science Association Organized Section on Qualitative Methods 4, no. 1:2–33.

Qualitative Sociology. 2006. *Qualitative Sociology* 29, no. 3:257–412. Special issue on political ethnography.

Rabinow, Paul, and William M. Sullivan, eds. 1987. *Interpretive Social Science: A Second Look.* Berkeley: University of California Press.

Ragin, Charles. 2000. *Fuzzy-Set Social Science.* Chicago: University of Chicago Press.

Ragin, Charles C., and Howard Becker, eds. 1992. *What Is a Case?* Cambridge: Cambridge University Press.

Ragin, Charles C., Joane Nagel, and Patricia White. 2004. *Workshop on the Scientific Foundations of Qualitative Research.* Arlington, Va.: National Science Foundation.

Randall, Vicky. 1982. *Women and Politics.* London: Macmillan.

Rao, Vijayendra, and Michael Walton, eds. 2004. *Culture and Public Action.* Stanford Social Science. Stanford, Calif.: Stanford University Press.

Rasing, W. C. E. 1994. *"Too Many People": Order and Nonconformity in Iglulingmiut Social Process.* Nijmegen: Katholieke Universiteit Faculteit der Rechtsgeleerdheid.

Rasinski, Kenneth A. 1989. "The Effect of Question Wording on Public Support for Government Spending." *Public Opinion Quarterly* 53, no. 3:388–94.

Read, Benjamin. 2006. "Site-Intensive Methods: Fenno and Scott in Search of a Coalition." *Qualitative Methods,* Newsletter of the APSA Organized Section on Qualitative Methods 4, no. 2:10–13.

Regan, Donald T. 1988. *For the Record: From Wall Street to Washington.* San Diego: Harcourt Brace Jovanovich.

Reid, Carolina Katz. 2004. *Achieving the American Dream? A Longitudinal Analysis of the Homeownership Experiences of Low-Income Households.* Working Paper 04-04. Seattle: Center for Studies in Demography and Ecology, University of Washington.

Renzi, Fred. 2006. "Networks: Terra Incognita and the Case for Ethnographic Intelligence." *Military Review* (September–October): 16–22.

Repairing Houses, Preserving Homes: Philadelphia's Home Repair Crisis and What We Can Do about It. 2005. Philadelphia: Women's Community Revitalization Project, Association of Community Organizations for Reform Now, United Communities of Southeast Philadelphia.

Research for Democracy [a collaboration between the Eastern Pennsylvania Organizing Project and the Temple University Center for Public Policy, with assistance from Diamond and Associates]. 2001. *Blight Free Philadelphia: A Public-Private Strategy to Create and Enhance Neighborhood Value.* Philadelphia.

Retsinas, Nicolas P., and Eric S. Belsky, eds. 2002. *Low-Income Homeownership: Examining the Unexamined Goal.* Washington, D.C.: Brookings Institution Press.

Reuters. 1998. "Soccer—Democratic Congo Warns of Magic Ahead of Key Match." 24 February.

Rich, Adrienne. 1986. "Notes toward a Politics of Location (1984)." In *Blood, Bread, and Poetry: Selected Prose 1979–1985,* 210–31. New York: W.W. Norton.

Richards, Paul, ed. 2005. *No Peace No War: An Anthropology of Contemporary Armed Conflicts.* Athens: Ohio University Press.

Richardson, Laurel. 1994. "Writing: A Method of Inquiry." In *Handbook of Qualitative Research,* ed. Norman K. Denzin and Yvonna S. Lincoln, 516–29. Thousand Oaks, Calif.: Sage.

Ricoeur, Paul. 1970. *Freud and Philosophy: An Essay on Interpretation.* New Haven, Conn.: Yale University Press.

Ries, Nancy. 1997. *Russian Talk: Culture and Conversation during Perestroika.* Ithaca, N.Y.: Cornell University Press.

Rogers, Dennis. 2006. "Living in the Shadow of Death: Gangs, Violence, and Social Order in Urban Nicaragua, 1996–2002." *Journal of Latin American Studies* 38, no. 2:267–92.

Rogin, Michael Paul. 1967. *The Intellectuals and McCarthy: The Radical Specter.* Cambridge, Mass.: MIT Press.

Rogowski, Ronald. 1995. "The Role of Theory and Anomaly in Social Scientific Research." *American Political Science Review* 89:467–70.

Rohter, Larry. 2006. "Embattled Brazilian President Fails to Win on First Round Ballot." *New York Times*, 2 October.

Røryvik, Emil André. 2006. "Troops, Tropes and Troubles: Rendering Corporate Management a Privileged Ethnographic Object." Presented to the European Group on Organizational Studies Annual Conference, Bergen, Norway, 6–9 July.

Rosaldo, Renato. 1986. "From the Door of His Tent: The Fieldworker and the Inquisitor." In *Writing Culture: The Poetics and Politics of Ethnography*, ed. James Clifford and George E. Marcus, 77–97. Berkeley: University of California Press.

Rosander, Eva Evers, and David Westerlund, eds. 1997. *African Islam and Islam in Africa: Encounters between Sufis and Islamists*. Athens: Ohio University Press.

Ross, Dorothy. 1991. *The Origins of American Social Science*. Cambridge: Cambridge University Press.

Rudolph, Lloyd I., and Susanne Hoeber Rudolph. 2003. "Engaging Subjective Knowledge: How Amar Singh's Diary Narratives of and by the Self Help Explain Identity Politics." *Perspectives on Politics* 1, no. 4:681–94.

Rudoph, Susanne Hoeber, and Lloyd I. Rudolph, with Mohan Singh Kanota, eds. 2000. *Reversing the Gaze: Amar Singh's Diary, A Colonial Subject's Narrative of Imperial India*. Delhi: Oxford University Press.

Rueschemeyer, Dietrich. 1986. *Power and the Division of Labour*. Stanford, Calif.: Stanford University Press.

Rundstrom, Robert A. 1990. "A Cultural Interpretation of Inuit Map Accuracy." *Geographical Review* 80:155–68.

Ryabinska, Natalya. 2006. "Media Framing and Citizens' Engagement in Public Life: The Case of Ukrainian and Polish Press." Paper presented at the Seminar in Contemporary Ukrainian Studies, University of Ottawa, 14 October.

Sahlins, Marshall. 1981. *Historical Metaphors and Mythical Realities: Structure in the History of the Early Sandwich Islands Kingdom*. Ann Arbor: University of Michigan Press.

———. 1987. *Islands of History*. Chicago: University of Chicago Press.

———. 2004. *Apologies to Thucydides: Understanding History as Culture and Vice Versa*. Chicago: University of Chicago Press.

Said, Edward. 1979. *Orientalism*. New York: Vintage Books.

Sakombi Inongo. 1992. "Confession publique d'un ancien baron du président Mobutu." *Elima*, 22 April, 9.

Salemink, Oscar. 2003. "Introduction: Ethnography, Anthropology and Colonial Discourse." In Salemink, *The Ethnography of Vietnam's Central Highlanders: A Historical Contextualization, 1850–1990*, 1–39. Honolulu: University of Hawai'i Press.

Samson, Fabienne. 2005. *Les marabouts de l'Islam politique: Le Dahiratoul Moustarchidina wal Moustarchidaty, un mouvement néo-confrérique sénégalais*. Paris: Karthala.

Sand-Jensen, Kaj. 2007. "How to Write Consistently Boring Scientific Literature." *Oikos* 116:723–27.

Sandoval, Chela. 2000. *The Methodology of the Oppressed*. Minneapolis: University of Minnesota Press.

Sassen, Saskia. 2006. *Territory, Authority, Rights: From Medieval to Global Assemblages*. Updated edition. Princeton, N.J.: Princeton University Press.

Schaffer, Frederic C. 1998. *Democracy in Translation: Understanding Politics in an Unfamiliar Culture*. Ithaca, N.Y.: Cornell University Press.

Schatz, Edward. 2004. *Modern Clan Politics: The Power of "Blood" in Kazakhstan and Beyond*. Seattle: University of Washington Press.

———. 2007. "Methods Are Not Tools: Ethnography and the Limits of Multiple-Methods Research." Working Paper 12, Committee on Concepts and Methods, International Political Science Association, January.

———. 2009. "The Soft Authoritarian 'Tool Kit': Agenda-Setting Power in Kazakhstan and Kyrgyzstan." *Comparative Politics* 41, no. 2:203–22.

Schatzberg, Michael G. 1974–75. "Field Log." Lisala, 28 April 1975.

———. 1979. "Conflict and Culture in African Education: Authority Patterns in a Cameroonian Lycée." *Comparative Education Review* 23, no. 1:52–65.

———. 1980. *Politics and Class in Zaire: Bureaucracy, Business and Beer in Lisala.* New York: Holmes & Meier, Africana.

———. 1981. "Ethnicity and Class at the Local Level: Bars and Bureaucrats in Lisala, Zaire." *Comparative Politics* 13, no. 4:461–78.

———. 1984. "Zaire." In *The Political Economy of African Foreign Policy: Comparative Analysis,* ed. Timothy M. Shaw and Olajide Aluko, 283–318. Farnsborough: Gower.

———. 1986. "Two Faces of Kenya: The Researcher and the State." *African Studies Review* 29, no. 4:1–15.

———. 1988. *The Dialectics of Oppression in Zaire.* Bloomington: Indiana University Press.

———. 2001. *Political Legitimacy in Middle Africa: Father, Family, Food.* Bloomington: Indiana University Press.

———. 2006. "Soccer, Science, and Sorcery: Causation and African Football." *Afrika Spectrum* 41, no. 3:351–69.

Schedler, Andreas. 2006. "The Logic of Electoral Authoritarianism." In *Electoral Authoritarianism: The Dynamics of Unfree Competition,* ed. Andreas Schedler, 95–112. Boulder, Colo.: Lynne Rienner.

Scheele, Judith. 2007. "Recycling *Baraka*: Knowledge, Politics, and Religion in Contemporary Algeria." *Comparative Studies in Society and History* 49, no. 2:304–28.

Schram, Sanford F. 1995. *Words of Welfare: The Poverty of Social Science and the Social Science of Poverty.* Minneapolis: University of Minnesota Press.

———. 2004. "Beyond Paradigm: Resisting the Assimilation of Phronetic Social Science," *Politics and Society* 32, no. 3:417–33.

———. 2006. *Welfare Discipline: Discourse, Governance and Globalization.* Philadelphia: Temple University Press.

Schuman, Howard, and Stanley Presser. 1981. *Questions and Answers in Attitude Surveys: Experiments on Question Form, Wording and Context.* New York: Academic Press.

Schwartz-Shea, Peregrine. 2003. "Is This the Curriculum We Want? Doctoral Requirements and Offerings in Methods and Methodology." *PS: Political Science & Politics* 36:379–86.

———. 2006. "Judging Quality: Evaluative Criteria and Epistemic Communities." In *Interpretation and Method: Empirical Research Methods and the Interpretive Turn,* ed. Dvora Yanow and P. Schwartz-Shea, 89–113. Armonk, N.Y.: M. E. Sharpe.

Schwartz-Shea, Peregrine, and Dvora Yanow. 2002. "'Reading' 'Methods' 'Texts': How Research Methods Texts Construct Political Science." *Political Research Quarterly* 55: 457–86.

Scott, James C. 1977. *The Moral Economy of the Peasant: Subsistence and Rebellion in Southeast Asia.* New Haven, Conn.: Yale University Press.

———. 1985. *Weapons of the Weak: Everyday Forms of Peasant Resistance.* New Haven, Conn.: Yale University Press.

———. 1990. *Domination and the Arts of Resistance: Hidden Transcripts.* New Haven, Conn.: Yale University Press.

———. 1998. *Seeing Like a State: How Certain Schemes to Improve the Human Condition Have Failed.* New Haven, Conn.: Yale University Press.

Seesemann, Rüdiger. 2005. "The Quotidian Dimension of Islamic Reformisn in Wadai (Chad)." In *L'Islam politique au sud du Sahara,* ed. Muriel Gomez-Perez, 327–46. Paris: Karthala.

Sewell, William H., Jr. 1996. "Three Temporalities: Toward an Eventful Sociology." In *The Historic Turn in the Human Sciences,* ed. Terrence McDonald, 245–80. Ann Arbor: University of Michigan Press.

———. 1999. "The Concept(s) of Culture." In *Beyond the Cultural Turn: New Directions in the Study of Culture and Society,* ed. Victoria Bonnell and Lynn Hunt, 35–61. Berkeley: University of California Press.

Shapiro, Ian. 2004. "Problems, Methods, and Theories in the Study of Politics, or: What's Wrong with Political Science and What to Do about It." In *Problems and Methods in the Study of Politics,* ed. Ian Shapiro, Rogers M. Smith, and Tarek E. Masoud, 19–41. Cambridge: Cambridge University Press.

———. 2005. *The Flight from Reality in the Human Sciences.* Princeton, N.J.: Princeton University Press.

Shdaimah, Corey, and Roland Stahl. 2005. "The Perils of Low-Income Homeownership: Home Repair Problems and Policies in Philadelphia." Policy Brief 2. Bryn Mawr, Pa.: Center for Ethnicities, Communities and Social Policy, Bryn Mawr College.

———. 2006. "Reflections of Doing Phronetic Social Science: A Case Study." In *Making Political Science Matter: Debating Research, Knowledge and Method,* ed. Sanford F. Schram and Brian Caterino, 98–113. New York: New York University Press.

Shehata, Samer. 2006. "Ethnography, Identity, and the Production of Knowledge." In *Interpretation and Method: Empirical Research Methods and the Interpretive Turn,* ed. Dvora Yanow and Peregrine Schwartz-Shea, 244–63. Armonk, N.Y.: M. E. Sharpe.

Sherraden, Michael, ed. 2005. *Inclusion in the American Dream: Assets, Poverty, and Public Policy.* New York: Oxford University Press.

Shively, W. Phillips. 1995. "Review of Designing Social Inquiry." *Journal of Politics* 24: 424–27.

Shweder, Richard A. 1997. "The Surprise of Ethnography." *Ethnos* 25, no. 2:152–63.

Sider, Gerald. 1986. *Culture and Class in Anthropology and History: A Newfoundland Illustration.* Cambridge: Cambridge University Press.

Siegel, James. 1998. *A New Criminal Type in Jakarta.* Durham, N.C.: Duke University Press.

———. 2000 [1969]. *The Rope of God.* Revised edition. Ann Arbor: University of Michigan Press.

———. 2006. *Naming the Witch.* Stanford, Calif.: Stanford University Press.

Sil, Rudra, and Peter Katzenstein. 2005. "What Is Analytical Eclecticism and Why Do We Need It? A Pragmatist Perspective on Problems and Mechanisms in the Study of World Politics." Presented at the Annual Meeting of the American Political Science Association, Washington, D.C., 1–4 September.

Sluka, Jeffrey A. 1995. "Reflections on Managing Danger in Fieldwork: Dangerous Anthropology in Belfast." In *Fieldwork under Fire: Contemporary Studies of Violence and Survival,* ed. Carolyn Nordstrom and Antonius C. G. M. Robben, 276–94. Berkeley: University of California Press.

Smith, Rogers. 2002. "Should We Make Political Science More of a Science or More about Politics?" *PS: Political Science and Politics* 35:199–201.

―――. 2004. "The Politics of Identities and the Tasks of Political Science." In *Problems and Methods in the Study of Politics*, ed. Ian Shapiro, Rogers Smith, and Tarek E. Masoud, 42–66. Cambridge: Cambridge University Press.

Snyder, Benson R. 1973. *The Hidden Curriculum*. Cambridge, Mass.: MIT Press.

Soss, Joe. 2000. *Unwanted Claims: The Politics of Participation in the U.S. Welfare System*. Ann Arbor: University of Michigan Press.

Spiro, Milford E. 1996. "Postmodernist Anthropology, Subjectivity, and Science: A Modernist Critique." *Comparative Studies in Society and History* 38, no. 4:759–80.

Spradley, James P. 1979. *The Ethnographic Interview*. New York: Wadsworth.

―――. 1980. *Participant Observation*. New York: Wadsworth.

Stacey, Judith. 1991. "Can There Be a Feminist Ethnography?" In *Women's Words: The Feminist Practice of Oral History*, ed. Sherna Berger Gluck and Daphne Patai, 111–19. New York: Routledge.

Stack, Carol B. 1996. "Writing Ethnography: Feminist Critical Practice." In *Dilemmas in Fieldwork*, ed. Diane L. Wolf, 96–106. Boulder, Colo.: Westview.

Stahl, Roland, and Corey S. Shdaimah. 2008. "Collaboration between Community Advocates and Academic Researchers: Scientific Advocacy or Political Research?" *British Journal of Social Work* 38:1610–29

Stark, David, and Laszlo Bruszt. 1998. *Postsocialist Pathways: Transforming Politics and Property in East Central Europe*. Cambridge: Cambridge University Press.

Starn, Orin. 1999. *Nightwatch: The Politics of Protest in the Andes*. Durham, N.C.: Duke University Press.

Steinberg, Marc W. 1998. "Tilting the Frame: Considerations on Collective Action Framing from a Discursive Turn." *Theory and Society* 27, no. 6:845–72.

Stevenson, Jonathan. 2003. "Africa's Growing Strategic Resonance." *Survival* 45, no. 4:153–72.

Stevenson, Randy. 2005. "Making a Contribution: The Role of Fieldwork in Scientific Research Programs." *Newsletter of the American Political Science Association Organized Section in Comparative Politics* 16, no. 2:12–16.

Stocking, George W., Jr. 1968. *Race, Culture, and Evolution: Essays in the History of Anthropology*. New York: Free Press.

―――, ed. 1983. *Observers Observed: Essays on Ethnographic Fieldwork*. Madison: University of Wisconsin Press.

―――. 1992. *The Ethnographer's Magic and Other Essays in the History of Anthropology*. Madison: University of Wisconsin Press.

Stoker, Laura, and M. Kent Jennings. 2005. "Political Similarity and Influence between Husbands and Wives." In *The Social Logic of Politics*, ed. Alan Zuckerman, 51–74. Philadelphia: Temple University Press.

Stokes, Susan C. 1995. *Cultures in Conflict: Social Movements and the State in Peru*. Berkeley: University of California Press.

―――. 2005. "Perverse Accountability: A Formal Model of Machine Politics with Evidence from Argentina." *American Political Science Review* 99, no. 3:315–26.

Stoll, David. 1999. *Rigoberta Menchú and the Story of All Poor Guatemalans*. Boulder, Colo.: Westview.

Stone, Deborah. 2001. *Policy Paradox: The Art of Political Decision Making*. New York: W. W. Norton.

Strier, Roni. 2005. "Gendered Realities of Poverty: Men's and Women's Views of Poverty in Jerusalem." *Social Service Review* 79, no. 2:344–67.

Suárez-Orozco, Marcelo. 1992. "Grammar of Terror: Psychological Responses to State Terrorism in the Dirty War and Post Dirty Argentina." In *The Paths to Domination, Resistance and Terror*, ed. Carolyn Nordstrom and JoAnn Martin, 219–59. Berkeley: University of California Press.

Sutton, Robert I. 1997. "The Virtues of Closet Qualitative Research." *Organization Science* 8:97–106.

Swidler, Ann. 1986. "Culture in Action: Symbols and Strategies." *American Sociological Review* 51 (April): 287–94.

Tarrow, Sidney. 2005. *The New Transnational Activism*. Cambridge: Cambridge University Press.

Taylor, Charles. 1971. "Interpretation and the Sciences of Man." *Review of Metaphysics* 25:3–51.

Taylor, Matthew M. 2006. "Veto and Voice in the Courts: Policy Implications of Institutional Design in the Brazilian Judiciary." *Comparative Politics* 38, no. 3:739–66.

Thelen, Kathleen, and Sven Steinmo. 1992. "Historical Institutionalism in Comparative Politics." In *Structuring Politics: Historical Institutionalism in Comparative Analysis*, ed. S. Steinmo, K. Thelen, and Frank Longstreth, 1–32. Cambridge: Cambridge University Press.

Thomas, George. 2005. "The Qualitative Foundations of Political Science Methodology." *Perspectives on Politics* 3, no. 4:855–66.

Thomas, William I., and Florian Znaniecki. 1918–20. *The Polish Peasant in Europe and America: Monograph of an Immigrant Group*. Boston: Richard G. Bader/Gorham Press.

Thompson, E. P. 1978. *The Poverty of Theory and Other Essays*. New York: Monthly Review Press.

Thoreau, Henry David. 1854. *Walden; or, A life in the woods*. Available online: xroads .virginia.edu/~HYPER/WALDEN/hdt01.html.

Thornton, Patricia M. 2002. "Framing Dissent in Contemporary China: Irony, Ambiguity and Metonymy." *China Quarterly* 171:661–81.

Tickamyer, Ann R., Debra A. Henderson, Julie Anne White, and Barry L. Tadlock. 2000. "Voices of Welfare Reform: Bureaucratic Rationality vs. Participant Perceptions." *Affilia* 15, no. 2:173–92.

Tilly, Charles. 1999. "The Trouble with Stories." In *The Social Worlds of Higher Education: Handbook for Teaching in a New Century*, ed. Marco Giugni and Florence Passy, 256–70. Thousand Oaks, Calif.: Pine Forge Press.

———. 2001. "Mechanisms in Political Processes." *Annual Review of Political Science* 4: 21–41.

———. 2006. "Afterword: Political Ethnography as Art and Science." *Qualitative Sociology* 29:409–12.

Tobin, Beth. 1999. *Picturing Imperial Power: Colonial Subjects in Eighteenth-Century British Painting*. Durham, N.C.: Duke University Press.

Trickett, Edison J., and Mary Ellen Oliveri. 1997. "Ethnography and Sociocultural Processes: Introductory Comments." *Ethos* 25, no. 2:146–51.

Trouillot, Michel-Rolph. 2003. *Global Transformations: Anthropology and the Modern World*. New York: Palgrave Macmillan.

Tsing, Anna Lowenhaupt. 1993. *In the Realm of the Diamond Queen: Marginality in an Out-of-the-Way Place*. Princeton, N.J.: Princeton University Press.

Tufte, Edward R. 1990. *Envisioning Information*. Cheshire, Conn.: Graphics Press.

Turner, Graeme. 1996. *British Cultural Studies: An Introduction*. 2d ed. London: Routledge.

Tyler, Stephen A. 1986. "Post-Modern Ethnography: From Document of the Occult to Occult Document." In *Writing Culture: The Poetics and Politics of Ethnography*, ed. J. Clifford and G. E. Marcus, 122–40. Berkeley: University of California Press.

Unzueta, José Luis. 1980. "La Va Asamblea de ETA." *Saioak* 4, no. 4:3–52.

Van Bruinessen, Martin. 1998. "Studies of Sufism and the Sufi Orders in Indonesia." *Die Welt des Islams* 38, no. 2:192–219.

Van de Walle, Nicolas. 2002. "Africa's Range of Regimes." *Journal of Democracy* 13, no. 2:66–80.

Van Maanen, John. 1988. *Tales of the Field*. Chicago: University of Chicago Press.

———. 1991. "Playing Back the Tape." In *Experiencing Fieldwork: An Inside View of Qualitative Research*, ed. W. B. Shaffir and R. A. Stebbins, 31–42. Thousand Oaks, Calif.: Sage.

Varshney, Ashutosh. 2002. *Ethnic Conflict and Civic Life: Hindus and Muslims in India*. 2d ed. New Haven, Conn.: Yale University Press.

———. 2006. "Recognizing the Tradeoffs We Make." In "Symposium: Ethnography Meets Rational Choice: David Laitin, for Example." *Qualitative Methods*, Newsletter of the APSA Organized Section on Qualitative Methods 4, no. 1: 20–26.

Verba, Sidney. 1996. "The Citizen as Respondent: Sample Surveys and American Democracy. Presidential Address, American Political Science Association, 1995." *American Political Science Review* 90, no. 1:1–7.

Verdery, Katherine. 1996. *What Was Socialism, and What Comes Next?* Princeton, N.J.: Princeton University Press.

———. 2003. *The Vanishing Hectare: Property and Value in Postsocialist Transylvania*. Ithaca, N.Y.: Cornell University Press.

"Victory for Political Scientists." 2000. *Nature* 406 (10 August). Available at: http://www .nature.com/nature/journal/v406/n6796/full/406547a0.html.

Vikor, Knut S. 2000. "Sufi Brotherhoods in Africa." In *The History of Islam in Africa*, ed. Nehemia Levtzion and Randall L. Pouwells, 441–76. Athens: Ohio University Press.

Villalón, Leonardo. 1995. *Islamic Society and State Power in Senegal: Disciples and Citizens in Fatick*. Cambridge: Cambridge University Press.

———. 2007. "Senegal: Shades of Islamism on a Sufi Landscape." In *Political Islam in West Africa: State-Society Relations Transformed*, ed. William F. S. Miles, 161–82. Boulder, Colo.: Lynne Rienner.

Vincent, Joan. 1990. *Anthropology and Politics: Visions, Traditions, and Trends*. Tucson: University of Arizona Press.

———, ed. 2002. *The Anthropology of Politics: A Reader in Ethnography, Theory, and Critique*. London: Blackwell.

Wagner-Pacifici, Robin Erica. 1986. *The Moro Morality Play: Terrorism as Social Drama*. Chicago: University of Chicago Press.

Wallerstein, Immanuel. 1974. *The Modern World-System: Capitalist Agriculture and the Origins of the European World-Economy in the Sixteenth Century*. New York: Academic Press.

Walsh, Katherine Cramer. 2004. *Talking about Politics: Informal Groups and Social Identity in American Life*. Chicago: University of Chicago Press.

———. 2007. *Talking about Race: Community Dialogues and the Politics of Difference*. Chicago: University of Chicago Press.

Walzer, Michael. 1983. *Spheres of Justice: A Defense of Pluralism and Equality*. New York: Basic Books.

Warren, Dorian T. 2005. "A New Labor Movement for a New Century? The Incorporation of Marginalized Workers in United States Unions." Ph.D. diss., Yale University.

———. 2007. "Politics, Power and Inequality in 'Real-Time': The Perils and Promises of a

Political Ethnography." Presented at the fourth session of the Seminars in Organizational Ethnography, "Power and Politics in Ethnographic Research," 9 May.

Warren, Kay B. 1998. *Indigenous Movements and Their Critics: Pan-Maya Activism in Guatemala.* Princeton, N.J.: Princeton University Press.

Weaver, Catherine. 2008. *Hypocrisy Trap: The World Bank and the Poverty of Reform.* Princeton, N.J.: Princeton University Press.

Wedeen, Lisa. 1998. "Acting 'As If': Symbolic Politics and Social Control in Syria." *Comparative Studies in Society and History* 40, no. 3:503–23.

———. 1999. *Ambiguities of Domination: Politics, Rhetoric, and Symbols in Contemporary Syria.* Chicago: University of Chicago Press.

———. 2002. "Conceptualizing Culture: Possibilities for Political Science." *American Political Science Review* 96, no. 4:713–28.

———. 2004. "Concepts and Commitments in the Study of Democracy." In *Problems and Methods in the Study of Politics,* ed. Ian Shapiro, Rogers Smith, and Tarek E. Masoud, 274–306. Cambridge: Cambridge University Press.

———. 2006. "NSF [National Science Foundation] Memo for Workshop on Scientific Foundations of Qualitative Research."

———. 2007. "The Politics of Deliberation: *Qat* Chews as Public Spheres in Yemen." *Public Culture* 19, no. 1: 59–84.

———. 2008a. *Peripheral Visions: Publics, Power, and Performance in Yemen.* Chicago: University of Chicago Press.

———. 2008b. "Scientific Knowledge, Liberalism, and Empire: American Political Science in the Modern Middle East." Available online: www.ssrc.org/program_areas/global/june2007_meeting/Wedeen_FinalDraft_June08.pdf.

Wedel, Janine R., Cris Shore, Gregory Feldman, and Stacy Lathrop. 2005. "Toward an Anthropology of Public Policy." *Annals of the American Academy of Political and Social Science* 600:30–51.

Wendt, Alexander, and Ian Shapiro. 1992. "The Difference That Realism Makes: Social Science and the Politics of Consent." *Politics and Society* 20, no. 2:197–224.

West, Harry G. 2005. *Kupilikula: Governance and the Invisible Realm in Mozambique.* Chicago: University of Chicago Press.

———. 2007. *Ethnographic Sorcery.* Chicago: University of Chicago Press.

White, Hayden. 1978. *Tropics of Discourse: Essays in Cultural Criticism.* Baltimore: Johns Hopkins University Press.

———. 1987. *The Content of the Form: Narrative Discourse and Historical Representation.* Baltimore: Johns Hopkins University Press.

Wiktorowicz, Quintan, ed. 2004. *Islamic Activism: A Social Movement Theory Approach.* Bloomington: Indiana University Press.

Wildavsky, Aaron. 1971. *The Revolt against the Masses, and Other Essays on Politics and Public Policy.* New York: Basic Books.

———. 1993. *Craftways: On the Organization of Scholarly Work.* 2d ed. New Brunswick, N.J.: Transaction.

Wilkinson, Claire. 2008. "Positioning 'Security' and Securing One's Position: The Researcher's Role in Investigating 'Security' in Kyrgyzstan." In *Fieldwork in Difficult Environments: Methodology As Boundary Work in Development Research,* ed. Caleb R. L. Wall and Peter P. Mollinga, 43–67. Berlin: Lit Verlag.

Willis, Paul. 1981. *Learning to Labour: How Working Class Kids Get Working Class Jobs.* New York: Columbia University Press.

Wilson, Thomas M. 1990. "From Patronage to Brokerage in the Local Politics of Eastern Ireland." *Ethnohistory* 37, no. 2:158–87.

Witvliet, Charlotte van Oyen. 1997. "Traumatic Intrusive Imagery as an Emotional Memory Phenomenon: A Review of Research and Explanatory Information Processing Theories." *Clinical Psychology Review* 17, no. 5:509–36.

Wolf, Eric. 1982. *Europe and the People without History.* Berkeley: University of California Press.

Wood, Elisabeth Jean. 2003. *Insurgent Collective Action and Civil War in El Salvador.* Cambridge: Cambridge University Press.

———. 2006. "The Ethical Challenges of Field Research in Conflict Zones." *Qualitative Sociology* 29, no. 3:307–41.

———. 2007. "Field Research." In *The Oxford Handbook of Comparative Politics,* ed. Carles Boix and Susan Stokes, 123–46. Oxford: Oxford University Press.

Woodruff, David M. 1999. *Money Unmade: Barter and the Fate of Russian Capitalism.* Ithaca, N.Y.: Cornell University Press.

Yanagisako, Sylvia. 2002. *Producing Culture and Capital: Family Firms in Italy.* Princeton, N.J.: Princeton University Press.

Yanow, Dvora. 1976. "Community Organization: Theories and Practices." Unpublished paper.

———. 1996. *How Does a Policy Mean?* Washington, D.C.: Georgetown University Press.

———. 2000. *Conducting Interpretive Policy Analysis.* Newbury Park, Calif.: Sage.

———. 2001. "Learning in and from Improvising: Lessons from Theater for Organizational Learning." *Reflections* 2:58–62.

———. 2003. "Accessing Local Knowledge." In *Deliberative Policy Analysis: Understanding Governance in the Network Society,* ed. Maarten A. Hajer and Hendrik Wagenaar, 228–46. Cambridge: Cambridge University Press.

———. 2006a. *Academic Foxes, Ethnographic Hedgehogs: Evidence, Local Knowledge, and Interpretive Analysis.* Amsterdam: Faculteit der Sociale Wetenschappen, Vrije Universiteit.

———. 2006b. "Neither Rigorous nor Objective? Interrogating Criteria for knowledge Claims in Interpretive Science." In *Interpretation and Method: Empirical Research Methods and the Interpretive Turn,* ed. Dvora Yanow and Peregrine Schwartz-Shea, 67–88. Armonk, N.Y.: M. E. Sharpe.

———. 2006c. How Built Spaces Mean: A Semiotics of Space." In *Interpretation and Method: Empirical Research Methods and the Interpretive Turn,* ed. Dvora Yanow and Peregrine Schwartz-Shea, 349–66. Armonk, N.Y.: M. E. Sharpe.

Yanow, Dvora, and Peregrine Schwartz-Shea, eds. 2006. *Interpretation and Method: Empirical Research Methods and the Interpretive Turn.* Armonk, N.Y.: M. E. Sharpe.

———. 2008. "Reforming Institutional Review Board Policy: Issues in Implementation and Field Research." *PS: Political Science & Politics* 41:483–94.

Yanow, Dvora, Harrison Trice, Janice Beyer, Joanne Martin, Gideon Kunda, and Linda Smircich. 1995. "Writing Organizational Tales." Crossroads symposium. *Organization Science* 6:225–26.

Young, Iris Marion. 1990. *Justice and the Politics of Difference.* Princeton, N.J.: Princeton University Press.

Yurchak, Alexei. 2003. "Soviet Hegemony of Form: Everything Was Forever, Until It Was No More." *Comparative Studies in Society and History* 45, no. 3:480–510.

Zaller, John R., and Stanley Feldman. 1992. "A Simple Theory of the Survey Response: Answering Questions Means Revealing Preferences." *American Journal of Political Science* 36:579–618.

Zamenga Batukezanga. 1975. *Sept frères et une soeur*. Kinshasa: Editions Saint-Paul-Afrique.

Zemon Davis, Natalie. 1983. *The Return of Martin Guerre*. Cambridge, Mass.: Harvard University Press.

Zinn, Howard, with David Barsamian. 2006. *Original Zinn: Conversations on History and Politics*. New York: HarperCollins.

Zirakzadeh, Cyrus Ernesto. 1985. "The Political Thought of Basque Businessmen, 1976–1980." In *Basque Politics: A Case Study in Ethnic Nationalism*, ed. William A. Douglass, 265–83. New York: Associated Faculty Press.

———. 1989. "Economic Changes and Surges in Micro-Nationalist Voting in Scotland and the Basque Region of Spain." *Comparative Studies in Society and History* 31, no. 2:318–39.

———. 1991. *A Rebellious People: Basques, Protests, and Politics*. Reno: University of Nevada Press.

———. 2000. "Some Quotidian Meanings of 'Frame' and 'Framing' and Some Non-Democratic Tendencies in Social-Movement Theory." In *Proceedings of the Sixth International Conference on Social Movements: Alternative Futures and Political Protest*, vol. 2, ed. Colin Barker and Mike Tyldesley, 1–13. Manchester: Manchester Metropolitan University.

———. 2004. "Farm Workers Labor Movement." In *The Encyclopedia of American Social Movements*, vol. 3, ed. Immanuel Ness, 822–34. Armonk, N.Y.: M. E. Sharpe.

———. 2006. *Social Movements in Politics: A Comparative Study*. 2d ed. New York: Palgrave Macmillan.

CONTRIBUTORS

JESSICA ALLINA-PISANO is an associate professor in the School of Political Studies at the University of Ottawa and an associate of the Davis Center for Russian and Eurasian Studies at Harvard University. She received her Ph.D. in political science from Yale University in 2003. She is the author of *The Post-Soviet Potemkin Village: Politics and Property Rights in the Black Earth* (Cambridge: Cambridge University Press, 2008). Her research on Russian and Ukrainian politics and political economy has appeared in journals such as *World Politics, East European Politics and Societies, International Labor and Working Class History, The Journal of Peasant Studies,* and *Otechestvennye zapiski,* and as chapters in edited volumes. She is currently working on two monographs: an analysis of façade institutions in post-Soviet states, and a political history of surveillance in a Hungarian village currently divided by the Ukraine–European Union border.

ENRIQUE DESMOND ARIAS is an associate professor of government at the John Jay College of Criminal Justice, City University of New York, and in the Criminal Justice Doctoral Program at the Graduate Center, CUNY, where he is also a Fellow at the Bildner Center for Western Hemisphere Studies. His book *Drugs and Democracy in Rio de Janeiro: Trafficking, Social Networks, and Public Security* was published by the University of North Carolina Press (2006), and he has published articles in the journals *Latin American Politics and Society, Qualitative Sociology,* and *Journal of Latin American Studies.* He has held two Fulbright awards and a Dorothy Danforth Compton Fellowship from the Institute for the Study of World Politics.

MYRON (MIKE) ARONOFF received his Ph.D. in anthropology from Manchester University and his Ph.D. in political science from the University of California at Los Angeles. He is an emeritus professor at Rutgers University. He was previously affiliated with Tel Aviv University and Manchester University. At present he is a visiting professor at the University of Michigan. He was twice a fellow in residence of the Netherlands Institute for Advanced Studies. His research has been funded by the Ford Foundation, the social science research councils of both the United States and the United Kingdom, and the American Council of Learned Societies, among others. He has authored and edited a dozen books, mostly on Israel and political anthropology. His most recent book is *The Spy Novels of John le Carré: Balancing Ethics and Politics* (New York: St. Martin's Press, 1998). He is coauthor with Jan Kubik of the forthcoming *Anthropology and Political Science: Culture, Politics, and Identity*. Aronoff has published widely in refereed journals and scholarly collections. He edits the journal *Political Anthropology* and is past president of the Association for Political and Legal Anthropology as well as the founding president of the Association for Israel Studies.

LORRAINE BAYARD DE VOLO is an associate professor of women and gender studies and affiliated faculty of political science at the University of Colorado, Boulder. She is the author of *Mothers of Heroes and Martyrs: Gender Identity Politics in Nicaragua, 1979–1999* (Baltimore: Johns Hopkins University Press, 2001), as well as of articles in journals such as *Comparative Politics, Mobilization, Gender & Society, PS: Political Science and Politics*, and *Social Politics*. She is currently working on a comparative project on women and war in Colombia, Cuba, Mexico, and Nicaragua, and is writing several articles on women and militarization in Cuba. She received funding for these projects from the National Science Foundation and the U.S. Institute of Peace.

CÉDRIC JOURDE is associate professor at the School of Political Studies, University of Ottawa. His main research themes concern the evolution of neo-authoritarian regimes in West Africa, the various trajectories of political Islam in the Sahel, and the interaction between cultural practices and political domination. His current research project focuses on the politics of ethnicity and Islam in Senegal and Mauritania. He has published articles in *International Studies Quarterly, Comparative Politics, Journal of Contemporary African Studies*, and *African Issues*. He is the author of chapters in edited volumes that analyze issues such as U.S. foreign policy in West Africa, the fate of former single parties in West Africa, and Islamist movements in Mauritania.

JAN KUBIK holds a master's degree in sociology from Jagiellonian University in Krakow, Poland, and a Ph.D. in anthropology from Columbia University. He is an associate professor of political science at Rutgers, The State University of New Jersey, and recurring visiting professor of sociology at the Centre for Social Studies, Polish Academy of Sciences, Warsaw. He is the author (with Grzegorz Ekiert) of the award-winning book *Rebellious Civil Society: Popular Protest and Democratic Consolidation in Poland, 1989–1993* (Ann Arbor: University of Michigan Press, 1999) and sole author of *The Power of Symbols against the Symbols of Power: The Rise of Solidarity and the Fall of State Socialism in Poland* (University Park: Penn State University Press, 1994). He has also published articles in such journals as *World Politics, East European Politics and Societies, Communist and Post-Communist Studies*, and *Polish Sociological Review*, and in several edited volumes, including *Capitalism and Democracy in Central and Eastern Europe: Assessing the Legacy of Communist Rule,* edited by G. Ekiert and S. E. Hanson (Cambridge: Cambridge University Press, 2003).

TIMOTHY PACHIRAT holds a Ph.D. from Yale University and is an assistant professor in the Department of Politics at The New School for Social Research. His research and teaching interests include comparative politics, the politics of Southeast Asia, spatial and visual politics, the sociology of domination and resistance, the political economy of dirty and dangerous work, and interpretive and ethnographic research methods. He is currently working on a political ethnography of an industrialized slaughterhouse in the Great Plains of the United States to explore how violence that is seen as both essential and repugnant to modern society is organized, disciplined, and regulated.

EDWARD SCHATZ is an associate professor of political science at the University of Toronto. He received his Ph.D. from the University of Wisconsin–Madison in 2000. He is the author of *Modern Clan Politics: The Power of "Blood" in Kazakhstan and Beyond* (Seattle: University of Washington Press, 2004), as well as articles in journals such as *Comparative Politics, Slavic Review, International Political Science Review, Nationalism and Ethnic Politics, Ethnic and Racial Studies, Nationalities Papers,* and *PS: Political Science and Politics.* His current research examines the impact that changing images of the United States have on social mobilization in ex-Soviet Central Asia.

MICHAEL G. SCHATZBERG is a professor of political science at the University of Wisconsin–Madison, where he served from 2004 to 2007 as director of the African studies program. He holds a Ph.D. in political science from the University of Wisconsin–Madison (1977). His major teaching and research interests include African politics, comparative politics, and political culture. He also teaches an occasional graduate seminar on qualitative methods. His books include *Political Legitimacy in Middle Africa: Father, Family, Food* (Bloomington: Indiana University Press, 2001), *The Dialectics of Oppression in Zaire* (Bloomington: Indiana University Press, 1988), *Politics and Class in Zaire: Bureaucracy, Business, and Beer in Lisala* (New York: Holmes & Meier, Africana, 1980), and *Mobutu or Chaos? The United States and Zaire, 1960–1990* (Philadelphia: Foreign Policy Research Institute, 1991). He has also published articles in numerous professional journals. His current research project deals with the politics, economics, and culture of football (soccer) in sub-Saharan Africa.

SANFORD F. SCHRAM teaches social theory and social policy in the Graduate School of Social Work and Social Research at Bryn Mawr College. He has published articles in *American Political Science Review, American Sociological Review, Perspectives on Politics,* and numerous other journals. His first book, *Words of Welfare: The Poverty of Social Science and the Social Science of Poverty* (Minneapolis: University of Minnesota Press, 1995), won the Michael Harrington Award from the American Political Science Association. His most recent book is *Welfare Discipline: Discourse, Governance, and Globalization* (Philadelphia: Temple University Press, 2006).

COREY SHDAIMAH is assistant professor at the University of Maryland, Baltimore, School of Social Work. She studies how people and professionals work around, against, and within policies that they find hostile and oppressive. She has articles published or forthcoming in the *Journal of Sociology and Social Welfare, Journal of Progressive Human Services, British Journal of Social Work,* and *Social Work,* and she has published essays in a number of edited volumes. Her forthcoming book is entitled *Negotiating Justice: Public Interest Lawyering, Low-Income Clients, and the Pursuit of Social Justice* (New York: New York University Press).

ROLAND STAHL is a senior researcher and lecturer at the Lucerne University of Applied Sciences and Arts (Switzerland). He is the author of a number of published articles, including "Collaboration Between Community Advocates and Academic Researchers: Scientific Advocacy or Political Research" (*British Journal of Social Work* 38: 1610–29). He teaches in the areas of comparative social policy, poverty, and community-based research.

KATHERINE CRAMER WALSH holds a Ph.D. from the University of Michigan (2000). She is an associate professor in the Department of Political Science and the Morgridge Center for Public Service Faculty Research Scholar at the University of Wisconsin–Madison. She teaches and does research on deliberative democracy, public opinion, political communication, and civic engagement. She is the author of *Talking about Race: Community Dialogues and the Politics of Difference* (Chicago: University of Chicago Press, 2007) and *Talking about Politics: Informal Groups and Social Identity in American Life* (Chicago: University of Chicago Press, 2004), and coauthor (with the members of the American Political Science Association's Task Force on Civic Engagement and Civic Education) of *Democracy at Risk: How Political Choices Have Undermined Citizenship and What We Can Do about It* (Washington, D.C.: Brookings Institution, 2005).

LISA WEDEEN is professor of political science at the University of Chicago. She is the author of *Ambiguities of Domination: Politics, Rhetoric, and Symbols in Contemporary Syria* (Chicago: University of Chicago Press, 1999) and *Peripheral Visions: Performing Politics in Unified Yemen* (Chicago: University of Chicago Press, 2008). She has also published numerous articles in professional journals, including *American Political Science Review, Comparative Studies in Society and History,* and *Public Culture.*

ELISABETH JEAN WOOD is professor of political science at Yale University and research professor at the Santa Fe Institute. She is the author of *Forging Democracy from Below: Insurgent Transitions in South Africa and El Salvador* (Cambridge: Cambridge University Press, 2000) and *Insurgent Collective Action and Civil War in El Salvador* (Cambridge: Cambridge University Press, 2003). Her current research is on patterns of sexual violence during war.

DVORA YANOW holds the Strategic Chair in Meaning and Method at the Vrije Universiteit (Amsterdam). Her research has been shaped by an overall interest in the communication of meaning in organizational and policy settings. She is the author of three books: *How Does a Policy Mean? Interpreting Policy and Organizational Actions* (Washington, D.C.: Georgetown University Press, 1996), *Conducting Interpretive Policy Analysis* (New York: Sage, 2000), and *Constructing "Race" and "Ethnicity" in America: Category-Making in Public Policy and Administration* (Armonk, N.Y.: M. E. Sharpe, 2003), which was awarded the 2007 Herbert Simon-APSA and 2004 ASPA Research Section best book awards. She is also the coeditor of five books and the author of numerous articles published in professional journals. She received her Ph.D. in planning, policy, and organizational studies from MIT.

CYRUS ERNESTO ZIRAKZADEH is professor of political science and associate dean of the College of Liberal Arts and Sciences at the University of Connecticut. He earned his college degree from the University of Michigan, his master's from Stanford University, and his doctorate from the University of California, Berkeley. He is the author and co-author of four books, and has published articles in several political science and multidisciplinary journals, including *Polity, Review of Politics, Journal of Theoretical Politics,* and *Comparative Studies in Society and History.* In 1998, his *Social Movements in Politics: A Comparative Study* (London and New York: Addison Wesley Longman) received an "Outstanding Academic Book of the Year" award from *Choice* magazine.

Made in the USA
Lexington, KY
27 February 2014